DANISH MEDIEVAL CASTLES

SPØTTRUP *in Salling was built by Jørgen Friis, Bishop of Viborg, in the first decades of the 16th century and was very advanced for its day. A number of latrine shafts led down from the attic level, where the castle's work-force or garrison would have been housed, to the moat. One such shaft can be seen here on the outer wall of the east wing.*

DANISH MEDIEVAL CASTLES

By Rikke Agnete Olsen

With photos by Janne Klerk

To David with
kindest regards
from Rikke

Aarhus University Press

*The earthwork named **DANEVIRKE** winds through the landscape from Slien Fjord in the east and on to the marsh areas in the west beside the Rivers Ejder and Trene. Parts of the rampart system date from the 7th century. A stretch of the main rampart east of what is known as "Valdemar's Wall" can be seen here.*

Contents

VESBORG, *on the south-western tip of Samsø, was a strong fortress for a short time in the 14th century. It was built on several mounds. Much of the castle/site has now slipped down into the sea. Ruins of one of the castle buildings can still be seen from the shore below the remains of the mound where the lighthouse is now placed.*

Preface

This book, originally in Danish and now in English, is the only comprehensive overview of Danish medieval castles. It describes their development and places them in their historical context – a context that may at times be difficult to find one's way in, for readers who are not very familiar with Danish history. To help provide linkages and landmarks, a chronological list of kings and genealogical tables can be found at the end of this book.

In its Danish version this book has reached its third edition, which comprises a significant revision of the two earlier editions, in that, for instance in a number of the sections concerning particular castles, it now incorporates and discusses the latest excavation results and publications, and thus provides a description of the latest state of play in castle research at this time.

Danish medieval castles have been a focus of my work over a period of almost forty years, and many of the results of that work are available in the form of articles in diverse foreign periodicals and in *festschrifts* for colleagues in a range of countries; here those results are now available in a collected volume and moreover in English.

Throughout the years that I have worked on this subject I have found a great deal of inspiration in contacts with colleagues both in Denmark and abroad, and I would like here to express my sincere thanks to them all.

The fact that this book can now be published in English is the consequence of a generous donation from the foundation *A.P. Møller og Hustru Chastine McKinney Møllers Fond til almene Formaal,* to which I owe a deep debt of gratitude.

I also owe warm thanks to the Director of Aarhus University Press, Claes Hvidbak, who provided support and encouragement for the first edition of my book about Danish medieval castles, and who took the initiative to publish this third edition. And likewise to former university lecturer Hans Blosen, who has been responsible for the German summary. The photographs by Janne Klerk which illustrate the book, infused with qualities of soul and immediacy, make it entirely special, and our collaboration in this work has developed into a warm friendship which I very much appreciate.

The same applies to my cooperation and friendship with Joan Frances Davidson, whose thoroughness and always dependable sense of the quality of language have made the English edition truly English.

Alrø, March 2014.
Rikke Agnete Olsen

A corner of one of the mounds of **BRATTINGSBORG,** *at Hald. One can just make out where the moat was.*

I

The Medieval Castle: The fortified dwelling

What is a castle?

All through the ages people have found ways of protecting themselves and their possessions from attack and assault. They have turned features of nature to advantage, for instance hiding themselves and their valuables in caves or on inaccessible islands in lakes, marshes or bogs, but they have also done what they could to improve the protection afforded by natural features, by means of building ramparts, moats and other physical obstructions.

Collective strongholds set up in inaccessible places, town fortifications, border walls, citadels and forts with garrisons in particularly vulnerable areas are all known in many cultures and from many different periods. They reflect the societies in which they were created and illustrate the needs experienced at that time, by states or individuals, for protection, security and prestige, as well as being an expression of the economic context in which they came into being.

This also applies to the medieval castle, which belongs to the forms of society and of warfare that prevailed in the time of its origins. Where it differs from other forms of fortification is in the fact that it is both a dwelling and a fortress at the same time. Kings, princes, bishops and aristocratic secular landowners built and owned castles, and the wealthiest and most powerful might own several of them, in which case they were run by stewards or bailiffs. In some cases there was room for a large complement of men, almost like a garrison, but the large castles were never just barracks, because they were also the family home of the owner, or that of his administrator. The smaller castles, often privately owned, would also usually be the main premises of an agricultural complex, or might protect some other income-producing enterprise, such as iron production or toll collection. In many cases the castle was the administrative centre for a large or small area.

At borders, harbour entrances, good vantage points and other strategic sites there were fortified towers or citadels which might be defended by organised manpower, but which could not function independently without guaranteed delivery of supplies. These were advance-guard positions in the context of an actual castle nearby, and thus formed parts of a larger fortification system.

In everyday life the castles were to a great extent self-supporting entities, and life in them, as in other types of farming, was dependent on the seasons and

*Among the various round churches on the island of Bornholm **ØSTERLARS,** dating from c.1200, has the most defence features. Here, beside an internal staircase at the level of the loft, the light comes in through a machicolation.*

the crop yields. Castles situated in or near a town of course had to have supplies brought in from elsewhere. The major castles of the realm that were intended to provide protection from external enemies, and to maintain law and order in the country, naturally had a different social significance from that of small local structures which were only meant to protect their owner and his property. The difference between the major castles which could withstand enemy attack for months, and the small strongholds that could be overrun by a couple of dozen men within a few days became particularly conspicuous in times of actual warfare.

No matter what size they were or what degree of fortification they offered, castles provided the setting for upper-class life in many countries, and norms of life-style and daily routines were very similar, whether those routines were taking place in half-timbered structures behind palisades, in stone houses surrounded by walls with towers and pinnacles, or on a country estate without fortifications. Neither the most powerful people in the realm nor ordinary people ever had fortifications to protect all their property, but in all the buildings of the upper and powerful classes there was also an element of prestige.

Castles in Denmark and elsewhere

There were many castles in Denmark in the Middle Ages, but they did not all function throughout the whole of that period and it was far from the case that all of them lived up to posterity's ideas of a castle. In many instances nothing is known about what the structure consisted of, and several have been lost without trace or are difficult to identify on site. A few have been rebuilt so radically that the original building is unrecognizable, while others are still present as grass-covered earthworks or ruins, for example Hammershus on the island of Bornholm. That is the largest castle ruin in the Nordic region, and it is on a scale comparable to the grandest structures in other countries where many more castles have been preserved, even taking into account the relative size of those countries. One reason for the more extensive preservation of castle-remains elsewhere is that when they had fallen into disuse they did not become stone-quarries – as they did in Denmark, where stone is in scarce supply – providing material for re-use by peasants, town-dwellers or by the Crown itself.

The term *voldsted,* meaning "castle mound" was used as early as in the Middle Ages to refer to sites where there had been a castle, for instance at Hastrup in the Vejle district in 1419. Sometimes the site of a former castle was referred to just as a *vold,* meaning "rampart", as in the case of Bjørnkær near Odder in 1427, when it was handed over to the Bishop of Aarhus. In present-day Denmark there are some 1,000 known castle mounds, and this corresponds to approximately one in every second parish. In the areas of Southern Sweden which were part of Denmark in the Middle Ages there are a few hundred castle mounds and in Schleswig there are about 50 sites south of the present border. The castles were not evenly distributed over the whole country. In some parishes there are several castle mounds, but that does not necessarily mean that there were several castles. There could have been one castle which was moved, for reasons which we do not now

KARLSTEIN, *southwest of Prague, was built in 1348 as the residence of Emperor Charles IV. The castle was built at several different levels on the top of the mountain and has space for the court and the imperial family, ceremonial reception rooms and chapels. It withstood the test of war during the Hussite Wars in the early 15th century and later underwent several reconstructions. Archive photo.*

know. In other parishes apparently there was no castle, and it can be difficult in individual cases to find an explanation for the circumstances, even if one knows who owned the land and estate.

In many other countries the history of castles has been well established. There is knowledge about who ordered them built and when that happened, and some of them are still lived in, even in a few instances by descendants of the original owners. This does not apply in the Danish context. Here many castle-structures are completely anonymous, while the knowledge we have of others has been pieced together from scattered oddments of not always reliable information in the few preserved written sources. It is only through the application of archaeological and modern scientific dating methods that it has become possible to compose a reasonably coherent overview of the history of the castle in medieval Denmark.

Our ideas about Danish medieval "knights' castles" have been assembled from the evidence of fortifications in other countries, with strutting towers and pinnacles, curtain walls with wall walks and loopholes, drawbridges, secret passages, deep dungeons, etc. Some of these features are familiar to us from castle buildings that were restored in the 19th century, when romantic notions about "the Age of Chivalry" flourished almost as profusely as they do today, and their present incarnation often has more to do with the ideas of the restorers than with the realities of the Middle Ages. Not every castle, by any means, either in

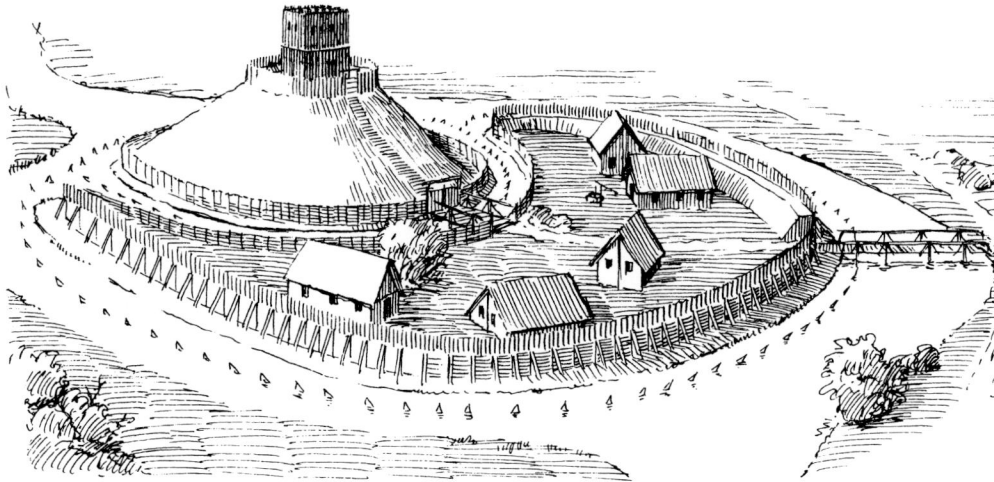

Denmark or elsewhere, was equipped from the start with the whole spectrum of fortification features. Some never acquired them – even though the castles that survived through centuries underwent many alterations.

The history of the castle varies from country to country, because in all cases it was closely related to broader historical development and it was also determined by specific political conditions. In Denmark castles began to appear relatively late. The Viking Age did not fade out until the 11th century, and the old Nordic world was not subject to much influence from Europe before the century that followed – and certainly not in the matter of fortifications.

The birth of the castle

The origins of the medieval castle have to be sought in Charlemagne's immense Franco-German empire. There, during the course of the 9th and 10th centuries, it became common for major landowners to protect their estates with defensive structures of earth and wood. Constructions of a particular type arose, now known as "motte and bailey". The motte consisted of a mound, either natural or constructed, and it was surrounded by one or several sets of ramparts and moats, often with a wooden tower protected by a palisade on the motte. The tower would often take up almost all the space at the top of the mound; in its earliest forms it was intended exclusively for defence and was only in use during battle. It was the strongest point of the building complex and the last refuge of the defenders, so the conditions of access were made as difficult as possible. Close beside the motte, perhaps on a low island or on a separate mound with its own rampart or palisade and moat, one would find the house, stables, barn and everything else that would be associated with farming on a certain scale. This was the bailey, and there could be more than one bailey linked to a motte.

Many structures of this type have been excavated on the continent of Europe and in Britain, so the type of construction is well-known, and there are also pictures of castles like this dating from the time when they were in use. On the Bayeux tapestry, the famous embroidered work from the end of the 11th century

HUSTERKNUPP, *east of Aachen, was the "family" castle of the Counts of Hochstaden, and the site was fortified from before the year 900 until sometime in the 14th century. From the 12th century onwards the castle was what is known as a motte-and-bailey structure, consisting of one mound with a tower and another with agricultural buildings and living quarters. Reconstruction drawing from A. Herrnbrodt:* Der Husterknupp, *Vol 6. Bonner Jahrbücher 1958.*

CONTRA ... DINANTES: E[T]

DINANT, *in the province of Namur in Belgium, was one of the castles that were fought over in the period before William the Conqueror achieved victory in England in 1066. On the Bayeux tapestry, the embroidered pictorial wall hanging from the end of that century, the battle at Dinant is depicted, and it is evident that it takes place around a wooden tower on a mound surrounded by a rampart and moat – a motte. Photo: Tapisserie de Bayeux.*

which illustrates the story of the Norman Conquest of England in 1066, there are depictions of some of the battles in Normandy prior to the invasion of England. One of them took place at the castle of Dinant. It was clearly a motte, and Duke William and his Normans took that form of fortification with them to England, where until that time it had not been customary for landowners – even major ones – to fortify their property.

Motte and bailey castles were usually private fortifications and were commonly to be found in the western part of the Carolingian realm, in what later became Northern France, as it underwent a period of internal strife, weak central power and frequent attacks by Vikings. Around the middle of the 9th century a large Viking army in fact reached Paris and laid siege to the town in the well-established fashion, which the Norsemen rapidly mastered to perfection. Local landowners built private castles both as a defence against these "wild Norsemen" and as protection against each other. The Vikings themselves also built castles once they had settled in the territory, and in 911 one of their chieftains became Duke of "Normandy", and that became the name by which this part of the country thereafter was known. But the Vikings did not bring the castle home with them to the Nordic region. Society there was not set up in such a way that castles were necessary.

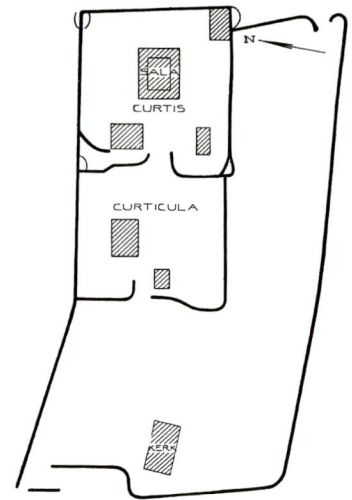

The society behind the castle

Charlemagne had built up his power and governed his massive empire by using loyal landowners and henchmen who each administered their local and more manageable districts or provinces on his behalf and under a degree of supervision by itinerant imperial inspectors. That system worked well in the time of Charlemagne, but under his successors, and after the empire was divided, it proved to be a two-edged sword and led to the weakening of central authority. The provincial royal or imperial representatives virtually became independent princes in their own areas, which were handed down through inheritance within powerful families. Power within the realm was divided up among many by use of the form of social organisation known as feudalism – which is not related to the use of that term in Marxist economic theory.

Historically feudalism is a political and judicial concept that belongs to the Middle Ages; in principle the feudal state was constructed in the shape of a pyramid with many steps, with reciprocal connections between adjacent steps two by two, but otherwise no direct contact between the different steps. The king or emperor sat at the top of the social pyramid, the dukes were their vassals belonging below, and they in turn had counts beneath them. The latter did not have duties relating to the king, but divided up their land among a number of land-holders who were even further from central authority. This continued right down to the bottom of the pyramid, where protection and subsistence were exchanged for service and obedience, so that all had positions that were clearly defined in relation to their surroundings. While that was the ideal, reality was less clear-cut, the result being nonetheless a weakening of central authority. This was in part due to the fact that the Church was built up in the same way, and since it was also a major landowner there could be overlapping of the two parallel hierarchies.

The feudal system's method of allocating rights, responsibilities and duties in connection with the use of land and the carrying out of functions in society left scope for great independence on the individual steps of the pyramid. This could lead to total fragmentation of power and weakening of central authority, to the point where it could not fulfil its obligations in society. In that case the king or princely ruler was not able to maintain rule of law, ensure the defence of the realm or implement policies that safeguarded the interests of the country. Then the individual local landowner had to protect himself and his family and possessions and ensure peace in his own area. The castle became the means to do this, first in Northern France, and later in the rest of Europe, including areas where feudalism never took root. The feudal state was a short-lived Utopia, but feudal law left traces in all the countries where the law was written in Latin.

Turbulent conditions can occur anywhere, and central authority can be weakened for many reasons. Private strongholds were always a threat, and even as early as the second half of the 9th century attempts were made by French kings to call a halt to the building of fortifications of that type, but with no success. They did not have the necessary power to enforce their orders.

One of the fortresses of the Carolingian Empire was situated near **DORESTAD** *in the Netherlands. With its almost geometrical ground-plan it was related to Roman citadels. The central house in the inner courtyard contained the living quarters for the owner – the emperor -when he visited the place. From A. Tuulse:* Borgar i Västerlandet. *Scale 1: 2500.*

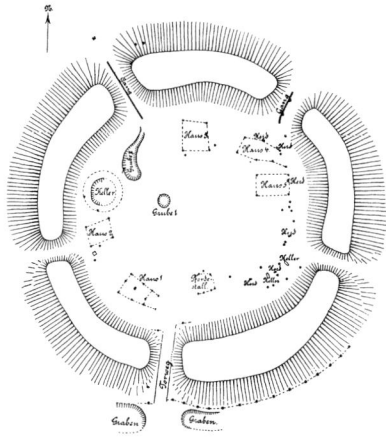

PIPINSBURG *near Geestemünde, not far from Bremerhaven, is a ring fort with defence features in the form of earth ramparts and moats. Fortresses of this type were common in the eastern part of the Frankish Empire from the time of Charlemagne and later. From A. Tuulse:* Borgar i Västerlandet. *Scale 1: 1700.*

<

The Donjon in BEAUGENCY, *on the Loire between Blois and Orleans, is from the end of the 11th century. Now only the 36 m high outer walls are left of the "Caesar Tower", which was part of a larger castle complex after rebuilding in the 16th century, but suffered damage in a fire during the religious wars. In 1840 the vaulting between the storeys collapsed. The large windows in the upper storey show that the tower was lived in until a relatively late date. Archive photo.*

The TOWER OF LONDON *seen from the Thames in the mid-17th century. The massive Norman keep from the end of the 11th century was gradually surrounded by many more buildings, and a system of curtain walls turned it into a concentric construction. Engraving by Wenceslaus Hollar. British Library, London.*

The development of the castle

The Carolingian rulers had of course built defences at the borders in the eastern part of the kingdom. In some cases these were fortresses to house guards and were surrounded by walls and had clearly been influenced by Roman camps; in other cases they were round fortresses inspired by or directly taken over from Saxon or Slavonic defence structures as those peoples were gradually subjugated. Both types of fortified sites became the background for the development on German territory of castles with curtain walls. Some time was still to elapse, however, before the rulers there fortified their palaces, and before private castles began to multiply, even though the motte and bailey structure was also known from an early date; castle-building developed differently in the western and eastern parts of the old Carolingian Empire.

In Northern France and Normandy fortresses of stone began to be built by the end of the 10th century, and in time some immense tower-structures – veritable stone mountains – were erected. They functioned at one and the same time as motte and tower, but also housed living quarters that could be both spacious and splendidly equipped. In these towers, or *donjons*, the living quarters and fortifications were fused together, so one can think of them as consisting of the dwelling area moving onto the motte. It was this type of castle that William the Conqueror brought with him to England, and that other Normans had already introduced to Sicily and thus to Italy. *Donjons* of this kind from the 11th century are still to be found, but in the century that followed, this type of structure became fully developed in France and in England, where the large tower containing living quarters became known as the "keep".

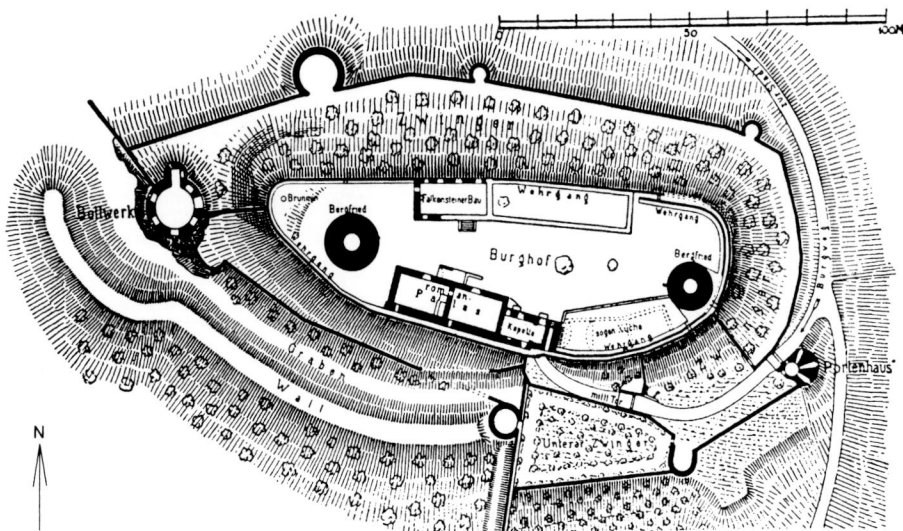

MÜNZENBERG *in Wetterau, north of Frankfurt am Main, had two stout Bergfried towers within the castle courtyard from around 1200. The castle was extended during the Middle Ages and was abandoned after c.1600. From A. Tuulse:* Borgar i Västerlandet.

On the Bayeux tapestry one can see mottes and wooden towers, and those types of structure were not abandoned because new ones began to be built in stone, but they acquired a different role from their previous one. Not everyone could afford to build a keep. It called for enormous resources in terms of both money and manpower, and the building process was lengthy. A motte with a wooden tower and palisade could be rustled up in a short time by a practised crew or by the estate's own people. As a permanent castle the motte and bailey type eventually became a second-rank structure – the minor dignitary's fortification – but the motte remained useful in war. This can clearly be seen if one follows in the footsteps of William the Conqueror as he travelled through England after the Battle of Hastings in 1066. The route and the events are well-known, from when the fleet landed at Pevensey, on the coast of southern England, after crossing the Channel. Although the Battle of Hastings was of decisive importance, it was nevertheless by means of the construction of a number of mottes on strategic sites, together with the use of campaign-forts in troublesome situations, that the country was conquered during the brief period that followed. On particularly important sites the new Norman overlords rapidly began to build stone castles, and for instance the Tower of London was completed before 1100. Both there and in e.g. Colchester there was still masonry standing from the time of Roman occupation of England, and this was re-used by the new Norman rulers.

The large stone-built buildings meant that power could be maintained. The urgently erected wooden structures built on hastily thrown up castle-mounds were soon replaced by keeps and larger castles from which the Norman overlords ruled the country as the representatives of their king. Before the Conquest private castles were virtually unknown in England. Now they came to play a major role both during the Conquest and in its aftermath in support of the monarchy, but as generally happened elsewhere they also became a threat. In time more and more of them were built, and they were not always in the hands of subjects loyal to the Crown. The situation in England did not deteriorate to the same extent as

COUCY, *near Laon in Northern France, was the most splendid nobleman's castle in France in the period around the middle of the 13th century. It was situated on a high hill, together with a fortified village. The nobleman who built the castle coveted the crown; he considered that his family was superior to and older than the royal family. The large donjon, with walls seven metres thick, was blown up by the Germans in 1918. Four other strong towers projected from the curtain walls.*

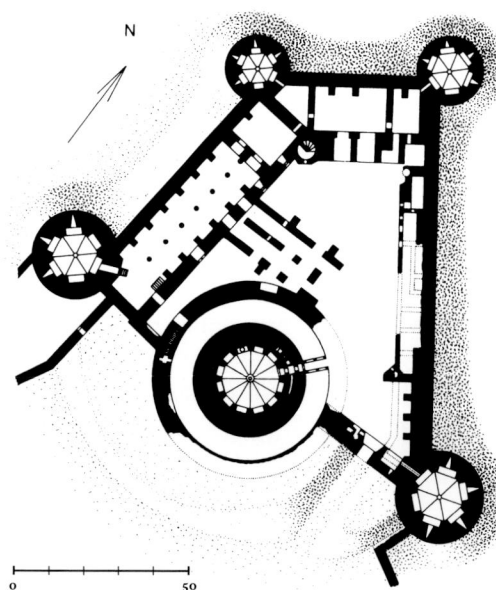

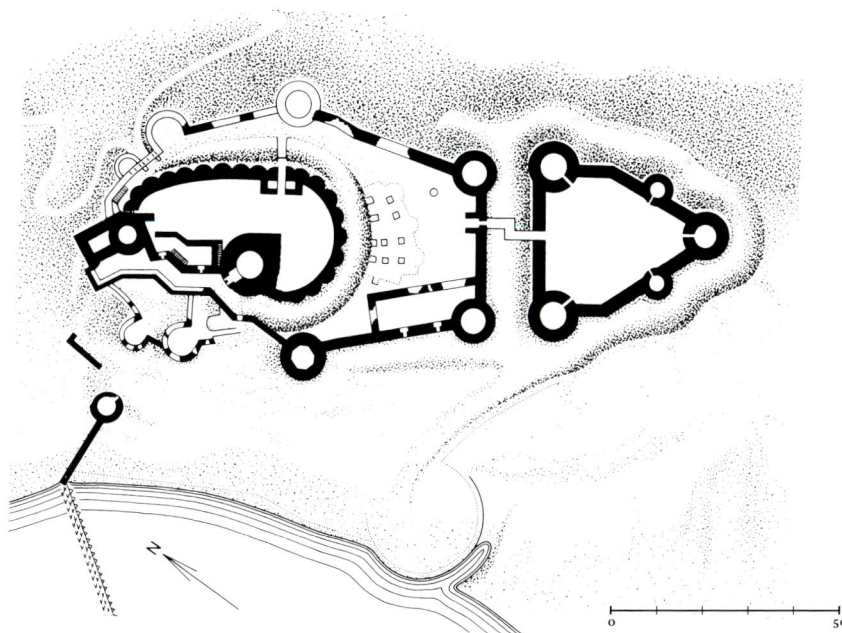

CHÂTEAU GAILLARD (plan) on the Seine south of Rouen was the ultimate in castles. Richard the Lionheart had the central part built a few years before 1200 and called the castle his "beautiful daughter". The French king conquered the castle a few years after it was built, and it never afterwards came to have real significance, although it resisted a siege in 1419. From the 16th century onwards it fell into disrepair.

CHÂTEAU GAILLARD is now an impressive ruin. Here the remains of Richard the Lionheart's castle are seen from the east. Archive photo.

in France, however. The Dukes of Normandy had been the most unruly vassals of the French king; as kings of England they did not allow the noblemen under them much independent power, and from as early as the end of the 12th century they insisted on enforcing the Crown's monopoly of the right to build castles. This was a safety measure, but it was also a good source of income for royal power, since noblemen could buy a "licence to crenellate", i.e. to build battlements and decorative towers on their manor houses, so that one could see that it was people of high social standing who lived there.

In spite of their size the *donjon* and keep could not in the long run accommodate all that was necessary for the housekeeping and other operations associated with them; there were requirements for stables, kitchens, store-rooms, soldiers' quarters, etc. Buildings for all manner of purposes sprouted up around the tower, and the whole area was surrounded by a curtain wall, in some cases from as early as the 12th century. At major sites there could be a development of a whole system of several curtain walls with outer courtyards surrounding the core of the castle.

In Germany and Central Europe towers were also to be found, but there the curtain wall tended to be the primary feature. Towers with living quarters were to be found from an early date, but the German *Bergfried* never became as massive as the *donjon* or keep, and it was not a dwelling-tower. It was first and foremost a defence structure. Whether a *Bergfried* was placed in the curtain wall or in the middle of the castle courtyard among all the castle's other buildings, it was the strongest element of the fortress and the last place of refuge for its defenders, except where it was built purely for prestige purposes and intended to impress with its height. As part of the defence fortifications a *Bergfried* was thus a motte with the wooden tower pulled into the bailey. German castles were to a great extent adapted to suit the terrain, and throughout the 11th century, when powerful men began to take names from their fortresses, and the 12th century, when minor noblemen followed suit, castles sprouted up on cliff-tops and other suitable sites across the whole empire as evidence of the weakening of imperial authority.

Castles were well-known and widespread throughout large areas of Europe by the year 1200. In general they made use of the interplay between walls and towers, and gradually it often became the case that several towers were included in a single castle-structure, for instance to protect the gate, sometimes with a whole castle-like construction in front of it, a barbican. Almost everywhere castles were by this time built of stone, like other monumental buildings, but ramparts and moats were still used as outer protection and natural features of the landscape were exploited as much as possible.

For this reason it is of only limited use to attempt to define typologies for castles or to set up criteria for dating them on the basis of categories such as "raised castles" or "water castles", dry or wet moats or more or less formally organised castle layouts. A certain type may be characteristic of an area or a kind of terrain. Some builders of castles may have had models they preferred, but each individual structure is in fact unique and special. It is a reflection of its owner's economy and need for security. It tells us something about the localities over which he had power, and his desire to demonstrate who he was. This can of course all change for the particular structure from one period to another, but as a fortified dwelling the castle-concept was in fact fully developed before 1200. All features that came to be added later were refinements.

Refinements of castle-building

New features came both from further afield and from times past. In the First Crusade, 1097-99, and in waves during the centuries that followed, princes, noblemen and others flocked to make the journey from Europe to the Holy Land to liberate Christ's Grave in Jerusalem from the "infidels", i.e. the Muslims. At first the Crusaders fared well, and they created a number of small "kingdoms"around Jerusalem and along the coast towards Asia Minor. The Christian victors constantly remained a small minority in relation to the local population, however, and they had to shore up their domination with strong fortresses. When the Muslim leaders managed to rally and counter-attack, the Crusaders found themselves living in

HARLECH *in Wales is one of the castles Edward I of England had built to secure English dominance in the region. It was a curtain-wall castle without a central tower, but the gateway to the east was particularly strongly fortified, with no fewer than seven forms of impediment that had to be overcome. Harlech was built between 1283 and 1290. Archive photo.*

The castle of **CATANIA** *on Sicily was built between 1239 and 1250 as the residence of Frederik II, King of Sicily and Holy Roman Emperor. The ground-plan is that of a fortress, but the living conditions were very comfortable. The castle survived both cannon-fire and earthquakes and today houses Catania's museum.*

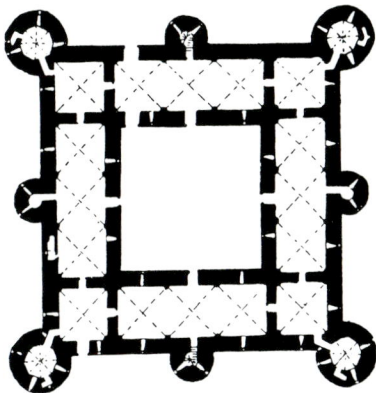

a constant state of siege, and the Christian orders of chivalry, the princes and even the more modest noble landowners built gigantic castles which in many cases can still be seen as impressive ruins today. In the Crusaders' castles one could find all the details of fortifications that had been known from antiquity, as developed in the Roman and not least the Byzantine Empires, and which the Arabs to some extent had adopted. The Christian warriors also learned from their opponents, and all the latest innovations were rapidly carried back home to Europe.

The devices in question were such features as projecting towers, overhanging wall walks, imposing angled bases etc., but what was important was that the construction was thoroughly thought out and systematically built up in such a way that each element in the fortifications provided security and was in turn secured by other parts. Loop-holes and machicolations were used to ensure that there were no blind angles that could be used for cover by the enemy during an attack, and the castle came to consist of a whole series of defences that had to be breached one by one before it was conquered. The Crusaders' castle-building became an art of fortification in the course of the 12th century because that was

necessary. By the end of the century the same techniques were all in use in Europe too; Richard Lionheart of England, the most famous of all Crusaders, for instance created a synthesis of the art of fortification in Château Gaillard, the castle he had built overlooking the Seine during the last years of the 12th century.

In the centuries that followed, castle-building reached its heyday in the areas where the castle had first developed and spread, perhaps most of all in France. New constructions and extensions to existing buildings became ever more carefully thought out, and the interplay between the individual parts of the fortification and the surrounding natural elements became more and more refined. Experiments were carried out with diverse types of symmetrical quadrangular structures, and where the site-conditions allowed, with completely symmetrical fortified constructions, e.g. in Catania in Sicily and in some of the castles Edward I built to secure his conquest of Wales in the years after 1282. Round or octagonal towers became more common, and the variations in the use of fortification elements were evened out throughout Europe, while the *donjon,* keep and *Bergfried* kept their particular characteristics. On the whole the castles became larger, because wars were waged on a larger scale than before, and became the business of princes at national level. On account of that, specially large and strong new royal castles were often built at the border of newly conquered areas, or in the

CRAIGEVAR, *west of Aberdeen in Scotland, was completed as late as 1626. It has the appearance of a toy castle, but the intention behind it was serious enough. The unruly conditions in Scotland at the time made it necessary to build private castles. Seen from the south. Archive photo.*

*The castle of **ELTZ,** on the Mosel northeast of Trier, was an important family seat from the mid 12th century. The castle grew and through the years became the residence of many branches of the same family. It was a fortified residence rather than a fortress, and it was never destroyed; now it is a unique example of living conditions in the Middle Ages and slightly later. Seen from the north. Archive photo.*

middle of them, as in Wales. The princely courts also grew, so that there was a requirement for substantial space for the many people and animals belonging to the court households.

The ordinary local potentate could at best only count on fortifying himself against his peers, against roving gangs of robbers or rebellious peasants. He would perhaps not even be granted permission to fortify his estate. Fortified buildings were originally a royal prerogative, because the king's original first duties and responsibilities were to organise war-waging and ensure peace both within the country and in relations with the external enemies of the realm. Wherever and whenever central power functioned well there was no need or place for private castles.

In turbulent areas, near borders or just far from central power, for a long time it was sufficient in many cases to have a tall stone-built house – sometimes so tall that it was called a tower-house. There might also have been ramparts or a wall and a little moat around the house and out-buildings. In the later Middle Ages some individuals with a little more power and greater need for security built small-scale castles as in the old days, in situations where they did not live in such a place already, but in many locations the mildly fortified manor – or completely unfortified version of it – became the most common form of home for the nobility in the late Middle Ages. Now and then it might have a castle-like appearance, for instance with a battlement on a tower-like feature, or with a moat around the main building, but that did not make it into a fortress. In England this meant, as already mentioned, that one had a "licence to crenellate", in France that the king had given his permission for the building, and everywhere it was a demonstration that the owner was superior to the common herd. Throughout all of Europe in the 16th century those who had control over their circumstances built spacious homes disguised as castles – in France *"châteaux manoirs"*, in England "manor houses" and in Germany *"Adelssitze"*. In Denmark they have since become known as *"herreborge"*.

The history of the castle starts off very differently in different countries. The end of story, on the other hand, happened more-or-less at the same time, from around 1500 and onwards in the first half of the 16th century, when social and

SØBORG *in North Sealand was one of Denmark's earliest castle structures. It functioned from the beginning of the 12th century until the end of the 16th century. Today there are only faint traces of ruins on the castle mound.*

religious unrest threw many European countries into conflict situations. Wars were waged with large armies of mercenaries and effective firearms, and they demonstrated that the castle was out-of-date as a defence structure. It could not withstand attack with cannons and could not contain a garrison sufficient for effective defence in conjunction with counter-attack on the attackers.

The two functions of the castle were then separated out, and in later times fortresses were built for war purposes, whereas palaces and mansions were built for living in. The houses of the powerful were often still called castles, but no-one dreamt of thinking of them as fortresses. Such houses were often given names ending in "borg", but no-one imagined that e.g. the royal residences of Amalienborg, Fredensborg, or Christiansborg, which now houses the Danish parliament, could be considered fortresses.

II

Denmark: the first stages the earliest castles

The large circular fortresses of the Viking Age fell out of use as early as the beginning of the 11th century. There were a few towns that had been enclosed in sturdy surrounding ramparts in the Viking Age, and several were fortified in the turbulent years in the middle of the 12th century. Strongholds continued to be used as places of communal refuge, some of them far into the Middle Ages, and Danevirke, the earthen rampart on the border between Denmark and Germany, was significant – it was reinforced as late as in the latter half of the 12th century and in the early 13th – but those structures were all fortifications, not actual castles.

In the Middle Ages Denmark was larger, as a country, than it is today. Scania, Halland and Blekinge were then part of Denmark but have belonged to Sweden since 1660, and the Duchy of Schleswig – Southern Jutland, as it was called originally – was conquered by Prussia in 1864 and was German until 1920, when the northern part of Schleswig returned to Denmark after a plebiscite. In the whole of what was then Danish territory one finds the same type of ruins and remains of the same kinds of castles. In Schleswig and the southern Swedish territories the castles and castle mounds often have a different history from that of their counterparts in the rest of the kingdom, however, since there were particular circumstances in play there.

In Denmark there is no positive proof, written or archaeological, of the existence of castles, either royal or private, before the first half of the 12th century, and the earliest traces of evidence relate only to very few: Haraldsborg near Roskilde, Søborg and Bastrup in North Sealand, Pedersborg near Sorø and perhaps Borren in Højby parish in the Ods Herred district. They are all on Sealand, which was the centre of the kingdom, and where the important struggles for power took place, but apart from Søborg none of them was still in use after 1200, perhaps because they had already been demolished before then. The written sources are few and the information in them sparse, but archaeological evidence of definite traces of other early castles is also lacking – particularly of private ones, even though in recent years strenuous efforts have been made, with good reason, to find them.

Throughout the middle of the 12th century there were turbulent times in Denmark. The members of the royal family and their supporters fought over the Crown and over power in the realm and in the end the country was close to being split between three of the contenders for the throne, Svend, Knud and Valdemar. There were powerful forces at work, also beyond Denmark's borders: even the

DANEVIRKE: *part of the main rampart east of Valdemar's Wall.*

Denmark in the Middle Ages
Market town
Bishop's seat
Monastery / Convent
Other places of historical importance
SKAGERAK
NORWAY
Bohus
Nya Lødøse
Opensten
Kongsbakke
Øresten
Hunehals
Kindahus
SWEDEN
GOTLAND
Skagen
Hjørring
Børglum
Sæby
VENDSYSSEL
Ås
Varberg
HALLAND
Trolleborg
Skt. Jørgensbjerg
Tisted
Aalborg
Svenstrup
Vitskøl
KATTEGAT
Falkenberg
Vestervig
HIMMER-SYSSEL
Nykøbing
Pliksborg
Spøtrup
Halmstad
Hobro
Mariager
Laholm
Lemvig
Skive
Tap Hede
Viborg
Båstad
Finderup
Randers
Grenå
Hald
Holstebro
Grate Hede
BLEKINGE
Kullen
Rønneby
Kalø
Luntertun
Elleholm
JUTLAND
Æbeltoft
Aarhus
Hjelm
Herrevad
Ringkøbing
Ry
Søborg
Gurre
Helsingborg
Bækkeskov
Sølvesborg
Skanderborg
Esrum
Hærvejen
SCANIA
Om
Isøre
Helsingør
Væ
Åhus
Landskrone
Bosø
Horsens
Nykøbing
Slangerup
Dysiebro
Vidtskøfle
Skibby
Refsnæs
Jelling
København
Lund
Øved
Holbæk
Varde
Vejle
Kalundborg
Lejre
Roskilde
Dalby
Simrishamn
Tommarp
Malmø
Børringe
SEALAND
Dragør
Bogense
Slimmingehus
Lindholmen
Haraldsted
Ystad
Kolding
Middelfart
Trelleborg
Sorø
Fjenneslev
Køge
Skanør
Odense
Slagelse
Ringsted
Trelleborg
Ribe
Falsterbo
Sprogø
Antvorskov
Fotevig
Hammershus
FUNEN
Gram
Korsør
Skovkloster
St. Heddinge
Assens
Nyborg
BORNHOLM
Haderslev
Hagenskov
Næstved
Lilleborg
Rønne
Skælskør
Neksø
Løgum
Åbenrå
Fåborg
Svendborg
Præstø
Vordingborg
BALTIC SEA
MØEN
NORDFRISLAND
Trøjborg
Stege
Urnehoved
Tønder
Sønderborg
Stubbekøbing
Nakskov
Sakskøbing
LANGELAND
FALSTER
Flensborg
Ryd
Maribo
Nykøbing
Arkona
LOLLAND
Husum
Slesvig
FEMERN
RYGEN
Danevirke
Gottorp
Lo Hede
Kiel
Ejderen
Rendsborg
Bornhøved

Holy Roman Emperor was involved. These circumstances could have formed a natural environment for private castle-building. The reason that such a development did not take place may be that the struggle for the Crown was played out at a high level and did not impinge on society in depth, but it could also just as well be the case that the structure of the old Nordic society was stronger than influence from the countries south and west of Denmark. In the Nordic region fighting over castles did not begin until the mid 13th century. Until then and for a long time afterwards power struggles were decided in battles on open fields, e.g. Grathe Hede near Viborg, where Valdemar, later known as Valdemar the Great, won against Svend after the bloodbath of Roskilde in 1157, when the third contender for the throne, Knud, was murdered. Queen Margrete's victory over Albrecht of Sweden at Falen or Åsle in 1389 is another example, and it was the same in other countries, for instance at the famous battles of Crécy in 1346 and Agincourt in 1415 during the Hundred Years' War between England and France.

DENMARK IN THE MIDDLE AGES

The earliest written sources that mention castles in Denmark and provide evidence of their role are chronicles from the 12th century. The oldest is the Roskilde Chronicle from around 1140, but the best-known and most detailed is Saxo's chronicle, *Gesta Danorum*, written around 1200, describing the deeds of the Danes. It is a biased account, designed to glorify the Valdemars and in particular Archbishop Absalon, who had commissioned Saxo's work. In Saxo's writing the general trend and the opportunity to use fine language – genuine silver-age Latin, full of quotations from the authors of antiquity – are more important than the absolute truth, and in matters of warfare, battles and castles it has to be borne in mind that Saxo was a scholar who evidently had never served in the field, even though he came from one of the families that had been involved in the conflicts over the royal succession.

Saxo for instance describes the castle of Arkona on the island of Rügen using the words with which the Roman historian Justin depicted the temple in Delphi. Excavations at Arkona have shown, however, that it was built of earth and wood, as a Slavonic type of ring fort, typical of its time and of the people who built it. Furthermore, Saxo's lifetime was later than many of the events of which he gives an account, but we must all the same take his stories about castles into consideration and compare them with what other sources, such as his contemporary Svend Aggesen, can tell us. Svend Aggesen was no doubt knowledgeable and well-educated, but unlike Saxo he was not a man of the Church.

The earliest "castle" mentioned by Saxo is situated either in or near the town of Schleswig, and was being used as a prison for unfortunate members of the royal family and for other distinguished and dangerous individuals in the years after the murder of Duke Knud Lavard in 1131. The Roskilde Chronicle says that it was a castle, but the building is often interpreted as a tower, probably because castle towers were later used as prisons for dangerous political enemies, so that "to be put in the tower" came to mean imprisonment. Saxo did not use either the word

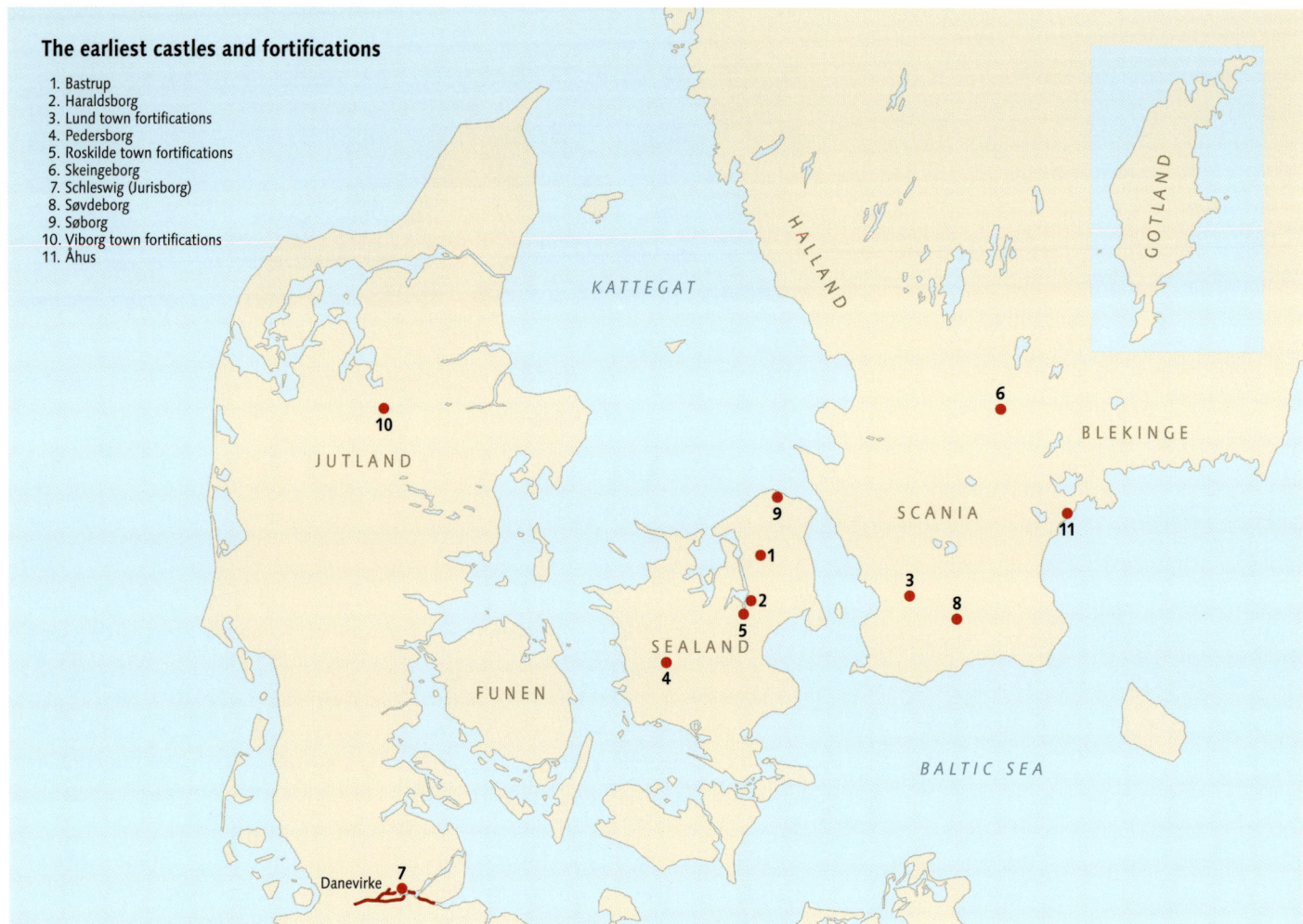

The earliest castles and fortifications

1. Bastrup
2. Haraldsborg
3. Lund town fortifications
4. Pedersborg
5. Roskilde town fortifications
6. Skeingeborg
7. Schleswig (Jurisborg)
8. Søvdeborg
9. Søborg
10. Viborg town fortifications
11. Åhus

"tower" or the word "castle", however; he writes only about a "prison". The little island of Mågeø in the fjord named Slien, near Schleswig, was the site of what later became Jurisborg, where the toll had to be paid to the authorities, and from where the harbour was guarded up to around 1200. It was possibly there that King Erik Plovpenning met his brother Abel in 1250, and where instead of negotiating a peace treaty the King was killed and thrown in the fjord. Quite how much fortification there was in the first half of the 12th century is not possible to establish, since the traces of the structure are badly damaged, but there would hardly have been space for a major construction on the island.

In the town of Schleswig there was an important royal seat, which first the kings and later the dukes of Schleswig used as a residence until the middle of the 13th century, when they moved to Gottorp. At the beginning of the 1130s King Niels sought refuge from the victorious avengers of Knud Lavard at the royal estate in Schleswig, but he did not find sanctuary there from the inhabitants of the town, who apparently killed him. In recent years traces have been found in the

MAP SHOWING DENMARK'S OLDEST CASTLES. *Some are mentioned in written sources, particularly by Saxo. Others have been found by archaeological investigation.*

town of solid building-structures which are thought to be possible remains of the royal property, but not enough has been found to justify calling this a castle.

The murder of Duke Knud Lavard led to civil-war-like conflict over the accession to the throne in Denmark during the next quarter century. Knud Lavard was the son of King Erik Ejegod and thus a member of the fertile and extensive royal family whose innumerable members could all with almost equal justice lay claim to the throne – if they were men. Denmark did not have a hereditary monarchy, and the king was chosen by the great men of the kingdom, but at any rate from the time of Gorm the Old onwards they had all been from a particular family. Since the death of King Svend Estridsen in the 1070s five of his many sons had succeeded him on the throne, one after the other. Their sons and their brothers' and sisters' sons then fought with and against each other for decades, supported by the most powerful families in the country, until it ended with Knud Lavard's son Valdemar becoming undisputed king in 1157, after the country had been divided for a time between him and his cousin Svend and their half cousin Knud.

It is thus possible, more-or-less, to follow the traces of the conflicts and the changing coalitions, and to detect that castles play a remarkably small role in the battles. According to the sources, important towns like Lund, Roskilde and Viborg had fortifications by this time, and some of them have been brought to light now by archaeological investigations. But they were not castles. On the other hand, the "Castles of the Belt" – no doubt Storebælt, the channel between the Danish islands of Sealand and Funen – which Svend Grathe is said to have built as protection against pirates, and on which Valdemar waged war in the mid 1100s, may actually have been castles in the medieval interpretation. Nothing is known about them however – not even where they were sited or whether they were perhaps forerunners for the major royal castles of the Valdemar Age (1157-1241), e.g. Nyborg on Funen and Tårnborg at Korsør Nor, which together with the tower on the island of Sprogø protected the crossing of the Belt and with it the cohesion of the regions of the kingdom.

Sealand was a rich area in the centre of the realm in the decades of the conflict over the succession; the members of the powerful Hvide family, who owned large quantities of land on the island, were important participants in the conflict between contenders for the throne, but there were other powerful interests involved. The Church also had a role to play – at least in the person of its leader, Eskil, the second archbishop of the realm and nephew of the first, Asser. Eskil himself came from a powerful family, the Thrugot or Trund family, and he had a daughter who was married to a grandson of Knud the Holy, so in addition to Eskil's interest in maintaining the strength of influence of the Church, the matter of who sat on the throne was also of personal importance to him. As members of the royal family, his daughter's sons were just as eligible as many other male descendants of Svend Estridsen, and in addition to being the foremost prince of the Church in the kingdom and a major landowner Eskil was also an internationally-minded person with important contacts in Europe. It may seem surprising that an archbishop had children and grandchildren, but clerical celibacy was not imposed until 1139, and by then Eskil already had children.

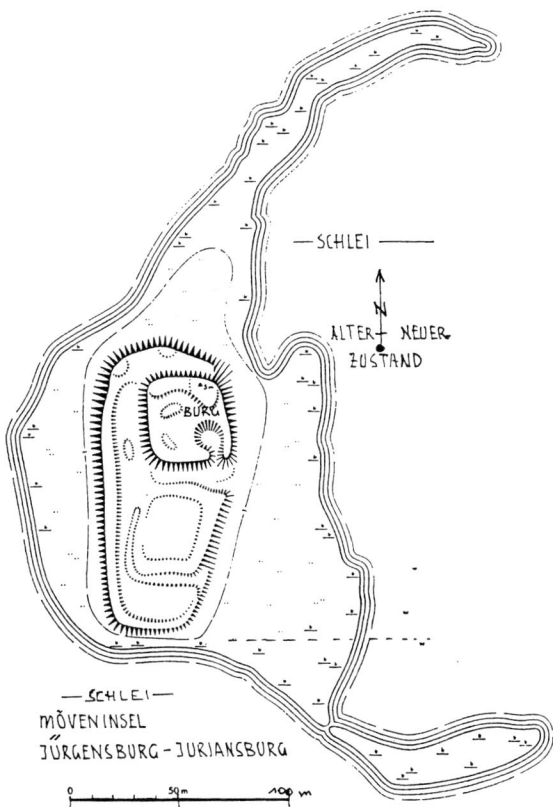

JURISBURG *on Mågeø, an island in the harbour of the town of Schleswig, probably dates from the 13th century, and perhaps it was there that Duke Abel had his brother King Erik Plovpenning murdered in 1250. From Arthur Dähn:* Ringwälle und Turmhügel in Schleswig-Holstein.

Well into the middle of the 12th century Archbishop Eskil had participated in the conflict over the throne and at several times he had been the enemy of the reigning king. He had been in conflict with a succession of kings in Scania, and to strengthen his position he had built a castle in north Sealand on a little island in what was then Søborg Lake. The lake was drained in the late 18th century. He also built Åhus at the mouth of the river Helgeå on the south coast of Scania, on a site which he may have received from Svend Grathe in 1149, but it was probably not a castle from the start. On that site there are still the ruins of a fine stone-built house, a *palatium,* and Eskil may not have had the same need to protect himself in Scania as he had on Sealand.

The ruin of the palatium *of* **ÅHUS** *has walls that are still standing to a height of over two metres, so one can form an impression of the lower floor, 19 x 10.5 m. Possibly Archbishop Eskil's fine house was more of a residence than a castle, but later there was a real castle on the site.*

KNOWN CASTLES
from the first half of the 12th century

THE BASTRUP TOWER

Overlooking Bastrup Lake, north of Farum on Sealand, lies the ruin of a mighty round tower. It was built on a peninsula that reached out into the lake, and the site was cut off from the mainland by a moat and possibly a rampart. Not many traces of the other houses that must have surrounded the tower have been found, so they can be assumed to have been light wooden or half-timbered buildings without deep foundations.

The Bastrup Tower was built of calcareous tufa, travertine from hill-slopes, which was used for the construction of most of the early stone buildings in Denmark. The walls of these buildings were built in cofferwork, i.e. with well-shaped ashlars on either side of a core of boulders and rubble fused together with mortar. The ruin of the Bastrup Tower still stands several metres high, with six-metre-thick walls and an external diameter of 21 m a little above the base, and the preserved cellar space provides a good impression of the colossal size and strength of the original tower. On account of both its size and the high quality of the masonry-work the Bastrup Tower is unique not just in Denmark but also by international standards. Not even French donjons from that time are so massive, and nothing even remotely similar is known in Danish medieval architecture. In the era of the Bastrup Tower there was, however, an almost equally immense and older round tower in Hamburg.

There are no records about the site of the Bastrup Tower. So nothing is known about its history and one can only guess at who had it built, what its purpose was and how long it stood there intact. Such a splendid building must have belonged to the highest and wealthiest social circle, and perhaps the owner and person responsible for its construction was a member of the important family that posterity has dubbed the "Hvide" family. They became staunch supporters of Knud Lavard's son Valdemar, so that it was actually because of them that he could take the throne and come to be known as Valdemar the Great. Throughout the whole period of his reign – and the reigns of his sons Knud and Valdemar the Victorious, a period known as the Valdemar period, from 1157 to 1241 – the Crown was strong in collaboration with the Hvide family. These were people with strong contacts abroad; they travelled often and had no doubt seen castles both in

In the lower level of the **BASTRUP TOWER** *the ashlars of calcareous tufa can be seen to best advantage. Tufa or travertine is a building material commonly found in Denmark's earliest masonry buildings. View over a frozen Bastrup Lake.*

Germany and in France, and in relation to Danish conditions they possessed almost unlimited wealth.

Sealand was "Hvideland" rather than Crown land, and in a letter from the time of King Niels there is mention of an "Ebbe de Bastetorp", who may be identical with Ebbe Skjalmsen, Absalon's father's brother and Knud Lavard's foster-brother. He played a large and active part in the battles on Sealand for many years and may well have had need of a castle, but what the Bastrup Tower was more specifically intended to protect is difficult to say; it could have been a strategic stretch of road of which there is now no other evidence. Even though quite a lot is known about the fighting over the succession, there is insufficient information about specific situations for it to be possible to explain the strategic function of the Bastrup Tower, but it is

The ruins of the **BASTRUP TOWER** *still rise to an impressive height above ground level. The base of the tower shows the quality of the building-work, but we can only guess at who was responsible for having the tower built, and likewise it is impossible to calculate the original height of the tower. Seen from the northeast.*

Old plan of the **BASTRUP TOWER** *with indications of the thickness of the walls. Danish National Museum.*

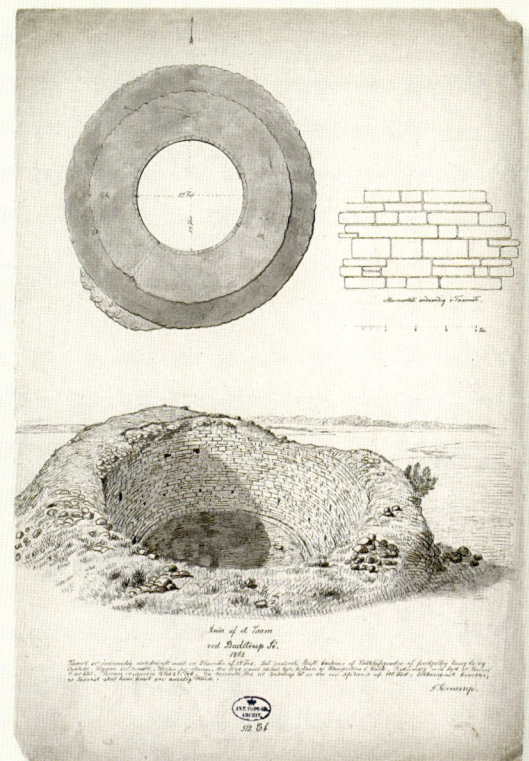

nevertheless reasonable to see it as an element in the Hvide family's support for the avengers of Knud Lavard.

Means to provide for the construction of the tower and a context that could justify it were also in the possession of Ebbe Skjalmsen, and since his descendants owned estates and other land near the site of the Bastrup Tower, it could well have belonged to him. The dates fit with the building material and place the Bastrup Tower at the beginning of the 12th century. Despite its splendour and impressive strength it could only have had a short period of function, however, since it is not mentioned in any context in written sources. The Herman de Bastrop who is mentioned in the "Femernlist" in King Valdemar's *Jordebog* (i.e. the register of royal properties) from c.1231 cannot be associated with any context that could link him to Bastrup. There have not been many finds at the site, but a small treasure hoard of coins from Svend Grathe's time – around 1150 – may possibly indicate that the building was still in use at that time. That would also have been to be expected.

PEDERSBORG

At the northern end of Pedersborg Lake, where it connects with the adjacent Lake Tuelsø, Pedersborg Church towers up on a natural mound about 15 m in height; the sides of the mound have been cut away to leave steep slopes and the churchyard now surrounds most of it. The surface at the top measures 35 x 70 m, and before the church was built, probably in the first half of the 13th century, it was the site of a castle that had at least one fine stone building, i.e. a round church in a style similar to two others – the one in Bjernede, which was built c.1170-75 by Sune Ebbesen, and Archbishop Eskil's church in Søborg. A large section of the masonry-work of the round church at Pedersborg can still be seen in the northern slope of the churchyard, where it tumbled down, no doubt in connection with the clearing of the top surface of the mound. Masonry remains have also been found on the top of the mound, and they may come from a curtain wall or perhaps from a large stone-built house.

The castle mound is situated in an area of some 9 acres which is surrounded by a stout semi-circular rampart leading down to the shores of the lake; the

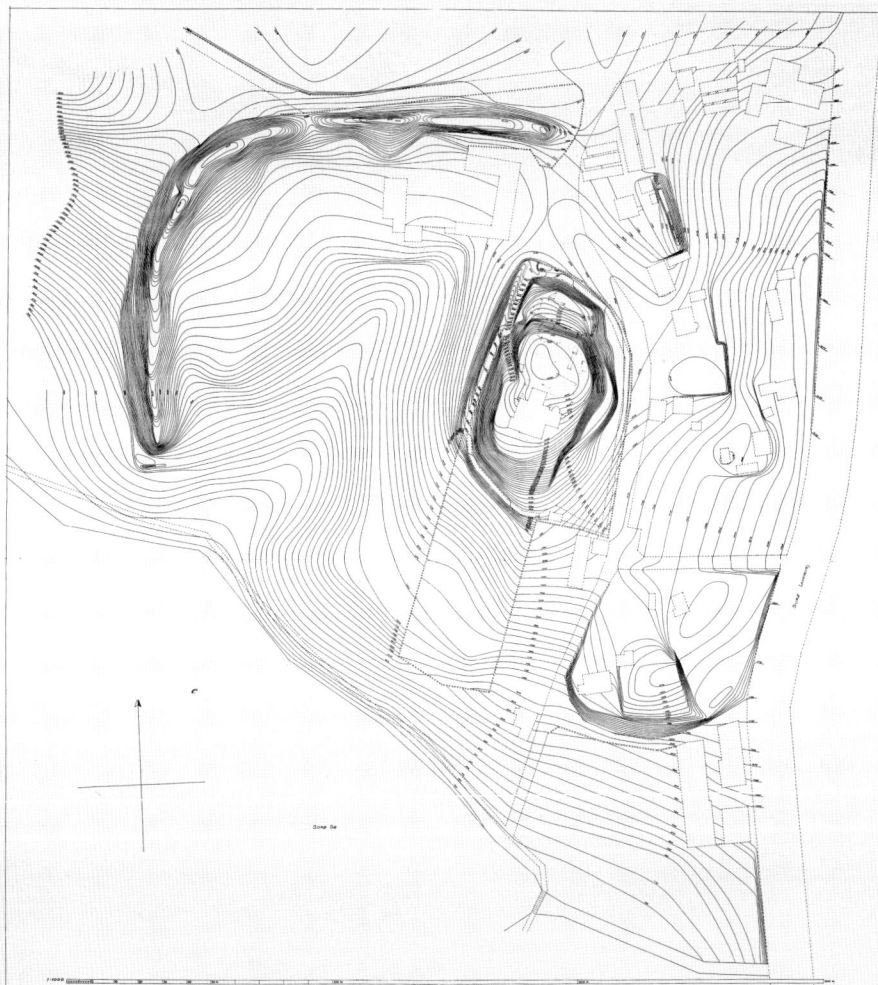

Plan of **PEDERSBORG** *showing the area within the rampart from the 7th century. The church is now situated on top of the mound, and at the bottom of the mound one can see the outline of the stone-built house that was of slightly later date than the castle.*

rampart is 17 m wide at its base and in some places still has a height of up to 4 m. It is part of a prehistoric fortification, with its earliest phase dating to about 600 BC, and whoever commissioned the building of Pedersborg thus chose to make use of a pre-existing defence feature when he built his castle, probably in the middle of the 12th century.

In all probability the initiator of the castle-building was Peder Torstensen, who was married to Skjalm Hvide's daughter Cecilia – the sister of "Ebbe de Bastetorp" and aunt of Sune Ebbesen in Bjernede – so Peder belonged to the powerful Hvide clan. If Saxo is to be believed, he distinguished himself in the campaigns against the Wends in the reign of Valdemar the Great, and his daughter's son Ulf presented Pedersborg to the monastery in Sorø in 1205. By that time several buildings had been erected on the south side of the castle mound, including a *palatium*, a grand stone-built house, which had no doubt been occupied by the influential family's household.

It was a relief for the monks to acquire Pedersborg, or "Borg", as the place was originally known, since Peder had evidently made life difficult for the monastery when he could. The monastery had no use for the castle, and in due course the present church was built on the top of the mound.

Peder Torstensen doubtless enjoyed his castle in ways other than annoying the monks in Sorø, and his motives for building it were probably the same as his brother-in-law Ebbe's, i.e. to offer support to the young future King Valdemar. But apart from these two structures nothing more is known about private castles, either in the Hvide family's possession or in the hands of other major figures in the first half of the 12th century, and those two structures did not survive the Valdemar period.

PEDERSBORG *on a misty winter day. The castle mound has become a churchyard, and part of the castle site is now an asphalt-covered parking area. Seen from the west.*

HARALDSBORG

All traces of this structure were totally eradicated in connection with the building of a residential neighbourhood on the north-eastern edge of Roskilde in the 1920s, and now it is only street-names such as "King Valdemar's Road" that testify to the fact that there was once a royal castle there. It functioned as a royal estate until the civil war in Denmark in the 1530s, when it was burned down. By that time Haraldsborg was an administrative centre rather than a fortress; it is referred to as *"curia"*, farm, and not *"castrum"*, castle, but its history goes back to the years of turbulence in Denmark after the killing of Knud Lavard in 1131, and it was not the king who had the castle built, but another member of the royal family, Harald Kesja.

Harald Kesja was Knud Lavard's step-brother and was for a time one

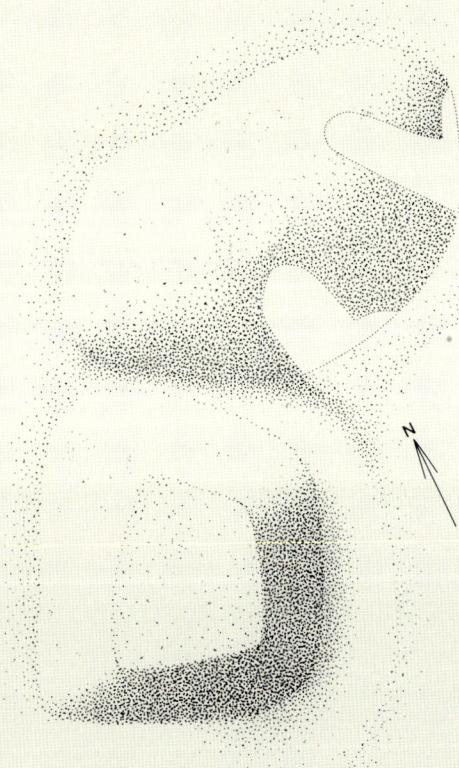

The mural painting on the north wall of the nave in **AAL CHURCH** in West Jutland, from the early 13th century, shows an equestrian battle scene, probably a depiction of one of the battles in the Old Testament. The conflict is raging around the strange tower on "stilts" seen in this detail from the painting. Photo from www.kalkmalerier.dk.

of the group that sought to avenge his death, but then he decided to seek power for himself. This brought him into conflict with Erik Emune, who was step-brother both to himself and to Knud Lavard, but who chose a wiser path than Harald and through remaining allied with the Hvide family achieved access to royal power for a number of years.

During the long conflict over the throne, between 1131 and 1157, there were few long spells of peace. Many battles were fought between different parties, both on land and at sea, but only on one single occasion is there mention of a battle at a castle. That was in 1132, when

Erik Emune and his army laid siege to Haraldsborg. Saxo gives a detailed and exciting account of this, explaining that Harald Kesja had built the castle, and setting out what he had heard about the battle. Some of it had clearly surprised him, and perhaps because of that there is useful information to be extracted from his text.

As far as Saxo knew, the fortifications were of earth and wood. The castle was surrounded by a rampart, probably with a palisade on top of it, and inside

Drawing of the remains of **HARALDSBORG**, near Roskilde, from 1903. The plan shows a type of structure which was common between c.1250 and 1350, but it does not correspond to Saxo's description from around 1200.

the ramparts "they had a strange house that could turn when given the slightest push just like a door on a spindle". This sounds really peculiar, and impractical. It may have been a post mill, but there would hardly have been any windmills in Denmark at such an early date, and a mill of that type would not have been of use for defence purposes. There might instead have been a fortress tower on poles, a "tower on stilts" like the one to be seen on on the mural equestrian frieze from around 1200 in Aal Church in western Jutland. Finally it is possible that the whole story has been distorted in the course of the years, so it does not serve any useful purpose to try to imagine what kind of tower there was on Harald Kesja's castle.

On the other hand it is interesting to know that Erik Emune and his troops made little impression on the fortifications, even though they were a large force and were equipped with siege engines. According to Saxo they were not used to using these weapons, and had to seek help from some Germans fetched from the town of Roskilde. The Germans had no problems making the machines work. The tower was crushed by a well-aimed shot, and this scared the defenders so much that they fled on horseback during the night down the "dark side of the rampart " – whatever that meant.

At any rate, there is not much to be learned from this, apart from the little piece of evidence that the Danes were not used to the weaponry of siege warfare. Around the castle area several finds have been made of coins from Erik Emune's time or later, and of old precious silver objects, some of them from distant places. This shows that the castle belonged to a wealthy and important milieu.

How the castle buildings were otherwise arranged is something we can only guess at. There is a survey of the area from 1903, before the site was destroyed by the subsequent house-building, but it shows two mounds which were probably not part of the original site. Castles were often altered over the course of time, in order to adapt to newly-developed weapons of attack and to changing circumstances, and on the drawing from 1903 the castle structure shown is one that would have been common in Denmark in the period between c.1250 and 1350.

THE HARALDSBORG TREASURE HOARD *contains a quantity of coins, mainly from Erik Emune's time, and diverse silver objects, including a lid that suggests oriental inspiration, with animal motifs, and a gilded silver bowl with inlays of blue and green glass. Possibly these valuable objects were hidden in the context of the fighting in the 1130s. They must have come from a refined environment, and some of them are of a sufficient age to have perhaps been heirlooms by the time they were hidden away. The hoard is now in the Danish National Museum. Photo Danish National Museum.*

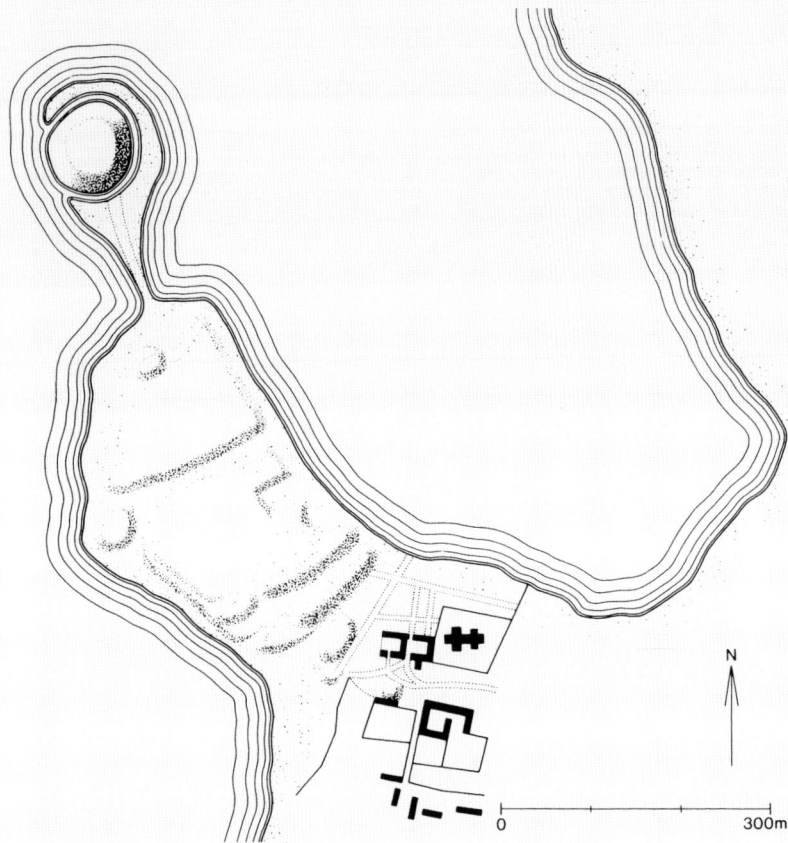

SØBORG is the oldest castle with a curtain wall known in Denmark, but at first there was only a tower surrounded by a palisade on the island. This is marked with black on the plan. The outline with grey hatching shows the next phase, in which a curtain wall with towers surrounds a palatium – a distinguished stone-built house – along with a little round church and another stone building. The later extension of the castle, no doubt from the time of the Valdemars, is shown with a clear hollow outline. From C.M. Smidt, 1930.

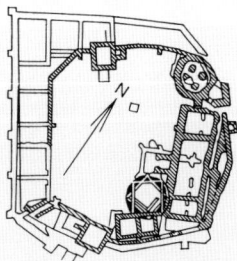

SØBORG

If we are to make the date and the age fit, Archbishop Eskild must at the earliest have built his castle in the 1130s, i.e. when the conflict over the throne was being waged in earnest. He was born in c.1100 and would have had to have reached a certain maturity and acquired land before he could plan to build. From 1134 onwards he was Bishop of Roskilde and thus commanded the richest diocese in Denmark; in 1137 he succeeded his uncle, Asser, as archbishop. How he acquired the site for the castle is not known, but it was possibly in an exchange of land with King Erik Emune, whom he supported for a time. This is a matter excavations cannot solve; they can only show us something about the date and structural arrangement. Saxo, who is the main source of our knowledge about the castle, does not call it by the name "Søborg", but describes a "castle the archbishop had built in Lethre peat-bog". Even making allowances for any possible uncertainty, this can hardly be anything other than Søborg. If Saxo is right in saying that the archbishop built the castle it must have been after 1137.

The site was well-chosen, on the outermost of three islets in the lake. On the inner one there is still today a church from around 1200 and the village of Søborg, which in the Middle Ages was an important market town with a town charter. On the middle island, which is protected by two solid ramparts – of unknown age, but as far as can be judged dating back to prehistoric time – finds have been made of graves and brick-kilns. It can therefore be assumed that there were many people associated with the castle from an early stage; Saxo re-

The huge ramparts in front of the headland at **SØBORG** *most likely date from prehistoric time. It was probably here that Valdemar the Great's troops drew up their siege engines in 1161. Seen from the southeast.*

fers to it as *"urbs"* – town – and not *"arx"* or *"castrum"* – castle.

On the outermost little island there was the castle itself. It has been thoroughly excavated several times and is frequently mentioned in written sources. Through the years Søborg has also played a role in works of literature, e.g. in B.S. Ingemann's novels, written in the first half of the 19th century. For many years his works were so popular that they became part of the "national identity" and the castle and its history became an important part of the Danish national heritage. Archaeological investigations at Søborg have shown that the first fortifications on the site, which measures c. 60 x 60 m, consisted of a rampart running along the shore of the island. It was probably topped by a palisade, and at some point an octagonal stone-built tower was constructed on the castle site, before it was extended and reinforced relatively few years later.

A horse-shoe shaped moat was dug to the north, east and south-east, surrounding the island. The castle site was raised, and so was the rampart outside the moat. Then a curtain wall was added along the rim of the mound, and the entrance on the south side was protected by a robust gate-tower. Another sturdy tower was added to the north wall and a smaller one to the east. Both projected slightly forward from the outer wall, so that the castle could be protected from enemy attack, by men shooting arrows along the wall. Within the castle site, towards the east there was a fine stone-built house, a *palatium,* and north of that a little round church which was the castle chapel. South of the *palatium* there was another stone building, and there were probably a number of lighter buildings of wood and half-timbered construction within the castle walls.

Projecting towers were among the fortification features the Crusaders brought back with them to Europe in the 12th century, so the fact that they are found here may mean that Søborg's oldest curtain wall dates from after Eskil's time. It is therefore possible that the castle which was besieged by Valdemar the Great's troops and conquered in 1161 was at that time still surrounded by a rampart and palisade, but it was situated out in the middle of the lake and

was at any rate a strong fortress. Saxo recounts that now the King's troops had become used to siege warfare and knew how to use weapons of bombardment, i.e. trebuchets and other versions of artillery in use at the time, but even so they could not conquer Søborg.

So they had to resort to stratagem. One of Eskil's two grandsons was attending school in Esrum Abbey not far from Søborg. He was fetched and a large gallows was erected, so that the defenders of the castle could see it and understand that the boy would be hanged if the garrison did not surrender. At the same time a forged letter from the Archbishop was slipped into the castle, containing the message that the defenders should surrender rather than let the Archbishop's grandson die. In this way King Valdemar took the castle, and it then remained the property of the Crown. Saxo

is enthusiastic about the cunning fabrication, which he attributes to the King, so one can fully understand that the boy and his brother became enemies of King Valdemar and sought to stir up rebellion against him when they were old enough to do so.

In the years around 1200 Søborg seems to have been rebuilt and extended; the curtain wall was extended, stone-built houses were added along it, and at the same time a church was built on the innermost islet, where the town was also expanding. Søborg was an important place for the monarchy up until the late Middle Ages, for a long time as the state prison for dangerous political opponents. These were people such as Prince Buris, who was part of the royal family but did not support King Valdemar in his attempts to keep the succession in his own branch of the family by hav-

KING SAUL FIGHTING AGAINST THE AMMONITES. *The hand-to-hand fighting was extremely violent, and the head of one of the warriors was split through his helmet; this was back when men were men. The troops were firing trebuchets, and all in all it is a lively representation of a battle at the time when the depiction was made. Illustration in* The Crusader Bible *c.1250. The Morgan Library & Museum, New York.*

ing his eldest son acknowledged as heir to the throne while he himself was still alive. Legend has it that Buris further offended King Valdemar by falling in love with the King's sister, but the gruesome tale of the death of the lovers and their burial in a common grave in Vestervig,

in northwest Jutland, is pure fiction. King Valdemar did not have a sister that Buris could have fallen in love with.

Another enemy was Bishop Valdemar of Schleswig, who was incarcerated in Søborg for fourteen years from 1193. He was politically dangerous because he was the son of one of the contenders for the throne, Knud, who had been murdered in the bloodbath in Roskilde in 1157; moreover, the Bishop did little to conceal his desire to achieve power. Archbishop Jens Grand had become the bitterest opponent of the Crown as a consequence of the conflict between the sons of Valdemar the Victorious after the latter's death in 1241; according to a chronicle's account of his imprisonment he suffered torment in the prison in Søborg, spending a year and a half, from 1294, in the tower, until a cook helped him to escape.

In the days when the novels of B.S. Ingemann were known by virtually every child and adult in Denmark, most people had a clear mental image of how badly treated the Archbishop was, until the cunning cook "Morten Madsvend" arranged his escape. In reality distinguished prisoners were not normally very badly treated; imprisonment involved relatively free and amenable living conditions, and a large royal castle provided both a suitable environment and a safe place of detention for such prisoners.

Søborg does not seem to have had great military significance after it became royal. There was certainly a fight for the castle in the 1340s in connection with Valdemar Atterdag's unification of the kingdom, but that is mostly evidence of how far the kingdom had slipped into disintegration. By that time there were

SØBORG CHURCH *was built of brick in c.1200. The fine red walls here on the north side give some idea of what the castle buildings would have looked like, out in the lake in the time of the Valdemars. Seen from the northeast.*

many castles, including private ones, over the whole realm.

In addition to being a state prison, Søborg Castle was an important administrative centre until the 1530s, when the fief of Søborg was placed under Kronborg, and the castle was allowed to fall into disrepair.

Two of these four early castles disappeared during the Middle Ages; one fell into a state of decay in the 16th century and the traces of the last were destroyed in more recent times. There are also structures whose history is not known, but where there have been finds which identify a period of functioning that suggests they were constructed in the time of the conflict over the succession. Borren in Højby parish in Ods Herred is such a site; it seems to have been fortified before or around the mid-12th century and to have fallen out of use after that. There was a round tower there, smaller than the Bastrup Tower. All that can be seen are the foundations of granite boulders, and no owner can be associated with the site, which lay on a peninsula that was divided off from the rest of the mainland by a stout wall of granite boulders.

It is difficult to believe, however, that the Crown or the royal contenders would not have had castles or fortifications in Denmark in connection with the decades of war in the 12th century. There were many battles, because the conflict came to have the nature of civil war, with shifting positions and alliances, and because the Wends – Slavonic pirates – in those turbulent days constantly ravaged the country's shores. And undeniably the few structures that are known show that the techniques of building castles had been fully mastered.

In a period when central power breaks down and cannot ensure peace within the kingdom or in relation to other countries it is extremely important for the population to have secure places of refuge; this is where communal strongholds – places of refuge similar to the simple forts of earlier times – come into the picture. It is evidently more difficult for an individual landowner to protect himself, because the possessions of both large and small estate owners were often spread out, sometimes in several parts of the country, as were the Crown properties. It was impossible, even in the case of the royal properties, and even later in the Middle Ages, to fortify all the estates; viewing this from today's perspective it is not possible to see why some locations were fortified and others not.

The communal strongholds had a role to play far up in time; for example St Albert on Ærø was used in the 13th century. On the island of Bornholm there were several such places; with its position in the middle of the Baltic the island was vulnerable to attack, and there were no local potentates who built their own castles, but from around 1150 a number of fortified round churches were built, in which people could defend themselves and protect their belongings against acute attacks. The stores of the islanders' merchant-farmers might be contained there, for example, and there was a real need for this both then and in the century that followed, but the churches could hardly contain a whole settlement's population with cattle and crops, so the strongholds were still indispensable.

Such strongholds were often strategically placed for defence at some distance from the dangerous coasts, and this may also have been the reason for the location of the Crown's earliest real castles. At any rate there are in a few places examples of structures of a relatively great age and with a clearly defensive location away from the coast, which are royally-owned when one advances so far in time that something is known about their ownership. This applies to Lilleborg on Bornholm, Refshaleborg on the island of Borgø in Maribo Lake, and perhaps

ØSTERLARS CHURCH on Bornholm is from c.1200, like the other round churches on the island, and it was equipped with various defence features, for instance a sentry walk. The island was vulnerable to attack from the sea, and the rich trading-farmers used the fortified round churches as store-houses. The local population could also seek refuge there when under attack. The pointed roof and stout buttresses are later additions. Seen from the north.

also Gammel Brattingsborg on the island of Samsø. Søborg and Pedersborg and even Haraldsborg were situated, like Borren, some distance inland. Skanderborg in central Jutland is the example, among all the castles belonging to the Crown, that is situated furthest inland. Its history cannot be traced further back in time in written sources than to the mid-13th century, but at that time it was an important royal castle. The castle mound is in such a ruined state, however, that it is questionable whether archaeological investigation would provide further information. *(continued on page 54)*

GAMLEBORG *in Almindingen on Bornholm is the largest of the castle-refuges on the island. It has roots in the Iron Age or possibly the Viking Age, and had room for many people and animals. It covers an area as large as the site of Hammershus when the latter was in full function, and it seems to have been built as late as around 1100. There is a stone wall around the site, the access is strongly fortified, and there is a rampart around the wall, but Gamleborg is a castle-refuge and not a royal castle by medieval standards.*

THE IMPORTANCE OF LOCATION

LILLEBORG

The clearest example of a castle or fortification placed at a distance from the coast is to be found on Bornholm. In Almindingen, in the centre of the island, there are two very different structures. The older, Gamleborg, is the largest of the strongholds on the island; it was in use at the beginning of the 12th century but is far too large to be a medieval castle.

Lilleborg, on the other hand, fits that description well. It is situated near Gamleborg, on a rocky outcrop on the shore of the lake named Borresø, which during the active lifetime of the castle surrounded it completely, because the water-level was raised by dams. Lilleborg corresponds in size to the central part of Hammershus and is half the size of the actual castle building of Vordingborg. At Lilleborg there are also ruins of medieval stone houses and distinct medieval fortification features, e.g. at the entrance, which was protected by a massive tower. It is difficult to determine a date for the construction of the castle, but as far as can be judged from the finds that have emerged from the excavations on the site there is nothing that would contradict a dating to around the middle of the 12th century.

The castle was later extended and reinforced, but was still not able to withstand attack in 1259, when King Christoffer I's powerful enemies, including

both the Archbishop and Prince Jarmer of Rügen, laid siege to it and captured it, so that in consequence it could no longer have been a bastion of royal support. Excavations have revealed traces of fire and damage to the structure of Lilleborg, and this has been associated with the battles in 1259, but there are also indications that it was lived in for some time after the conquest. In the decades that followed there was also a need for a stronghold on the island, and because of its situation Lilleborg was a particularly good place to take refuge, even if its defences as a castle were ruined, so this may explain its continued use as living quarters. The country was at war again, and after the destruction of Lilleborg Hammershus was left as the only medieval castle on Bornholm; through most of the Middle Ages it was in the hands of a succession of archbishops who were for much of the time enemies of the Crown.

LILLEBORG is situated high up on a rocky outcrop near Borresø in Almindingen, not far from Gamleborg, and it is one of the castles that may have been royal property before castle-building in general began in Denmark. Tradition has it that the castle was built by Svend Grathe in the mid-12th century, but that is not certain. The castle was abandoned after it was conquered in 1259, but continued to function as a place of refuge for some time.

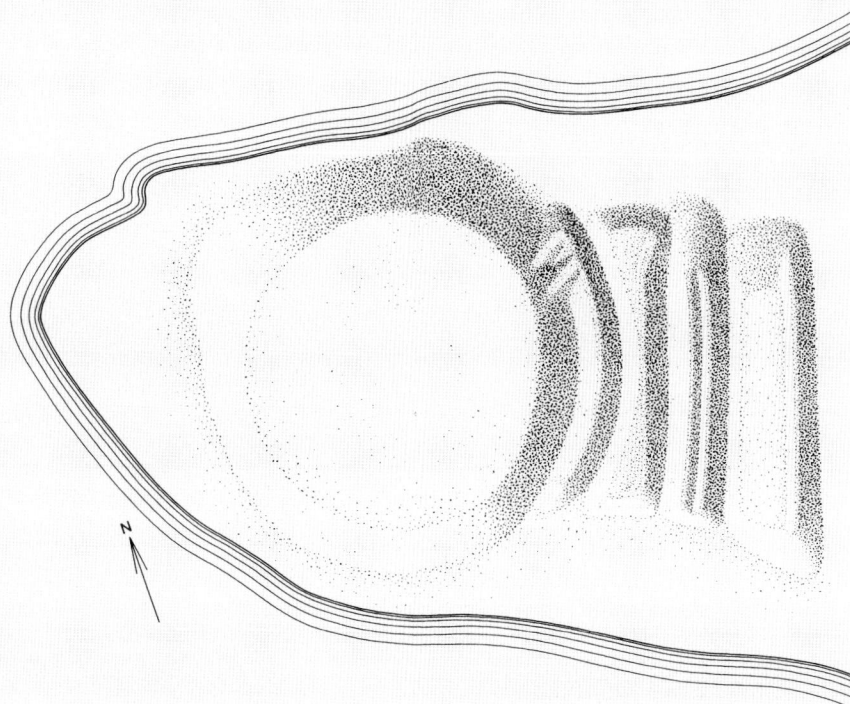

REFSHALEBORG

The western point of the island of Borgø in Søndersø Lake near Maribo is the site of the fortified structure named Refshaleborg, which was a strong royal castle until it was destroyed in 1256 in the same context that resulted in the ruin of Lilleborg. Written sources inform us that it was local peasants who were responsible for the devastation: "the farmhands went mad with clubs", according to several of them, while the Visby Chronicle adds the word "bang". Christoffer I was in conflict with the Archbishop and his allies, including Prince Jarmer of Rügen, and had problems with his subjects. But if it was farmhands who destroyed the castle there must have been exceedingly many of them, or else the castle had only a few men guarding it, or had perhaps fallen into disrepair.

Refshaleborg had however been an impressive structure and had been in use from at least some point in the 12th century. The castle mound, which has a

REFSHALEBORG on the island of Borgø in Maribo Lake was abandoned, like Lilleborg, after it was conquered in the mid-13th century; perhaps the location was no longer strategically important. The castle was a strong fortress with many moats and ramparts to the east, but it was also situated rather far from the coast, so its functions must have been for local protection rather than coastal defence.

diameter of 90 m, is protected to the north, south and west by steep slopes running down to the lake, while to the east it was shielded by five moats with ramparts between them. At some time after brick came into use in Denmark, during the reign of Valdemar the Great, a rather slight curtain wall was erected around the castle mound. It was perhaps some 1 m thick and apparently built of

HJORTHOLM *on the little island in Stavns Fjord consists of two large mounds. Excavations in the summer of 2011 revealed that these are enormous earthworks which were never completed or taken into use. There are no archaeological finds that can date the structure, so one is left to guess that it belonged to the war with Norway after the murder of King Erik Klipping in 1286, or that it should be seen in the context of Queen Margrete's pirates' conflict with the Hanseatics at the end of the 14th century. The layout could fit with either context. Seen from the southwest.*

bricks in unusual sizes and firings, so they were perhaps early bricks like the large ones from the tower on Sprogø which Valdemar the Great had built. This may mean that the site's fortifications were reinforced in his time, but in that case the work was not significant enough to be mentioned by Saxo or by Svend Aggesen, or by any other source. The castle was linked to the mainland at the north of the island by a wooden bridge, 250 m long and 5 m broad; about 75 of the support posts for the bridge are preserved. Using dendrochronology their felling-date has been established as between 1135 and 1193, so the structure was important enough to the Crown to keep it maintained for about 100 years,

but after the destruction at the end of the 1250s it was no longer in use, and the buildings on the site were probably used as stone-quarries by the Crown or by the local population.

GAMMEL BRATTINGSBORG

The name Brattingsborg is known from many places in Denmark. It is also found in ballads and has romantic associations, but it does not often date from long ago, and Brattingsborg in Tranebjerg, in the centre of the island of Samsø, has no links with the large present-day estate on the island. The site is on a fenced-in field on the edge of the village; there are only faint traces in the terrain, and it is not easy to interpret the site. It has also undergone change in the course of time; for a while, for instance, there was a windmill on the top of the castle mound.

During extensive excavations at Gammel Brattingsborg in the summer of 2008 remains of strongly-built walls, burials, and a ruined chapel came to light. Finds of objects were few in number, and most of them suggest a date of use in the 13th century and not later. The context has not been clearly identified, however, and the chapel with adjoining graveyard, which was connected with the castle, does not make the interpretation of the structure any easier. If there was in fact a castle here in the 12th century, its function must have been essentially defensive, however, in contradistinction to the other castles of the Valdemar period, even though at that time it would have been possible to sail closer to the site.

There is no doubt that the structure was royal. Samsø belonged to the Crown throughout the Middle Ages, even though during brief periods in the 14th century it was enfeoffed as a duchy together with the now Swedish province of Halland. Several important meetings were held on the island over the course of time; for instance in 1215, when most of the powerful men in the country assembled there and acknowledged Valdemar, the eldest son of Valdemar the Victorious, as successor to his father. There is no mention of a castle in that connection. In 1216, in a royal letter, the property is referred to as a "curia", and

BRATTINGSBORG in the village of Tranekær on Samsø may well have been the earliest royal structure on the island. New excavations have revealed traces of buildings from the early Middle Ages, including a little church. Old sketch. Danish National Museum.

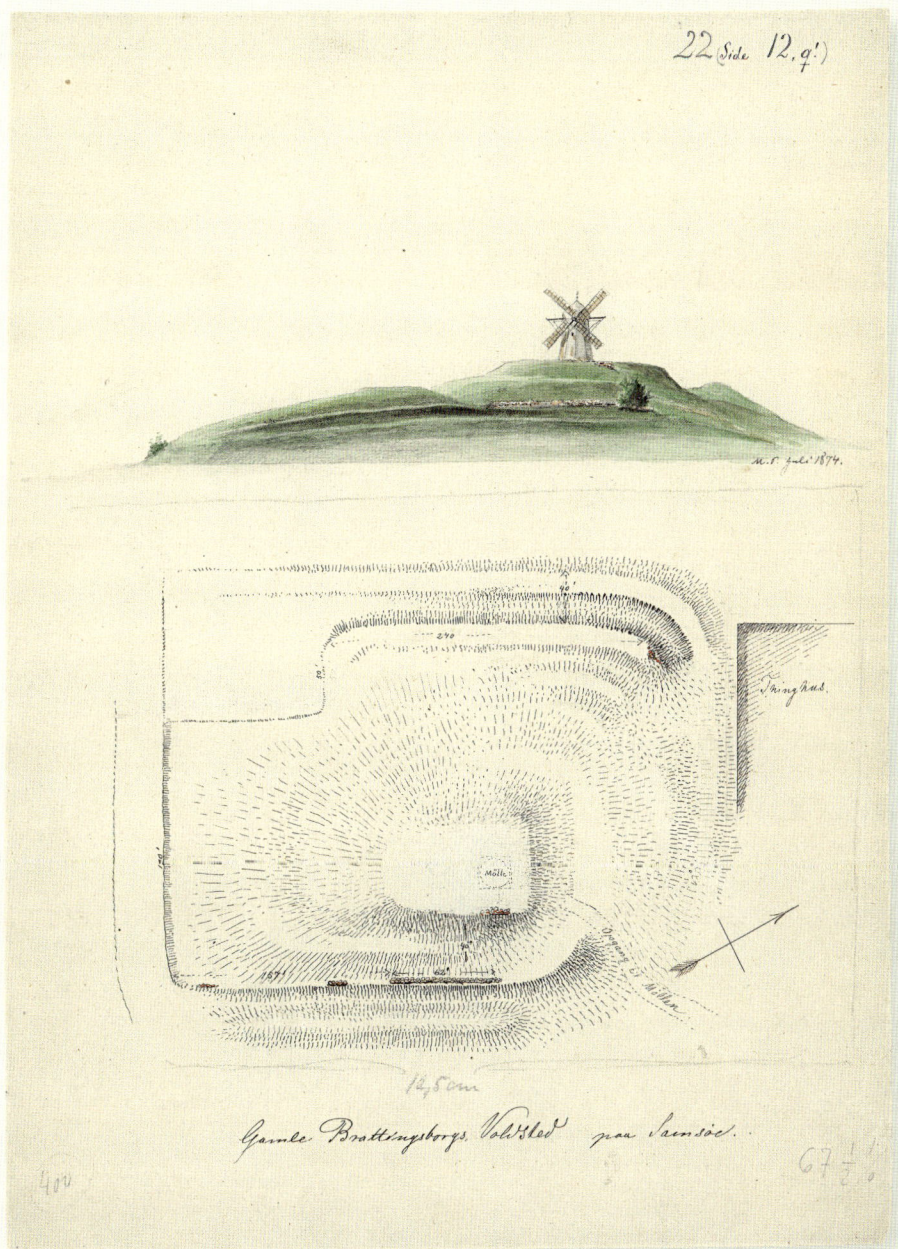

it was certainly part of a royal estate on Samsø.

One of the medieval sources, the Lund Chronicle, mentions that in 1289 "Marsk Stig destroyed/demolished a castle – or the castle – on Samsø". As the commander of part of the Norwegian fleet Marsk Stig Andersen, who had been outlawed in 1287 as one of the murderers of King Erik Klipping, led the men in the marauding Norwegian ships which plagued Samsø that year, according to the chronicle, and then burned Tårnborg "with the church" on the coast of Korsør Nor in western Sealand, destroying several other places around the coasts, including Nykøbing on Falster, before joining forces with the Norwegian king on the island of Amager. The joint fleets then sailed together to Grønsund off southern Sealand, stormed the castle of Stegeborg on Møn and burned the town of Stubbekøbing before the whole fleet sailed home to Norway in the middle of August. It was not until the following year that Stig Andersen and his followers sailed south again to build the castle on the island of Hjelm, turning the island into a dangerous Norwegian base in the middle of Danish waters.

This information is to be found in a long passage that was inserted into the chronicle at a later date. It also relates that the summer campaign lasted from the middle of July to the middle of August, so Stig Andersen and his warriors must have moved fast, if the rest of the account can be believed. The location of Gammel Brattingsborg and the solid masonry that has been found on the site make it improbable that during a campaign of naval skirmishes and coastal raids there would have been sufficient manpower and weaponry to besiege, conquer and demolish the structure.

Such a feat could not be accomplished from one day to another, nor would it have been the purpose of the Norwegian king's sea offensive against Denmark, but it would fit well with the fact of the absence of finds at the fortified site from the period after the 13th century. Previously it was thought that it could have been Vesborg, on the southern tip of Samsø, that was destroyed by Stig Andersen, but recent excavations have shown that the castle there was not built until the mid-14th century. A third fortified site, Bisgård in the parish of Onsbjerg, also seems to date from after 1289.

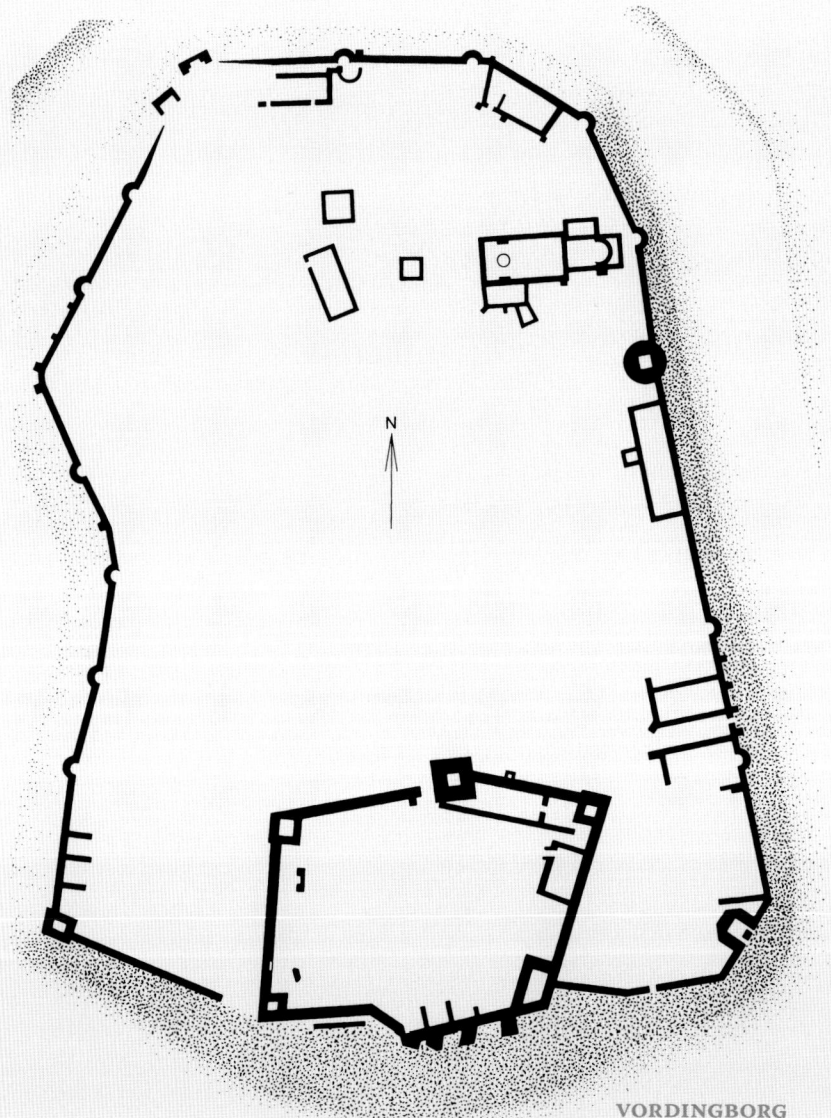

VORDINGBORG

Plans of **VORDINGBORG, HAMMERSHUS** *and* **LILLEBORG.** *Hammershus succeeded Lilleborg as the important fortress on Bornholm early in the 13th century. Vordingborg was the most important royal castle in Denmark for long periods. In all three structures the inner castle is of more-or-less the same size.*

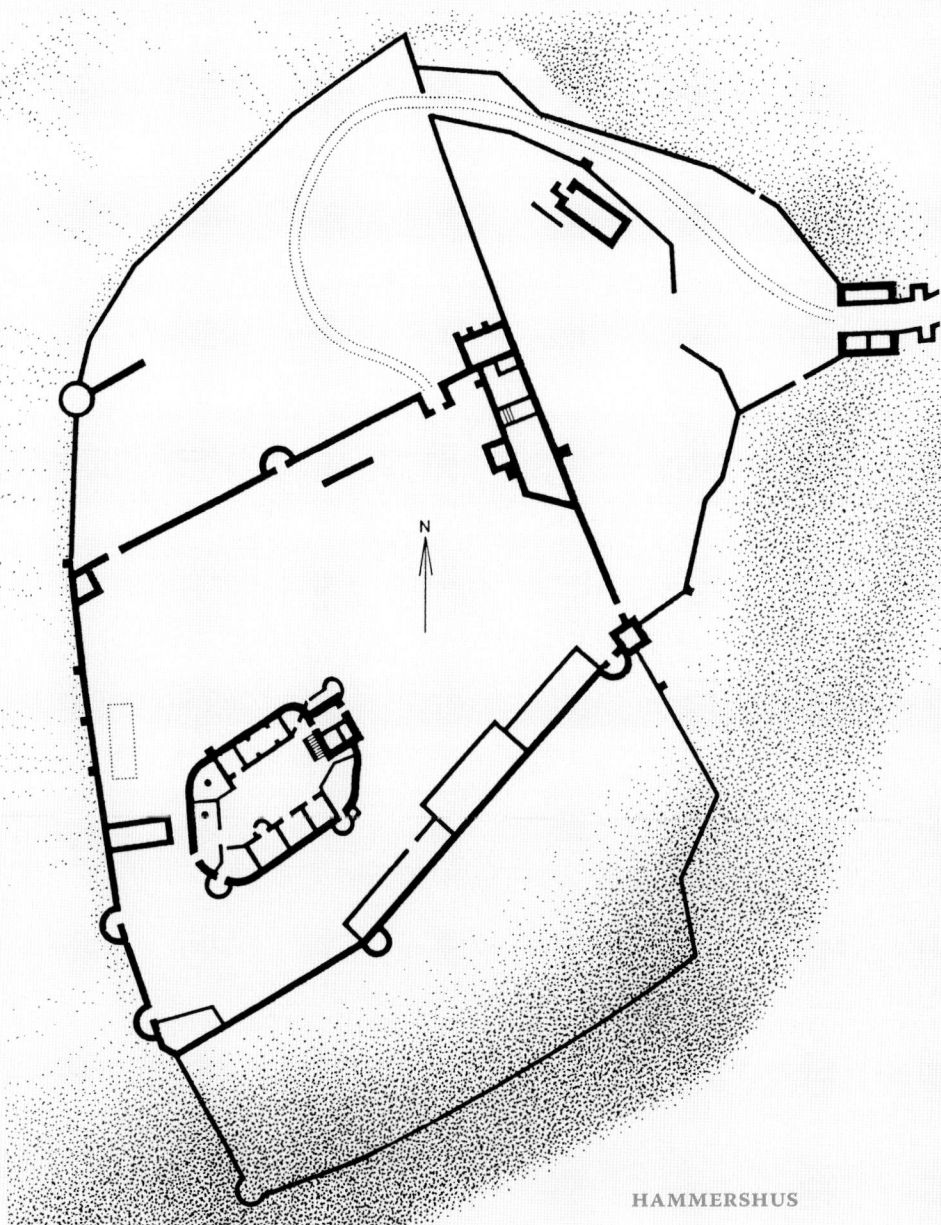

HAMMERSHUS

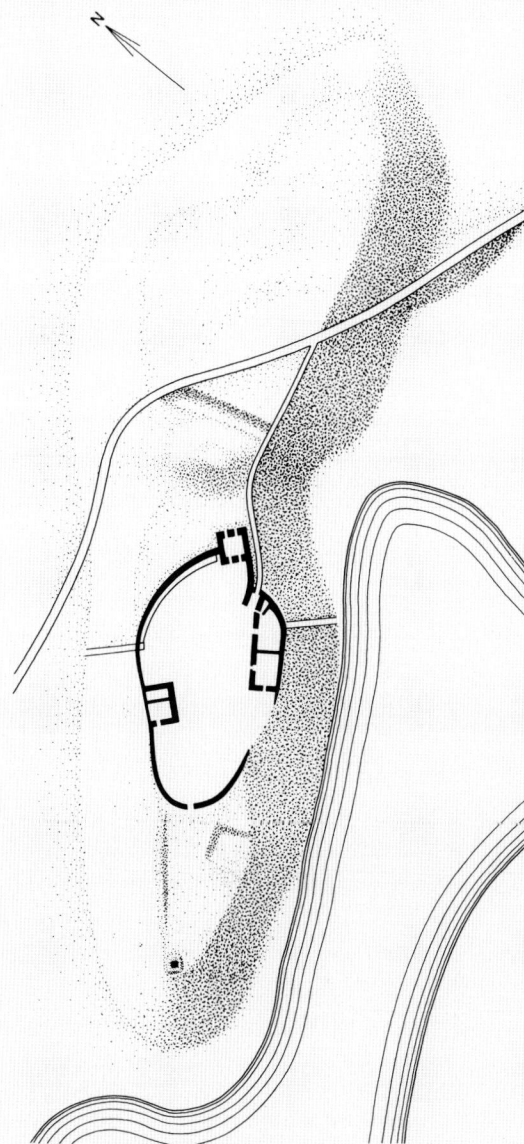

LILLEBORG

There may have been other fortified structures that are unknown to us, and maybe Søby Volde on the island of Ærø and Skarreborg on Mors also belong among the 12th century castles. Søby Volde can be dated archaeologically to that century, but it is difficult to find common denominators shared by those two structures other than a certain similarity. Søby Volde may have been royal, but nothing at all is known about Skarreborg. The earliest version of Vordingborg is possibly also among the very early royal constructions; traces have been found of fortifications under the oldest curtain wall structure.

Apart from the few early constructions that did not last long it is not easy to find evidence of private castles built by aristocrats in the 12th century. In some cases there is a tradition concerning a person who commissioned a building – e.g. that Absalon built Bistrup, the present-day St Hans Hospital at Roskilde. There the building-remains and finds suggest that there was once a prestigious building, but it is not possible to say whether it was a palace or a castle. Dragsholm near Fårevejle in Ods Herred also belonged to the Bishop of Roskilde. Absalon's nephew Peder Sunesen possibly built a palace there, traces of which can still be detected in the present buildings, but at what point in time Dragsholm became a castle is hard to say.

There may well have been private fortifications consisting of earthworks and timber constructions, built in response to specific political situations, but which have not resulted in evidence left to us either in written sources or in archaeological remains. Castles of that type could be erected quickly and altered easily, and it is difficult to find traces of them today, but a provisional conclusion is that the powerful figures in the kingdom managed to survive for a long time without fortified sites. The Crown and the Princes of the Church also did so in many cases, and the extensive royal castle-building of the later Valdemar period was not intended as protection against internal strife in the realm.

Apart from the battle over Haraldsborg and the conquest of Søborg there is only one known reference to a military encounter over a castle in the kingdom in the 12th century; it underlines the rarity of castles and throws some light on the social context in which they were to be found.

In 1180 there was unrest in Scania, where Absalon had succeeded Eskil as archbishop and had soon aroused opposition among the people, who asserted their traditional rights and vehemently opposed paying the new church taxes which Absalon wanted to introduce. On one occasion, Saxo recounts, the hostility reached a point where a large and wildly agitated crowd pursued Absalon and his men all the way to "a castle the Archbishop had built in a lake", and were ready to attack. The prospects for the Bishop's men were not good, because apart from the fact that the castle was situated on a small island a short distance from land there were few fortifications. The Bishop's people had to hasten to collect horses in from the meadow and build a blockade of carriages on the road out to the island, "where the Archbishop later built a wall of brick". Some went out to collect stones for slings, and the whole description is reminiscent of a Western in which the Indians attack the settlers' caravans.

The site is called Søvdeborg or Sigosta and is to be found in the now dried-up

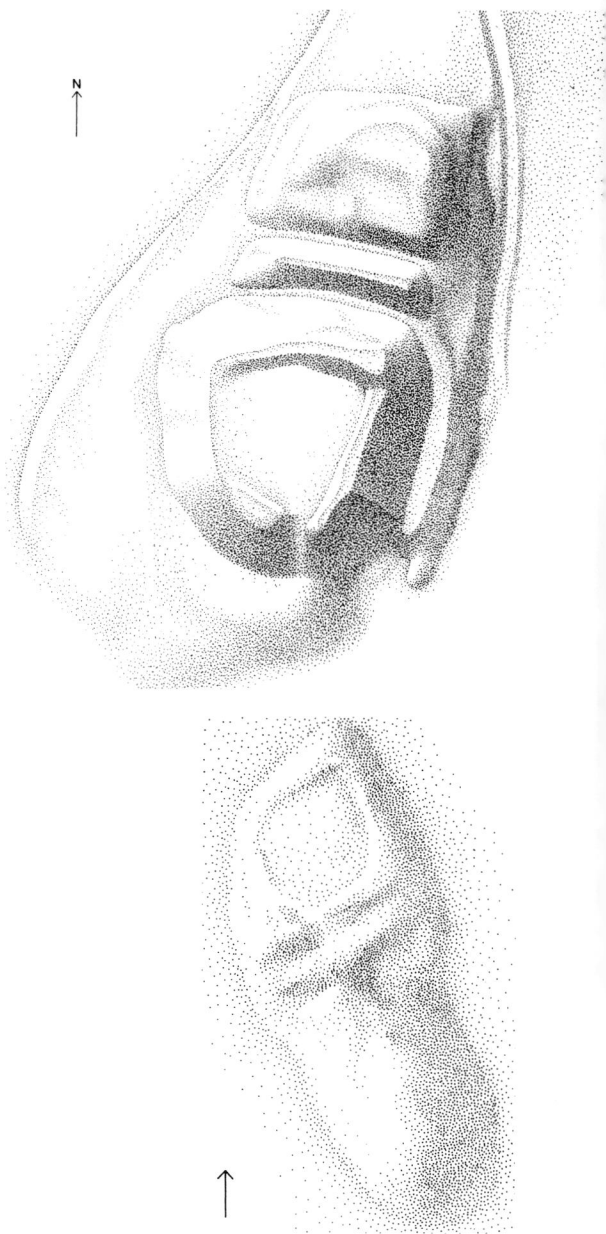

SØBY VOLDE *on Ærø (above) and* **SKARREBORG** *on Mors (below) are possibly both examples of early royal fortresses, but excavations on those sites would be needed before anything can be established with certainty.*

DRAGSHOLM, *not far from Fårevejle, belonged to the Roskilde bishopric in the Middle Ages, and Absalon's nephew Peder Sunesen built a splendid* palatium *there in the early 13th century. It is now completely hidden by later phases of rebuilding which turned Dragsholm into a strong castle, but in the south wall one can still detect traces of the group of three tall windows, the tallest in the centre, which adorned Bishop Peder's house.*

Søvde Lake in the Malmøhus district in southern Scania. Either it was not a real fortress or possibly it had not been completed in 1180. Today there is nothing to be seen at the site, but during excavations traces have come to light of a brick wall c. 1.5 m thick, which is interpreted as the one that Absalon had built. The result of the conflict was that the Archbishop fled from Søvde and took refuge in the castle he had had constructed, with the King's permission, in the little trading station named Havn, which later became Copenhagen. And the angry Scanians burned Søvdeborg.

Now there is a lighthouse towering over **SPROGØ,** where Valdemar the Great built a castle to secure the coasts of the country and the sea crossing over the Great Belt against the threat from pirates. The castle could receive assistance from **TÅRNBORG,** on the shore at Korsør Nor, where a fleet could be well sheltered. Seen from the northeast.

Absalon was not popular in Scania and might well have had good reason to seek to protect his possessions and revenues, and those of the archbishopric, and on those grounds among others it has been suggested that he was responsible for building the unique and remarkable castle structure of Skeingeborg in the parish of Verum in Scania. There one finds the remains of an octagonal curtain wall surrounding a fortified site with a diameter of some 40 m. The wall is still a couple of metres in height, but has originally been much higher. Within its perimeter traces have been found of a large stone-built dwelling and various smaller buildings, but apart from coins there are few finds that can be used for dating. The suggestion that Absalon may have commissioned the building arises primarily from the fact that the area belonged to an estate in the archiepiscopal see, and also because of Absalon's poor relations with the Scanians; the coin finds on the site appear to indicate that the castle fell out of use around the middle of the 13th century. What happened to it is not known, and it had been totally forgotten until 1924. No parallels to this structure are known either in Denmark or elsewhere. In that respect it has some similarity to the Bastrup Tower.

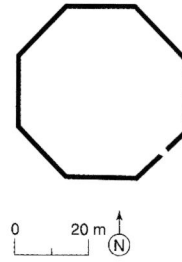

0   20 m   N

SKEINGEBORG in northern Scania, close to the border with Småland, is distinctive with its unusual octagonal curtain wall enclosing the castle's buildings. From Anders Ødmann: Borgar i Skåne.

The BASTRUP TOWER was skilfully built of calcareous tufa, travertine. This can still be seen in the remains of the base section. Seen from the northeast.

III

The castles of Valdemar the Great

In **VALDEMAR THE GREAT'S** *grave in St Bendt's Church in Ringsted there was a lead plaque on which his greatest achievements were listed. They were that he had driven out the Wends, strengthened Danevirke with a wall of "fired stones" (bricks) and built the castle on Sprogø. Photo Danish National Museum.*

Protecting the realm

The first and most important function of the monarch, from time immemorial, has been to ensure peace within the kingdom. The monarch was the commander of the military forces of the kingdom, and so he had the right to control the kingdom's defence structures and to use them as resources in war. King Valdemar himself was also responsible for the building of important castles and fortresses. On a lead tablet that was found in his grave in St Bendt's Church in Ringsted, where he was buried in 1182, there is an enumeration of the important feats for which he deserved particular praise. He is described as the conqueror of the Wends, the liberator of the fatherland and the keeper of peace. All these are consequences of his successful wars, and he is praised especially for having reinforced Danevirke, Denmark's frontier rampart in southern Jutland, by building a wall of "fired stones" i.e. bricks, and for having built the castle on the island of Sprogø. Previously the little island had been a pirates' lair, and it was an ideal look-out post. A lighthouse now stands where the castle-tower rose up, surrounded by a curtain wall, similar to the structure at Tårnborg on the coast at Korsør Nor; from there one would have been able to see enemy ships from a great distance and take measures to ensure that they were kept away. There would either have been ships at the ready on the island or else those manning the castle would have signalled for reinforcements.

Tårnborg, on the shore of the cove at Korsør in western Sealand, was perhaps also founded in King Valdemar's time; the castle there was at any rate an important part of the context in which the tower on Sprogø operated. It could only do so in collaboration with a more influential support-point on the mainland, and the cove provided a safe harbour for the ships of a guard-fleet until such time as there came a message or a signal from Sprogø about a sighting of an enemy. Furthermore, the Tårnborg construction is designed almost exactly in the same way as the site on Sprogø where the lighthouse is now situated. They were of roughly the same size, but the castle-area at Tårnborg became much larger in the course of the Middle Ages. Exactly how large is not known, but it was one of the places

that was fought over long and hard in the 1320s, as was Vordingborg. The church on the site belonged to the castle area, and during excavations it has been possible to establish that there was a trading area on the shore below the fortress and the church. The trading place and thus also the fortress can be said, on the basis of coin finds etc., to have been in use far into the 14th century, until Tårnborg's role was taken over by Korsør, right out on the coast. It is not possible to ascertain the extent of the destruction wrought by Marsk Stig and the Norwegian king in 1289.

There were many possibilities, even in the Middle Ages, for sending messages and reports over long distances. Pigeon post was in common use, as it still is, but one could also raise a flag or use some other signal that had a pre-arranged meaning. One could light a bonfire, and that could be seen better than a flag e.g. at night. On the basis of what were later known as "beacons" it has been suggested that Denmark was covered by a network of beacon mounds from a period early

VALDEMAR'S WALL *at Danevirke, built for the protection of the realm, is one of the achievements for which Valdemar the Great is praised. Brick was an innovative building material in Denmark at that time. Bricks could be fired almost everywhere in Denmark, but the process called for fuel – firewood – and that was expensive in the Middle Ages. So only the rich and powerful could build in brick. Here the wall is seen from the south, from the enemy's side.*

in the Middle Ages; they were possibly called *"warther"* and were equipped with a tower so that once a fire was lit the message of danger could be spread in relay rapidly over the country and send the signal to mobilise the defence forces. This is not very credible, however. The place-names including *"warth"* are on the whole not old, and the sites suggested tend not to be either. And there is no evidence, either archaeological or historical, that central power in the kingdom was organised in such a way that it could have made use of such messages before the late Middle Ages at the earliest. Beacons are not mentioned before the 15th century, while there is no record of beacon-watches, i.e. permanent manning of beacons, before as late as 1444, and the fact that the system was fully developed in the 17th century does not provide us with any evidence of conditions in the Middle Ages. In fact the fighting force of the kingdom, the *Leidang*, was not at all organised in such a way that it could be used in this manner in the early Middle Ages. But of course there could have been systems for raising the alarm at a local level.

One of the locations that has been mentioned as a possible *"warth"*, because of its name among other reasons, is Vordingborg. There was a fortress there, beneath the later castle, and the *Leidang* fleet traditionally assembled there for campaigns, particularly against the Wends, that were organised in common by all the fighting forces of the different parts of the country. The Wends were from Slavonic tribes living in the Baltic coastal area around the island of Rügen, which was the departure-point for their ravaging raids on Denmark. The population of Wendland and the area further east was still heathen in the 12th century and the beginning of the following century, and the campaigns against the Wends during the Valdemar period were also directed against their old gods. Christian warriors could not be satisfied with letting pagan beliefs persist, and not least the conquest of Rügen, with the fortress of Arkona which contained the shrine of the god Svantevit, is described by Saxo in detail and with vivacity. There must have been grieving among the vanquished when the statue of the god with the four faces ended up as kindling under the pots of soup for the Danish troops.

It would be exaggerating to describe Valdemar the Great's wars as crusades, however, even though Svend Aggesen praises the King for having forced the inhabitants of Rügen at sword-point to "allow themselves to be born again in the water of Holy Baptism", and Absalon himself, as the leader of the Church, enthusiastically took part in the combat. He had his own interpretation of loyalty, and for instance in the context of the besieging and conquest of Søborg he had taken the King's side against his superior Archbishop Eskil, because he considered that his oath of loyalty to the King was the most important. The Pope was also further away. The conversion of heathens was not the first object of the campaigns against the Wends – creating peace and security in the kingdom was the primary purpose. That is what King Valdemar is praised for on the lead tablet in his grave, and both Saxo and Svend Aggesen extol his achievements in securing the borders, the coasts and the harbours, and thus creating safe conditions in the realm.

For these reasons Vordingborg is of course not a crusader castle. It is not situated in conquered land as a power-base for Christianising and dominance, as was the case of e.g. the castles of the German Order. Vordingborg was one of the

TÅRNBORG CHURCH *belonged within the castle area, but the limits of that area are not clear. The castle was important, and it was fought over both in the 14th century and later. On the shore of the inlet below the castle there was also a trading place. Seen from the north.*

TÅRNBORG, *near Korsør, was one of the impor-*
tant early castles from the time of the Valdemars.
The fortress had the same ground plan and size
as the one on Sprogø.

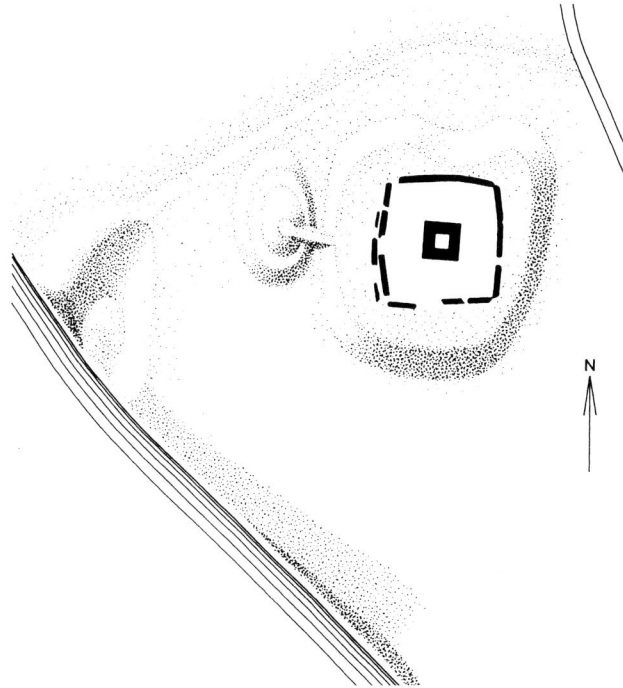

most important royal castles in Denmark, and at times possibly the most important of them. In recent years excavations have been carried out in several places
in the large castle area, which contained, apart from the central castle buildings,
a town-like settlement with a church behind a curtain wall like that at Kalundborg and perhaps Tårnborg. The whole structure has been rebuilt and reinforced
several times over, but it is clear that Vordingborg was of major importance to
Valdemar the Great, and he stayed there often. He also died there in 1182.

The extension of the central fort and the construction of the massive outer
curtain wall, which together with the broad moats covered the area including the
church and was crowned by the Goose Tower, belong to a later period in the active lifetime of the castle, i.e. to the second half of the 14th century, when Valdemar Atterdag radically reinforced the construction in connection with, amongst
other things, his wars against the Hanseatic League. In his time Vordingborg was
virtually the capital of the kingdom, but even in the 1320s, when Christoffer II was
trying to hold onto power, it was a formidable stronghold that could not easily
be overrun by the Holstein mortgage-holders and their well-trained professional
troops. Vordingborg was King Christoffer's last stronghold in the country until
he was forced to leave the castle after a long siege in 1326. He left with the Crown
Jewels, which have never been seen since.

After the Middle Ages Vordingborg gradually lost its significance, and the
castle was demolished in the 18th century. The remains, with Valdemar Atterdag's
Goose Tower and the large area of ruins around it, are still impressive today.

King Valdemar the Great's strongest supporters helped to build the defences
of the realm. His chief allies, Absalon and Esbern Snare, were his foster-brothers.
He had grown up with them in their home in Fjenneslev, just as his father had
lived in their grandfather's household. They supported him in his wars and gave

*From the top of the **GOOSE TOWER** at Vordingborg one can look far out to sea towards the south. From here Valdemar the Great and his men could see the* leidang *fleets assembling for battle against the Wends..*

Vordingborg's **GOOSE TOWER,** *the tower in Korsør and that of Kärnan in Helsingborg (Scania) are the only preserved medieval castle towers in the old Danish territory. Here part of the interior of the Goose Tower can be seen. The staircase is enclosed in the wall, and the toothing visible in the masonry has once carried the vaulting over the room.*

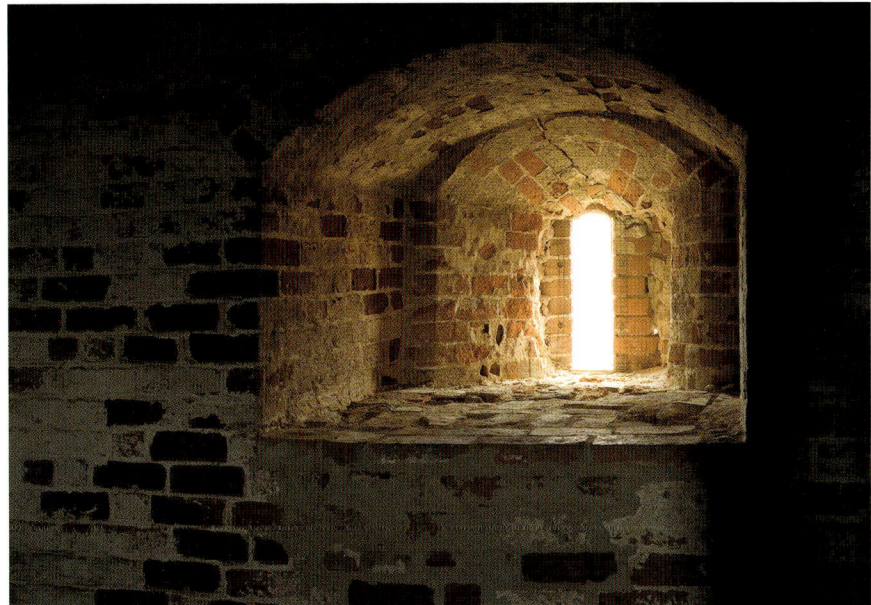

The castle beside the harbour in **KORSØR** *replaced Tårnborg at some point in the late Middle Ages. The tower of the castle is still preserved. This is one of the light-apertures in the tower.*

(continued on page 72)

him unconditional loyalty. The family had helped him to ascend to the throne and the ties between the three of them were certainly more than merely political. Absalon's view that his loyalty to the King was more important than his duty to the Church was a provocative stance in the second phase of the "investiture conflict" between the secular powers and the ecclesiastical authorities over who should have the greatest authority in the kingdoms. This had also been the root of the disagreement between Archbishop Eskil and successive kings, but with the backing of the Hvide family and Absalon assured to him, Valdemar the Great emerged

ROYAL CASTLES BUILT BY LICENCE

THE CASTLE IN HAVN
(Copenhagen)

Deep in the cellars underneath present-day Christiansborg, now the seat of the Danish Parliament, lie the ruins of Absalon's castle, which was begun in 1167 on a site donated, with a generous amount of land, by King Valdemar to his friend and staunch supporter, who was then Bishop of Roskilde. Saxo recounts that the castle was intended as protection against pirates, that it took four years to build it, and that it functioned well for

its purpose. The site has seen buildings and alterations, destruction and rebuilding many times over, until the present palace was erected, so that despite excavations it is difficult to clarify the details of what Absalon's castle looked like, but it was at any rate surrounded by a limestone wall and had stone buildings within the castle area. The remains of the earliest castle and ruins of other old editions of Copenhagen Castle have been exposed and can be visited in the cellars under Christiansborg.

Later in the Middle Ages both the

King and various successive Bishops of Roskilde claimed that the castle in Havn belonged to them, and in the mid-13th century, when the Archbishop and the Bishop of Roskilde, along with other members of the Hvide family abandoned the King in favour of the Duke of Schleswig, the King's troops attacked the castle. In the years that followed Copenhagen Castle fell into a succession of different hands, including those of creditors in the era when it had been pawned or mortgaged away. The castle was attacked and defended, and in 1368 it was

The ruins of the medieval **COPENHAGEN CASTLE** *can be seen today in the cellars under Christiansborg. The black outline shows what it has been possible to identify as Absalon's building from the 1160s.*

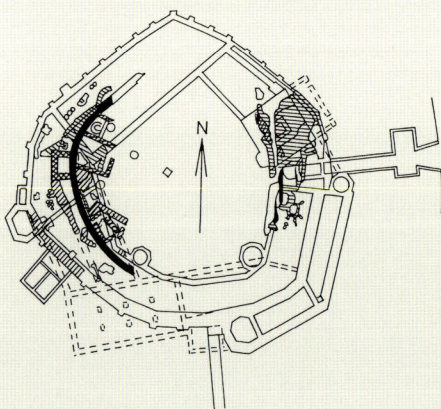

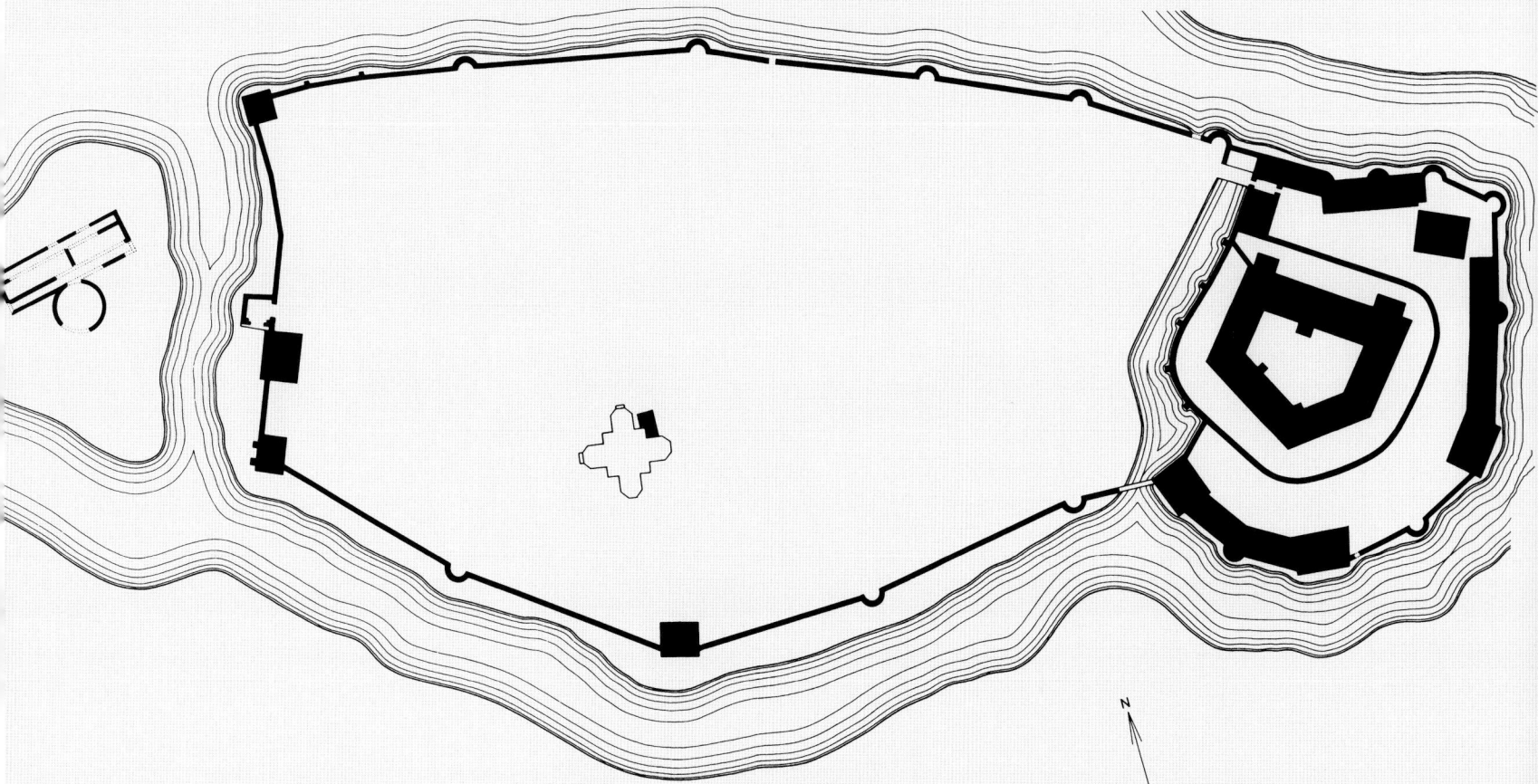

KALUNDBORG *was founded by Esbern Snare in c.1170. It is not known how large his castle was or how it was laid out, but it was probably situated on the mound furthest to the west. The upper town with its unusual church and the castle in the west developed in the course of the Middle Ages, and Kalundborg became both the largest of the royal castles in the realm and one of the most important. Some of the towers in the eastern castle had special names: one was known as "Father's Hat" and another as "the Foal". The state archives were kept here for a long time.*

A mural painting from the second half of the 13th century, in **HORNSLET CHURCH** *on Djursland, shows a battle scene beside a town gate. It is no doubt a scene from the Old Testament, but the warriors' equipment is from the era when the sons of Valdemar the Victorious were at war with one another. Photo from www.kalkmalerier.dk.*

razed to the ground by the Hanseatics, who at that point had conquered it. Successive kings constantly asserted their right to the place, and at least from the time of Eric of Pomerania there was no further challenge to Crown ownership of Copenhagen Castle, which gradually acquired greater significance than the other royal castles. Kings increasingly came to spend more time at the castle, which was situated conveniently in the middle of the kingdom, and against this background the town of Copenhagen eventually became the capital.

The old Copenhagen Castle, with alterations, remained standing until 1730, when it was pulled down. Christian VI's Christiansborg was built on the site and was completed in 1740. It burned down in 1794; a new Christiansborg was inaugurated in 1828, but it in turn burned

down in 1884. The present building was completed in 1928, but never became a royal residence.

KALUNDBORG

The pirates, i.e. the Wends, had exploited the weakness of the realm in the 12th century and had made the waters around the kingdom unsafe and dangerous. The inner reaches of Kalundborg fjord provided good conditions for surprise counter-attacks on the pirate ships, and it was there that Esbern Snare made his contribution to the defence of the realm, in around 1170.

In the course of the Middle Ages Kalundborg became one of Denmark's strongest castles and perhaps the largest. The fortified area came to include the

KALUNDBORG'S fortifications have virtually all disappeared, but viewing it from the northwest one can still gain a sense of the castle's strength.

The tall house in Præstegade in KALUNDBORG is one of the few preserved medieval brick houses in Denmark. There were similar buildings to be found in the castle courtyards and on castle mounds at the larger locations in the 14th century and onwards.

town and its unusual church with five towers and a castle at either end of the town, to the west and to the east. It is thought that the western castle and the town were built under Esbern Snare's orders, but that the church was not added until after his death in 1204, and that the town's curtain wall with towers was added in connection with the building of the eastern castle, perhaps in Erik Menved's reign from the end of the 13th century. At that time Kalundborg was indisputably royal property, and there had actually never been doubt about that, even though Esbern Snare's daughter Ingeborg and her husband lived in the castle

after Esbern's death. This did not change anything, because her husband, Peder Strangesen, was also a loyal supporter of the Valdemars. He died at the same time as the last of them, in 1241, but Ingeborg lived for a long time after his death – long enough to become a victim of the changed political conditions during the conflict between the sons of Valdemar the Victorious, from 1241 onwards – and she had to hand over Kalundborg to Erik Klipping in 1263.

After that there was never any doubt that the castle belonged to the Crown, even though during the period of dissolution of the realm Kalundborg changed hands several times. For a while, for instance, it was part of the Duchy of Samsø and Halland, which Christoffer II governed before he became king, and which was later in the hands of Knud Porse, who was married to (another) Ingeborg, mother of the Norwegian-Swedish King Magnus Smek. Kalundborg was one of the many castles Valdemar Atterdag had to conquer in the 1340s in his battle to regain royal power. The eastern castle and the town fortifications were reinforced in his reign, and after his time Kalundborg was one of the strongest fortresses in the country and an important administrative centre. National assemblies were held there, important prisoners kept there, as in Søborg, and one of the sturdy towers in the eastern castle, called Folen, housed the national archives.

As late as at the beginning of the 16th century the eastern castle was reinforced with another curtain wall to the north, and for many years Kalundborg was a safe and suitable prison for the deposed Christian II. The castle was destroyed during the Swedish Wars in 1658 and after that it was left to fall into disrepair.

The castles and fortified refuges of the Valdemar Era

1. Arreskov
2. Brattingsborg
3. Dragsholm
4. Dronningholm
5. Falsters Virke
6. Gamleborg
7. Gottorp
8. Gurre
9. Hagenskov
10. Hammershus
11. Haraldsborg
12. Helsingborg
13. Hindsgavl
14. Jungshoved
15. Jurisborg
16. Kalundborg
17. Copenhagen
18. Lilleborg
19. Nordborg
20. Nyborg
21. Pedersborg
22. Refshaleborg
23. Skanderborg
24. Skanør
25. St. Albert
26. Sprogø
27. Stegeborg
28. Søborg
29. Søby Volde
30. Sølvesborg
31. Sønderborg
32. Søvdeborg
33. Tranekær
34. Tårnborg
35. Vordingborg
36. Ørkil
37. Åhus

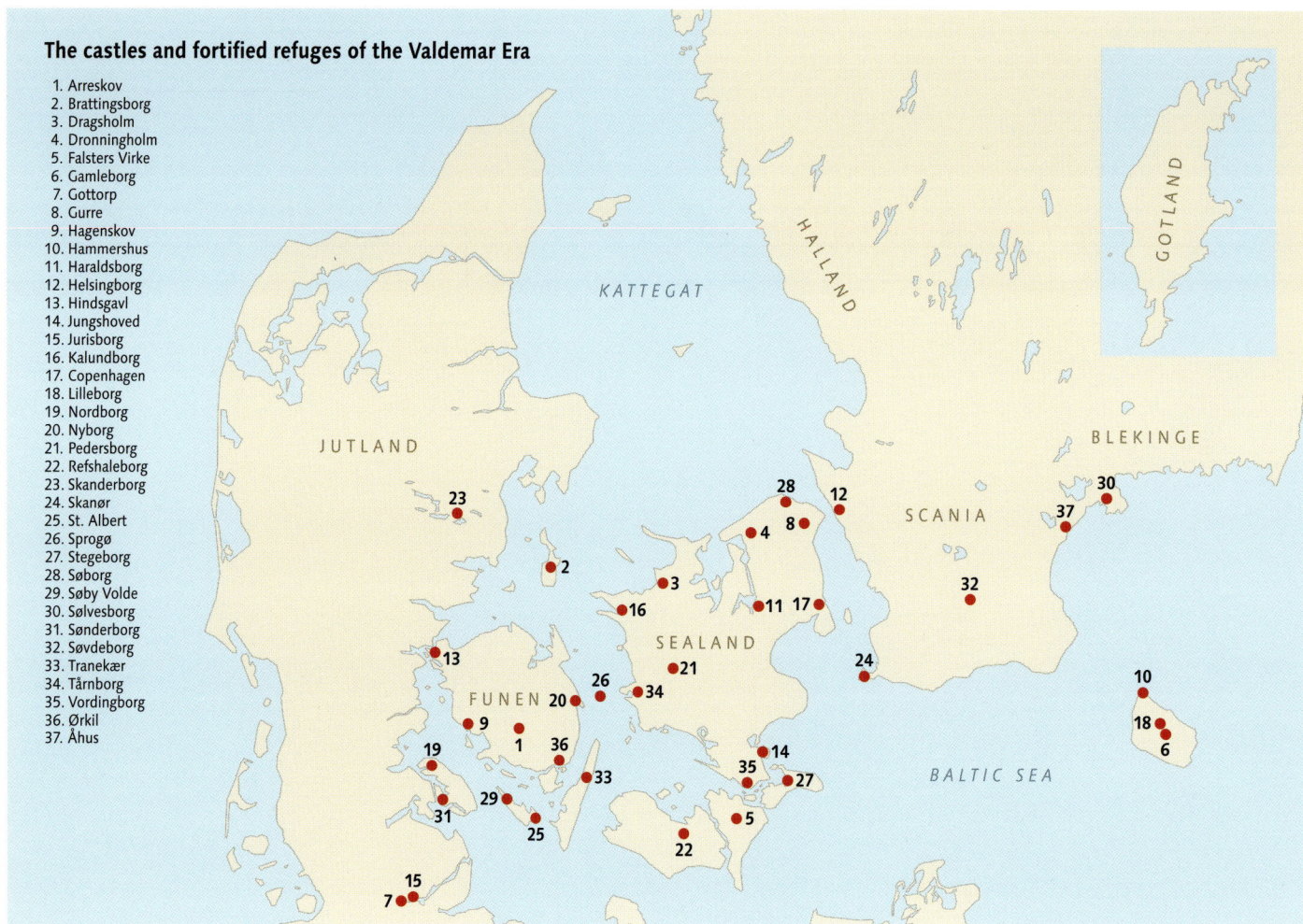

The **CASTLES OF THE VALDEMAR ERA** – *the map shows they protected the borders and crossing points around the shores of the country.*

as the victor in his own territories. King Valdemar could safely allow men such as Absalon and Esbern to build castles for him, and both Absalon's "Havn" ("Harbour": later Copenhagen) and Esbern's Kalundborg have to be seen in the context of the Crown's other properties.

It was not because of lack of knowledge about fortifications that there were so few castles in Denmark in the time of the Valdemars. Even the earliest of the Danish castles were fully on a level with what was to be found at the same time in the rest of Europe. The Bastrup Tower was virtually in a league of its own, as was Skeingeborg. Søborg was certainly rather fragile, but had a completely modern curtain wall structure with strategic interplay between walls, towers and nature; the prestige dwelling in the castle, the *palatium* with the round chapel at the gable, was built according to the tradition of the German imperial palaces. This was the way both powerful landowners and the Crown chose to build, e.g. at Pedersborg and Helsingborg. On Sprogø and at Tårnborg brick-built towers surrounded by a curtain wall functioned as citadels; they had room for a garrison and had special observation duties. In Kalundborg and Vordingborg the castles were part of a whole town complex, and it can be seen that natural conditions were used to full advantage, also in cases where the fortifications consisted of earthworks and perhaps more wood than stone, as at Refshaleborg on the island of Borgø in Maribo Lake.

It was the fully developed castle, refined over the course of a few centuries elsewhere in Europe, that was taken into use in Denmark in the 12th century. It came in particular via Germany, as can be seen from the size of the towers and their placing in the curtain wall and as gate-defences. They are mostly too small to contain dwellings, and they are known as *"barfred"*, which is a Danish version of the German *Bergfried*. But inspiration came from other sources too. The Bastrup Tower is older and more like a "dwelling tower" – a keep or a *donjon*, as known from France – but in addition to the great tower in Hamburg there were other round towers in Europe at the time when the Bastrup Tower was built. The tower at Borren was also large enough to contain living quarters, as was the Mantel Tower at Hammershus, from the beginning of the 13th century, and in the course of time at least one other *donjon* or keep was built at Helsingborg.

As can also be seen in Danish churches, European architecture was well known to the powerful in the country, and they chose freely from the abundant range of features used elsewhere.

It is possible that several of the old strong royal castles – Helsingborg, for instance – have roots that go right back to the reign of the first Valdemar, but otherwise they were built by his sons, who succeeded him on the throne – first Knud, who was the fourth, but is known as the sixth, because Roman numerals caused problems in those days too, and then Valdemar, known as the Victorious, but who can also be said to have bungled away his opportunities, at any rate where foreign relations were concerned. The period of reign of those three kings, from 1157 to 1241, is known as the Valdemar period.

That period was a time of strengthening for Denmark. The parts of the kingdom which had been about to separate off from each other were gathered together and bound more closely to each other. Knud VI and Valdemar the Victorious followed in their father's footsteps and continued to strengthen the kingdom in relation to surrounding countries through many battles, always waging them at the border and in other people's territory, never on Danish ground. They were supported, as their father had been, by the Hvide family and with them by the Church, with the most important ecclesiastical offices, the archiepiscopal see and the bishopric of Roskilde held almost as inherited posts in the family. From the beginning it had been important to secure peace in the kingdom, and that had not been entirely easy, even though Haraldsborg and Søborg are the only known examples of castles in the kingdom that were a threat to the king's authority. Neither in Halland, where Archbishop Eskil's rebellious grandsons were dukes, nor in Schleswig, where Bishop Valdemar held power, is it possible to identify instances of significant castle structures that were meant to be directed against the Crown.

The royal family had many members, and Valdemar the Great had to weed out many who were not loyal to him in order to ensure safety for himself and his

successors, but the problem re-emerged in the following generations. At the same time that the royal fathers were fighting their own generation's possible opponents within the family, they also saw to it that all their sons were provided with lands, titles and positions, even the younger ones and the illegitimate ones. For a long time it proved possible to keep the peace and preserve order. If that had not been the case there would have been royal castles in all parts of the country, not just on exposed coastlines and borders, and there would have been many private fortified sites. The property of the Crown was spread out over all areas of the country and in many cases was administered from unfortified royal estates, just as other aristocrats ran their properties from farms without fortifications. This was how it had been from before the kingdom had been united, and how it had been in England before the Norman Conquest. The Valdemars built their authority on the basis that the kingdom became a state governed by laws, and there was order in the laws, which were now written down and came to be applied systematically. Close cooperation with the Church was an additional source of strength, and it was also important to have the support of the powerful men of the country.

The country's defences were extended with a number of castle structures that were turned towards enemies from outside, in particular the Wends. The castles were strategically sited at borders and landing places, on exposed coastlines and perhaps also beside important roads. Apart from Skanderborg in Jutland,

SKANDERBORG is one of the important old royal castles that has now virtually disappeared. The castle mound has been levelled out so that it almost looks like a park area in the middle of the town's churchyard. The church dates from Frederik II's 16th century buildings on the site. Seen from the north.

*The palatium at **NYBORG** has been rebuilt and enlarged several times, so that it now extends over the whole length of the west side of the curtain wall, c. 60 m. Seen from the east.*

NYBORG *became important both because of its location and because it was there that meetings were held of* Danehoffet, *the assembly of the powerful men in the country. The plan shows the layout in the 13th century, when parts of the palatium on the west side had already been built and shared the outer wall with the curtain wall. The large tower to the east protected the entrance.*

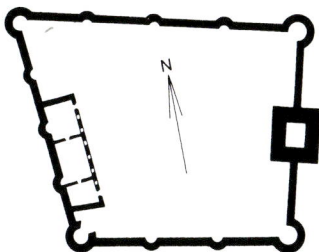

some of the castles on Funen and a few others, all of the castles are situated in areas subject to external threat. Some other structures, known because they were involved in battles in the mid 13th century, e.g. between the sons of Valdemar the Victorious, must have been built prior to that; this is possibly also true of Gottorp. Valdemar the Great and his two sons all managed, however, as warlords to bring conditions of peace, security and splendour to the country so effectively and to such popular satisfaction that the phrase "in King Valdemar's time" came to mean "in the good old days".

The Wends, as pirates in the best Viking tradition, had for many years taken advantage of the period of weak central power in Denmark. They had raided and plundered in many areas and made settlements, possibly even extensive ones, on Lolland and Falster, where after a while they became assimilated into the former population. Their homeland had been weakened both by the Danish campaigns against the Wends, including the wars – successful for a certain time – led by Valdemar the Victorious, and by the inroads on their territory made by German princes and Christian orders of chivalry.

The Valdemars drove the pirates out of the Danish waters and took the battle beyond the boundaries of the country by making conquests around the whole coast of the Baltic from Rügen up to and including Estonia. The numerous wars abroad in many cases involved sieges, and even if there were differences between

the round Slavonic earthwork structures and the more normal medieval castles in Holstein, e.g. Rendsburg and Hamburg, the methods of attack and the tactics were basically the same. The campaigns became crusades, while at the same time they had a pragmatic political background. On the Christian value scale of the time, the Estonian campaigns of Valdemar the Victorious, with Papal authorisation, ranked just as high as crusades to the Holy Land. Archbishop Anders Sunesen was not only Absalon's nephew and an equally staunch supporter of the Crown, but just like both Absalon and Eskil he was a Papal Legate and thus had the right to lead a crusade. It is doubtless in that context that the construction of Hammershus should be seen, probably as a joint building venture undertaken by Valdemar the Victorious and Anders Sunesen in connection with the campaigns in the Baltic, and it is probably because of this that the Crown so often tried to

HAMMERSHUS on Bornholm was from its origins a combined royal and episcopal construction, but it was frequently fought over, especially when the Crown and Church became enemies in connection with the conflict between the sons of Valdemar the Victorious and their descendants from the mid-13th century. The large building in the foreground was a storehouse for the wares collected as taxes from Bornholm. Seen from the south.

The great tower of the inner castle at **HAMMERSHUS** *is known as the* MANTEL *Tower. The word is German and means "cloak". The tower is integrated into the curtain wall, which in German is called "Mantelmaur". The name is a relic of the time when the town of Lübeck was in possession of the castle. The tower is both gate-tower and dwelling-tower, and it has been extended upwards several times, so that the original tower-house became a gigantic tower.*

wrest the castle away from the archiepiscopal see. It did not succeed in doing so for a long time, but like the struggle between the Crown and the Bishop of Roskilde over Copenhagen, the conflict shows how royalty tried to assert its monopoly of building and possessing the fortresses in the kingdom.

During the time of the Valdemars it became firmly established that the position of Denmark's border in the south of Jutland was fixed. The annual assemblies of the *Leidang* fleet at Vordingborg contributed to linking the different parts of the country together and to keeping disruptive elements occupied, even though at times it was difficult to keep order in the assembled forces from all parts of the country. If Saxo is to be believed, there were particular problems with the Jutlanders. They had a tendency to go home if they had to stay so long that the provisions they had brought from home had been eaten up.

In the middle of the 12th century a new building material was introduced to Denmark. This was the brick, or "fired stone", as mentioned on the lead tablet in Valdemar the Great's grave. It came to Denmark direct from Lombardy and was the ideal building material in a country like Denmark, where there is clay everywhere and virtually no access to natural stone except if one collects boulders from the fields. Many churches were built of brick in the Middle Ages, particularly in market towns and where there were monasteries, and both at Søborg and in most of the royal castles brick constructions were used on top of bases of boulders. Brick is not a cheap building material, however. Firing and transport presuppose a good economy and many resources, and for a long time the use of brick was a distinguishing characteristic of upper class building. Brick buildings never became common in association with small private castles, but they came to distinguish the buildings of the Crown, of the Church and of the highest local potentates, not least their castles.

The Mantel Tower at **HAMMERSHUS** *is now a ruin, but inside it the many traces of windows, doors, stoves and chimneys tell us about the building-history of the tower.*

IV

Interlude – and more castles: The political background

Valdemar the Victorious died on 28 March 1241, "when the crown truly fell from the head of the Danes", according to the author of the Ryd Chronicle, who then proceeded to describe all the unhappy events that were subsequently to befall the country. The crown, truth to tell, had begun to wobble some twenty years earlier, when the King and his eldest son and co-regent, Valdemar the Younger, were taken captive during a hunt on the island of Lyø, south of Funen, and had to endure a lengthy period of imprisonment in Germany "in the tower" at the mercy of Count Henrik of Schwerin as revenge for all the conquests around the shores of the Baltic. During this time the King's Council ruled Denmark. The royal prisoners were released on payment of a large ransom, which for a long time contributed to destroying the economy of the Crown, and the war campaign that was intended to reassert Danish authority in Northern Germany ended with King Valdemar being defeated at Bornhøved in Holstein in 1227. Despite this, general conditions within the kingdom remained stable during his lifetime, and significant advances were made in generalising and enforcing law in the realm. An important step was the issuing of a written version of *"Jyske Lov"* – the law of Jutland. Each of the lands which together made up the realm of Denmark had its own collection of laws, but *Jyske Lov* was the first comprehensive law text issued under the authority of the King. After the old King's death everything went wrong.

King Valdemar left three sons born in wedlock; in the course of only a few years all of them came to reign, and they were in a constant state of conflict with each other. Erik had been his father's co-regent when the eldest brother, Valdemar the Younger, died. Abel then succeeded Erik as Duke of Schleswig, and Christoffer became ruler of Lolland and Falster. In addition there were a couple of illegitimate sons: Niels, who became Count of Halland, and Knud, who was the outcome of a relationship between Valdemar the Victorious and Helene, the wife –or possibly widow – of Esbern Snare, and who became Duke of Reval and later Duke of Blekinge. The Hvide family really provided the monarchy with all conceivable support! All the sons took part in the conflict after their father's death, either for the purpose of winning the throne or in order to gain the maximum sovereign power in the area under their control. This was to have consequences far into the future.

Even though this was not a case of dissolution of a feudal system as in France or Germany, the unity of the kingdom was under threat. This was clear to the

The thick walls of the castles and towers were put to use; little useful spaces and stairways were built into them. This is a view down into the spiral staircase at **KÄRNAN** *in Helsingborg.*

successive kings. In time as they came to the throne each of the brothers, Erik Plovpenning – named after the taxes he imposed – followed by Abel and then Christoffer, took a hard line over the family members' striving for power and independence. Erik was killed by Abel, whose reign lasted for only two years. Erik left only daughters, and it was Christoffer's descendants who retained the throne, while Abel's sons had to make do with the Duchy of Schleswig, although Christoffer had been the youngest son. Partly for that reason Abel's descendants were particularly eager to become independent of the kingdom, and they were powerfully supported by their maternal family, the Counts of Holstein. Throughout many years more and more frequent and open conflict broke out between "the King" and "the Duke" on the border between their possessions, and this led to the construction of a number of castles on the boundary between the kingdom and the duchy. The dividing line followed to a large extent the route of the river named Kongeåen.

There was also unrest within the kingdom, because members of the royal family, in addition to their entailed princely estates, had inherited property in other parts of the country, and they claimed princely rights over all that they owned. Two of Erik Plovpenning's daughters were married to kings in the neighbouring countries in Norway and Sweden, and they thus came to have unwelcome influence over internal Danish conditions. An attempt was made to put the two youngest daughters into a convent, but the strong-willed ladies escaped and demanded their inheritance. The Duke of Schleswig and several of the members of his family, Count Jacob of North Halland and the husbands and children of the two Plovpenning daughters in Norway and Sweden all claimed what was due to them. It would have weakened the Crown to divide up so many of the royal possessions among so many claimants. King Erik Klipping (son of Christoffer) allowed the process of settlement to drag out. This just made everything worse.

The many years of strife led to the creation of factions among the major landowners and other influential people in the land, who took up the cause of

different members of the royal family, and perhaps the worst aspect was that the Church became involved. The leaders of the Church were for the most part members of the country's most prominent families, and as bishops and abbots they ran huge estates almost like a state within the state. The Church had grown large and powerful and had become an independent authority which no longer stuck to supporting the monarchy, but on the contrary could actually make demands of it. In the conflict between the Crown and Abel's descendants a number of successive archbishops, and along with them the majority of the power-holders in the Church, chose to support the Abel dynasty. The second half of the 13th century was deeply marked by the bitter fight between the monarchy and the Church, and in the "Great Archbishop Conflict" both parties used every method available to them. The Archbishop responded with excommunication and interdict when the King had him thrown in prison, and both measures were resorted to more than

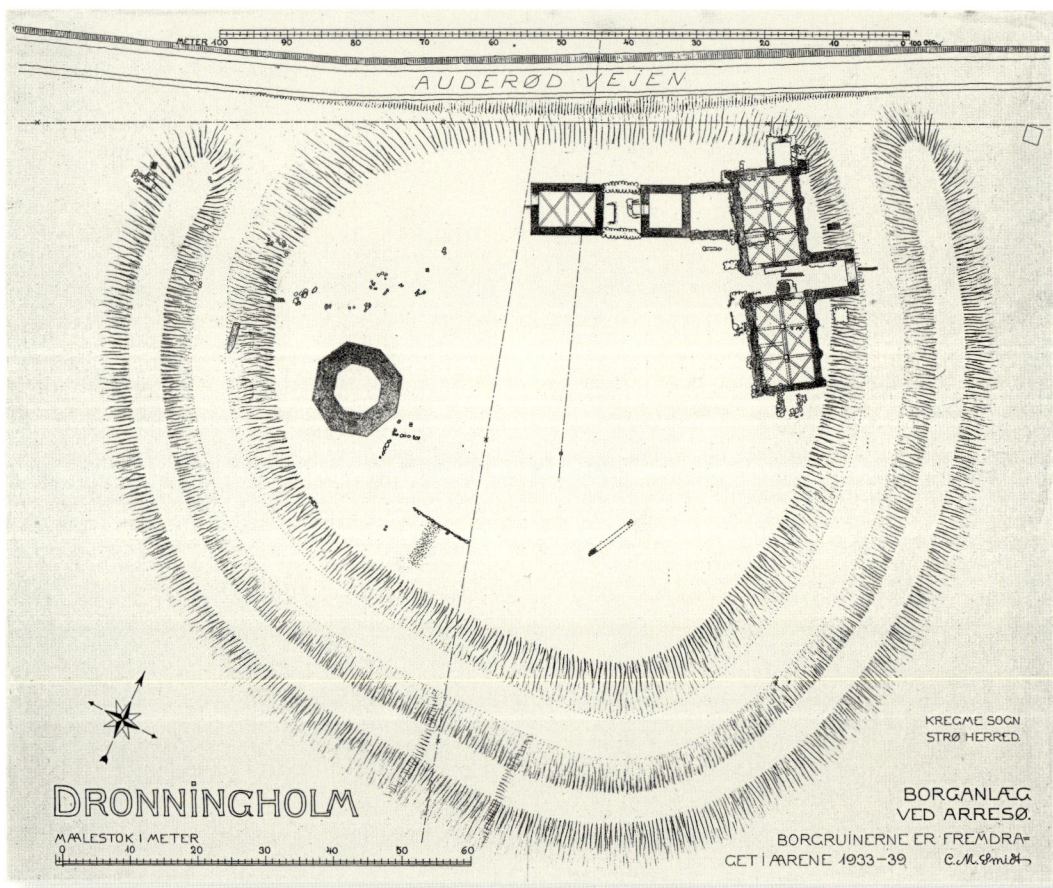

RIBERHUS *was built in the 1260s, like Koldinghus, in connection with the battles between the King and the Duke, and for centuries the two structures played their part in marking the boundary between the kingdom and the duchy. Now there is only a mound with some ruins left of the castle as it was after Christian III's rebuilding. Above it stands a statue of Valdemar the Victorious's queen, Dagmar, whom he received here on her arrival in Denmark.*

DRONNINGHOLM *on the shore of Arresø Lake was once a royal castle with a curtain wall and fine Romanesque brick houses.*

The ruin of **DRONNINGHOLM** *is now overgrown with grass, so that it is difficult to see the outline of the building-remains and to perceive the extent of the castle.*

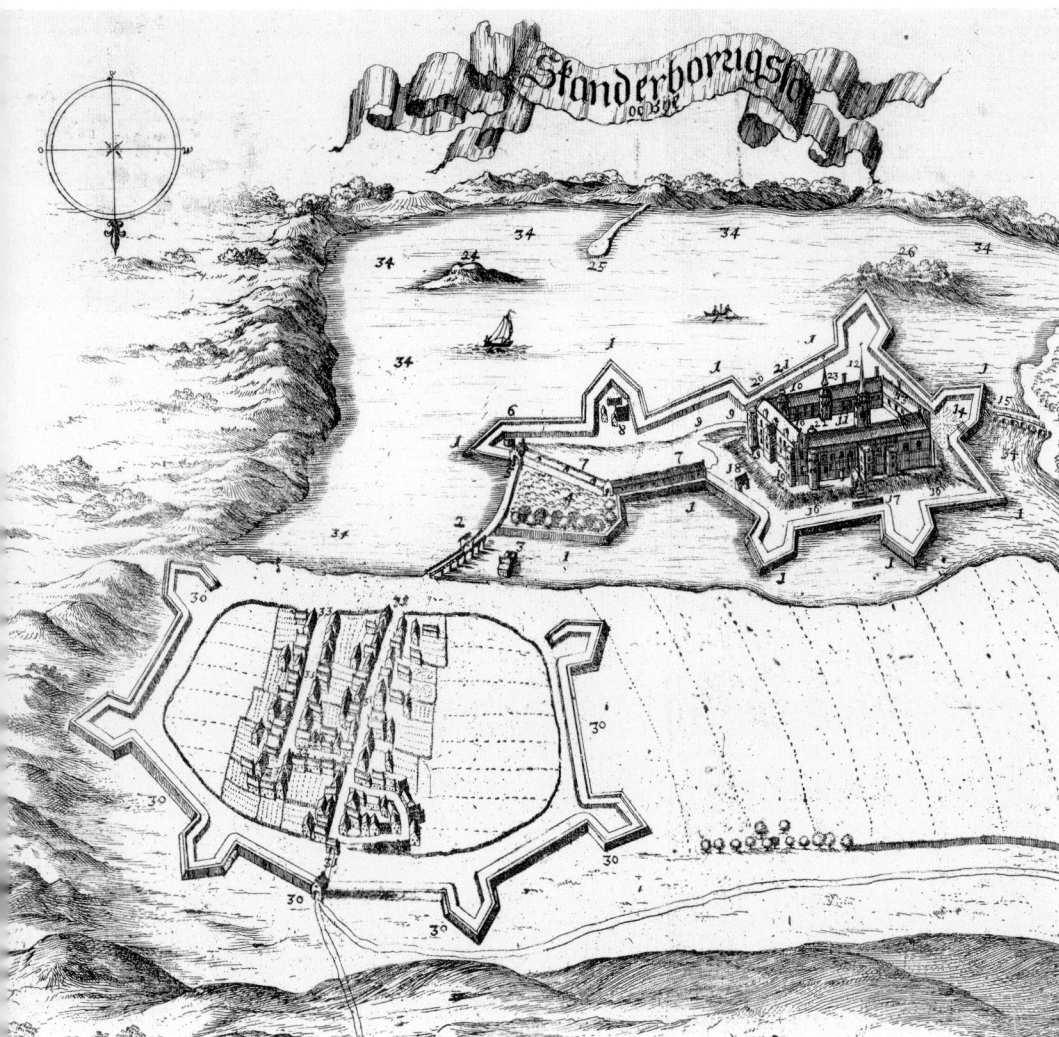

once, so the King and country had to manage without ecclesiastical support in much of the kingdom for long periods. The exception to this for some while was the diocese of Ribe, because the Church was not united in its views either, but finally a very large majority of the secular aristocrats in the country also came to hold the opinion that the power of the monarchy should be limited.

What made matters worse was that the monarchy's finances were steadily diminishing. The economic legacy of Valdemar the Victorious was negative because of his many wars. The large ransom that had to be paid to Count Henrik of Schwerin to gain the release of the King and his eldest son was also a heavy burden on the budget. In addition the conflicts between his successors were especially costly in that they took place within the country and affected the surrounding inhabitants, and even in the years immediately following King Valdemar's death it proved necessary to raise extra taxes – *inter alia* on arable land – a measure that gave rise to King Erik's nickname of "Plovpenning" meaning "plough-penny". The extra tax liability continued after his reign and led to increasing discontent and unrest among the populace. The situation became more acrimonious in the time of Christoffer's son Erik Klipping, who ended up murdered in Finderup Barn near Viborg in 1286. "King Erik was killed in his bed on St Cecilia's Eve by those he loved best, and he had 56 wounds", according to the account by a monk from Ryd Monastery, and that is about the limit of what is known today about Denmark's last regicide.

There was certainly a verdict pronounced in the case at Whit the following year, in the Danehof, or Danish medieval parliament, in Nyborg; nine men from the country's most influential families were declared outlaws for the murder of King Erik, but it has never been proven who actually used the daggers, and there were people even at the time who thought that the verdict was a miscarriage of justice. Those convicted were some of the most powerful men in the kingdom, and the judgement was a political decision about the division of power in society between the monarchy, the church and the leading landowners. It brought to a close for a time the power struggle that had culminated with the murder in Finderup, which can be traced through records in contemporary annals, but not everyone was pleased with the outcome. When Erik Klipping had acceded to the throne as a child, the monks in Øm Monastery, near Skanderborg in central Jutland, wrote in their chronicle: "Unhappy the land whose king is a child and whose princes feast at daybreak". The same thought no doubt struck many in Denmark when his son, also named Erik, in turn became king as a child.

The entries in the chronicles are short and more or less copied from one to the next, but even so one can see that castles came to play a larger and larger role in conflicts. It is in this period that they came into their own in Denmark. The sources tell us that the warring parties destroyed each other's castles and property. That became the way that one weakened one's opponent, not least because over time much of the management of land and property took place in the castles. The new kind of war also cost much more than was produced by the ordinary revenues of the Crown or of major landowners. It in fact required quantities of very costly building and structural work, and the military resources of the country were insufficient. Expensive mercenaries had to be added to the mix.

The course of the war

Already in the first year after the death of Valdemar the Victorious, conflict broke out between his sons King Erik Plovpenning and his brother, Duke Abel. The King led an army to take Kolding, which did not yet have a castle. Soon King Erik's other brothers also joined the conflict, and the King took Christoffer prisoner, along with Duke Knud of Blekinge. Then Abel took Ribe, which also had no castle at this time, but there must have been a royal seat there, since it was there that Valdemar the Victorious had received his Queen, Dagmar, and it was also there that the wedding of Valdemar the Younger had been held. Germans raided Copenhagen, which may have included the castle, and the King burned Svendborg, which Abel had provided with fortifications, and where there was a castle. The King took Ribe

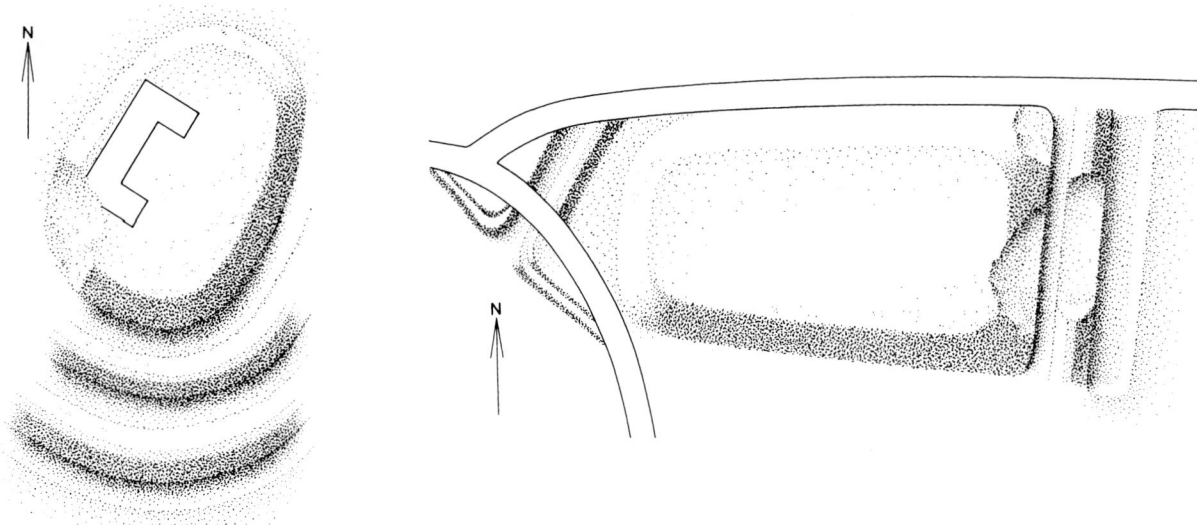

back, went on to attack Abel's castle at Arreskov on Funen, and eventually took "all his brothers' castles and all their property", according to the Lund Chronicle. Meanwhile Queen Jutta sat in the important royal castle at Skanderborg and bled the area white, according to the Øm Monastery Chronicle.

It cannot be any surprise that the King became short of money and had to claim more of the hated land taxes. In Jutland he gathered them in, but in Scania the people refused, as often before and since, and in their anger the farmers and country-people chased the King from Lund to Helsingborg, where they besieged the castle. King Erik escaped, however, and in the end no doubt collected some money before he went off campaigning against the Frisians. When that campaign failed he went straight to Schleswig, where he was killed on the orders of his brother Abel. All this took place in the course of less than ten years, and as the Ryd Chronicle expresses it: "the strife amongst the brothers destroyed the country".

The periods of reign of Abel and of Christoffer, taken together, were just as short as that of Erik, but no less tempestuous. There was fighting on the Scanian peninsula of Skanør – over the castle there – in 1252, and in the same year Abel died during a campaign against the Frisians. Christoffer became king and in 1253 he gave Abel's son, Valdemar Abelsen, Schleswig as an entailed estate. This meant that he recognised his nephew's right to the territory, but his intention was possibly to give himself free hands for the battle with the German knight Henrik Æmeltorp, who played a major if brief role in Denmark, in which in the course of a year he took control of the island of Møn and built a castle at Skelskør on Sealand. The castle was taken by the King, Svendborg was burned down again, and the peasants rose up in protest, not least on Sealand. Several chronicles, as already mentioned, relate that 1255 was the year that the "farmhands went mad with clubs". In the following year Refshaleborg was laid in ruins for ever, but there were no doubt other castles that also suffered damage. The King took Nykøbing on Falster – probably the castle – and Tranekær – in that case certainly the castle – and defeated the peasants emphatically at Lejre Bro on Sealand. Important battles were still fought and decided in open fields, but the peasants of course didn't have any castles. The conflict with the Church, which had begun already during

ARRESKOV *on Funen has two medieval castle mounds. Not much is known about them, but they are both large and testify to the importance of the place during the conflict between the sons of Valdemar the Victorious.*

JOMFRUHØJ *with its two mounds, in the woods at Lundsgård, south of Kerteminde, is typical of this period, since the unrest in the country caused landowners to build fortifications. Coin finds indicate that the site was still in use in the early 15th century.*

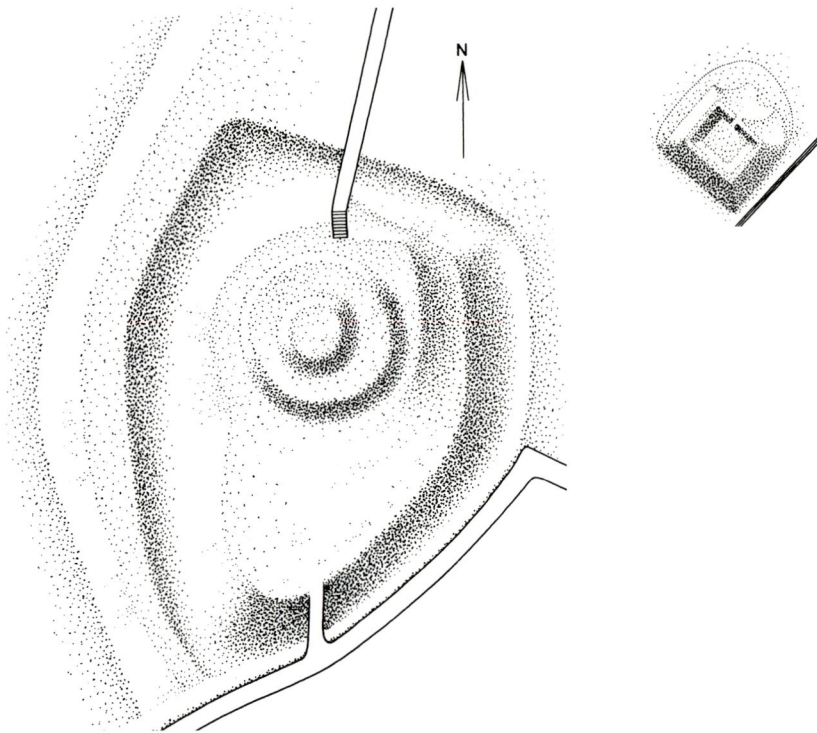

HAGENSKOV on Funen was known as Frederiksgave for a time, but was given its original name again in 1962. Here there are the remains of both a large and a small fortification from the Middle Ages. It was probably in the larger one that Christoffer I held Archbishop Jacob Erlandsen prisoner in 1259.

INITIAL LETTER, a large splendidly decorated "D" from a text in a 14th century Bible. A knight receives his sword from a prince in return for swearing an oath of fealty – i.e. promising obedience and faithfulness – on certain conditions. Durham Cathedral MS All, 3, fol 225 V. Photo reproduced with the permission of the Chapter of Durham Cathedral.

Erik's reign, culminated provisionally with the capture of Archbishop Jacob Erlandsen in 1259. He was taken to the castle of Hagenskov on Funen and according to one source put "in the tower", while another says "in chains", and a third says he was "imprisoned in a dark cell". At any rate he was imprisoned, but perhaps the conditions were not so very bad. In any case he regained his freedom the same year.

Christoffer died in Ribe in 1259. Evil tongues suggested that he was helped on his way by poison from the hand of a man of the Church. His underage son Erik (Klipping) succeeded to the throne. This was not an improvement in circumstances but rather the opposite, since it meant that Abel's family was again bypassed, and they thought they should take precedence by right of seniority; through most of Erik Klipping's reign the Duke of Schleswig was probably the monarchy's most dangerous opponent. But there were many other major problems, and the enemies of the Crown readily grouped themselves together.

Prince Jarmer of Rügen was causing havoc on Sealand and his men killed many peasants near Næstved; together with the Archbishop's brother he is reported as having destroyed the King's fortress on Bornholm in 1259. That was no doubt Lilleborg, for which the King perhaps no longer had much use anyway, since the Archbishop had taken control over virtually the whole island and had secured for himself the major castle of Hammershus. Christoffer's widow, Dowager Queen Margrete, held the regency during the childhood of the underage King Erik. She was known as "Margrete Sprænghest", a nickname which implied that she ruled the country with a hard hand, in the same way that she rode her horse. She was forced to accept that Abel's son Erik became Duke of Schleswig, succeeding his brother Valdemar, but this did not create peace. In 1261 open con-

THE STORMING OF A TOWN. *Assorted troops with many different weapons are on their way up the wall on siege ladders during the last phase of the conquest. The episode took place in the middle of the 15th century.* Chroniques de Charles VII *by Jean Chartier, Ms. fr. 2691, fol. 264v. Bibliothèque Nationale, Paris.*

flict broke out between the Queen and the Duke, south of the town of Schleswig and Danevirke; they fought at Lohede and the royal troops lost. King Erik and his mother were taken prisoner. The Queen was soon released, however, and for a year she ruled Denmark with Duke Albrecht of Braunschweig as a harsh co-regent. His role in the kingdom was just one of several signs that relations with other countries were unstable and partly determined by relationships within the Danish royal house. Both Norway and Sweden took an increasingly hostile stance towards Denmark because of the inheritance claims of Erik Plovpenning's daughters, and at the same time other descendants of Valdemar the Victorious also laid claim to a share of royal riches in the form of privileges and property. The country was subject to papal interdict, the King and Queen had been excommunicated, and Albrecht of Braunschweig, chief among others, was ravaging the property of the Church. The Church itself was divided, however, and some of the bishops were loyal to the Crown. This did not simplify matters.

*The west wing of **NYBORG** seen from the north. At one stage there was a plan to install cannons in the corner tower, but the vibrations when they were fired would have been too strong.*

Erik Klipping had hardly reached home after a couple of years of imprisonment by the Margrave of Brandenburg, with whose daughter he had had to enter into a betrothal pact without dowry, before he destroyed Arreskov on Funen in 1264. In the following year the Duke of Schleswig destroyed Møgeltønderhus, the predecessor of Schackenborg, the property of the royalist Bishop of Ribe, and the King then built castles in Kolding and Ribe in 1267 or -68. Those two towns had often been fought over since the beginning of Erik Plovpenning's reign, and this happened again in 1271. Then Schleswig was attacked by the Germans, i.e. the Holsteiners, and there are reports that the King began to lay waste the Duchy. Relations with the Church did not improve, although the interdict was lifted, and then fighting began in Sweden also; there the Danes had fortune on their side. Conditions within the kingdom had by then become intolerable for the majority of leading landowners, however, and at meetings in Helsingborg, Nyborg and finally in Vordingborg the King had to give in to their demands and allow e.g. his cousin's son Valdemar Eriksen to take the Duchy of Schleswig and a slightly more distant relative, Jacob, to become Count of North Halland.

Soon the King took up his arbitrary ways again; he threw Duke Valdemar and his seneschal in prison in Søborg and destroyed the Duke's castle of Tønderhus. They were released again the following year, in 1286, but by then many had had enough, and King Erik was murdered in Finderup Barn at the end of November. The monk who wrote out the chronicle in Ryd Monastery near Flensborg fjord, where Glücksborg Castle now stands, formulated the following verdict on King Erik on behalf of the contemporary Church: "He did many evil deeds and plundered the churches. Those who came to him with complaints of injustice received no justice from him. The monasteries his forefathers built he left impoverished by his royal progresses with horses and dogs. In his time the Holstein Counts ravaged large sections of the Duchy, and Jarmer laid waste large parts of Sealand". According to this man of the Church Erik Klipping had been a really bad king, unable to secure the kingdom from external threats or to keep the peace internally. He was an unjust ruler, a *"rex injustus",* the complete opposite of the Valdemars, and it is made to seem almost a good deed to free the country from him. This is the account of an opponent, but Ryd was in fact a Cistercian monastery and was faithful to the Archbishop. Abel had been the patron of the monastery, and there were significant reasons for the monks in Ryd not to view Christoffer's son with sympathy. Or vice versa: rumour has it that it was Abbot Arnfast from Ryd monastery who had poisoned King Erik's father – and even that he had done so while administering Holy Communion!

The castles

During the 45 years after the death of Valdemar the Victorious more castles were built than have been mentioned here, for example Duke Erik Abelsen's Gottorp in Schleswig. We do not have names for all of them, and there are no doubt some we do not know anything about, but in those years the castles became the most

important places in the country, in political and military terms. From them the population was governed and administered, it was there that important meetings were held, and dangerous people were imprisoned. Those who held the castles had power in the realm.

For that reason both Copenhagen Castle and Hammershus on Bornholm went on being bones of contention. The bishops of Roskilde claimed that Absalon's old castle in Copenhagen was theirs and not the Crown's, while the kings continued to insist that only the Crown could own the defences of the realm. Hammershus was one of them, but the archbishops had wanted to take over Bornholm, and even the whole archdiocese, as their own property, as if it formed a princely feudal estate, and the castle had become the archbishops' fortress against the Crown. The other bishops in the country in many cases had their own castles, and they could be used in the power struggles in the kingdom, as in the case of the Bishop of Ribe's Møgeltønderhus.

Some of the castles that are mentioned in written sources between 1241 and 1286 had apparently existed right from the beginning of this period, and possibly before that, and they would have belonged, like the castles of the Valdemar period, to those in the uppermost layer of society. The same would apply to most of the structures that can be dated to the period before Erik Klipping's death. Several castles are situated at points around the kingdom where Crown land met the boundaries of princely feudal estates and other properties belonging to the royal dynasty, and it was there that battles took place between the rival parties. The

OLS CHURCH *on Bornholm is one of the island's fortified round churches. The local inhabitants could take shelter in the loft during an attack.*

OLS CHURCH *has a sturdy free-standing belfry, as do the other round churches.*

In the mound beneath the later main building at **EGHOLM** on Sealand lie the remains of a castle structure originating from the 13th century, when the site belonged to Count Jacob of North Halland. He was a member of the royal family, but was also an enemy of the Crown. One can still see a fine vaulted room lying deep below the top of the mound.

>

NÆSHOLM is situated in a low-lying meadow which was once covered in water. The posts which carried the bridge over to firm land provide a date of 1278-79 for the construction of the castle. It functioned until the mid-14th century, when it was destroyed after a battle. Seen from the southeast.

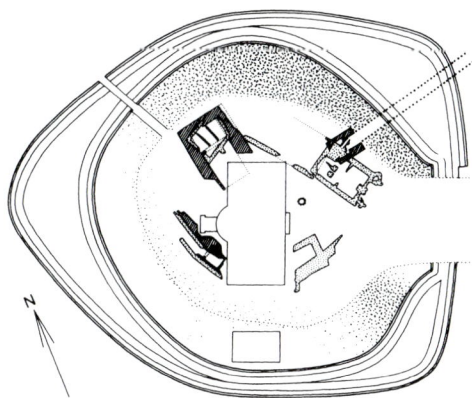

*Plan of **EGHOLM** with traces of buildings from several of the castle's building phases.*

NÆSHOLM in North Sealand is the most thoroughly excavated castle mound in Denmark, and it was probably a royal castle. The Crown had many possessions in addition to the national castles, and in times of unrest it could be necessary to fortify many of them. At Næsholm part of the mound has been carved away and strengthened with a tower made of brick. There were several buildings of lighter construction on the mound, and one of them had a gallery-walk.

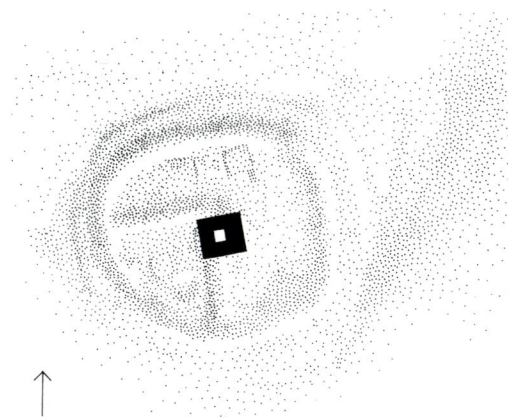

border between the kingdom and the Duchy of Schleswig is the clearest example, with the construction of the royal castles in Kolding and Ribe, but Arreskov and Hagenskov on Funen, the fortification of Svendborg, Tranekær on Langeland and Henrik Æmeltorp's castle at Skelskør belong to this pattern.

There is one castle that is not mentioned in the written sources before c.1400 and that has been dated by archaeological investigations to around the middle of the 13th century or a little later. It is Egholm in Sæby parish, in the Voldborg district on Sealand; remains have been found there of buildings from several different periods, so it is possible to see how the site has been altered in the course of time. From the earliest phase there is the ruin of a stylish brick Romanesque building. The ownership of the site was a puzzle for a long time, but it has now by indirect means been shown that the probable owner was the Jacob already mentioned who was confirmed as Count of North Halland in 1284. He was from the royal family but in opposition to Erik Klipping, who was unwilling for a long time to recognise his right to the title, in the same way that he wavered over recognising the right of other members of the royal family to inherit landed properties in the kingdom. Count Jacob was among those declared outlaws for the murder in Finderup; he no doubt had good reason to want to establish his status in the years of unrest, and he could afford to do so in style. Egholm was an estate which his heirs would be willing to struggle to regain.

The castle of Næsholm, on the Ods Herred peninsula in north-west Sealand, can also be dated archaeologically. The castle mound is one of the few almost totally excavated castle mounds in Denmark. It is not mentioned in any written source, but there are many coin finds from the century of unrest between the mid-13th century and the period around 1340, when Valdemar Atterdag won his kingdom by fighting for it more or less castle after castle, particularly on Sealand. The excavations showed that the castle had been destroyed in battle, and a dendrochronological dating of some of the posts carrying the bridge that gave access to the mainland has given a date of 1278, so despite the evidence of the coins that must have been the year of construction of the castle.

Næsholm was a relatively modest structure. Its brick tower was the only masonry building, and the castle mound is divided into two parts by an angled ditch – a strange and rather impractical feature. This is not the headquarters of a powerful person, but was more probably a large landowner's secondary property or a local overlord's fortified farm. The later land-owning history of the area could suggest that Næsholm was a lesser royal property that would have been run by a bailiff, but this is not certain. The estate may have changed hands many times between the 14th century and the point when it appeared in the archives; the castle itself is never mentioned.

There are several castle mounds in the area, and one of them is Borren, an old and remarkable site very close to Næsholm. The others may be of later date. Together they demonstrate that castle mounds are so different, one from the other, that one cannot hope for much success in trying to date them typologically.

The notes in the chronicles, the larger number of castle structures and the texts of laws provide evidence that castles became important elements of warfare

This scholarly man with his doctor's hat, seen on a mural painting from the first half of the 14th century in **KELDBY CHURCH ON MØN,** *is sitting with his inkwell and a book. He may well be writing about contemporary events. Photo from www.kalkmalerier.dk.*

in Denmark from Erik Plovpenning's time onwards, even though castles were not built in some important and fought-over places such as Kolding and Ribe until rather late. The texts of laws about the working duties of peasants indicate that there was extensive fortification-building in the period, and if one examines in chronological order the texts about castle-building in the successive kings' coronation charters, they show the development in the division of power between the monarch and the other powerful figures in the kingdom.

The oldest is the document relating to the "Abel-Christoffer provisions" from the beginning of the 1250s. It is referred to in this way because it is not completely clear which provisions relate to Abel and which to Christoffer. One of the paragraphs of this law states that no-one can be forced by the king or by knights to build fortifications in the sowing or harvesting season except in cases of the greatest need. "Planking and ditching" are the terms equivalent to the Danish version of the text, meaning putting up palisades and constructing moats. So that was what peasants could be used for, while constructing masonry buildings and walls required specialists. From Erik Klipping's final years, when he had to give in to the opposition, there are a number of regulations that in slightly different forms say that the peasants could not be forced to repair or build mills, farms or castles (for the king), without directives from the State Council and in situations of the greatest need, or more than in King Valdemar's time unless they did so voluntarily.

Christoffer II and Valdemar III were required to demolish royal castles, and King Oluf also had limits imposed on him, but the prohibition on castle-building issued by his mother, Queen Margrete, in 1396, was the expression of complete re-establishment of the power of the Crown.

These legal provisions show how the authority and the demands for power had grown on the part of the aristocracy and landowners, and it is interesting that the "knights" also claimed the right to make the peasants build fortifications in the mid-13th century. What is particularly important is that there was clearly a significant amount of castle-building taking place in the country, and that work on the royal fortresses was increasing the burden on the peasants beyond what was tolerable. The war waged by the great figures in the country had begun to have costs for the small in society, but the country was still far from being generously sprinkled with castles.

Even though the ordinary people in rural Sealand had furiously swung their clubs in Christoffer I's time, the political power struggles were still restricted to the highest level of society, and took place between the king, the duke, the other members of the royal family and the major ecclesiastical and secular aristocrats. It was expensive to build castles that could really serve a purpose in battle at that level, and besides, there was no-one who used money and labour to build fortifications for themselves unless it was genuinely necessary.

But soon that was how things turned out. The 14th century translator or continuer of the Ryd Chronicle described the whole period with a quotation that can be found in Matthew, Mark and Luke: "A kingdom divided against itself cannot stand". A house split internally has to fall.

He wrote from experience, because that was what had happened.

V

The century of the castle in Denmark

The consequences of regicide

At the Danehof, or National Assembly, in Nyborg in 1287 nine of the country's most powerful and influential subjects were declared outlaws for the murder of King Erik Klipping. They included Count Jacob of North Halland, as well as the former Lord High Constable, Marsk Stig Andersen, and Chamberlain Rane Jonsen; most of them fled to Norway, where King Erik Præstehader (Priest-hater) ruled, and at first they found refuge in the castle of Kongshelle in Bohuslen. King Erik Præstehader was the son of Erik Plovpenning's daughter Ingeborg and had inherited from her large areas of land in Denmark, particularly in Northern Jutland. He was no friend of Denmark, and could make use of these well-connected banished Danes. At the end of June 1287 he and his brother, Duke Håkon, took most of the condemned men and their followers into their protection and the outlaws changed allegiance, though not nationality. Count Jacob was not part of this arrangement; he had possibly already for some time been "Norwegian". Esquire Arvid Bengtsen was not on the list either. He was the only one of them convicted for having been at the site of the murder, so that was possibly the reason. Stig Nielsen, a knight, was not convicted, but had in any case chosen exile, and several others did the same in the following years. It was a long time before it was safe for the enemies of the new regime to be in Denmark.

The outlaws came without land-revenues, but they possibly had with them some gold and no doubt also men and ships. They could provide important links to circles in Denmark that were unhappy with the new regime and the judgement in Nyborg. The Norwegian King's new men came to take part in his war against Denmark, which had begun before the murder and continued throughout the years that followed, and indeed after several of the outlaws were dead – for instance Marsk Stig Andersen in 1293. The war was conducted with all possible means on land and at sea, and in many of the contemporary sources it is presented as if it was "the outlaws" and in particular "Marsk Stig Andersen" that were ravaging Denmark. That view was adopted by the poet and historical novelist B.S. Ingemann, and through his works, from the first half of the 19th century, this interpretation became deeply rooted in Danish minds and even in those of historians. The convicted men and their followers certainly came to play an important

AALHOLM *on Lolland was the principal residence of Count Johan of Plön during the time that he figured as one of the two mortgage-holders in Denmark in the period up to 1340. The castle with its sturdy curtain wall has changed considerably through time. Seen from the south.*

NYBORG CASTLE. *The northern corner of the west wing seen from the top of the rampart surrounding the castle.*

role in the Norwegian King's war, and for instance Rane Jonsen led pirate attacks in and around Denmark on his own account, as Norwegian leaders previously had done. But when Marsk Stig Andersen is mentioned very often in the sources, much more frequently than Count Jacob, it shows in fact how significant he had been in Denmark. He was known to all.

The Danish monarch did not have much control over Erik Præstehader's possessions in Denmark. At any rate nothing could be done to prevent him from

fortifying the little island of Hjelm in Kattegat, off the east coast of Jutland not far from Ebeltoft. It became a fixed base deep within Danish waters and directed against Denmark. The chronicles agree that this happened in 1290, and the purpose, amongst other things, was to render sea traffic unsafe for merchants and thus prevent them from trading in Denmark. On Hjelm there was also a scheme to strike forged Danish coins in order to destroy the economy of the kingdom. Marsk Stig Andersen was Erik Præstehader's captain on the island-fortress for the few years that he still had to live, while Count Jacob was captain at the castle of Hunehals at Kungsbacka in north Halland. On Hjelm Marsk Stig was not far from his own land in Jutland, which was no doubt situated near to the Norwegian properties, and he could possibly have fetched revenues from his land over to the island and contributed to the war in that way. Count Jacob built Hunehals after 1287 "on Lunde Church's ground" as the representative of the Norwegian King. Both places were bases for raids made on Denmark, and both were castles belonging to the Norwegian King. In Norway, as in Denmark, the monarch held the right to fortified sites, so the structures were not "the outlaws' castles", even though the two most important of those convicted were captains of them. But castles were necessary in war. Varberg Castle in Halland may also have played a part.

The new Danish king, another Erik, who became known as Erik Menved, was about 14 years old when he came to the throne, and for the first years the victorious group of aristocrats formed the government together with the Dowa-

Hjelm

1. Skådebakken protected the access
2. Fyrbakken was an independent defence-work
3. Kastelsbakken was an independent defence-work

Together they turned the whole island
into a fortress, an impressive castle

Østhage

Nordhage

2 Fyrbakken

3 Kastelsbakken

Skådebakken

1

Vesthage

Sydhage

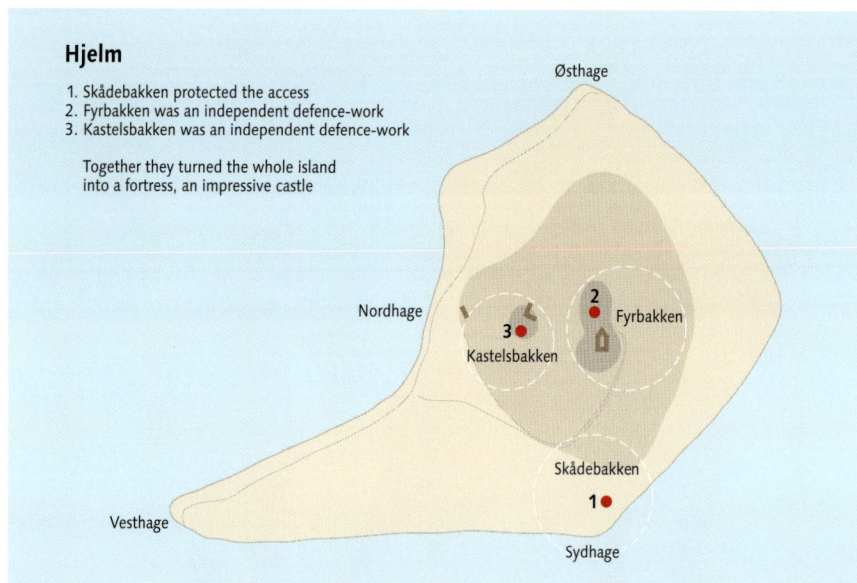

The Norwegian King Erik Præstehader was the son of one of Erik Plovpenning's daughters and had inherited land in Denmark. Possibly the island of **HJELM** *off the coast near Ebeltoft was among the properties he inherited. He had the island fortified in the context of the war with Denmark after the murder of Erik Klipping in 1286, and he made the former Lord High Constable of Denmark, Stig Andersen, into his warlord. Stig Andersen was one of those outlawed for the murder of the king. The plan shows the fortified sites on the island. It was previously thought that Skådebakken might be of earlier date than the other structures, but recent excavations have shown that all the fortifications date from the same period. From Pauline Asingh and Nils Engberg:* Marsk Stig og de fredløse på Hjelm, *2002.*

ger Queen Agnes. This was not an easy task; the monarchy was almost bankrupt, since from Christoffer I's time onwards parts of the Crown's properties had been mortgaged to generate money for war, and the conflicts in the country were still great. The government and later King Erik himself had to fight on many fronts for many years. The conflict with the Church flared up again, Duke Valdemar of Schleswig became the enemy of the Danish king once more, and yet again an archbishop was taken prisoner, in 1294 when Jens Grand was imprisoned in Søborg, and a new interdict was placed on the country. The war with Norway took centre stage, and some of the outlaws carried on a more or less independent enterprise of pirate raids, ravaging the coastal areas just as the Wends had done in their time, so that the whole population came to be affected. Now and then Duke Valdemar of Schleswig also intervened; he pulled down his father's old castle at Gottorp in order to build a new and stronger one. There was fighting from Jutland to Lolland, on Funen and on Sealand, with fortune changing sides throughout more than fifteen years, occasionally broken off for negotiations and cease-fires. Eventually everyone wanted peace. The outlaws from 1287 were almost all dead by this time, and their descendants wanted to go home and claim the right to their inheritance. The campaigns in Denmark had certainly disrupted the country and its people, but they had not overthrown the monarchy, and in the long run the merchants could not be kept away from a lucrative market.

It took time to reach agreement. In 1294 a truce was negotiated between Denmark and Norway at a meeting at Hindsgavl Castle. The truce was confirmed after some years, and the outlawed pirates gradually lost their military significance. But another source of conflict arose. The King's younger brother, Christoffer, soon came to cause difficulties, in the best of the family's traditions. He allied himself frequently with discontented aristocrats and assumed authority over areas and castles in the realm, so he had to be confronted with armed force, for

Popular ballad about the regicide in Finderup

Danish ballads have seldom originated at the same time as the events they describe, but the one about the murder of King Erik Klipping in 1286 is contemporary with the actual happenings. It relates how the murder was viewed by some people – or perhaps how some people wanted it to be viewed – and in the following centuries the ballad's version of the story was considered to be a true account.

The ballad describes how conditions in the kingdom had become wretched, because there were too many people who wanted to decide how the country should be ruled. Some of the King's enemies disguised themselves as Greyfriar monks and set off in pursuit of the King, who had gone hunting in North Jutland. They found him in a barn, Finderup Lade, near Viborg, where he had decided to stay overnight with his Chamberlain, Rane Jonsen, and other followers.

When the King heard noises outside the barn he became afraid and promised Rane Jonsen both his sister and half the kingdom if he would protect him. Rane said he would do so, but when the assailants came into the barn he did not draw his sword against them but pointed instead to the roof beams and showed them the heap of straw under which the King lay hiding.

The attackers soon found him and despatched him with several lethal stabbings. All this was witnessed by a "little young boy", a page in the service of the King, and he slipped out to saddle the white horse – no doubt the King's and thus the best and fastest – and rode to Skanderborg, where the Queen was staying with her sons, to tell her about the murder.

The clever lad warned the Queen: "You will have to look out for your kingdom, and you will have to look out for your property, and you will have to look out for your young son who will have to reign and command in Denmark." As a reward for his

efforts the young lad was promised a place at the Royal Court, with his clothing and his keep – as long as he and the Queen should live.

Each verse of the ballad has the refrain: "Because the country is in peril" – but the peril and wretchedness in the country was doomed to last for a long time after these events.

The contemporary ballad about the murder of **KING ERIK KLIPPING** *at Finderup Barn in 1286 contributed to creating an image of the event in popular consciousness. This was the last case of regicide in Denmark's history.*

Poul Steffensen's illustrations in B.S. Ingemanns popular novels cemented the generally accepted view that the outlaws did murder King Erik Klipping in 1286. Here the Chamberlain points to where the King has hidden himself.

instance at Kalundborg in 1297. The connection between Norway and Sweden became stronger through dynastic alliance and therefore threatened Denmark, so Erik Menved, who was now grown up and of age to rule independently, threw himself into new campaigns both in Sweden and beyond the Nordic region. He had ambitions to become a powerful ruler over the Baltic countries like his great-grandfather Valdemar the Victorious.

Erik Menved's wars and castles

Erik Menved proved that he was a talented field commander who could defeat his opponents, but he went on to wage war on too many fronts, and the wars became ever more costly. It required manpower on a large scale and massive material resources to wage war on towns and castles, and it was expensive to build and

HINDSGAVL'S *castle mound rises steeply from low-lying meadows close to the coast. Seen from the southeast.*

>

HINDSGAVL *on the Funen side of the Little Belt is known from the end of the 13th century, but may be older. This was where an agreement was negotiated between Erik Menved on the one hand, and on the other the Norwegian king and others who had taken part in the war that broke out after the murder of Erik Menved's father.*

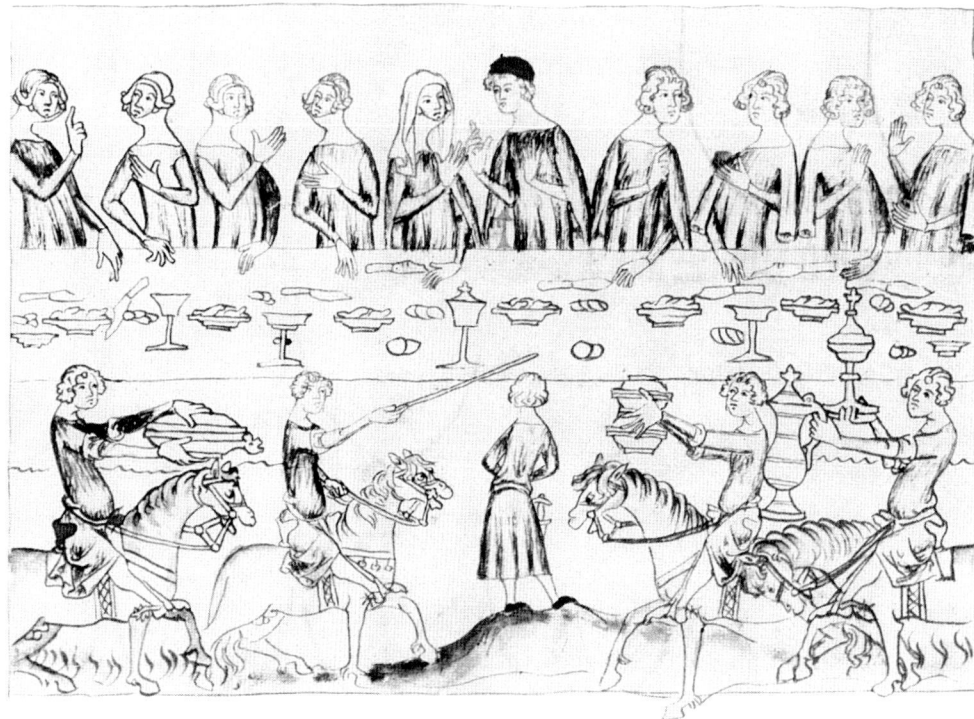

ERIK MENVED'S *efforts to gain land-conquests and influence in Northern Germany included holding grand festivities in Rostock in 1311. There he awarded knighthoods to many noblemen and provided magnificent hospitality. Food was possibly served on horseback as seen here on this picture from Ms. l c l in Landeshauptarchiv in Koblenz.*

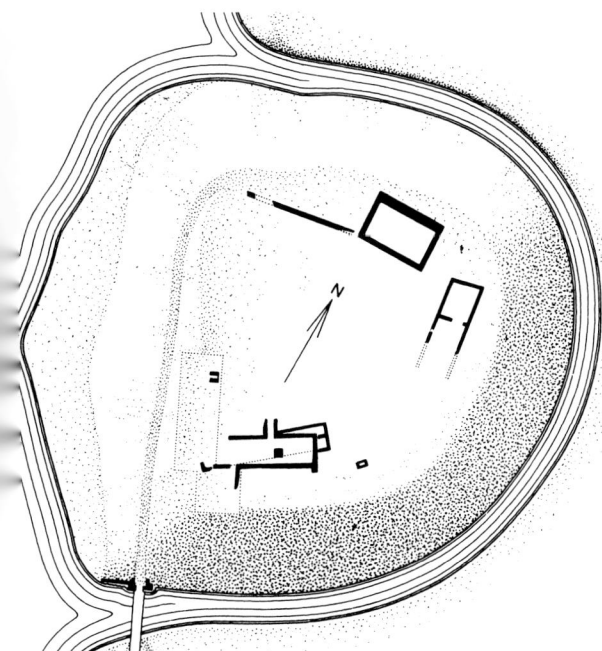

fortify. But war was necessary so long as there was no clear conclusion as to who held power in the kingdom.

The monarchy's conflict with the Church, "the Great Archbishop Conflict" was to some extent side-lined at the beginning of the 14th century. Relations with Norway and the heirs of the outlaws were settled either by agreements or by fights. King Erik conquered Hjelm in 1305 and tore down the once impressive fortifications there. There was war in Halland, which Count Jacob handed over to the Norwegian king in the same year, but there the Danish troops were not so successful. In 1307 Erik Menved intervened in Swedish matters to support his brother-in-law King Birger, who had serious problems with his brothers. This became a true family feud, and King Erik's brother Christoffer also became involved. At the same time King Erik was waging war, along with the German princes, against the trading towns on the Baltic coast. Gaining power over them would be of great advantage both to the Danish king and to the German rulers, and the war in Germany pitted the princes against the towns. Erik Menved had already taken control of Rostock in 1300. In 1311 he held a fantastic "Court" there – a huge celebration with tournaments and dubbing of knights and distribution of extravagant gifts. The fame of the event spread out through contemporary society, but it also played its part in weakening King Erik's finances, and the townspeople of Rostock were so little enamoured with his rule that they allied themselves with the townspeople of Wismar to go ravaging and burning in Denmark in the following year.

Both in Sweden and in Germany the battles were now fought castle by castle and town by town. In Halland Eskild Krage, who supported the King's brother Christoffer, took Laholm and Falkenberg and burned Ørkelljunga. The King won Nyköping, and so it went on, in Germany too. The castles had become a fixed fea-

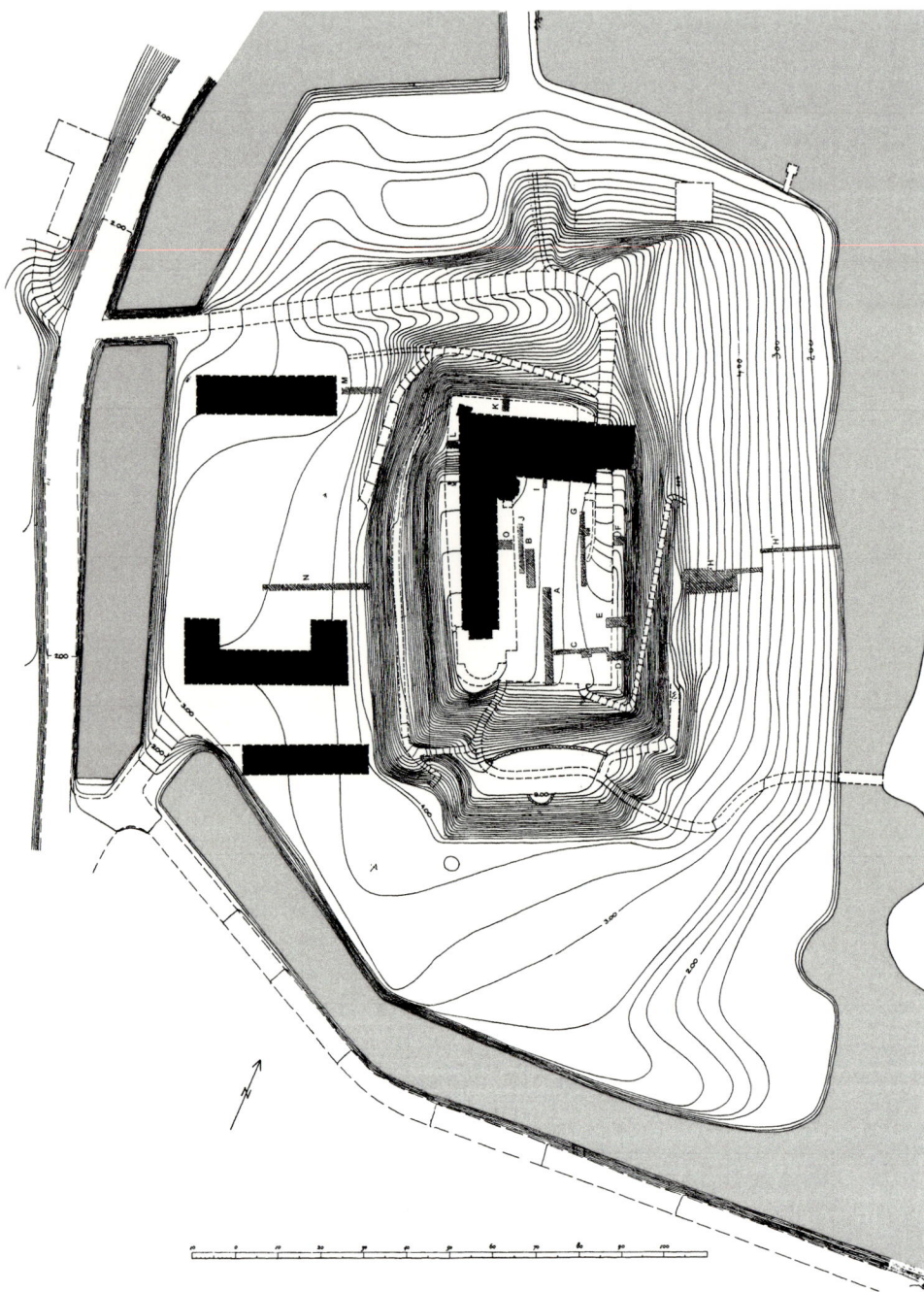

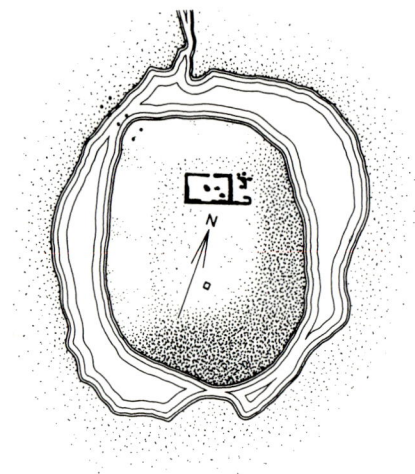

SKANØR, *just to the south of Malmø, was important for keeping control of the herring market and the sea traffic through Øresund.*

TRANEKÆR *on Langeland has a substantial preserved brick building, forming the north wing of the castle, from the 13th century. The castle was originally royal, but during part of the Middle Ages it belonged to the Duke of Schleswig. The plan also shows the extensively fortified surroundings.*

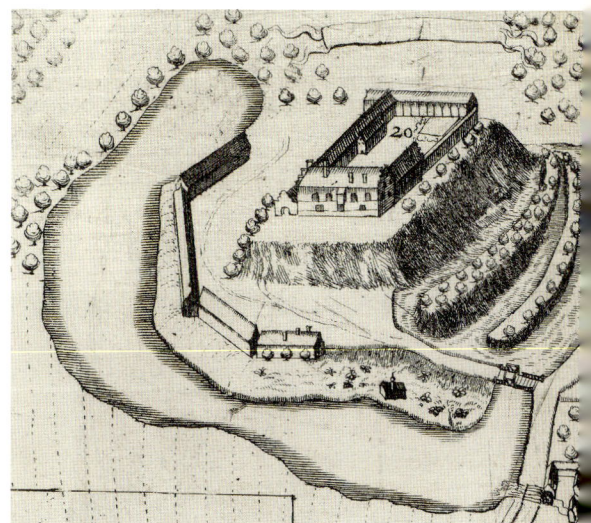

TRANEKÆR'S *thick walls are painted red, so that it is difficult to see the construction details. On the north side of the old building it is nevertheless possible to see a fine little window and a number of recesses which may be traces of cannon fire. This cannot have been from Valdemar Atterdag's siege of the castle, however, since that was before firearms were used in Denmark.*

<

From Resen's engraving from the end of the 17th century one can clearly picture that Tranekær was placed high up and well-protected, even though the ramparts had been planted with trees to give it a garden landscape.

ture of the cultural landscape, and they had a major role to play in the battles. One can of course conquer a country by skirting round the castles, but one cannot rule it without taking possession of the castles, and Erik Menved built new castles as well as reinforcing the fortifications of the old royal ones. He wanted the Crown to keep power.

In Denmark the number of private castles grew in step with the unrest in the realm, which was conditioned by the various levels of rivalry for power in the land. Denmark was never a feudal state, but the different members of the royal family treated their possessions as directly inheritable with full privileges. This was not recognised by the Crown, which saw the wider family members as subjects whose possessions were spread out around the country. Those who held princely entailed estates were considered, like all the Crown's vassals, to be officials. Some of them nevertheless built castles of a royal standard or sought to take over royal castles as their own. As long as he could, the King had to fight for his crown.

His situation was not made easier by the fact that he had used so many resources on the wars abroad. King Erik's wars were not success stories, even though technically he won virtually them all. There were too many of them and they arose so rapidly, one after the other, that he did not have sufficient troops with the men who were duty-bound to take part when the country was at war. Just as the peasants could not be forced to help construct the royal castles in the planting and harvesting seasons, they could also not be forced to take part in wars of aggression, and there were limits to how long the army could be required to serve. The participation of aristocratic land-owners was also limited in duration. So the King had to buy his soldiers, and that was expensive, particularly in a time of increasing demands for equipment and weaponry. He had to find the resources from the Crown's income, which was not in fact sufficient. That income was actually being steadily reduced because of the mortgaging off of property, and the next measure, inevitably, was to raise extra taxes, as had already been done in the time of Erik Plovpenning – but now the need was greater.

The consequence once again was rebellion among the harassed population. Both the peasants and their spokesmen had had enough. Many local potentates did not agree with the King; either they feared that his policies would give him too much power or they thought that he already had too much. Some possibly also thought that the King's extravagant policies might cost the country and the kingdom too much. The epithet "peasants", which is used by the sources, moreover has to be taken with a pinch of salt. The rebellious segments of the population consisted in large part of tax-paying peasants, but also included were large and small overlords and their discontented property-less workers who wielded the scythes and pitchforks that are always associated with peasant uprisings. If the rebellion was to be genuinely threatening there had to be a majority of disgruntled overlords, however. They understood how to use the real weapons of war.

The rebellion became an open conflagration in Jutland in 1312-13, after an attack by people from Lübeck on the Scanian town of Skanør and its castle, followed by an attack on Helsingborg and its castle. Erik Menved defeated the attackers, as he always did, but as always the victory proved to be an economic defeat and led to more conflict and greater expenses. When the King had beaten down the revolt in Jutland and taken the leaders' heads as examples to cause fear and dread, he had a number of castles built in Jutland in order to be able to control the population better in future. With these so-called "subjugation castles" he at length won control over the old obstinacy of the Jutlanders, according to the writer of the Sealand Chronicle. There had been no improvement since Saxo gave his account of the difficult Jutlanders who left the *Leidang* campaign and went home as soon as the food had been eaten.

What was new was that castles were being built to subjugate the country's own inhabitants. This shows that growing numbers of the populace had become involved in the political problems, and that the power struggles were no longer restricted to the highest levels of society. The basis for law was no longer stable, and royal authority had to use castles and military power to maintain peace. This time the unrest was mainly centred in Jutland, whereas previously it had been

BORGVOLD *near Viborg (above) and* BYGHOLM *near Horsens were two of the castles that Erik Menved had built after the rebellion in Jutland in 1312-13. "This was how he surmounted the old stubbornness of the Jutlanders", as the Sealand Chronicle says.*

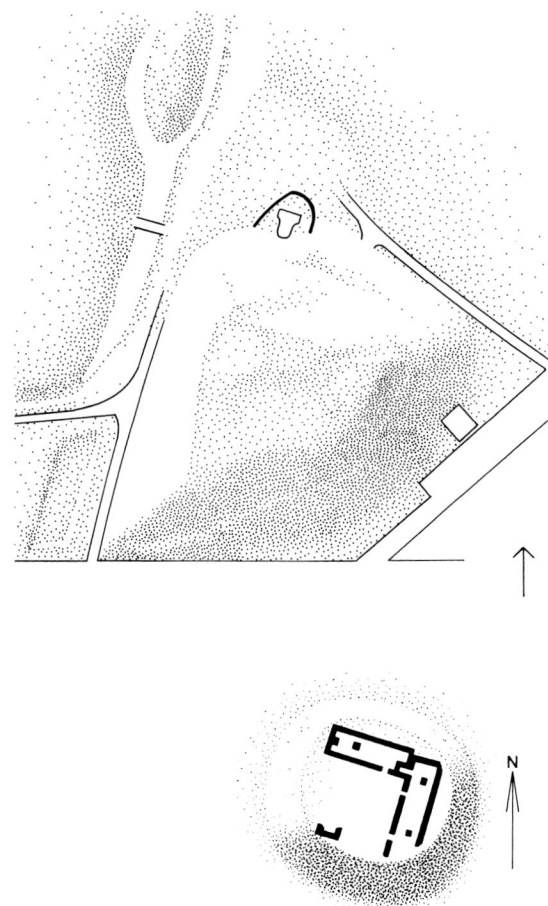

BYGHOLM'S *castle mound in Bygholm Park does not look impressive. It has been altered in the course of time to be integrated into its garden surroundings. Seen from the south.*

on Sealand that the farmhands had twirled their clubs, although there it had not been so necessary to build new fortifications. The old royal castles could in emergency be used against the country's own inhabitants. In Northern Jutland, however, Skanderborg was the only important castle from earlier times. Aalborg had perhaps come into play during the Valdemar period or just after, but as already mentioned even the towns of Kolding and Ribe, centres of conflict, did not have castles until the 1260s, after several years of war between kings and dukes.

Various chronicles mention the compulsory work on royal castles in 1313. In addition to the work the peasants were required to carry out to strengthen the fortifications at Kolding, castles were built at Horsens, in Viborg and on the island of Kalø. There is also mention of "Ulstrup on the Limfjord in the estate of the diocese of Ribe".

The bishopric of Ribe was loyal to the monarchy and continued to be so during the struggle between Crown and Church, and Bishop Christian, who wanted to retire from his post in 1310 because of old age, was persuaded to remain in office for the sake of King Erik. Ulstrup is now named Wolstrup and is a manor situated in the parish of Hjerm in West Jutland. The site has not been the subject of archaeological investigation, so nothing is known of what it would have been like in the Middle Ages when it was one of the administrative centres of the Ribe bishopric and became a fortified site in support of the Crown.

At Viborg and Horsens the castle mounds of Borgvold and Bygholm, respectively, are the remains of Erik Menved's castles. Both are rather high man-made castle mounds with rather modest top surfaces which would not have provided space for much more than living quarters, a kitchen and possibly the most essential stores. Farm buildings with barns and stables would have been at the foot of the mound or perhaps even further away. Excavations at Bygholm have brought to light the remains of a stone-built four-winged structure on top of the mound, but alterations had been made after the Middle Ages. Erik Menved's castle had perhaps replaced an earlier building, a royal manor, north of the town. At Borgvold timber was found that has been dated by dendrochronology to 1313, so in that case the archaeological evidence and the testimony of written sources fit together well.

(continued on page 118)

KALØ *was the strongest and most powerful of Erik Menved's castles. Although it is now a ruin it is still impressive, lying on its little island at the end of a long causeway leading to the shore. Seen from the east.*

KALØ

Kalø was significantly larger than the other new castles, and today it is still an impressive ruin, even though the castle was systematically demolished from the 1670s onwards and the building materials were shipped to Copenhagen, where they were used for the construction, at Kongens Nytorv, of Charlottenborg, then Gyldenløve's Palace. This tells us something about the price of bricks. Kalø's situation on a little island in the innermost curve of Aarhus bay is a splendid one. The ruin crowns a natural hill, and the remains of the castle's massive tower can be seen from a long distance inland. At Kalø the natural conditions are exploited to the best possible advantage. The castle mound rises steeply from the sea, so that ramparts and moats were only needed on three sides, but they are in fact impressive earthworks. The massive tower guarded the access to the inner castle courtyard and formed part of a whole series of

In his coronation charter from 1320 Christoffer II had to promise to demolish a number of castles belonging to the Crown, including **KALØ.** *It is difficult to see whether this was in fact carried out. The castle's main tower is still standing to a height of three storeys.*

The estate accounts from **KALØ** from the later part of the 16th century are preserved, and from them and from excavations of the castle one can gain an impression of what the castle looked like from the southeast. There is of course no guarantee that the details are correct.

The plan of **KALØ** shows the central castle, where the huge tower protected the access from the outer castle area to the main castle itself. Recent excavations on the "riding ground" outside the gatehouse and the drawbridge have shown that the mound was also fortified there, and that there was at least one large brick building on it.

defence works or barriers that began with the long causeway leading to the mainland.

Earlier excavations uncovered indications that the castle had been destroyed or demolished relatively soon after it was built, but was then rebuilt soon afterwards, mainly on the old foundations. After that there were only two minor alterations to the central castle right up to the time of its demolition at the end of the 17th century, and it is the medieval buildings of the main castle that are described in some detail in the estate accounts from the 16th and 17th centuries. On that basis, for once, we can put together a fairly clear picture of the upper floors of a castle and of how people lived in the space. This is particularly interesting because Kalø, which was similar in size to Kronborg at Elsinore, became one of the most important royal castles in Denmark in the course of the 14th century and provided the setting for many people's lives.

New excavations have brought to light remains of masonry and of stone buildings on the so-called Ridebane (riding ground) in front of the bridge leading to the central castle. The area was also protected by a solid palisade in the

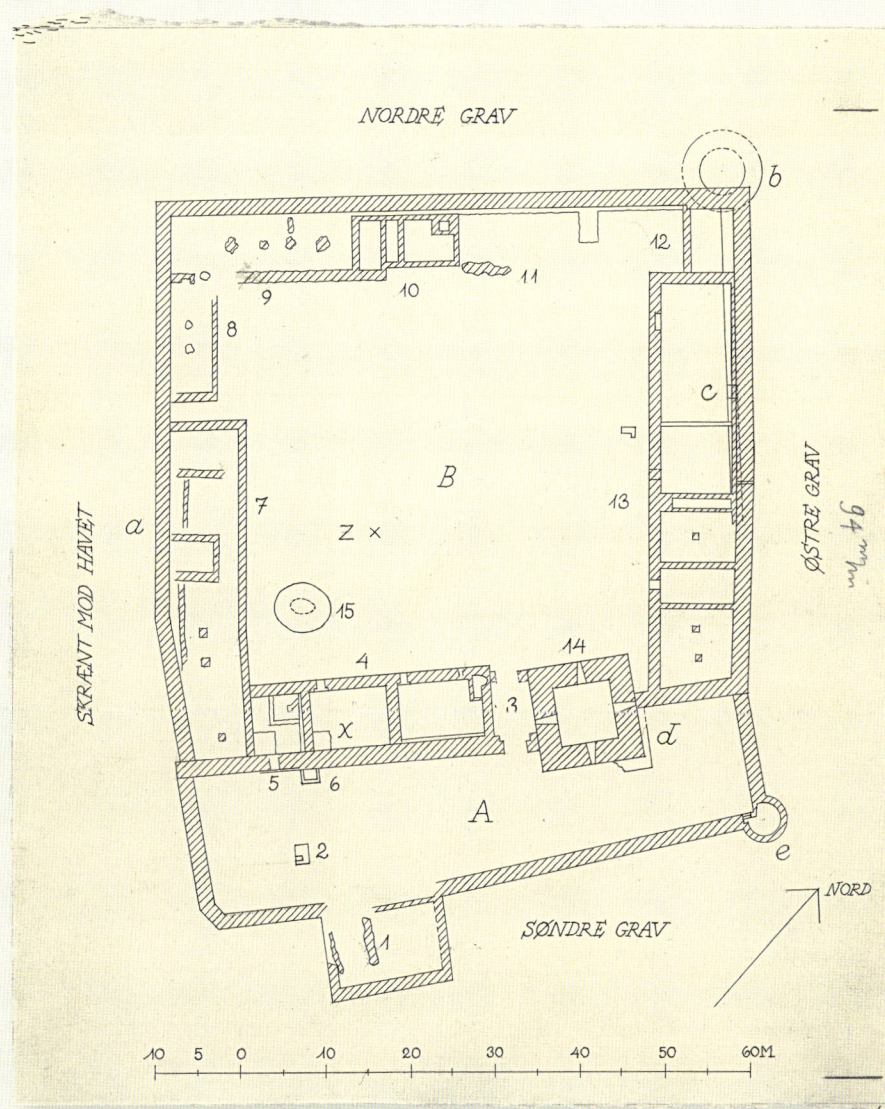

14th century, and the buildings may have been store-houses. This part of the castle is not described in the estate accounts and must have been demolished before the earliest description of the site from the end of the 16th century.

KALØ is situated on a natural mound that has been shaped and cut across by ditches so that large earthworks have been created.

Even when one has seen something with one's own eyes it can be difficult to remember it accurately. This is demonstrated by the drawing here, which represents the great tower at KALØ with windows and doors which it has never had. Drawing in the Danish National Museum's archives.

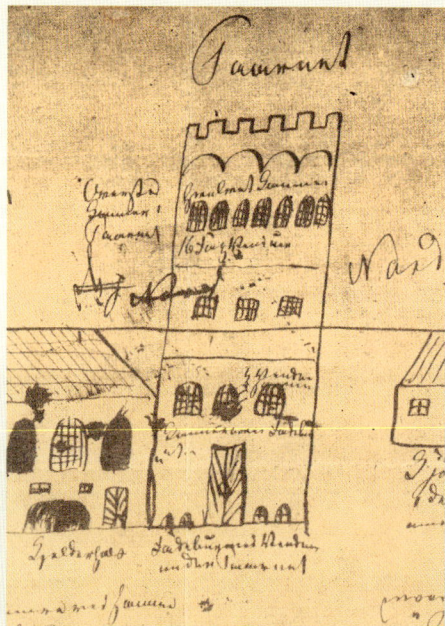

KÄRNAN *in Helsingborg was built in the 14th century and is a combined tower-dwelling. Originally the massive tower was surrounded by a slender curtain wall, so that it was a castle within a castle. Seen from the northeast.*

Castles were built in several other places on Crown property in King Erik's time, e.g. at Lindholm in Scania, but it is often difficult to see where new buildings were erected and where it was older buildings that were used by the monarchy. Major efforts were made, however, to strengthen several of the old royal castles, e.g. Kalundborg and Helsingborg; towers and other defence-works were also built in connection with the wars abroad.

Already in the Valdemar period the royal defence structures featured curtain walls, and in all the major castle buildings since then the fortifications had relied on the interplay between walls and towers. The new curtain-wall castles of the 14th century, however, were much more regular than the older ones; they had straight sides and the corners had right angles, even when they were built on natural mounds. In addition to King Erik Menved's castles, Count Johan of Plön's Aalholm on Lolland is a good example of this type of structure, which is particu-

Seen from a distance **TRANEKÆR** *clearly lies much higher than the surrounding land, and one can understand that it was a difficult place to conquer. Seen from the west.*

larly characteristic of the castles of the German Order on the Baltic coast.

In the battles that took place there it seems that the focus for attack and defence largely centred on towers from "King Valdemar's time" – no doubt those of Valdemar the Victorious – and it would have been interesting to see the castle that Erik Menved reinforced at the Warnemünde estuary. There the citizens had erected "a strong tower of brick" in connection with the revolt of 1311, and the Lübeck Chronicle relates that in the following year the Danish King came and laid siege to the tower together with the North German princes, until the defenders surrendered for lack of food. After that the King strengthened the tower with sturdy walls and moats, so that there was a curtain wall with a tower at each corner surrounding the strong tower in the middle. This sounds almost like a description of Valdemar Atterdag's Gurre, but the castle at Warnemünde only lasted for a short time.

Together with having to help build the "subjugation castles", the intractable Jutlanders were punished with yet another tax, known as "gold corn". Even that could not fill up the King's shrivelled coffers, however, and he continued like his predecessors to create funds by mortgaging property. This was an ill-fated route. The transactions could take several forms, in the worst case involving surrender of all royal income and legal authority. This could be for a defined period of time or for a lifetime and in practice could be inherited, because the mortgage could only with difficulty be redeemed on the death of the creditor, if the debt had not been paid. Each mortgaging transaction reduced the King's income and the territory over which he had power, and the likelihood of regaining the mortgaged land became smaller in time as the transactions of this type increased.

During Erik Menved's reign everything went so wrong that the once so strong royal power crumbled to pieces. When he died, in 1319, the Crown was on the verge of bankruptcy and power in the kingdom was in the hands of the mortgage-holders. They were Danish and foreign aristocrats, among whom the most important were two Counts of Holstein, who were both related to the Danish royal family. Gerhard III (the Great) was a very distant cousin, but was closely related to the family of the Schleswig dukes. Johan of Plön was the step-brother of the King from Queen Agnes's second marriage, to Count Gerhard II of Holstein-Plön. Through the years the Counts had raised considerable funds, at first for the purpose of helping the King and then with the aim of acquiring power in Denmark, but this needed far larger sums than they themselves could lay hands on. In order to procure those funds they had spread out loans among different sub-mortgage-holders, most of them aristocrats from Holstein, so there was a jumble of ownership relations in the kingdom. In the end there was no central authority that could maintain the rule of law.

For that reason castles came to be built all over the country. Some of them originally were defences against attack from Norway and the raids of the outlaws. Many were added as central power became progressively weaker. They were by no means all large stone- or brick-built structures with curtain walls, but the many new private castles were not intended to protect the realm or princely people and their property. Both for the new potentates who owned their own land and for the mortgage-holders of all categories it was a safeguard to have a castle situated on their lands. It gave added security and strength behind the administration of both large and small estates in their relations with neighbours who were possibly not entirely well-disposed or with roving gangs of robbers.

The second brother – Christoffer "Lackland" and his battles over the castles

Erik Menved and his queen died with no children, and the changed division of power in the country was clearly expressed in the coronation charter that King Erik's brother and successor Christoffer had to agree to on his accession to the throne. In 37 paragraphs he promised to rule according to conditions set by the

Counts Gerhard and Johan of Holstein, who were major mortgage-holders in Denmark, were also linked to the royal house. Gerhard was a very distant relative, and Johan was the son of Erik Klipping's widow, Queen Agnes, and her second husband. **THE COUNTS' SEALS** *are attached to several documents in the State Archives. Johan's is uppermost. Photo State Archives.*

>

GRØNHOLT *near Asminderød in Northern Sealand is one of the many castle mounds about which nothing is known. It is not mentioned in any sources, and no excavations have been carried out at the site. Seen from the northwest.*

aristocrats, but those conditions were so harsh that he actually had no chance to rule the country. The King's powers and resources were removed, and the charter required that the royal castles in Jutland should be demolished, apart from Ribe, Kolding and Skanderborg. All people should have returned to them what the Crown had taken from them. The heirs of the outlaws should have their due inheritance and the Archbishop should regain "his castle and property", i.e. Hammershus and Bornholm. All that Erik Menved had won by the sword was lost, and all opportunities to make new gains vanished, because all the taxes that had been imposed since "King Valdemar's time" were repealed. The war-service duties inflicted on the population were further reduced and those who lost anything in the King's wars were to have compensation. The Danish aristocrats who dictated the terms of the charter were also wary of the danger from the Holstein mortgage-holders. It was stipulated that no "German" could hold a castle, fief or bailiwick or be a member of the King's Council.

Christoffer did not get any chance to keep to these impossible conditions, nor did he make much attempt to do so. Right from the beginning he was immersed in conflict with his political opponents, and when King Erik's Seneschal, who had taken Hammershus for his King, refused to hand the castle over to the Archbishop, Christoffer had to reconquer it with force and great costs in order to live up to the conditions of his coronation charter. This resulted in a sixteen-month-long siege. In violation of the charter King Christoffer imposed additional taxes and soon found himself fighting on several fronts, both against the Danish

armed forces and against German mercenaries. This was an unfortunate combination, and his eldest son and co-regent, yet another Erik, was confined in Tårnborg and besieged, along with his German soldiers, by the men from Scania and Sealand whom he had actually assembled to fight for him. Tårnborg, as already mentioned, was a major fortification, much larger than the rather small ruin one can see today, but Erik capitulated after sixteen days and was taken to Haderslev and held in chains in the castle by the Holsteiners, who held the power in the Duchy. This is what the Sealand Chronicle tells us, and while it may not be accurate in its details, the gist of the story is no doubt true.

Meanwhile King Christoffer vanished in the dark of night from Vordingborg, taking with him the contents of the royal treasury, and there must have been something in it, because he came back shortly afterwards with fresh manpower. Then the Danish forces, in combination with the Holsteiners, laid siege to the castle for so long that at the end its inhabitants only had gruel made of chaff to live on, and the siege was lifted after negotiations. Christoffer was allowed to leave with his army, but he had nowhere to go. In order to raise money by the only means left to him he had mortgaged the last of the royal lands, so that now he had nothing left and no power to try to uphold.

The Holstein counts, on the other hand, had been strengthened and had gained increasing influence over Danish politics, because they had an interest in common with the major Danish mortgage-holders in free and unobstructed exploitation of their mortgages. In 1326 the leading aristocrats and mortgage-holders deposed King Christoffer, who showed no inclination to stop resisting the conditions of his reign, and who could not be expected to be willing to repay the Crown debt.

Christoffer was no longer someone to be reckoned with, and his nickname "Lackland" had come to fit well.

New king – no king

A king was something the country had to have, however, and he had to be from the royal family. Under strong influence from Count Gerhard the choice fell on Gerhard's own nephew, the eleven-year-old Duke Valdemar of Schleswig, who in return handed over the Duchy to his "dear Uncle Gerhard". As the young Valdemar's guardian the Count in reality was also in control of Denmark, or at any rate Jutland and Funen, where he held many mortgages.

Young Valdemar was the third of that name on the Danish throne. His coronation charter, from 1326, is even harsher than that of Christoffer II, and documents the complete eradication of royal power. It contains the same limitations as were imposed on Christoffer, but with additions. For instance all the royal castles in Halland and Scania, apart from Helsingborg, Skanør and Falsterbo, were to be demolished. There is no mention of the north Jutland castles, and it is not certain that they had been destroyed during Christoffer's reign, even though the Sealand Chronicle relates that that happened rapidly. If that was the case, they were soon built up again, because they functioned as important bases for support throughout many years that followed – particularly in the case of Kalø.

With the under-age Valdemar on the throne the situation was also different from when Christoffer was elected, and the royal castles in Jutland could be of use to Count Gerhard, who now as the guardian of the King was faced with the impossible task of maintaining order in the divided kingdom. After a few years he gave up the attempt, and Valdemar surrendered the empty crown and was given the title of Duke and the Duchy of Schleswig again, while Uncle Gerhard kept the castles he was holding in the kingdom and e.g. used Skanderborg as his main residence. "The bald Count", or "Count Gert" as he came to be known in Denmark, was the largest mortgage-holder of them all, and the power rested in the fortresses, but there were now too many private castle-owners with different interests for even the largest mortgage-holder to be able to control them. There was no longer any king, and it was impossible to substitute anyone else or anything else in his position.

Christoffer appeared on the scene again, however, supported by Count Johan, from 1330 until he died two years later. His reappearance in the kingdom took place entirely on the conditions set by the counts, and it turned out to be a brief and belligerent but also rather pitiful guest appearance, which was totally without significance for conditions in the kingdom. In one of the battles he lost, at Lohede in 1331, his eldest son Erik died. The second son, Otto, tried to win the crown a couple of years later, with support from abroad, but he was defeated by Count Gerhard at Taphede near Viborg. Major battles in open country never completely lost their importance – naturally. But the kingdom was in reality without a king, and thus without central power, until 1340.

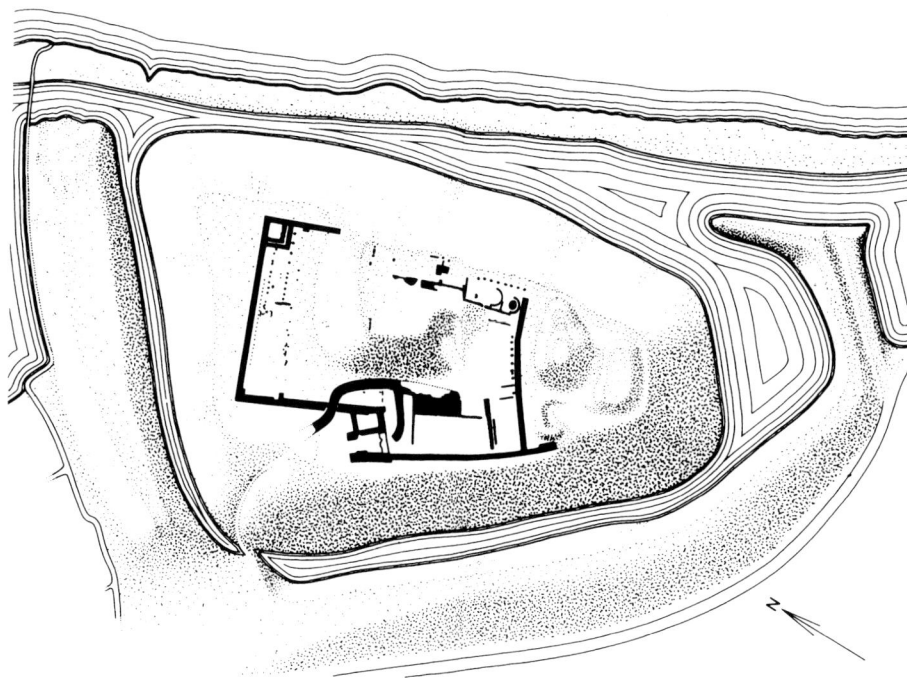

Plan of **RAVNSBORG** *showing traces of buildings on the mound. The ancillary buildings for this major complex were sited to the northwest of the mound, and to the west of them there was a watermill. Under the curtain-wall castle are the traces of an older castle site.*

The consequences of the weakened realm
– castles throughout the country

The lawless conditions prevailing over many years were reflected in the many castle structures, varying in layout and strength, that sprang up over the whole country. It was not just the major royal buildings or the main residences of the bishops or powerful secular aristocrats that were significant. The pattern was repeated among the lesser landowners, so that anyone who felt threatened – and who did not have reason for fear in those times? – fortified his property if he had the means to do so. The varied structures provide a good illustration of the wide range of conditions among the aristocracy and land-owning classes, even though many of those buildings, as mentioned, no longer exist or have only been partially or poorly investigated. With the support of the written sources it is nevertheless possible to gain some impression of the castles and their distribution, and occasionally it happens that a lost or previously unknown structure comes to light and extends the range of our knowledge. Excavations of course also do this.

In just the way that the innovative curtain-wall castle and tower fortifications were introduced and taken into use in the 12th century when they became necessary in Denmark, in the 14th century one finds examples of many different developments in castle-building around Europe, where the castle had originated. In Denmark they reflect not just a development, but also different social levels and degrees of necessity. Aalholm was a modern regular curtain-wall castle just like Kalø.

Halkær, which is now called Hedegård, in Northern Jutland near Nibe, was an old-fashioned and poorly fortified building situated on a low mound out in a bog-area. The building and its fortifications were of wood and the main building

was a hall with a long fire in the middle of the floor as might have been found in the Viking Age several centuries earlier. Boringholm, not far from Horsens, was also low-lying, in a bog-area, and consisted of wooden buildings. The finds on that site show that people of some standing lived there, and the site can be dated to the end of the 14th century. Many castles consisted, like Kærsgård south of Odder, of a quite steep little mound with a tower, often of wood, and a larger lower mound with space for a dwelling and farm buildings, enclosed by a rampart and moat.

This corresponds to the earliest motte and bailey structures in France and Germany, but one can also find earthworks of impressive dimensions such as Rugtved in Vendsyssel, which became royal property in Valdemar Atterdag's time, or Ravnsborg on Lolland, not to mention Tørning, to the north of Haderslev. That massive structure has hardly been investigated, but it had a chequered history from around 1300, when it was built as a royal castle, until in the 15th century, when it once more became incontestably royal.

RAVNSBORG *on the north coast of Lolland is a massive earthwork with extensive traces on top of it of a castle with a curtain wall from the 14th century. It may have been built by Count Johan, who also built Aalholm. Now the castle lies on the shore. Originally it was on a little island off the coast, and there was a long pile bridge that gave access to it. Seen from the east.*

BOESLUM NEAR EBELTOFT
– the story of a castle

In 1299 Erik Menved made an agreement with Archbishop Jens Grand in which, among other measures, the King ceded 1/6 of Boeslum. Because of this we know that the Crown owned land there, and in 1327, when the young Valdemar III mortgaged Boeslum among other properties such as Grenå and the royal estate there, to his Seneschal and others, a castle had just been built at Boeslum. This has been proven archaeologically, since the wooden bridge that led over the moat to the castle mound could be dated by dendrochronology. In 1331 Gerhard sold Boeslum to a certain Aage Pedersen, and after that ownership continued in private hands. Boeslum soon became more of a manor than a castle, and it was lived in for the next several centuries. Many finds of diverse objects illustrate life at Boeslum through the ages. Together with the results of the excavation and the written sources they both tell the story of the lifetime of the castle and illustrate how the once royal estate fell apart.

BOESLUM *near Ebeltoft was an important place in the 1320s. This can be seen from the objects found there, e.g. this hook for cocking a crossbow. It is cast in bronze and is so far the only known one of its kind. Photo Ebeltoft Museum.*

It goes without saying that a powerful landowner would have more dangerous enemies than a minor one. That is why Count Johan's Aalholm is so strongly fortified. Many of the smaller structures belonged to minor local landowners and only had to be protected from local enemies or itinerant bands of robbers. Other minor castles belonged to aristocrats who owned property spread out around the country, and the owner did not live in them all year round, but left day-to-day management to his bailiff, who was also expected to protect the property. It is impossible today to reconstruct the ownership-conditions of estates, which changed hands often, and for that reason one cannot explain why some particular sites were fortified and others not. Kærsgård, mentioned above, was possibly an estate with a bailiff, and the owner's main dwelling, in Gylling some ten kilometres from it, was not fortified. It is rare, however, to find written sources that provide information about these conditions, and even when they are mentioned little is given in the way of detail.

The real problem in the years of dissolution of the kingdom was perhaps not so much the actual conflicts between the warring parties at a high political level, but rather the level of ordinary insecurity that prevailed in consequence. A rebellion on Sealand or a battle at Lohede between the king and the counts was naturally unpleasant for the inhabitants of the area, but in the longer term it was worse and more unsettling that there were no prosecutions of people who stole their neighbours' grain or apple harvest because their own crops had failed, or

There is still a farm on the mound of **TORUP VOLDE,** *to the west of the road between Odder and Horsens. The buildings can be glimpsed at the end of the avenue. The castle mound is completely covered in trees, and nothing is known about the history of the place.*

BJØRNKÆR *near Hou is a typical structure from the time of unrest in the second half of the 13th century. By the beginning of the 15th century it was already dismantled.*

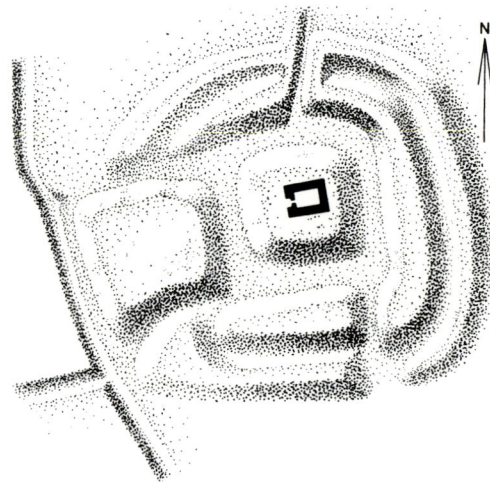

BJØRNKÆR'S *mounds are covered with tall trees and dug through by foxes. Seen from the west.*

On one of **BJØRNKÆR'S** *two mounds there was a little brick building. Excavation of the well in the cellar brought to light diverse remains of distillation apparatus. Seen from the southwest.*

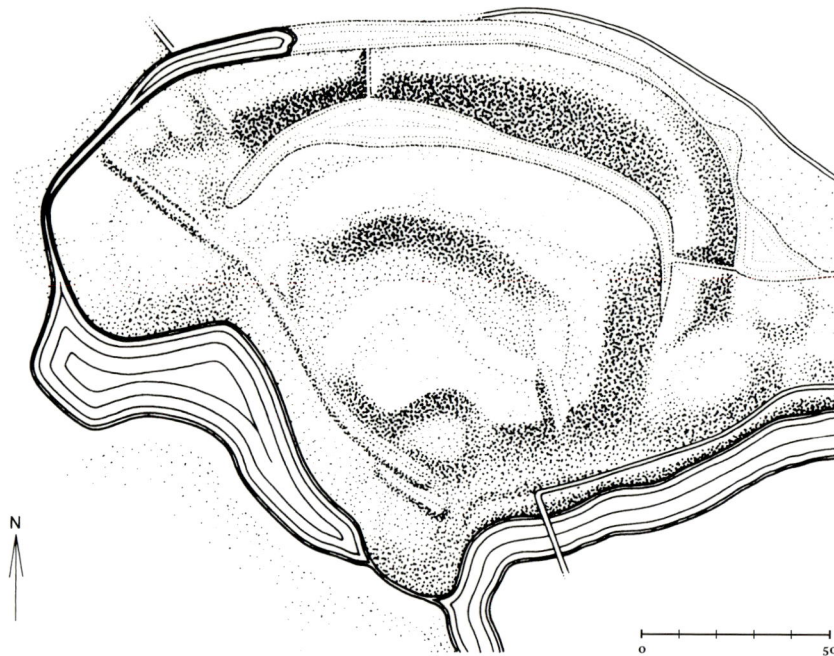

who stole pigs because their own fell sick. Robbers or attackers of this kind of course did not come in large groups – not like a real army. Against them palisades and obstructions to access were sufficient protection, but it was a burden to have to be always on guard, and it was time-consuming and costly to keep the fortifications in order.

Every farming estate occupied a large number of people, since farm production required the work of many hands. If there were just as many farmhands behind the palisade as there were men among the enemy's followers, one was well placed and could as a rule safely hold the enemy at bay, even if the farm's people were not real warriors, because the same was true of the neighbour's people. An attack by real troops could not be resisted by this type of structure for very long, and e.g. the excavation of Kærsgård seems to show that in that case the castle fell to an actual military attack.

The layout of the castles

It is perfectly possible to categorise the many different castle structures according to type. Some have two or more mounds behind the ramparts, while others have only one. There are structures on raised sites with dry moats, while others are low-lying and surrounded by wet areas, and there are naturally many of the latter in Denmark. The various types have been given more or less elaborate names: high castles and low castles, double castle mounds and *castrum-curia* structures. These terms are frequently used, but the term "motte and bailey" tends to be avoided in Denmark, because those castles belong to a different period and a different form of society. *Castrum-curia* means "fortress-farm" and refers to a fortified dwelling. One could actually just as well simply say "castle", since that term

RUGTVED *castle mound on the coast of Kattegat not far from Frederikshavn is in a poor state. It was given to the Bishop of Børglum in 1393 as part of Queen Margrete's payment of the Crown's debt to the Church.*

In connection with her wedding in the mid-14th century Cecilie of Gylling presented **A FINE BELL** *to her family church. Her father, Laurits Trugotsen, was a major landowner and one of the Crown's Danish mortgage-holders. The bridegroom, Markvard Rostrup, was Count Gerhard's captain in Skanderborg.*

Cecilie's bell still hangs in the tower of **GYLLING CHURCH,** *which is what is known as a "stilt tower".*

(Next pages) **KALØ'S** *inner castle enclosure is the same size as Kronborg's, but everything looks smaller without actual buildings. The large tower guarded the entrance from the outer courtyard and was connected with the sentry walk on the curtain wall. Seen from the west.*

can be used of structures with either one or two mounds. The easiest and clearest solution is to use "tower mound" and "farm mound(s)" or "castle mound(s)".

Type-terminology is well and good when it comes to describing structures. Where dating is concerned it does not contribute much, since in Denmark all these types are found within a very short period of time, viz. within the century of functioning of Næsholm Castle in Ods Herred, the northwest peninsula of Sealand. The castles were the products of their circumstances and purpose; they relate to their social context and were dependent on given natural conditions, and this is not strange. A castle is a functional construct, a tool, and by the time the castle reached the Nordic region it had found its optimal form, its position in society and in the landscape and its uses in different situations. For that reason, just like any other tool, it would not be likely to change fundamentally until the purpose for which it was used underwent change.

When we are puzzled, from today's perspective, over the placing and form of a structure in relation to its owner and his social position, as a rule it is because

*In some places there are church bells that are hung in wooden bell-towers. The one in **BIRKET ON LOLLAND** is from the 14th century, but has of course been repaired through the centuries since. The wooden towers on the tower-mounds of small castles would have looked like bell-towers such as this.*

we do not know enough – or perhaps know nothing at all – about the actual conditions and events that gave rise to the construction of the castle. People in days of old were of course better placed to understand their own situation and context than we can be in retrospect.

On the castle mounds there was seldom enough space for all the farm buildings inside the defence structures, and it is often difficult to say where they were situated. In some cases this seems to have been so far away that it would not have been possible to transport much in the way of provisions or valuables if it became necessary to to seek refuge in a hurry, but possibly there was always something hidden away behind the fortifications. It was common, far up in time, to keep grain in the lofts of the main buildings, as was done e.g. at Kalø. This could have happened in many places, even where there were only timber or half-timbered buildings. In the large castles with permanent garrisons and many people to be catered for in the everyday household there were extensive provisions and stores. It was there that the grain paid as tax was collected, along with other income paid in kind from the area that was administered from the castle, as can be seen for

(continued on page 138)

THE CASTLE MOUNDS AT HALD

Beside the lake at Hald, near Viborg in Jutland, there are two medieval castle mounds very close to each other. One of them, which is called Brattingsborg, like several other earthworks in Denmark of which we know little, is situated on a high, dry rise in a field which runs down to the lake, to the east of the present-day Hald. It consists of two mounds, one small, for defence or last refuge, and a larger one for a dwelling and some of the farm buildings. Around the whole site there have been moats about 20 metres in width, while the mounds together measure only some 40 x 23 metres.

The other castle mound, known as Gammelhald (Old Hald) or Niels Bugge's Hald, is situated on the lake shore at Bækkelund and consists of a high castle mound measuring some 70 x 90 metres, with traces of a perimeter rampart on the sides towards land. At that site there has also been an earth rampart in front, where there is now a damp stretch of meadow, but in the lifetime of the castle the water level in the lake was signifi-

GAMMELHALD, *or Niels Bugge's Hald, on the bank of Hald Lake, where the lake protected part of the mound.*

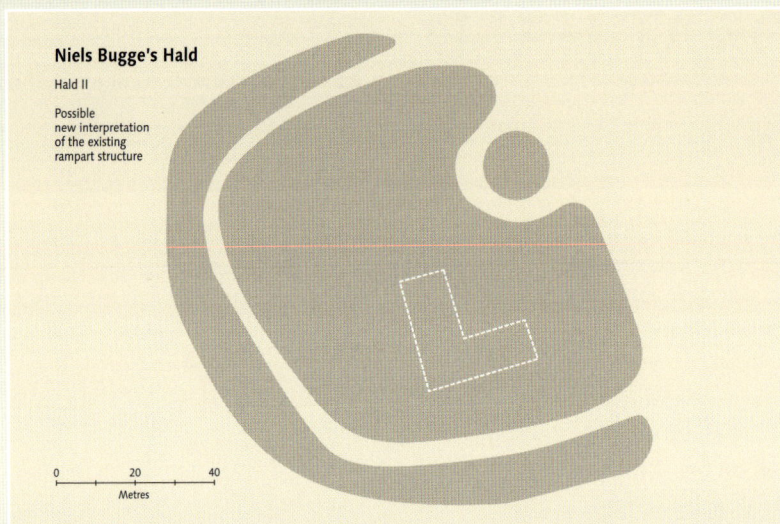

Niels Bugge's Hald

Hald II

Possible
new interpretation
of the existing
rampart structure

0   20   40
Metres

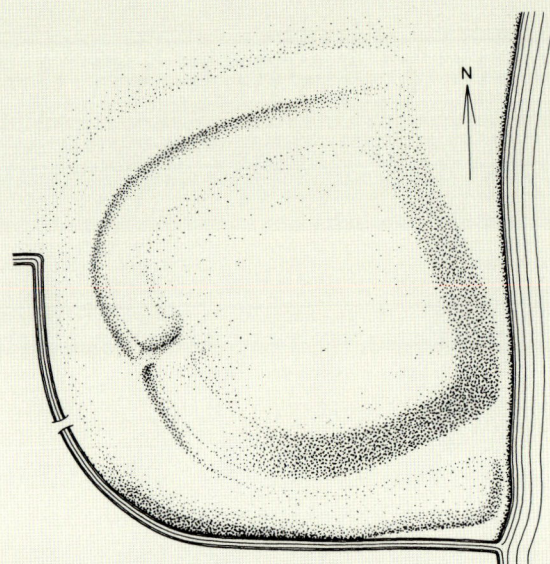

Two plans of **GAMMELHALD.** *New scientific technical analyses suggest that there was once a little detached tower mound at the edge of the castle mound.*

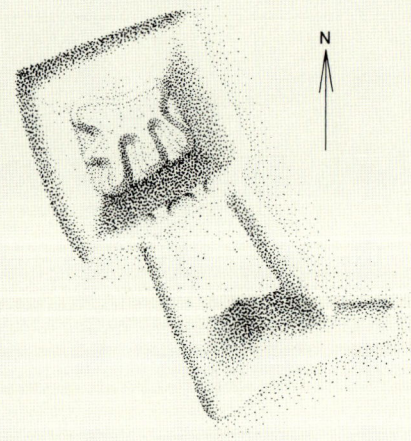

Plan of **BRATTINGSBORG** *near Hald.*

cantly lower, so then it would probably have been surrounded by dry moats. Traces have been found on the mound of buildings with masonry foundations, along with the remains of a hypocaust – a special oven for a warm air system – so the level of comfort was high in Niels Bugge's castle. There are also signs, however, that the castle mound was altered at some point from a construction with a very small tower mound separate from the farm mound, almost carved into it as at Næsholm. If that is the case the previous layout of the site was probably similar to many others – including Brattingsborg, before it became a massive castle, perhaps with a curtain wall. An excavation would be necessary to establish whether this is the case, however.

These two structures could well be contemporary, even if proof is found that Gammelhald was not altered, and they may both be from the 14th century. The two possible owners or commissioners of the buildings also belong to the same social layer. Both Niels Bugge and Ludvig Albertsen Eberstein, who is said to have built Brattingsborg and who

died in 1328, were in the first ranks of royal councillors, and both attempted to promote their own political ends. Ludvig Albertsen Eberstein came from an immigrant family of Saxon counts and served King Erik Menved first as Chamberlain and later as Lord High Constable (Marsk); it was he who conquered Hammershus for his King. In 1320 he was one of the major mortgage-holders in the country and contributed to dictating the conditions in Christoffer's coronation charter. The castle fell into disuse in the course of the 14th century and was possibly succeeded by Gammelhald.

Niels Bugge was a major landowner in central Jutland. His properties stretched from Nørre Vosborg near Ringkøbing to Hald, which he probably acquired in the 1340s. At one stage he had supported Count Gerhard, but later he became close to Valdemar Atterdag, both as a councillor and as an opponent. He was a leading figure in the rebellion of the Jutland landowners against King Valdemar at the beginning of the 1350s, and he was killed together with two other aristocrats in Middelfart in 1358 on his way home from a meeting with the King, who was blamed by some for the murder. The castle became Crown property in Valdemar Atterdag's time, and in 1393 his daughter Margrete donated it to the diocese of Viborg with the condition that the fortifications should be demolished.

Both these influential men, Niels Bugge and Ludvig Albertsen Eberstein, may have had good reason to want to protect themselves, and the written sources possibly imply that Brattingsborg is the earlier of the two castles. That cannot be judged from its size. It may be the case, for instance, that Ludvig Albertsen had his main residence in another place, while Niels Bugge lived here on his estate. Precise details of who owned what and when are lacking, and we only know about living quarters and defence features in the two castles. Where, for instance, were the farm buildings and how large were they?

BRATTINGSBORG'S *two mounds are openly exposed in the field above Hald Lake. Seen from the southwest.*

instance in the large storehouse at Hammershus, but both at major sites and even at royal castles the barns and other storage areas were apparently not fortified. For a long time they were also relatively small. The main farms with extensive manorial fields and large-scale farm buildings belong to the Renaissance and later times, when major landowners gradually collected their possessions in immense integrated estate areas. This happened late and by a slow process. In the 16th century a man's wealth was still calculated by the number of farms he owned. They could be scattered over the whole realm, some were small, others larger, and it was of course impossible to fortify them all. On the other hand it was less than likely that all the properties would be plundered at the same time.

It would probably not have been all landowners who fortified their properties in the 13th and 14th centuries. Some of the larger landowners might have held a particular castle that was mortgaged to them and lived in it. Less wealthy people could not have afforded to do so, even if they might have had good use of

SOLVIG *near Tønder was established and built at the beginning of the 14th century on four mounds which are now all northwest of the River Arn. By means of excavations it has been possible to trace changing buildings on some of the mounds, and to identify a manor-house site on the other side of the river that was taken into use at the end of the 14th century. A classic castle-site development. At Solvig it is also possible to follow the ownership-circumstances through time. That is not often possible.*

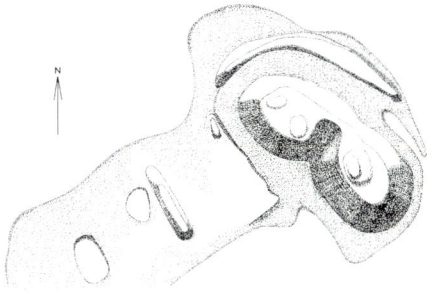

VITTSJÖ *in northern Scania, on the border of Småland, was possibly among the properties of the archiepiscopal see. It was the iron production on the mounds that the fortifications protected.*

Plan of **SOLVIG** *with the four low mounds marked to the west of the river.*

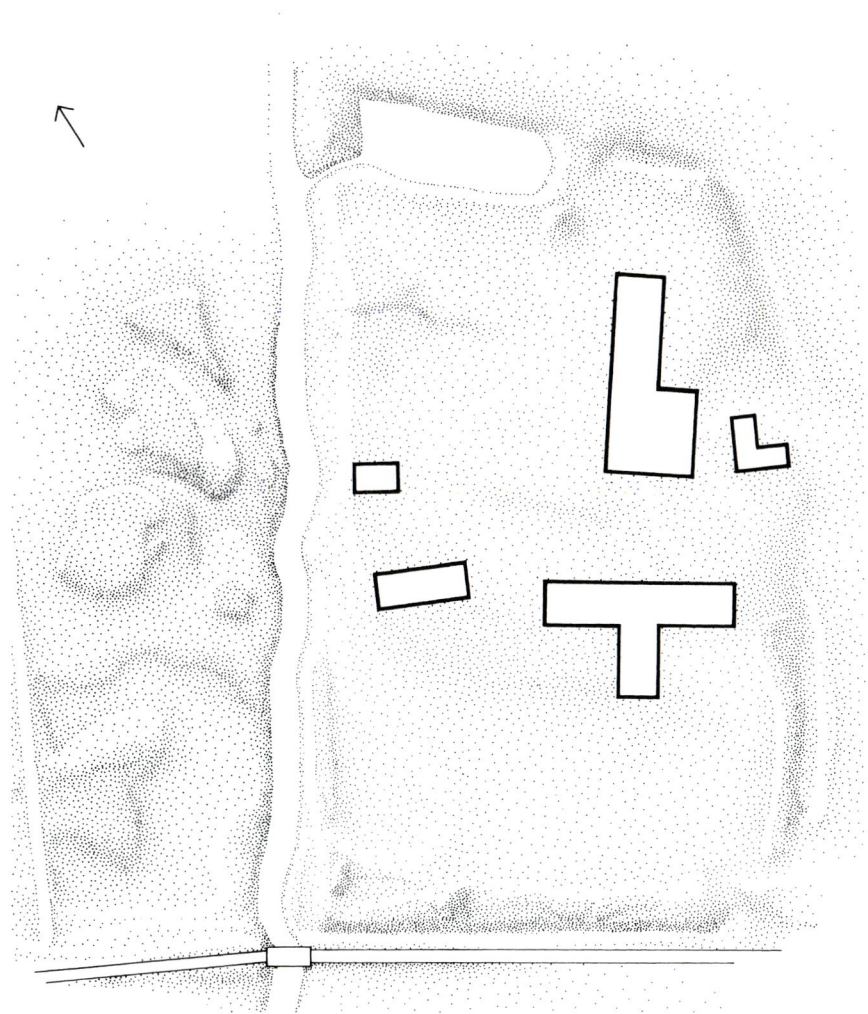

it. The Holstein sub-mortgage-holders who occupied estates in Denmark or ran the royal castles as head bailiffs for the Counts did not pay much attention to the laws of the land. They sought to obtain maximum gain from the mortgages they held in the period that they had them.

The end of the era of dissolution

The minor Danish gentry suffered under these conditions of exploitation by the more powerful, and from the end of the 1320s opposition to the Holstein domination arose, particularly among the Danish esquire class in Jutland. In 1329 the Holsteiners were attacked by the Jutlanders at Haderslevhus and Gottorp, and the Bishop of Ribe, who himself was from a family of esquires in Jutland, took an active part in the revolt, which forced Valdemar of Schleswig to abandon the Danish throne. The rebellion was quashed in the end, however, so there were no further direct consequences.

Unrest simmered on in the 1330s. The Bishop of Aarhus joined the cause of the discontented, the peasants on Sealand rose up, and Count Gerhard fanned the

PLANCTUS DE STATU REGNI DANIE
(scriptus anno 1329)

Geme, plange maesto more
dolorosa Dacia!
quia probo protectore
cares et audacia.
Gens eras fortissima,
virtute clarissima:
stravisti, vicisti
populum emulum
per terrarum spatia

**LAMENT FOR THE UNHAPPY
STATE OF DENMARK**

Moan and grieve with a gloomy heart,
O sorrowful Denmark,
for now you lack your virtuous protector
and your courage.
The populace was strong
and bright with virtue;
now scattered and defeated,
a people struggling
for a place among the nations

*(Translation from "Queenship and
Voice in Medieval Northern Europe"
by William Layhire, 2010)*

*The first verse of a long poem
of lament from 1329, describing
the unhappy state of Denmark
during the troubled regency of the
Counts of Holstein. All the royal
estates have been mortgaged,
there is hardly a kingdom any
more, and unrest and disorder
prevail.*

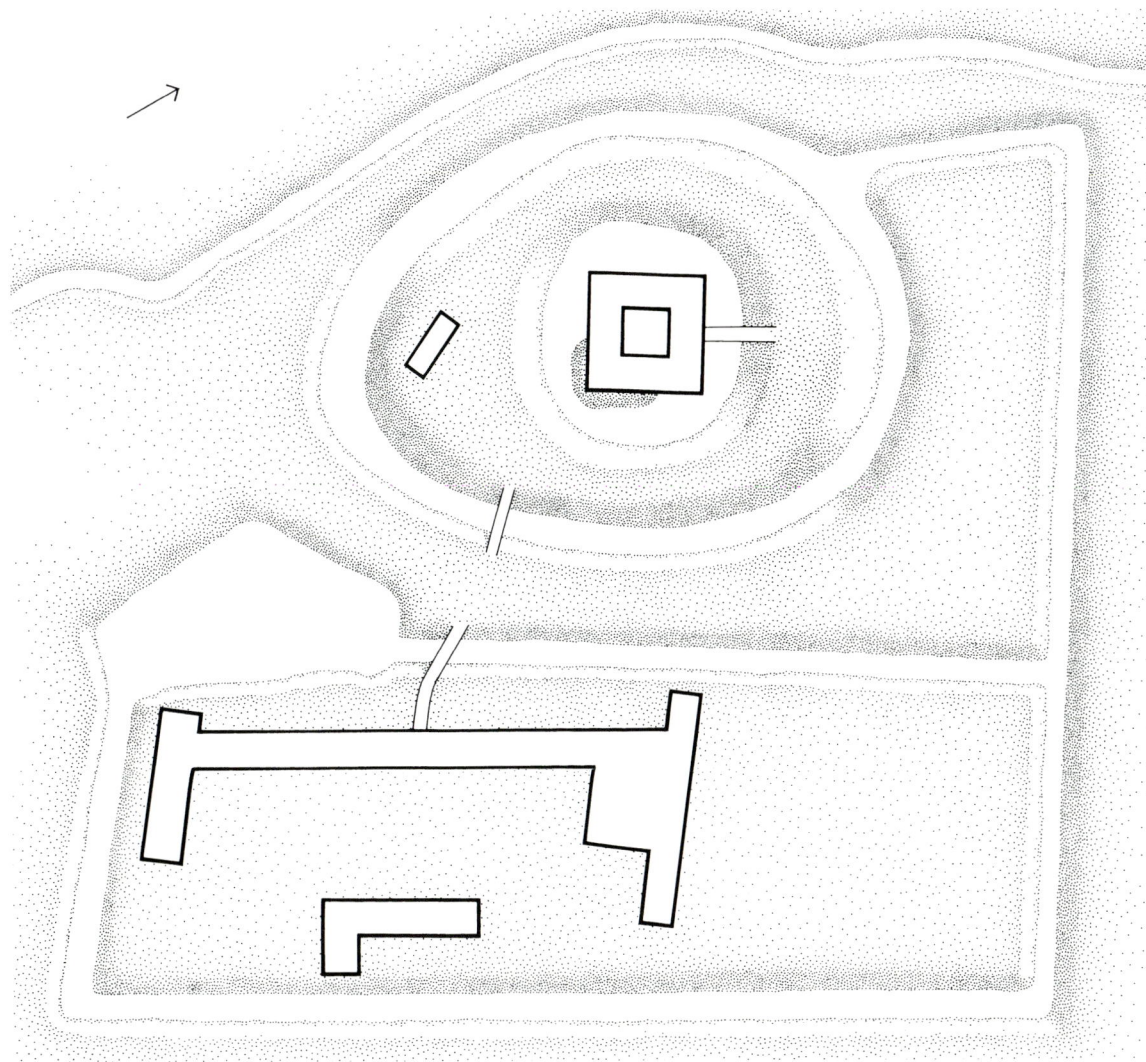

On **TRØJBORG'S** *medieval castle mound we now find the ruins of Peder Rantzau's Renaissance castle. In the 14th century the Limbek family owned the place for a long period. Queen Margrete bestowed the extensive Limbek possessions, in the Duchy of Schleswig, on the diocese of Ribe and they thus became Danish enclaves within the Duchy.*

TRØJBORG'S *castle mound was altered in connection with Peder Rantzau's rebuilding work. Traces of the earliest castle site are visible under the south corner of the Renaissance building.*

flames by demanding taxes from the churches and monasteries. "The Bald Count" had superior military forces, but the constant unrest considerably reduced his income from the substantial mortgaged lands he held in Denmark, and the troops were also expensive. The sub-mortgage-holders had to have their money in any case, so in the end it became a costly and unprofitable business to hold power in Denmark. Count Johan found it so difficult that he actually sold Scania to the Swedish king. After a while foreign interests also became involved in efforts to secure peace and a king on the throne in Denmark. The Hanseatic towns wanted peaceful conditions for trade, the North German princes wanted to keep a balance of power in the region, so that the Holstein counts did not become too powerful. The Margrave of Brandenburg was the son of the Emperor and married to the daughter of Christoffer II, but the dowry had not been paid and never would be unless Denmark had a king, so the Emperor and the Margrave were also willing to invest in the establishment of orderly conditions in the country. The various parties managed to cooperate and to find a candidate for the throne.

Their candidate was Christoffer's youngest son, Valdemar, who had been brought up in the Margrave's household and at the German imperial court, and at the end of the 1330s he began to put in appearances in the Baltic towns as the heir to the Danish empire. The time was ripe, since by then the Counts, not least Count Gerhard, were interested in a solution that would ensure that they would receive the money owing to them. Count Johan had already received a goodly sum from the sale of Scania, but there was still more that he wanted to claim. The Danish aristocrats and the churches in the country were looking forward to peace and to having the Holsteiners leave the realm. The populace at large no doubt felt the same way. A series of negotiations took place, but before they were completed Count Gerhard wanted to collect one last tax from Jutland, "the great silver beet", and he marched a large army up through the country. On 1 April 1340, however, he was murdered in Randers by Niels Ebbesen, a squire from Jutland, and after that the negotiations became productive, while the Jutland Chronicle relates that "in the same year, on 2 May, the same Niels Ebbesen killed many Germans by the River Skjern, where they were building a castle, causing the ruination of the Danes". No matter whether this was Lundenæs on the River Skjern in Western Jutland, or the castle of Skjern some 15 km from Randers, which belonged to Peder Vendelbo in 1347, this tells us much about the conditions in Jutland until Valdemar Atterdag took over the throne. The situation was intolerable, and new negotiations had to be embarked on.

Gerhard's sons met with the other parties involved, and the right of Valdemar Christoffersen – Valdemar Atterdag – to redeem the country was recognised. The mortgage sums had by now become enormous – 100,000 silver marks for Jutland and Funen, and on top of that there was Sealand and the islands and Scania as well, although it looked as if the latter had already been lost to the kingdom. When the sale of their territory had taken place the Scanians had willingly subjected to the authority of the Swedish King Magnus, nicknamed Smek, who now considered himself the entirely rightful lord of the Scanian territory and had no intention of giving it up.

King Valdemar was given a form of start-up capital, however; the land north of the Limfjord, with Aalborghus and Himmerland, became his dowry payment when he married Helveg, the sister of Duke Valdemar in Sønderborg in the early summer of 1340. He also gained the right to the incomes from the land, so he had something to work with, and in the treaty that followed the negotiations it was laid out in detail how the mortgaged land should be redeemed. Jutland was to come first, before Funen, and it was divided into four parts, each associated with a strong castle – Kalø, Horsens, Kolding and Ribe. The mortgage on Kalø, with a quarter of the land, was to be paid off first.

Valdemar Atterdag

King Valdemar later came to be known as Valdemar Atterdag, perhaps because he created new and better times for Denmark, or else because he often used the German oath "ach der Tage" – meaning something akin to "bloody Hell". He found

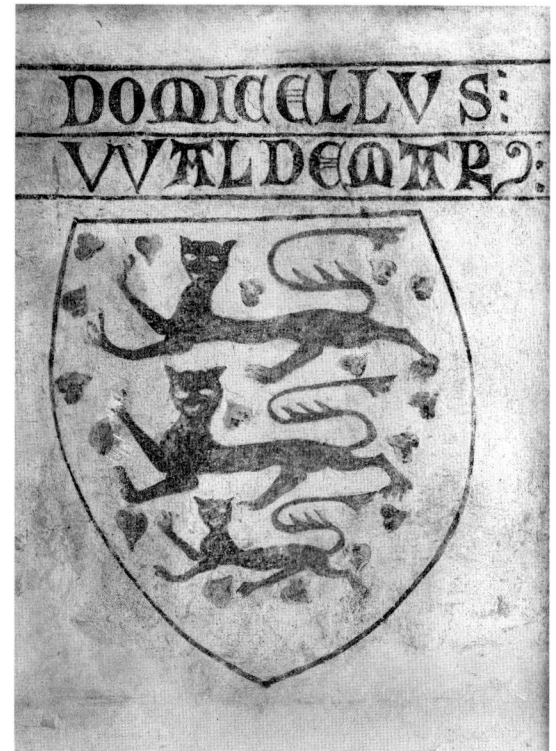

*The mural painting of **JUNKER VALDEMAR'S** coat of arms in Vor Frue Church in Aarhus is evidence of his aspiration to claim the throne. Bishop Svend was among his supporters and took part in the negotiations which resulted in the young prince becoming Denmark's king in 1340. Photo Danish National Museum.*

***ØLAND** in Thy is one of the country's smallest castle mounds, but in the 1350s it belonged to one of Valdemar Atterdag's opponents. In a later period the tower mound became for a while part of the garden landscape of the manor house alongside. This was probably situated on the farm mound of the castle, but it is now also abandoned and in poor repair.*

himself confronted with conditions that were to all intents and purposes no better than those that his predecessors had faced, but he went to work with the full support of the Church and solid back-up from the secular aristocrats. At the start he also had men and troops with him that his brother-in-law Margrave Ludvig and the Emperor had put at his disposition. In contemporary documents and particularly in the colourful descriptions in the Sealand Chronicle one can follow how Valdemar managed, throughout the whole of his reign, to redeem and conquer parts of the country step by step – i.e. castle by castle – and how he strove, by frequent journeys to attend local assemblies *(landsthing)* and by introducing a range of decrees and regulations, to put the country back on the right footing and make its institutions function once more.

Particularly in the first decade or so the King worked and fought from castle to castle, especially on Sealand. In spite of the fact that he gathered the funds for redeeming the mortgages, the payments did not always reach the true creditors, the sub-mortgage-holders, who naturally therefore did not want to cancel their mortgages. Problems also arose with the main mortgage-holders, because the counts could maintain that a particular estate was an inheritance and was not to be redeemed. Possibly some of the Danish aristocrats may also have resisted, because they were in the same situation as the Holstein sub-mortgage-holders. In addition, King Magnus of Sweden and the Hanseatics became involved in the conflict out of fear that King Valdemar might become too strong. That had not

The most distinguished room in **KÄRNAN,** *the King's Hall, is two storeys high and has vaulted rooms on its sides; the room on the left is a chapel.*

Elevation of **KÄRNAN** *with its many storeys. The King's Hall takes up levels 4 and 5. The walls are thicker towards the foot of the tower. The vertical shafts on the right lead down from the lavatories.*

Plan of **HELSINGBORG** *with* **KÄRNAN**. *The large tower from the 14th century had its own curtain wall and was built beside the place where the earlier tower had stood. The castle's little round church was situated in the southwest, adjoining the curtain wall.*

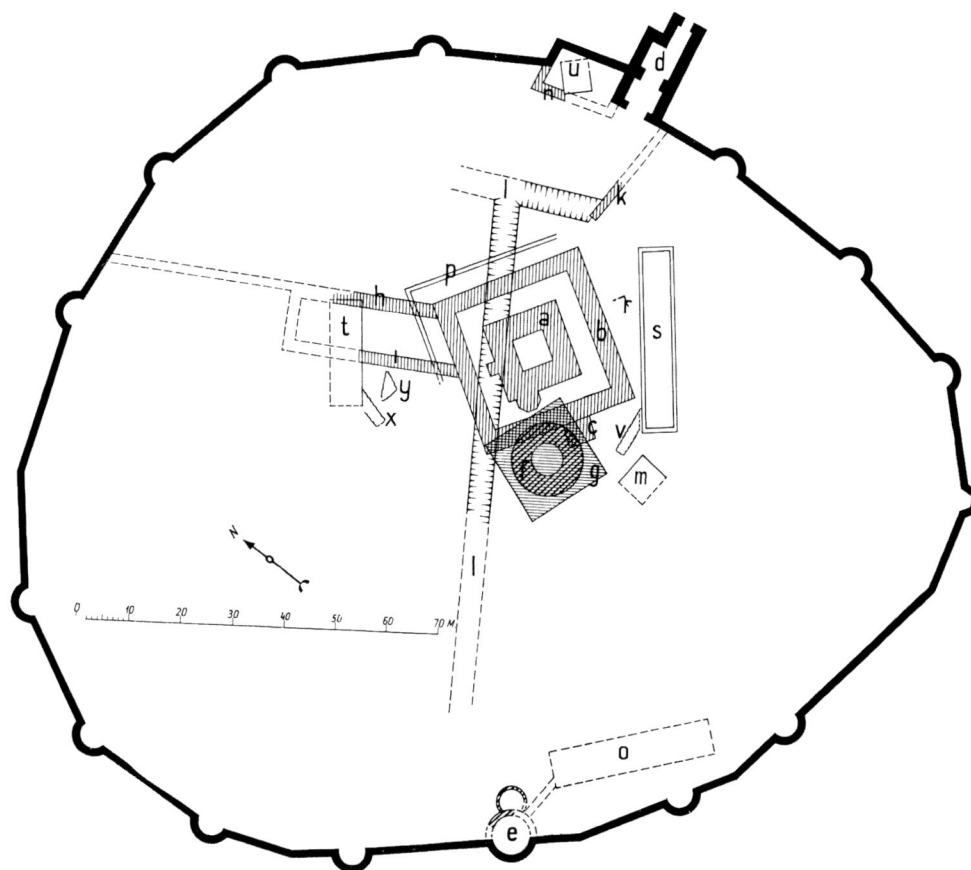

been the intention. In the various agreements and treaties between the parties concerned, castles invariably played an important role.

Independently of the King, the Jutland squires went into action again and took up the cudgels with the Holsteiners at Skanderborg where Niels Ebbesen was killed on 2 November 1340. Otherwise the retrieval of Jutland proceeded more-or-less according to plan, while King Valdemar in the early years was doing battle on Sealand. In 1341 he wanted to redeem Vordingborg, but this came to nothing, even though he had been given the silver chalices from the churches to help him; the mercenary troops wanted more in pay than he could raise. In the following year the King fought near Copenhagen, with his army and the Lord High Constable, against, among others, the captain of the Vordingborg garrison, and in 1343 there were totally chaotic conditions on Sealand. The army moved forward and back, turned up at Korsør and ended up in Ringsted, while the Bishop of Aarhus and the parish clerk of Roskilde were taken prisoner and kept in Padeborg, the present-day Sparresholm not far from Næstved. The castle there actually belonged to a Danish aristocrat, but he must either have been an opponent of the King and his policies, or else he had perhaps not received payments due to him. In any case, in 1345 the King's troops took the castle. Kalundborg was acquired in 1343. This was a time when opportunists changed sides many times over, but

The **GOOSE TOWER** at Vordingborg was part of the fortifications Valdemar Atterdag added to the castle. Inside the tower there is a stout wooden wall from a log-built house. There is only a narrow space around it.

Drawing of the wooden wall seen from the stairway.

Drawing of the smooth-planed inner side of the wooden wall. Both Danish National Museum.

Behind the **WOODEN WALL** a numbe of old finds from the castle are stored. What this space was originally used for is not known, but the wall was reused from another building, and it is the only example of this type of timber construction that is known in Denmark.

for a long time it was also difficult to see who would win in the end. Claus Limbæk, who had been Count Gerhard's man at Kalø, became the *"Drost"*, the King's Seneschal, in 1344. That was the most distinguished office in the realm – after the King himself the Seneschal was the most important person in the governance of the country. Søborg was won, and the Danes then tried their strength against a now unknown fortification near Næstved. In the following year they conquered and destroyed the nearby Gunderslevholm.

In 1346 everything seemed to have turned to King Valdemar's advantage. He took possession of Korsør and after a while of Vordingborg also. The Holsteiners were still fighting against him, however, and they landed on Lolland, but the Seneschal was there with an army and had surrounded the fortresses. One of them was no doubt Eriksvolde near Maribo. The castle site consists of two mounds, each with a very small surface area, surrounded by a stout rampart and moat. There would never have been room for civilian residence at the site, which also gives the impression of never having been wholly completed. The mounds are built up on culture layers from the 14th century, and timber from the site has been dated by dendrochronology to around 1343, so Eriksvolde was probably a campaign fortress built in a hurry by the Holsteiners and then besieged and won by the Seneschal shortly afterwards.

(continued on page 150)

GUNDERSLEVHOLM
– the history of a castle

The conquest of Gunderslevholm was a ferocious affair. When the *"Marsk"*– the Lord High Constable – finally succeeded in taking the castle in 1345, the garrison was cut down indiscriminately and the fortifications were destroyed. On the third day of the battle Jens Mogensen, "the founder of this place", died. Jens Mogensen, of the Grubbe family, had taken over the estate in 1333 and had needed a castle. It must have been built fast, because in 1339 he mortgaged it to a certain "Øllerik Skaft", i.e. Ulrik Skaft, or Schacht, probably a Holsteiner, maybe from the second generation. He was married, and happily married, to a Dane and evidently had no desire to give up Gunderslevholm; the indications are that he lived there with his wife, Inger. In his will, from 1341, drawn up at Søborg, he made a generous bequest to "the cook in Gunderslev".

Tradition has it that the King's troops attacked the castle because of problems with the mortgage. This cannot be verified today, but in any event Jens Mogensen died in battle at his King's side.

It is rare to be able to date the building of a castle so precisely as to within less than a decade and then to be able to follow its brief lifetime. The fortifications at Gunderslevholm were most probably destroyed in 1345, but the place was still lived in for some forty years after that, and it remained in the posses-sion of the Grubbe family for a couple of generations. The Grubbe family, and particularly Jens Mogensen's two sons, Mogens and Bent Byg were staunch supporters both of King Valdemar and of his daughter Margrete. Bent Byg held Gunderslevholm and many other properties on Sealand, and when he died in 1391 he left a will describing how it should all be divided up. He had also settled his economic transactions with Queen Margrete, who had been appointed guardian for the widowed Elene, and she took pains to see to it that everything was done by the rule book and according to Bent Byg's wishes. Everyone got what was due, including Elene, who sold all her valuables as well as the buildings at Gunderslevholm to pay for her upkeep and board in the St Klara Convent in Roskilde.

The buildings were then pulled down, and the materials were evidently of some value, but there is no mention of fortifications, and the family would not have had any particular reason to go to the expense of re-fortifying the buildings on the island in the river. A later owner built a house there again late in the 15th century, possibly on top of the old castle mound. That house did not last long either, and the castle mound is still lying there in the grounds of the present Gunderslevholm.

The coat of arms of the Grubbe family as depicted on the pulpit in **KONGSTED CHURCH** *in south-east Sealand. Photo Ane Krogh Nielsen.*

The castle in **KORSØR** succeeded Tårnborg at some point in the late Middle Ages. The tower at Korsør now stands amidst much later buildings in the fortress. As with all medieval towers the entrance is placed high up as a defence measure. The tower originally had four storeys with crenellations on the top; in the course of the Middle Ages the wall was strengthened on the inside and a stove was added in the room above the cellar. Two storeys were later added.

The battles continued with successes for the Crown, and Næsholm in Ods Herred was probably another of the structures that fell in that connection. Valdemar Atterdag could gradually begin to feel that his position was safe, and in 1347 he went on a pilgrimage to the Holy Land, where he was knighted on Christ's Grave. He returned to Denmark the following year and took the last castles on Sealand and some in Jutland, along with half of Funen, Nykøbing on Falster and Stege on Møn, while the fortress of Skjoldnæs near Ringsted was besieged. All this took place while the plague was ravaging the country.

In 1349 Valdemar Atterdag gave a report to the Sealand *landsthing* about what he had conquered and what it had cost. Some of it had been at the expense of the country, and the King had contributed by selling Estonia to the Teutonic Order. Then he opened negotiations with his allies and opponents over what was still to be done to forge a united country. In the years that followed he also undertook several war campaigns and journeys to Germany, some of them as a form of leader of mercenaries for his brother-in-law, Margrave Ludvig of Brandenburg, but ultimately for his own cause and that of Denmark.

A change of mood

It is remarkable to see how everything succeeded for King Valdemar, for a long time, even though periodically there were difficulties, and it is strange that he was able to leave the kingdom repeatedly at apparently critical points in time without his unifying policy falling into disintegration. He even did so in the 1350s, when he met opposition not only from the Holstein counts, but also from some of the Danish aristocrats. They had expected to gain great influence when they had disposed of the Holsteiners. Instead they found that their King was someone who wanted his own way and was able to take decisions.

In Jutland there was open insurrection, and Valdemar Atterdag had to carry on fighting on the home front, with shorter or longer intermissions, throughout the next decade or so. At the same time he built up a large volume of diplomatic activity and sought to play his opponents off against one another. The battles were always about and around the castles, but often the towns were also involved. Some of them, like Vordingborg and Kalundborg, existed in combination with a castle, while others had a castle closely tied to them, like Kolding, Ribe and many others. In 1351 the Crown buildings were fortified at great expense, and that was wise, because soon after that the Jutlanders and the counts laid siege to them. All negotiations and pacts stood or fell according to possession of the castles, and in the midst of it all Valdemar went off to Germany again, as if he didn't have enough to do in playing the role of army commander in his own kingdom. In 1354 an agreement was reached between the King and his opponents at a national assembly meeting in Nyborg, and then there was a breathing space, but from the end of the 1350s the conflicts broke out again from castle to castle. The King had to fight both the Duke of Schleswig and the counts – i.e. Gerhard's sons – as well as the Jutlanders.

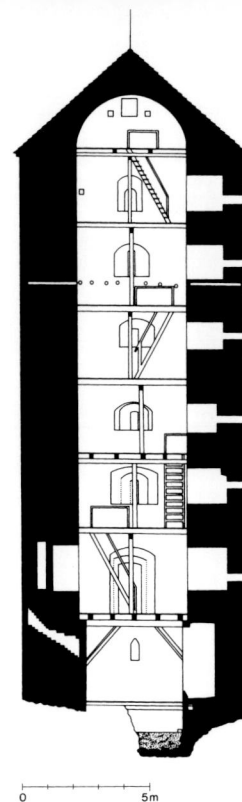

Elevation showing all eight storeys of the **KORSØR TOWER.**

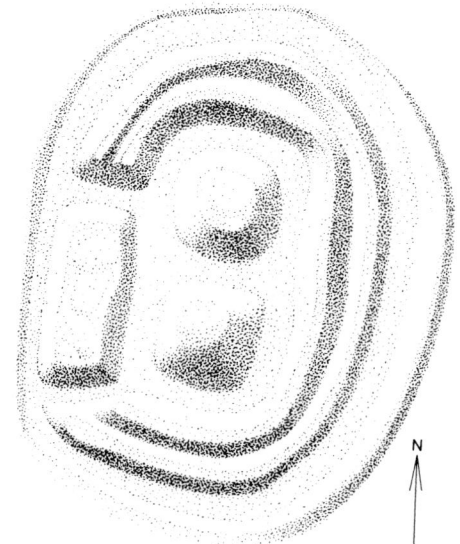

The castle mounds of **ERIKSVOLDE,** *just west of Maribo on Lolland, are both impressive and strange. For a while it was thought that the site was connected with Erik Emune and thus the 12th century, but later excavations showed that the structure was built in 1342-44, when Valdemar Atterdag was engaged in unifying the kingdom. The site was not in use for long, and it may have been one of the fortresses in which the Holsteiners entrenched themselves in 1344, when according to the Sealand Chronicle the Seneschal and the army were on Lolland and fighting with them.*

If one didn't know any better one might think that **TRANEKÆR,** *with its plastered walls and corbie-stepped gables, was a prestige building from the 19th century.*

On the elevation one can see that underneath all of it there is a hidden palatium *from the 13th century. Seen from the south. Elevation Danish National Museum.*

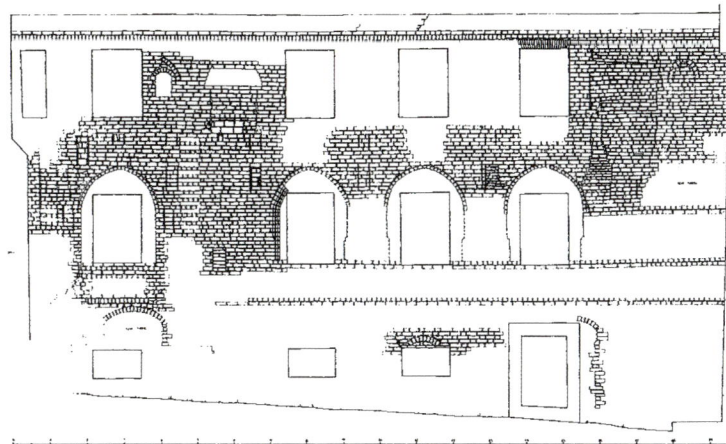

The enemies gathered forces and met the King in a battle at Brobjerg Castle on Funen. The location was probably near Urup in Rynkeby parish, midway between Odense and Svendborg. It was earlier thought to be at Gamborg on the coast between Middelfart and Assens, where there is an impressive castle mound, but the site at Urup is a reasonable conjecture, if one considers what the King and the counts held at the time on Funen. The example demonstrates how difficult it is, however, to judge the significance of individual structures within the whole context, if like Brobjerg in this case they crop up a single time in a particular connection, or like Næsholm and a few others they do not have any history attached to them other than what can be established by archaeology about when they functioned and whether they possibly succumbed in battle.

The King emerged victorious and gradually conquered all his opponents and took their castles. From the Duke of Schleswig he took Tranekær on Langeland and Nordborg on Als, where Sønderborg was also besieged using all the tricks

JUNGSHOVED *is situated on the coast south of Præstø. The place is mentioned as belonging to the Crown in 1231, but the castle may be older and could have been an element in the fortifications of the Danish coast constructed by the Valdemars. The nearby church was connected with the castle, which is now merely a mound on which sheep graze.*

Plan of **JUNGSHOVED** *with the remains of various buildings.*

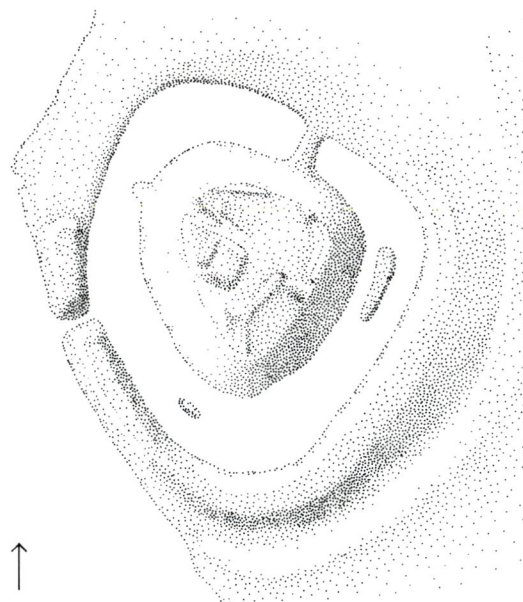

↑

of the trade – trebuchets, battering rams and other siege machines. The castle avoided being captured, however, because the Duchess Richiza, who held the castle in her husband's absence, was a wise woman and had the gift of the gab. Even so, on behalf of the Duke she had to agree to the King's conditions. He also captured Hindsgavl on Funen, and even though the Jutlanders won Tønder and the newly-built royal castle in Randers they were not given long to enjoy possession of it. The King's troops returned to Djursland and took not only Randers, but also Estrup, Katholm and Clausholm from the obstinate rebels. The Sealand Chronicle relates that the Jutlanders still refused to accept the authority of King Valdemar, because they saw how tyrannical his treatment of Sealand was. There their poor counterparts had had to build "castles out of mud and clay and did not even have straw". The Jutlanders themselves also had to do that at sites such as Boringholm, Hedegård and Sandgravvold, however.

Not all of Valdemar Atterdag's conquests lasted. He also lost a few of the battles in this war, but in the end he emerged the winner. The "King's Peace", which

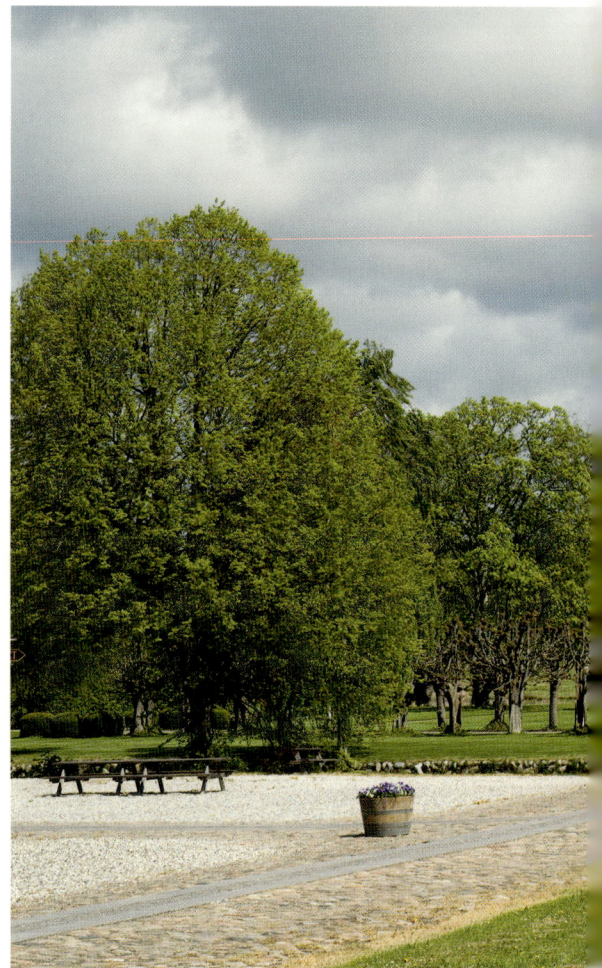

GAMMEL ESTRUP *was rebuilt as a Renaissance manor at the beginning of the 17th century. The west wing is the oldest building in the complex and dates from the end of the 15th century. This can be seen from the details in the wall on the side towards the courtyard.*

*The west wing of **GAMMEL ESTRUP** seen from the large courtyard, which is now part of the Museum of Agriculture. The old house had an old-fashioned gateway with a stepped gable and modern angled corner towers when it was rebuilt in 1616. Seen from the east.*

was settled in Kalundborg in 1360, shows that the King had the country and the land-owning elite behind him, as he had when in the same year he re-conquered the Scanian territories in a lightning campaign. This was a fine military accomplishment, and there was another in the following year when he conquered the island of Gotland in the Baltic Sea. The "King's Peace" was also a political achievement. The war in the kingdom had not increased King Valdemar's popularity, and nor was it improved by the fact that while the war was being waged he had worked to secure better juridical conditions – i.e. to strengthen royal power – and had also seen to it that the fortifications of towns and of various castles had been reinforced. This cost his subjects hard work and money, and the King had also used resources on troops and battles in other places, e.g. in the Ditmarshes and on the island of Femern.

After 1360 King Valdemar worked actively to win as much as possible of the lost Crown land back. Even though he had won the most important royal castles, many estates that had originally been Crown possessions were still in private hands. They had to be taken back, both for the sake of the revenue from them and to ensure a state of law and order, and also, not least, because it was important to gain control of the castles on that land. To a great extent Valdemar Atterdag used peaceful means and sought legal redress. He did not obtain all he wanted, by any means, and in many cases he had to be content with documents stating that the Crown had rights of possession after the present occupant's death. This could eventually be turned to advantage by his successor.

The enemies of the King and of his kingdom in other countries did not give up so easily. The Hanseatics were the worst and most threatening, and the conflict with them in the years around 1370 pulled in the King's other opponents, also those within the kingdom. The ungovernable north Jutland landowners raised the flag of dissent again, followed by the Duke of Schleswig, and by Count Gerhard's sons, Henrik and Claus. The Princes of Mecklenburg supported their kinsman Albrecht the Younger, who was adopted as king by Swedish aristocrats in 1364 instead of Magnus Smek, to whom Valdemar contributed military aid. All of this for the sake of the balance of power. They all saw the opportunity to weaken the all-too-powerful King of Denmark. But on the other hand, Mecklenburg should not be allowed to grow too powerful. The Treaty of Stralsund agreed with the Hanseatic League in 1370 was a defeat for Valdemar Atterdag, because among other things he had to cede the rights to the Scanian castles of Helsingborg, Skanør and Falsterbo for fifteen years. This gave the Hanseatics enormous revenues and great influence over the economy of the kingdom, and they wanted to hold on to that. They were therefore the decisive weight on the scales when it came to the balance of power around the Baltic. But danger had threatened before then, and it was not until the King died, in 1375, that it became pressingly menacing for Denmark.

Beside **KLEJTRUP** *Lake near Viborg there is a whole complex of earthworks and mounds which no doubt come from two fortified sites, one from the 14th century and the other of later date. The farm near the mounds is called Brattingsborg, and there are various legends linked with the place. Seen from the north-west.*

*The **GOOSE TOWER** at Vordingborg is incorporated in the curtain wall that surrounds the large castle area. The remains of the curtain wall rise some of the way up the wall beside the doorway that led out to the sentry walk. The tower acquired its name from the golden goose that Valdemar Atterdag is said to have had hoisted on the spire of the tower to mock his enemies from the Hanseatic towns.*

King Valdemar's castles

Valdemar Atterdag carried out building works at several of the Crown's important castles. Kalundborg was built out to its full extent in his time, and Vordingborg in particular was enlarged and fortified with walls, towers and broad moats that are still impressive today. The Goose Tower is a reminder of the King's battles with the Hanseatic towns, even though it is no longer crowned by the golden goose which he is supposed to have put there to mock them. It was probably also in his reign that Korsør took over Tårnborg's role in relation to monitoring the waters

of Storebælt. Whether there was still an interaction between the castle of Korsør and the fortress on the island of Sprogø is not known. The sources say nothing about the castle on the island. It is not mentioned after Valdemar the Great's time.

The war with the Hanseatic towns had also been about the castle in Copenhagen; the Hanseatics had conquered it in 1368 and had agreed to hold it until Helsingborg, on the Scanian coast, had been won. Then they would leave Sealand and the castle in Copenhagen would be pulled down. For that purpose it was decided that a number of towns, with Lübeck at their head, would send a group of their stonemasons and their tools – in all 46 men. It seems that they must have made the journey, and that they did their work thoroughly, so that not much of the old castle from Absalon's time remained.

Apparently Valdemar Atterdag must have managed to assert the Crown's right to Copenhagen, for when Queen Margrete allowed the Bishop of Roskilde to take over the town this did not mean that the Crown relinquished its rights. This makes it difficult to identify when the castle was rebuilt, however, and who did it, but it happened in the course of the last decades of the 14th century. King Valdemar also secured the Crown's right to Hammershus in a similar way, by making the Archbishop promise to relinquish the castle on the King's demand. That never became a reality, however.

Tradition has it that out of all his castles it was Gurre that Valdemar Atterdag liked best. He had had it built in North Sealand, possibly by extending an older structure. Letters show that he actually stayed at the castle frequently, particularly in his later life, and that he died there in 1375. Large meetings were held at Gurre, and agreements of international significance were reached there; the ruin that is left today covers only a small part of the castle area, but traces have been found of several other very different buildings. One of them, which was previously thought to have been a very large stable building, has turned out instead to have been a large house, on several storeys, with space for both stores and living quarters.

In the ruin with the four corner towers in the curtain wall around the rest of the tower or tower-house, which in many respects looks older than the wall, there would not have been room for the gilded halls which the 19th century poet Ingemann describes in a well-known Danish song *("På Sjølunds fagre sletter ...")*, but there could of course have been lively social activity in "the King's court" all the same. *"Curia regis"* is the term used for the Royal Court in the medieval chronicles, and it suits a place like Gurre well. In spite of its modest scale the castle's fortifications are reminiscent of some of the much larger crusader castles which King Valdemar could have seen on his journey to the Holy Land in 1347, but half a century earlier it had evidently been the same model that Erik Menved had used when he built the castle by the harbour at Warnemünde, and yet he had not visited Jerusalem.

Seen as a fortress Gurre was not at all at a level equal to that of the old royal castles, even though the proximity of the lake was a feature that could be used. The ruin was the only truly fortified part of the castle, but Gurre was not intended for use against a particular enemy. The castle was a symbol of royal power, and in King Valdemar's time its location sat safely in the middle of the Crown's possessions.

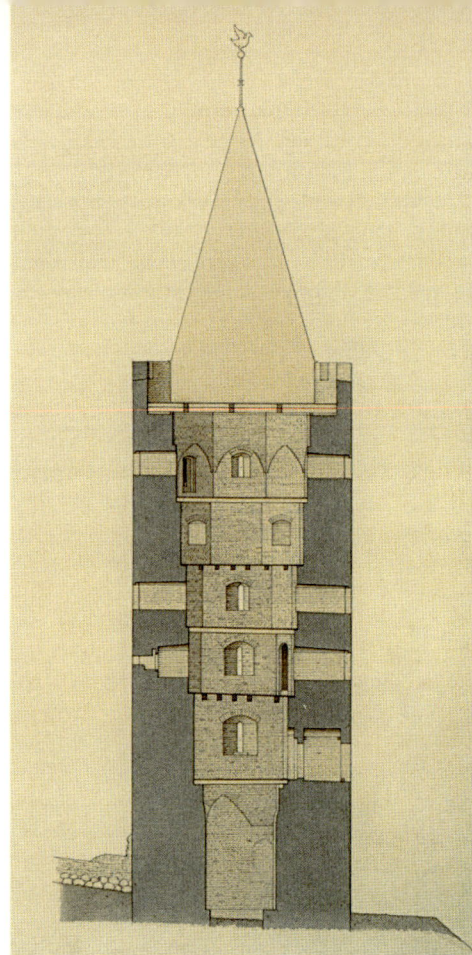

The **GOOSE TOWER** was a solidly fortified tower with very thick walls in relation to the interior space. Danish National Museum.

The whole area with the castle and town and church at **VORDINGBORG** rises high above the shore, where ships assembled for battle campaigns – and where enemy ships came sailing in.

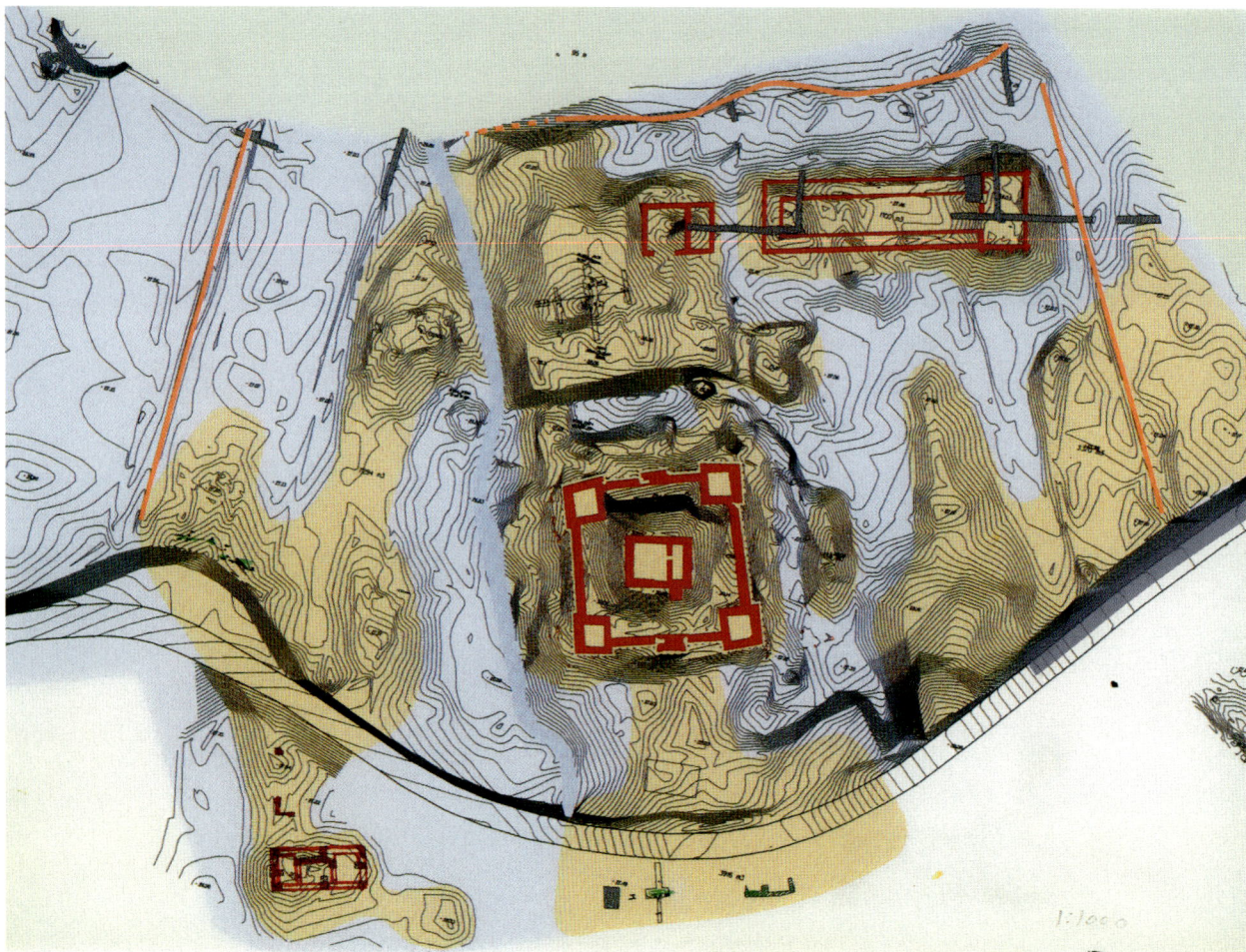

Søborg, not far from Gurre, was not modernised or reinforced in the 14th century, and various other Crown possessions, large or small – particularly the latter – were only lightly fortified or not at all, but they functioned all the same as administrative centres. In spite of rebellions and disagreements between the King and the aristocratic circles, the Crown must have been sufficiently strong for the system of control to function. This can also be seen from the fact that the King was able to travel abroad for rather long periods.

Completing the work

Towards the end of Valdemar Atterdag's reign there was peace in the kingdom and relations with other countries were relatively calm, but it was no doubt difficult for people within the kingdom to judge whether this was a durable situation. The peace was also more an expression of a balance between forces rather than a situation of absolute supremacy of government. Many castles, despite the King's efforts, were still in private hands and could in certain conditions become danger-

GURRE *in northern Sealand became an important royal castle in the time of Valdemar Atterdag, who often stayed there. When he died there, in 1375, there was a large Hanseatic delegation present in the castle. The guests did not find out that the King had died, so there must have been ample space for accommodation besides the little square castle area with the central tower which is visible today. Recent excavations have shown that many of the buildings associated with the castle lay spread around on small islands in the lake. All of this would not have been easy to defend, and in the central fortress the corner towers were water-reservoirs or were used for other peaceful purposes. The central tower may date from before Valdemar Atterdag's time. From Vivian Etting, Lone Hvass and Charlotte Boye Andersen:* Gurre Slot – kongeborg og sagnskat.

On the north and south sides of the central castle at **GURRE** there are symmetrical double stairways. They are very narrow, and clearly no-one could have ridden on horseback inside the curtain wall.

ous. It was not long ago that the Jutlanders had rebelled, and many of them were still alive and active. The grandees of the Church also had their own castles, and the support they had given the Crown in King Valdemar's time would not necessarily last forever. Previously the Church had for decades been the worst enemy of the Crown.

The aristocrats' loyalty to King Valdemar was to a great extent dependent on the King's and the nation's relations with other countries. The Holsteiners and other North German princes, Sweden and the Hanseatic towns were constantly on guard to ensure that Denmark did not become too strong, and the peace in the country was to some extent determined by the war with the Hanseatics. Because of it there were no resources for inner divisions. The King's councillors, who led the government in his absence and were left with the responsibility after his death, knew all too well that Denmark would be lost without strong central rule, and that required a king. There was no enthusiasm for having one from the family of the Dukes of Mecklenburg, however, even though King Valdemar had had to promise that one of the sons of his eldest daughter Ingeborg would have primacy when it came to the election of the next king of Denmark. There was already a Mecklenburg family member on the throne of Sweden. For that reason the Danish aristocracy agreed to support Valdemar's youngest daughter Margrete, who was Queen of Norway, and chose her young son Oluf as king. Perhaps they calculated that now the councillors would take power. If so, they turned out to be wrong.

Margrete showed herself to be a worthy heir to her father; she continued his policies, but used other means. She did not wage war against castles in Denmark, but by ingenuity – and some sources say trickery – she won many of them back for the Crown, including a high proportion of those held with promises to return them to Valdemar. That was true of e.g. Tordrup near Randers, which had belonged to one of the leaders of the Jutland uprising, Stig Andersen, who was the grandson of the Lord High Constable, Marsk Stig Andersen, who had been condemned as an outlaw in 1287.

Queen Margrete did not only acquire the castles; in many cases she had them pulled down. This was often attended to by the Church, because she transferred many estates and many castles to the Church, to which royal power in fact owed much, including cash sums. For instance, the Bishop of Viborg was given Hald, which had been held by Niels Bugge, who had been involved as one of the rebels against Valdemar Atterdag. Margrete used every conceivable legal ploy to take estates back for the Crown or at least to have the castles demolished, and she had a good degree of success in this, because she always took care to have the law on her side, and because the building materials from the demolitions had a high value. She doubtless made gains from this herself; in the case involving Archbishop Henrik of Uppsala , for instance, he took over the mortgage on Jämtland in 1402 on the basis that he would demolish the castle of Tibrantsholm. The materials from the castle were to pay off some of Margrete's debt to the Archbishop.

This was naturally not a policy that appealed to the aristocrats who had acquired some share of Crown property, but it says something about the state of law

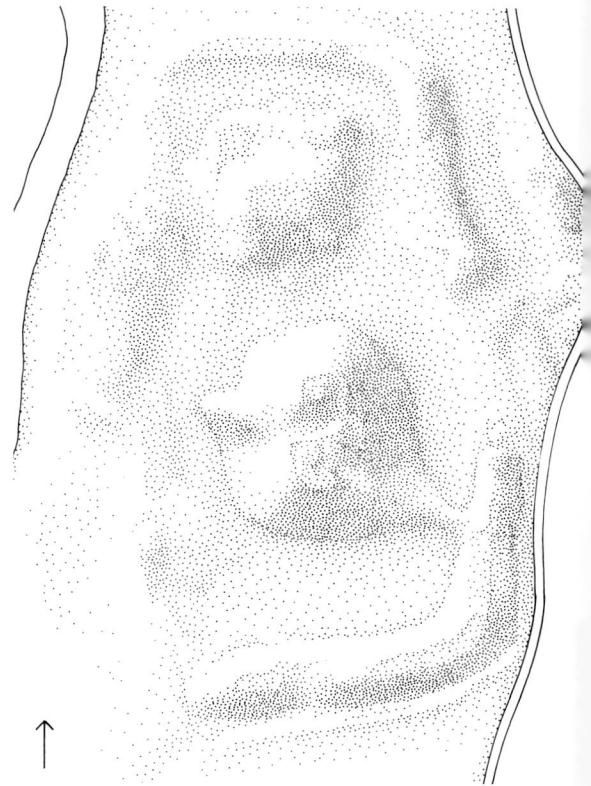

EGHOLM *in Himmerland is in fact two earthworks. The small mound had a wooden tower, erected in 1334, probably as a temporary place of refuge. The plan shows EGHOLM CASTLE, which perhaps replaced the little fortification after 1350. The castle was in the possession of Holsteiners for a time, and then Danes, until Valdemar Atterdag bought it. Queen Margrete gave the castle to Vor Frue Convent in Aalborg. The buildings were to be demolished and could never be rebuilt, but masses were to be held in the convent for the Queen and her parents for all eternity.*

Gutter in the corner between the curtain wall and one of the corner towers at **GURRE.** *The wall is double – i.e. built with two outer shells of brick with the hollow between them filled with stones stuck together with mortar. Seen from the north.*

QUEEN MARGRETE'S SEAL *is attached to various documents in the State Archives. She used a number of different seals. This one is the special court seal. Photo State Archives.*

ASSERBO, *on its very regular castle mound, is a noble family's estate and was probably not established until as late as the 15th century, more as a manor house than as a castle. Seen from the northeast.*

and order, and about the Queen, that it could be implemented. The reaction of the time – and of subsequent times – was partly admiration but also criticism that the Queen thus meddled in matters of inheritance and cheated young children and widows out of their expected inheritance, even where the case might involve her own friends or those of the Crown. In the case of the change of ownership of Gunderslevholm, however, she kept strictly to the agreements that had been made before the owner's death, and made sure that all received their due, including the childless widow. This also applied to Skarsholm, which she bought in 1408. It was an important part of her strength that her dealings were unassailable in law. But of course the woman who styled herself the "sovereign mistress" of the kingdom felt she needed to get rid of the private castles in the realm.

The essence of Margrete's perspective on the position of the powerful aristocrats in society can be understood from the decree she had issued in 1396, after her adopted son Erik of Pomerania had been crowned king in all three Nordic kingdoms. One of the paragraphs includes the following passage: "... because there has been exceptionally little justice that has issued from the strongholds that have been built until now, we hereby now forbid the building of any further strongholds or fortified towers, so that the land can all the sooner be brought in order and achieve greater peace and justice than has been the case until now, and we forbid bailiffs and officials to permit anyone to build castles and towers". This stipulation was also Margrete's political triumph, since it brought conditions back to the good old days before the conflict between the sons of Valdemar the Victorious, since the monarch now again had the monopoly of castle-building. Throughout all the years of unrest the Crown had gradually had to relinquish that right, until in the end everything was upside down, and the landowners were able to force successive kings to promise to pull down the Crown castles.

Now all was back to how it was "in King Valdemar's time", and there were certainly many in the country who were glad about that.

THE CASTLES IN ROYAL HANDS
at the time of Valdemar Atterdag's death

Valdemar Atterdag had at least six children with Queen Helvig. Only the youngest daughter, Margrete, survived him, but one of the older daughters had married Henrik, the son of Duke Albrecht of Mecklenburg, and she had lived long enough to have children. In 1371 Valdemar Atterdag had had to promise the son of Ingeborg and Henrik – another Albrecht – that he would be entitled to be elected king of Denmark. When the Danish King's Council instead chose Oluf, the son of Valdemar's youngest daughter, Margrete, the Meck-

lenburgs tried every possible means of asserting their rights, but without success. Among the strategies used, they gained the Emperor's support to claim that a number of Danish royal representatives should hand over the castles to the young Albrecht. Three letters about the case are known, all issued from Tangermünde on 12 September 1377. They concern only Funen, the southern Danish islands and Jutland, and it is not known whether there were now lost letters about the rest of the kingdom, or whether they were never issued.

The royal representatives were promised immunity even though "they had held the castles illegally".

HØNBORG *on the Jutland side of the Little Belt opposite Hindsgavl, was an important and royal property in the 14th century. It was there that Christian II stayed after he received the denunciation letter from the Jutland noblemen in 1523, and it was between Hønborg and Hindsgavl that he sailed irresolutely backwards and forwards during the night, when he had to decide whether to continue the struggle for power in the kingdom or abandon it for foreign shores. Seen from the north.*

The representatives and castles concerned were:

Anders Pedersen	and	Hagenskov
Jens Navnesen	"	Nyborg
Evert Moltke	"	Fåborg
Henning Berg	"	Kærstrup on Tåsinge
Jens Mus	"	Tranekær
Degenhard Bugenhagen	"	Ravnsborg
Niels Thomsen	"	Aalholm
Peder Nielsen	"	Grimstrup and all of Falster
Wrenzel van Bomenstorp	"	Stegeborg and all of Møn
Scarpenberg	"	Hønborg

There are two letters about the castles on the islands; Scarpenberg is only mentioned in one of them. Hønborg is situated on the Jutland side of the Little Belt, opposite Hindsgavl.

The representatives and castles concerned in Jutland were:

Henning Meinerstorp	and	Sønderborg, Nordborg, Brådeborg and Kegborg on Als
Spiker	"	Aabenraa
Nicolaus von Emer	"	Tønder
Bolzendal and Niels Skytte	"	the fortress of Zonkini (Sønnike's fortress?)
Rokit	"	Ribe, Skodborg and Varde
Ture Bosen	"	Lundenæs
Henning von Lancken	"	Bygholm
Erik Nielsen	"	Skanderborg
Jens Andersen	"	Kalø
Jacob Olufsen	"	Trudsholm (Kastbjerg s. N.E. Jutland)
Lyder Limbæk	"	Søgaard (Kliplev s.)
Gerlav Tun	"	Egholm
Henneke Limbæk	"	Trøjborg
Vendelbo	"	Aalborg
Henning Podebusk the Younger	"	Rugtved
Rekentin, Jens Lykke and Daget	"	(No castle named)
Fikke Moltke of Kyse	"	Bjørnholm
Jacob Nielsen	"	Hald

There are men from Danish families as well as others with German-Holstein and other foreign origins among the representatives in this list. The castles mentioned are all castles which were controlled by the Danish Crown and the King's Council, or by Margrete in Oluf's name, and nothing came of the demand to deliver them to Albrecht.

The castle
in the late Middle Ages

From castle back to farming estate

Queen Margrete continued to absorb estates into the ambit of Crown property until her death in 1412, and she had castles and fortifications demolished. In this way many of the fortified buildings that had been characteristic of the landscape for a long time now disappeared, and this process continued during the rest of the century and into the 16th century. Gradually, as the peace in the kingdom proved to be lasting, many people moved of their own accord out of their inaccessible castles situated in marshes and bogs or just far from the beaten track. When law and order prevailed there was no reason to make life difficult and take on unnecessary costs for maintenance of expensive defence works. Instead the powerful in the land now built wooden or half-timbered manor houses with three or four wings.

In several cases, such as at Lynderupgaard, not far from Viborg, a small stone house was extended by being joined onto or incorporated into half-timbered wings or a new main house. Smaller-scale houses were often made of boulders, sometimes mixed with bricks, and in some places it is no longer easy to distinguish them from the other buildings, because the old half-timbered houses were replaced, over time, by larger stone houses, e.g. at Krenkerup on Lolland.

At Østrupgaard near Fåborg, on Funen, there is a little granite-built house from c.1500. Stone houses of this type have no fortifications; they were not intended for defence against people, but they resisted fire better than the other farm buildings. They would have held the family's valuables, important documents, etc., and were thus a form of strongbox.

If resources could stretch to it, the living quarters would be set up in a stone- or brick-built house, as at the manor house Tjele near Viborg, where the oldest main building is a fine little brick house, probably from the beginning of the 16th century. It contained living quarters and stores distributed over its three floors, and is so well-preserved because it rapidly became too small. As a rule the manor houses were surrounded by moats, but there were seldom ramparts, and only rarely walls, around the mounds on which they stood. At Tjele there were not even moats, perhaps because the brick-built house provided all the prestige the owner could have wished. The moats were an indication that the inhabitants of

View of part of the servants' hall at **GLIMMINGEHUS.**

those buildings were people apart from, and more than, ordinary peasants; actual defence significance could not really be attributed to the moats, but they could be useful in keeping free-roaming domestic animals belonging to the village or to the manor itself at a distance from the landowner's residence. In order to emphasise that structures of this type were not castles, the earthworks on which they stood are known as manor-house mounds, and they are in fact evidence that Margrete's ban on castle-building was observed.

Long after the Middle Ages the nobility in large part continued to build and live in this way, and it is this type of manor house that is referred to in the bal-

LYNDERUPGÅRD *near Skals in central Jutland is one of the late medieval manor houses that match the descriptions of such houses in popular ballads which mention a little "stone house" amidst the other less solid buildings. The manor house lies on a low mound surrounded by a moat, so it is clear that people of status live here. But there are no actual fortifications. The estate belonged to the Viborg diocese until the Reformation. The little stone-built house in the west is the oldest and possibly dates from the end of the 14th century. The half-timbered houses around it are from the 16th century and later. Seen from the southeast.*

KRENKERUP *near Saks-*
købing on Lolland has been
much altered in the course of
the centuries, but in its walls
there is a little brick house
from the end of the 15th cen-
tury, along with the remains of
wings from the beginning of the
16th. At that time the estate
belonged to the wealthiest
man in the country, Seneschal
Mogens Gøye. Seen from the
south.

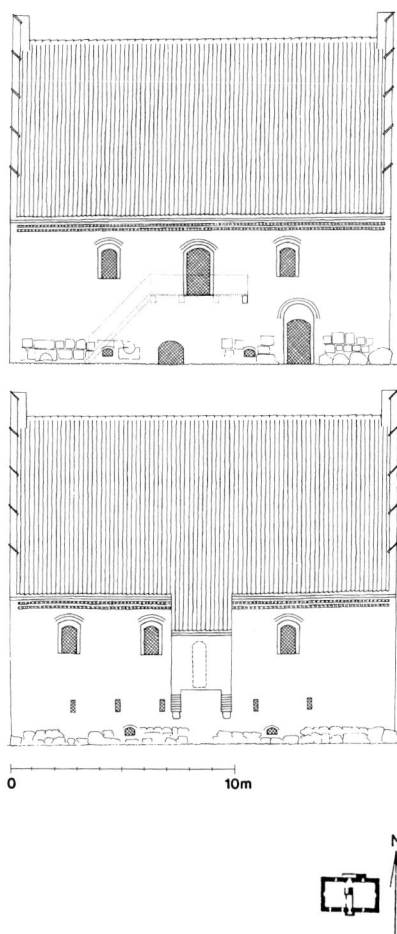

Elevation showing that each floor had its own entrance. There were stairs up to the door of the hall in the middle of the south facade, and there was a privy that projected from the middle of the rear wall. From Hans Henrik Engqvist: Tjele.

The little brick built house at **TJELE** *near Viborg provides space for full living quarters distributed over three floors, with stores in the cellar, dwelling rooms on the ground floor and a hall on the upper floor. It is from the beginning of the 16th century and soon became too small. Hence its good state of preservation. Seen from the south.*

lads that were collected and written down in the 16th and 17th centuries by noble ladies and others who were familiar with the contexts the ballads describe. It was not important that the narratives in some of the ballads might claim to have taken place several hundred years earlier. The ballads for instance tell of merry dancing on the grass-covered courtyard behind the entrance-gate. There are festive occasions in the main hall, people sleep and live in the upper storey and the space on the outdoor gallery is used for playing board-games and working on embroidery. One of the best-known ballads tells of the tragic fate of Ebbe Skammelsen. It mentions a stone house and a stone room, so Tjele, for example, where there was originally an outdoor gallery in front of the floor that held living quarters, could have provided the setting for this drama. Ebbe serves at the King's court and dreams one night that his mother and his beloved fair maiden are trapped in a burning building. A friend tells him that this means that Ebbe's brother has seduced his betrothed. Ebbe travels home immediately and arrives just as the couple are about to be wed. In wretched spirits he wants to leave again, but the family persuades him to stay and treats him as an honoured guest. He is placed at the head of the table, is in charge of pouring mead and wine, and even lights the way for the bride to proceed to the bridal chamber. On the high gallery outside the living quarters he reminds her of their past, but when she refuses to run away with him and in future will only be like a mother for him, he kills her. Then he goes to the stone room and kills his evil brother. In the commotion that followed he has to fight his way out, and he acquits himself well, since his father lost his left foot and his mother her right hand. "And that is why Ebbe Skammelsen is now an outlaw", as the refrain has it.

That can't be a surprise to anyone.

It was seldom however, that the living quarters in the manor houses of the 15th century were exclusively in stone buildings. Højstrup on Stevns, which is immortalised in the drama "Elverhøj" – a national favourite – had a little stone house at the beginning of the 15th century, when Queen Margrete took over the property from her faithful supporter Folmer Jacobsen Lunge. There was no tower or any trace of a fortification. Folmer had little need for a castle, and the Queen had none whatsoever.

There were stone buildings in several castles, including small ones, even before the 15th century, and it may have been difficult to distinguish between towers and small houses, as in the case of the tower mound at Bjørnkær near Odder, the ruin at Kelstrup in Ods Herred or even the central "tower" at Gurre. At Skarsholm, between Kalundborg and Jyderup, there are faint traces of stone buildings on two of the three castle mounds, and from a documented change of ownership in 1369 it seems that one of them must have had two storeys; the owners were in fact distinguished people, descendants of the illegitimate son, Knud, of Valdemar the Victorious. At Padeborg, now Sparresholm, there was both a curtain wall and a tower, but the remains lie on the castle mound under the present main building, so it is not easy to establish how old they are.

VOERGÅRD *in Northern Jutland belonged to successive Børglum bishops until the Reformation. The large brick-built house to the north was constructed on a low mound which was probably surrounded by a curtain wall, but it did not have serious fortifications. The courtyard is still surrounded by moats and is now particularly noteworthy because of Ingeborg Skeel's splendid house to the east from 1588.*

Properties with both stone and half-timbered houses

On private estates stone- or brick-built houses as main buildings did not occur until after the middle of the 15th century. One of the oldest is the fine house at Bollerup near Ystad in Scania, where an old house has been extended. At Gunderslevholm a stone house was constructed in the mid-15th century, but it has totally disappeared, while the oldest house at Gammel Estrup is now one of three wings. These were all properties that belonged to the wealthiest men in the country, and they were their main residences, but their stone or brick houses were not nearly as impressive as the old *palatium* at Pedersborg from before 1200. The fifteenth century brick houses, like the earliest main building at Tjele, normally only contained one dwelling consisting of a few rooms and housing the family's most precious belongings.

At Gammel Estrup there are traces, in the top storey, of some apertures that could look like loopholes or machicolations. Something similar can be seen at Svaneholm in Scania, but there are too few of them and they are too haphazardly-placed to have been of much use. The same applies to the Gyldenstjerne family's Kokkedal in Vendsyssel. That is otherwise an impressive building with three brick-built wings on a high mound surrounded by moats. The earthworks are perhaps older, but the buildings belong to the 16th century. The Bishop of Børglum's Voergaard, from 1520, also situated in Vendsyssel, was another case of a building

ODDEN *in Northern Jutland is situated on a large medieval castle mound. The two wings of the house are both from the 16th century, however, and completely without fortifications; they were later altered to create more symmetry in the 18th century style. Seen from the southeast. The unusual patriarchal cross or cross of Lorraine on the eastern gable of the oldest building, from the 1520s, is rare in Denmark; only one other example is known on a secular building, on the manor house of Krabbesholm, in Skive, Jutland.*

without actual defence structures, although there was a wall along the edge of the low mound on which it stood. There, as at the noblemen's estates, the machicolations or loopholes and moats were mostly testimony to the social status of the owner. This can clearly be seen at Bollerup. An arched cornice runs along the foot of the roof, so that it looks slightly like a series of machicolations, but it is in fact merely decoration. Bollerup, like many other Scanian houses, is built of stone.

There were influential secular figures in the country who retained their estates and their castles, and not all of them moved from peat bogs or peninsulas on lakes to live on more solid ground. In many places a later house replaced an old castle and was built on the former castle mound, so that it is now often impossible to find out how the buildings were arranged in the Middle Ages and whether there was really a castle there or, if so, for what period of time the defence features were maintained. Clausholm near Randers, for example, was one of the private castles that Valdemar Atterdag went to great lengths to conquer during the major Jutland uprising in the 1350s. Excavations around the present main building from the end of the 17th century have shown that there once were buildings situated on two small islands. Traces have been found of masonry houses, and with the help of written sources these can be dated to the end of the 15th century and beginning

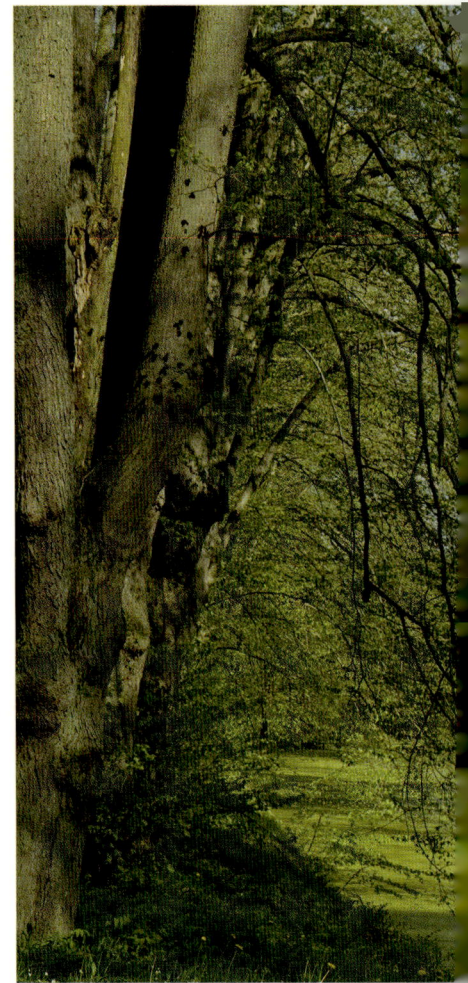

BOLLERUP *near Ystad in Scania is another unfortified house from the late Middle Ages. The house has been extended and rebuilt and provided with large windows over the course of time, but the blind arch friezes and the recesses in the gables still give the building a medieval character. The house is four storeys in height and formed a dignified setting for its distinguished owners, the Krognos family. It has been preserved because it made an excellent grain store when it became too out-of-date to live in. Seen from the southeast and the courtyard.*

KOKKEDAL, *near Brovst in North Jutland, is situated on top of a mound that was once a castle mound. Now it is a manor house, a fine dwelling from the early 16th century. Seen from the northwest.*

of the 16th, when the biggest landowner in the country, Mogens Gøye, owned the estate. At that time Clausholm was an enclosed four-winged structure, but the foundations are slight and do not suggest actual defence-works. Nor is there any suggestion of that in the written sources.

There is good reason to believe that 15th century landowners stopped living in castles. If they went on living in their old castles in marshes and bogs or on peninsulas in lakes they let the fortifications decay or else demolished them and made more comfortable arrangements. This was because of the castle-building ban and the prevailing economic conditions, but it was also because there was peace in the kingdom most of the time and in most places. The living quarters could certainly be appropriate to the owner's rank, even if the building was half-timbered, and the moat, as already mentioned, had become a marker of social status, even if it was for keeping ducks rather than for keeping enemies out. The right to build fortifications remained extremely important to the influential landowners, however.

(continued on page 180)

The castle in the late Middle Ages   **177**

GJORSLEV

The only large private brick-built house that is known from around 1400 and before 1500 is at Gjorslev on Stevns, the estate of the Bishop of Roskilde, Peder Jensen Lodehat, from c.1400. It is a grand building and its exterior is almost completely preserved. Apart from some changes to the roofing and on the facade Gjorslev's appearance is much as it was in the Middle Ages, but although it is impressive it is not a castle. There was a little chapel built out from the front facade into the courtyard, south of the entrance.

There were crenellations, however, and there still are loopholes high up above the central part of the house, which looks like a tower, but they would

Peder Jensen Lodehat's **GJORSLEV,** *seen from the southwest. At one time the cross-shaped house had stepped gables, and the formidable central building had crenellations at the top, but there were never ramparts or walls around the low mound.*

Some years ago excavations revealed traces of a little chapel on the east side of GJORSLEV'S main building. It is marked on the ground-plan of the house, but not on the overall plan of the site which shows later side buildings.

The little chapel at GJORSLEV still existed in the 17th century, as can be seen on the drawing. Pencil, watercolour and ink on paper. Between 1666 and 1715. Probably before 1682. Herzog Anton Ulrich-Museum, Braunschweig. Photo B.P. Keitner 1992.

never have been able to fulfil any practical function.

There are too many unprotected gables behind which an enemy could hide, and the "tower" is built in conjunction with the rest of the house and so has never been free-standing. There have always been large windows in the lower storeys, and the house lies open in the middle of its mound, which has never been surrounded by ramparts or walls. Gjorslev is a magnificent residence, a palace for the most important person in the kingdom except for the Queen he served so loyally; the ground-plan in the form of a cross was appropriate for a bishop. The house is also testimony to his wealth, since it was expensive to build in brick, and it was no doubt lack of funds that prevented more people from doing so.

Peder Jensen could afford whatever he wanted, and he complied loyally with the ban on building castles. Maybe, as the Queen's Chancellor, he was actually the person who formulated the ban. In any case, if everything went wrong, the bishops of Roskilde had always, from earlier ages, had other castles where they could seek refuge, for instance Dragsholm near the Sejrø bay.

Gjorslev belonged to successive bishops of Roskilde until the Reformation in 1536. Between 1540 and 1678 the house and estate were in private hands, and since 1743 this has also been the case. In the course of the years two wings have been built onto the old house.

PLAN OF GJORSLEV. *Before the side wings were added there were probably various other buildings on the site.*

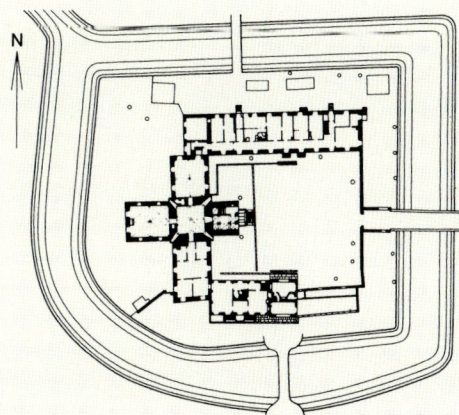

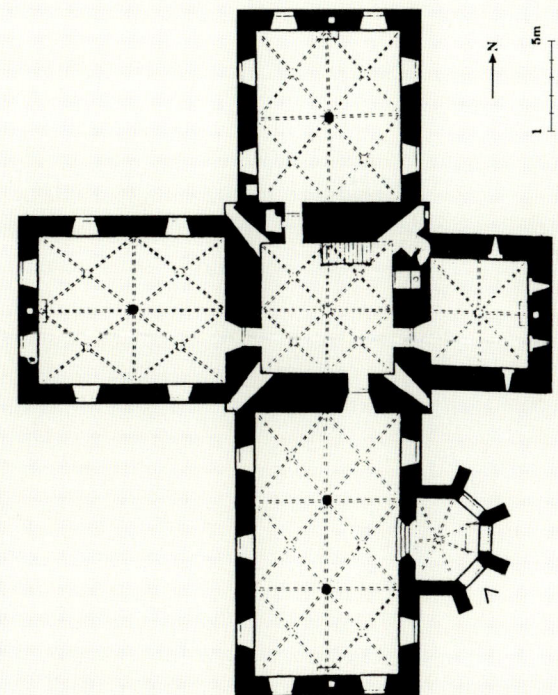

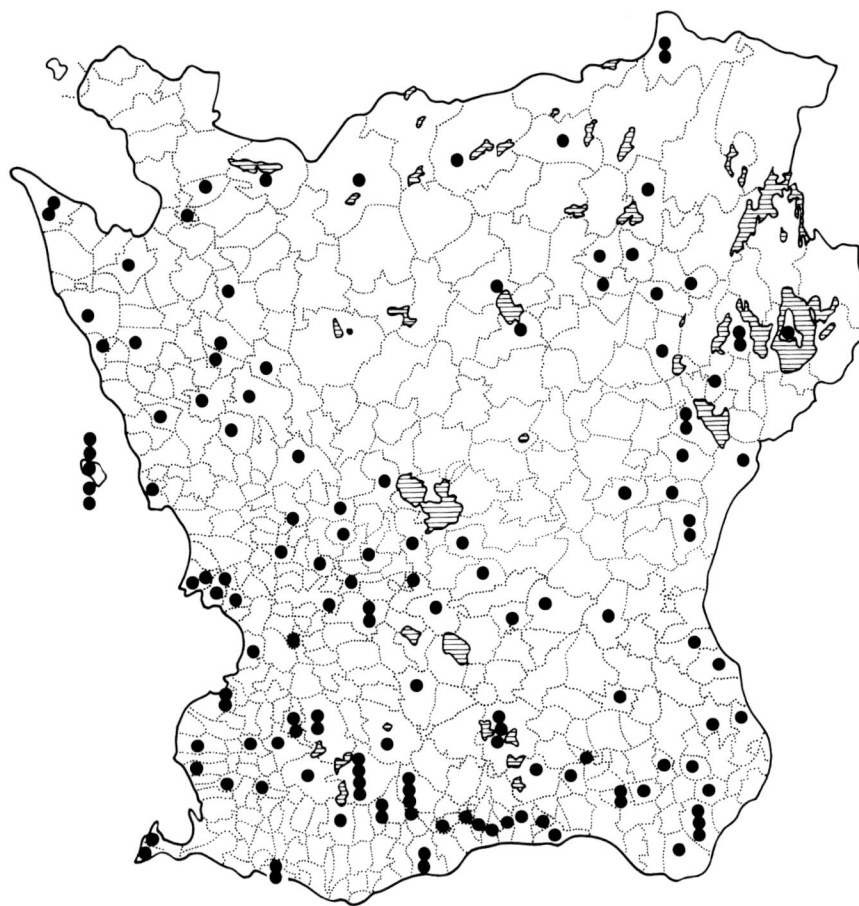

MAP OF SCANIA'S MEDIEVAL CASTLES.
From Anders Ødmann: Borgar i Skåne.

They had fought to share that royal prerogative for nearly 150 years, and they were not about to give up.

The coronation charter that King Hans had to agree to in 1483 is a clear expression of the powerful position of the nobility, and if the King had actually complied with the promises he made in the agreement he would have been completely unable to rule. One of the paragraphs annuls the ban on building castles. "Thus we shall have no power to obstruct or deny any men, spiritual or secular, in any of the realms [Denmark, Norway and Sweden, which Hans was to rule over as Union King] in fortifying or adding to their manors, which would be to the benefit of them and the realm."

Private castle-building was thus supposed to be of benefit to the kingdom. This could have been something a strong king could have exploited, if the occasion had arisen, but it never came to that. Times changed and warfare developed in new directions, and even the wealthiest private individuals were not able to meet the new criteria for adequately fortified buildings. The role of the castle had been played out by the beginning of the 16th century, and the provision in King Hans's coronation charter came to have mostly the effect of a permanent "licence to crenellate". Among the stone-built houses from the later part of the Middle Ages, Glimmingehus in eastern Scania is alone in resembling an actual castle.

(continued on page 184)

GLIMMINGEHUS

Glimmingehus in Scania was built by the rich and powerful royal representative on Gotland, Jens Holgersen Ulfstand, in around 1500, and it was a prestige project, a demonstration of wealth and a playground for important people. At that time the architect Adam van Düren, from Westphalia, was working in Denmark on Lund Cathedral, and he may also have worked for Jens Holgersen on Glimmingehus. He was a modern Renaissance architect, so it is in fact remarkable that Glimmingehus looks so much like a medieval castle.

There are loopholes and tiny windows in thick walls, and the conditions of access to the house are extremely difficult. There are more loopholes and murder-holes within the house, and on almost every step of the staircase a defender would be able to hit the enemy. That is, if the enemy came one at a time: there is literally only room for one defender and one attacker in the little building. Glimmingehus is much too small to play any role in real war or to be

*The entrance to **GLIMMINGEHUS** was well protected by a machicolation, down which the defenders could pour all sorts of vile things on the heads of the attackers. Beneath this there was a large aperture that could also be used for defence purposes. Above the door Jens Holgersen Ulfstand, the first owner, placed his coat of arms and those of his two wives.*

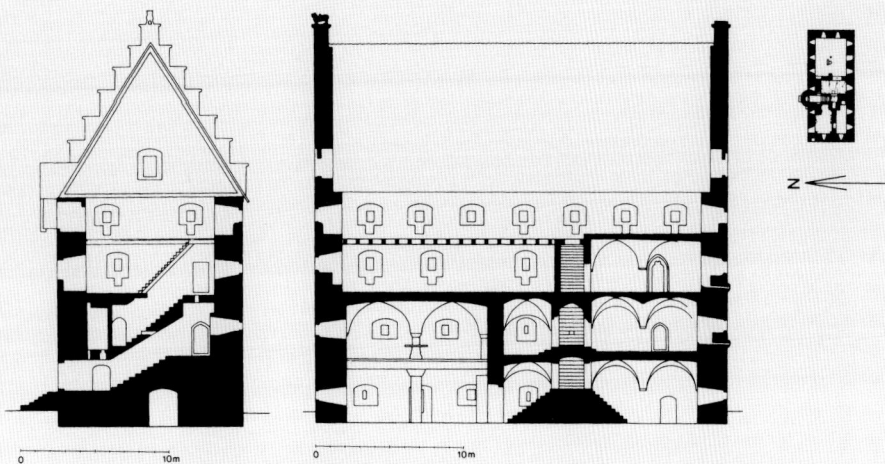

an asset to its owner and the kingdom, even though it was originally situated in the middle of a lake, while now there is only a moat around it. There were never any ramparts or walls around it, and even the fact that there are loopholes with room for firearms in the window-niches of the archers' loft is not enough to make Glimmingehus a strong fortress. The house was too small to contain even a limited crew of defenders or to house stores to provide for a siege of any length. But there is a well in the cellar.

It is, however, a very fine house with a servants' hall and a banqueting hall as well as two "apartments", and all of it is decorated with a wealth of strange pictorial stones and figures from churches on Gotland. Possibly this is the Nordic version of the Renaissance interest in Antiquity, in this case expressed in art from the Nordic region's own early history. At any rate, this was in line with King Hans's ideas. Jens Holgersen did not live permanently in Glimmingehus, even though it was situated on land that had traditionally belonged to his family. He was the King's representative on the island of Gotland and lived in the castle of Visborg there – a quite different and much larger kind of place. The modest-scale house in Scania seems like

a curious kind of toy – romantic chivalry, one might say – and at any rate it is an anachronism. It is deliberately conceived, and perhaps meant as a second home or occasional retreat, where the mighty official could feel that he was a knight of the old school and could remind the neighbourhood about who he was. The archaeological finds on the site also indicate that this was the case.

Glimmingehus remained in private hands until 1924, with only a brief interlude during the Great Nordic War, when the King confiscated the castle. It was immortalised in Selma Lagerlöf's charming book: Niels Holgersens Rejse (published in English as "The Wonderful Adventures of Nils"). Now Glimmingehus is open to the public and there is a small castle museum, containing finds from excavations on the site, in one of the newer wings.

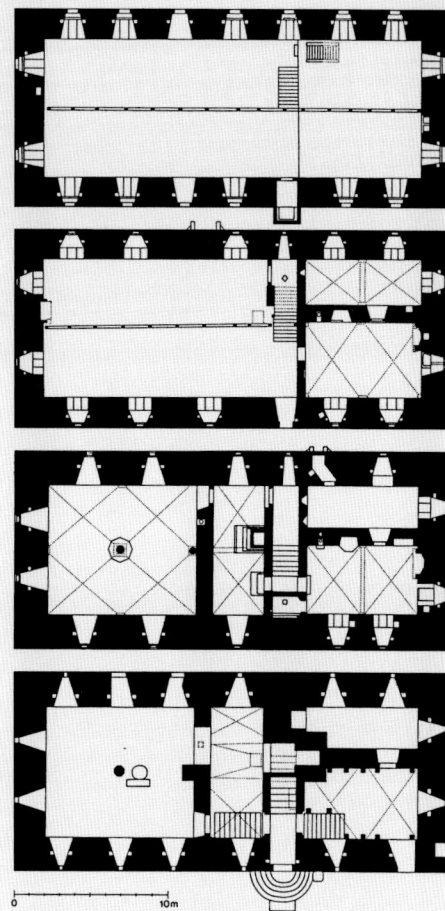

GLIMMINGEHUS in c.1500 was very small in relation to other castles of its time.

Each of the four floors of GLIMMINGEHUS contains several rooms behind the thick walls.

Down in the cellar were the kitchen and stores. On the next floor was the servants' hall, guardroom and a two-room apartment. Above that was another apartment and a hall. At the top was the archers' loft. The staircase was full of defensive features that could keep an enemy from the door – assuming that the enemy came one man at a time.

A peep into the uppermost and splendidly equipped apartment. Many of the decorations, for instance the images of saints, came from churches on Gotland, where Jens Holgersen was the king's representative.

In the kitchen at GLIMMINGEHUS there was a large fireplace and a well. Water was the most difficult thing to be without in a siege, but that never happened here.

Both Glimmingehus and Bollerup withstood rebellious bands of peasants in the 1520s, but that is another story. In those days a solid wall was good protection and could possibly be decisive in a fight even with a superior number of enemies, if they were badly organised and not used to fighting, or if they did not have time to conduct a siege. And stone does not burn as easily as wood; the sources actually relate that the peasants burned the big houses, except those that were made of stone. It may also be the case that the enemies just avoided them.

The royal castles in the time of
Queen Margrete and King Erik

Margrete's title of queen came from her marriage to Håkon of Norway. He was also for a time co-regent with his father, Magnus Smek, in Sweden, so Margrete could also call herself queen of Sweden. She also won power there after the battle at Åsle or Falen on 24 February 1389 against Albrecht of Mecklenburg. Like many other Swedish kings he had fallen out with some of the most leading elite, who had chosen to support Margrete as their ruler instead. After they were defeated Albrecht and his son Erik became prisoners of the Queen and remained in cap-

Erik of Pomerania built the strongly-fortified castle of **VISBORG** *in Visby on Gotland. He lived there for thirteen years and made the waters unsafe for seafarers. The castle was worthy of a prince. Illustration from* Svecia Antiqva et Hodierna.

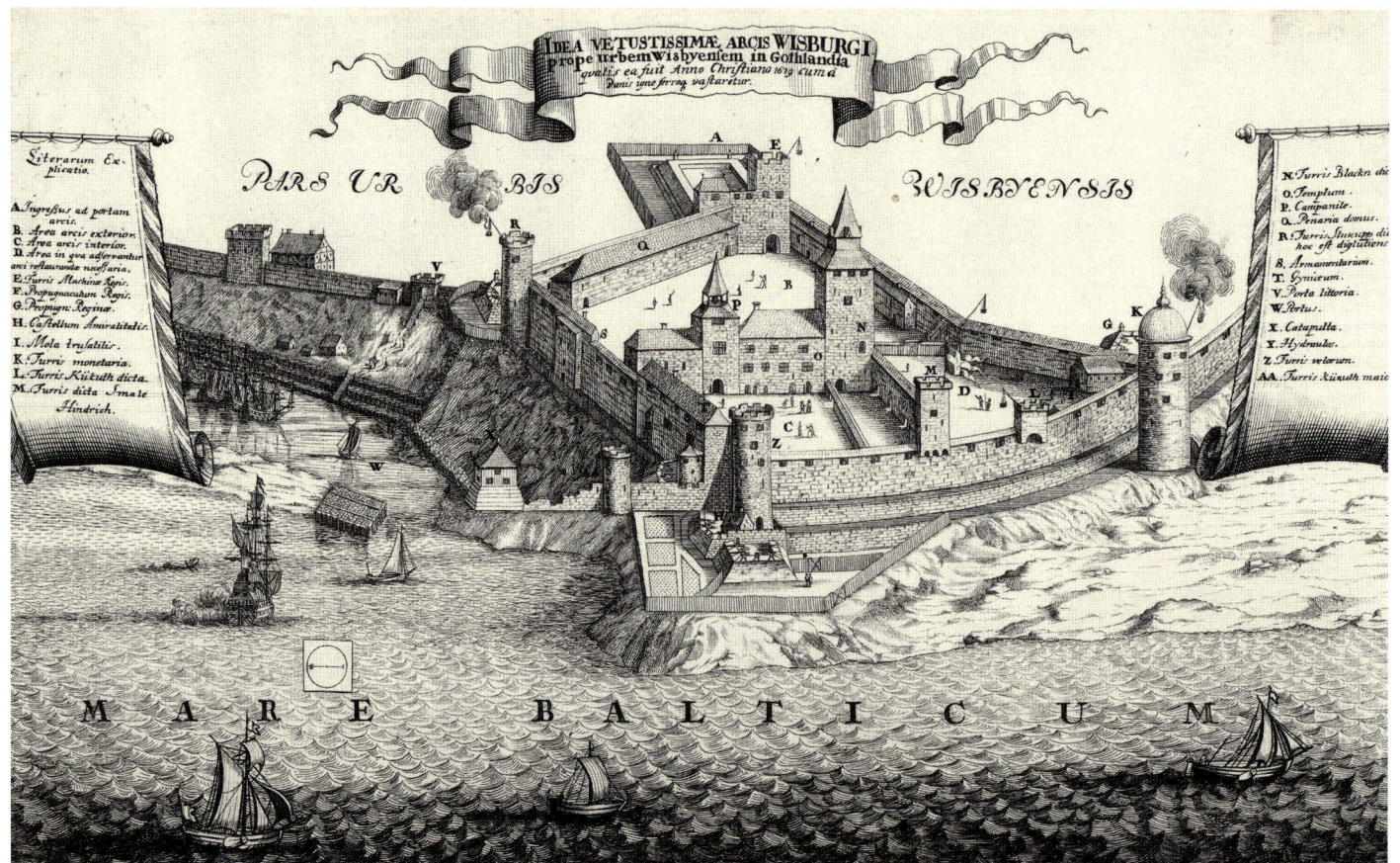

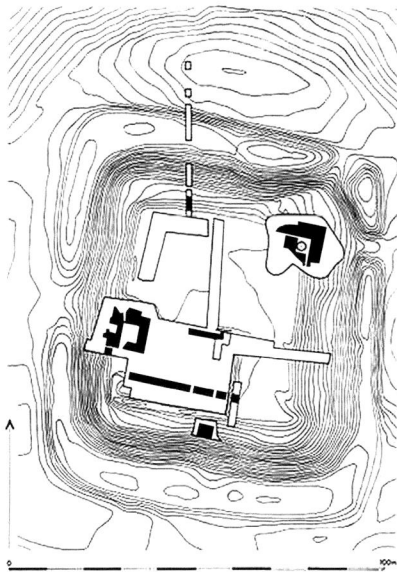

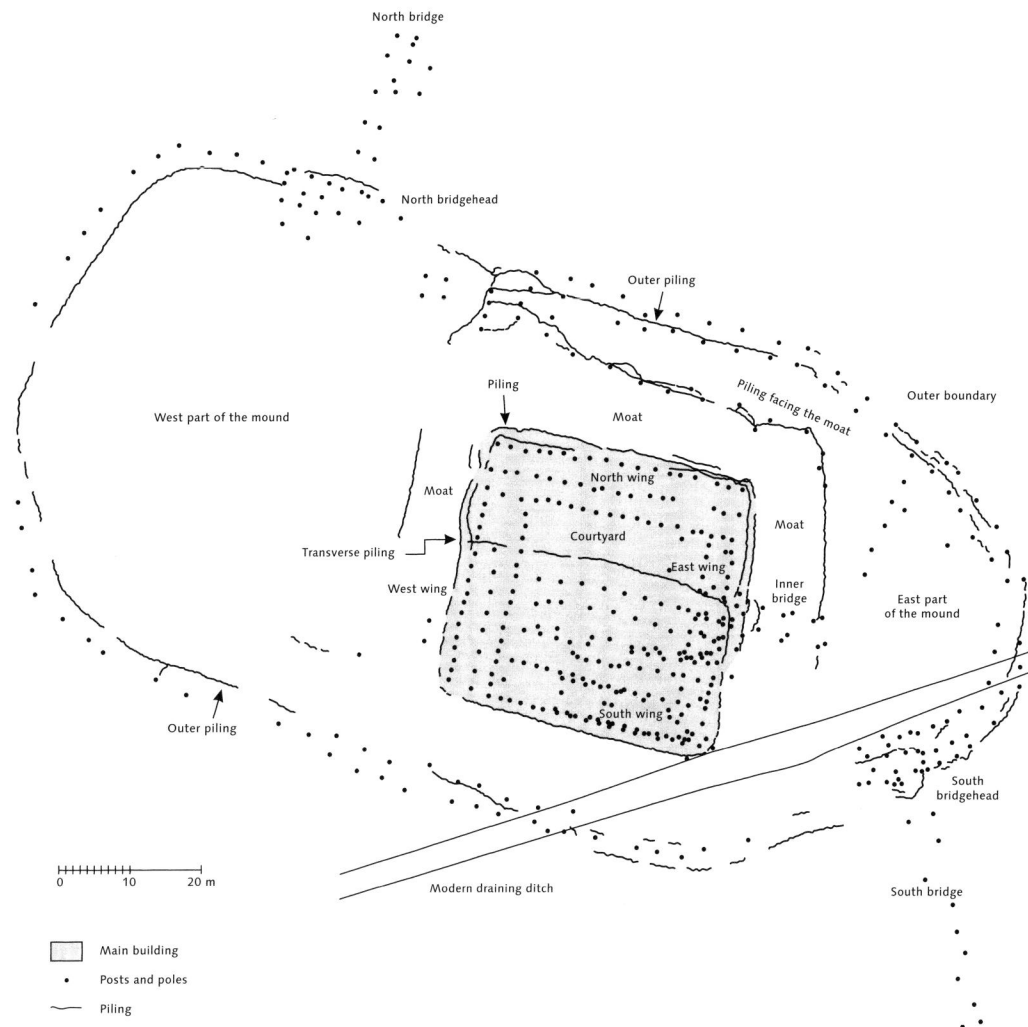

LINDHOLM *was one of Scania's strongest castles. It was here that the Swedish King Albrecht of Mecklenburg and his son Erik were imprisoned for a number of years after Queen Margrete had won the battle at Åsle in 1389.*

BORINGHOLM, *not far from Horsens, was still in use around 1400. With its wooden buildings on the low island in the marsh the estate may not look impressive, but abundant finds from the site are evidence of everyday life in the upper social layers at that time.*

tivity for six years in Lindholm Castle on Lake Børringesø in southeast Scania. This was one of the important royal castles in that part of the country, and it must have been considered secure enough to hold such important state prisoners as the Mecklenburg father and son. They were not set free until 1395, after an agreement had been negotiated at a large meeting in the castle. Two years later Margrete managed to create the Kalmar Union, uniting the Nordic Countries under one king, her adopted son Erik.

The royal or national castles – both the old ones and the more recent ones – naturally retained their significance as the defence structures of the realm and its borders, as administrative centres and as the venues for important meetings, negotiations and celebrations. Margrete certainly kept the old royal castles in good order, and she ensured that she had control over the most important, e.g. the Scanian castles of Helsingborg, Skanør and Falsterbo, which she compelled the Hanseatic towns to deliver back in 1387 in accordance with their old agreement with her father. She did not build many new castles, however, and she relied so much on the Church that strong bishops' castles were allowed to persist, and sev-

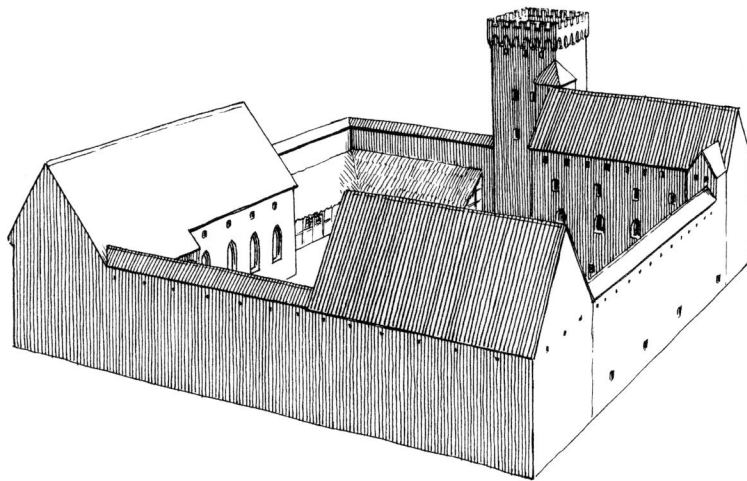

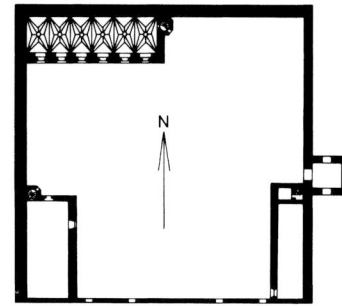

eral important national castles were mortgaged to bishops, e.g. Kalø, which the Bishop of Aarhus held until 1406.

Queen Margrete had inherited her father's fraught relationship with the Hanseatic towns, but she dealt with that by widespread use of piracy, organised by her representatives and other reliable henchmen, while she herself of course denounced it in negotiations with the towns. During the later years of her reign, and through the whole of Erik of Pomerania's, they worked by every possible means to win power over the Duchy of Schleswig. This was the last missing part needed to complete the reunification of the whole kingdom. Aabenraa in southern Jutland was given a new fortress, where Brundlund Castle is situated today, and Flensborg acquired a strong castle, later named Duborg. During the many battles in that part of the kingdom King Erik made use of rapidly constructed earthworks in the same way that Danish kings had done earlier in the Valdemar period in border struggles against opponents used to fighting over castles.

There were only two large and lasting constructions erected in the kingdoms by King Erik. One was Visborg in Visby on Gotland, where he himself lived for a decade or so, after he had been removed from the three Nordic thrones; the other was Krogen at Helsingør (Elsinore), which probably served as a replacement for the older Flynderborg, south of the town. It was from Krogen that it was possible to keep control, during several centuries, of the payment of the Øresund Toll by ships passing through the Sound – a system introduced by King Erik.

These new structures were strategically placed, like the old royal castles. Visborg and Krogen were curtain-wall constructions with straight stretches of wall and right-angled corners just like the 14th century castles, and Krogen was on the same scale as Kalø. This was the way the Teutonic Order built. They ruled over large areas of land, but always as conquerors and on military alert. The regularly-formed structures left their mark on the fortified buildings of the time.

The castle was not yet out-of-date as a resource of war, and through the rest of the Middle Ages it continued to be the seat of power. This can be seen for instance from the rules about when the castles of the realm should be at the disposal of the king, and when the King's Council should have power over them. Among the many factors that contributed to Erik of Pomerania being deposed as king was his attempt to secure castle-rights for his cousin Bugislav, whom he wished

Erik of Pomerania set up the Øresund Toll system, and to make sure that the toll was paid by all the ships that sailed through Øresund he built a castle, **KROGEN,** *on the coast, where the town of Helsingør (Elsinore) grew up. Krogen was a curtain-wall castle with buildings along the wall, which still today provide the framework around* **KRONBORG CASTLE.** *King Erik's castle may have looked like this reconstruction drawing, but the details are not known.*

In one of the rooms in **KROGEN** *there is a round window with a frame decorated with a number of mural paintings of coats of arms placed around that of Christ. To the left and right are the arms of King Erik and Queen Philippa, and others belong to bishops. It is not clear what the painting was meant to signify, but it was painted between 1421 and 1429.*

to succeed him on the throne. The King's Council was against this. Bugislav was not in the royal line of descent.

The Crown did not have a great need for castles within the kingdom when there was no war. The majority of the royal lands had always been administered from unfortified royal estates, and gradually more of these royal properties which were only lightly fortified, or not at all, appeared again. Ørum in Thy is an example of this, and Tordrup near Randers is another. Jutland in general had apparently not had many royal strongholds before the 14th century, and evidently the same was the case in the late Middle Ages, except in the area near the border with the Duchy of Schleswig. Haraldsborg near Roskilde is mentioned as an estate when it was destroyed during the civil war known as *Grevens Fejde* in the 1530s, and there is nothing to indicate that Jægerspris, the former Abrahamstrup, had defence features. Hagestedgård at any rate did not, and nor did the royal property in Grenå.

The peaceful functions of castles, and the power of the nobility

National policy-making continued to be formulated in the royal properties and especially in the royal castles. It was there that foreign ambassadors were received and important negotiations were conducted. Throughout the Middle Ages monarchs ruled the kingdom while travelling around; they were still elected and acclaimed in the *landsthing* for each part of the country, and all decrees were issued, if in rather uniform versions, in a specific edition for each *"land"*. On their journeys through the kingdom the monarchs tended more and more to stay in the large castles which could accommodate the growing court, and it was there that they lived and died. This also applied to the members of the most powerful families in the country, who held positions as the king's representatives in the most important Crown castles. They held onto those positions just as determinedly as the mortgage-holders had under Erik Menved and Christoffer II. The perpetual lack of royal funds also led, in the 15th century, to mortgaging of royal properties, on terms that were just as harsh as in earlier times. The noblemen who lived with their families in the royal castles had all the military security they could have wished at Crown expense, and therefore had no reason to fortify their own properties. In addition, there was peace in Denmark almost all the time. The battles to keep the Union together took place in Sweden.

JÆGERSPRIS *was called* **ABRAHAMSTRUP** *in the Middle Ages. It belonged to the Crown. The tall building in the middle is a late medieval brick house – rebuilt and changed, of course. The site has never been fortified. Seen from the north.*

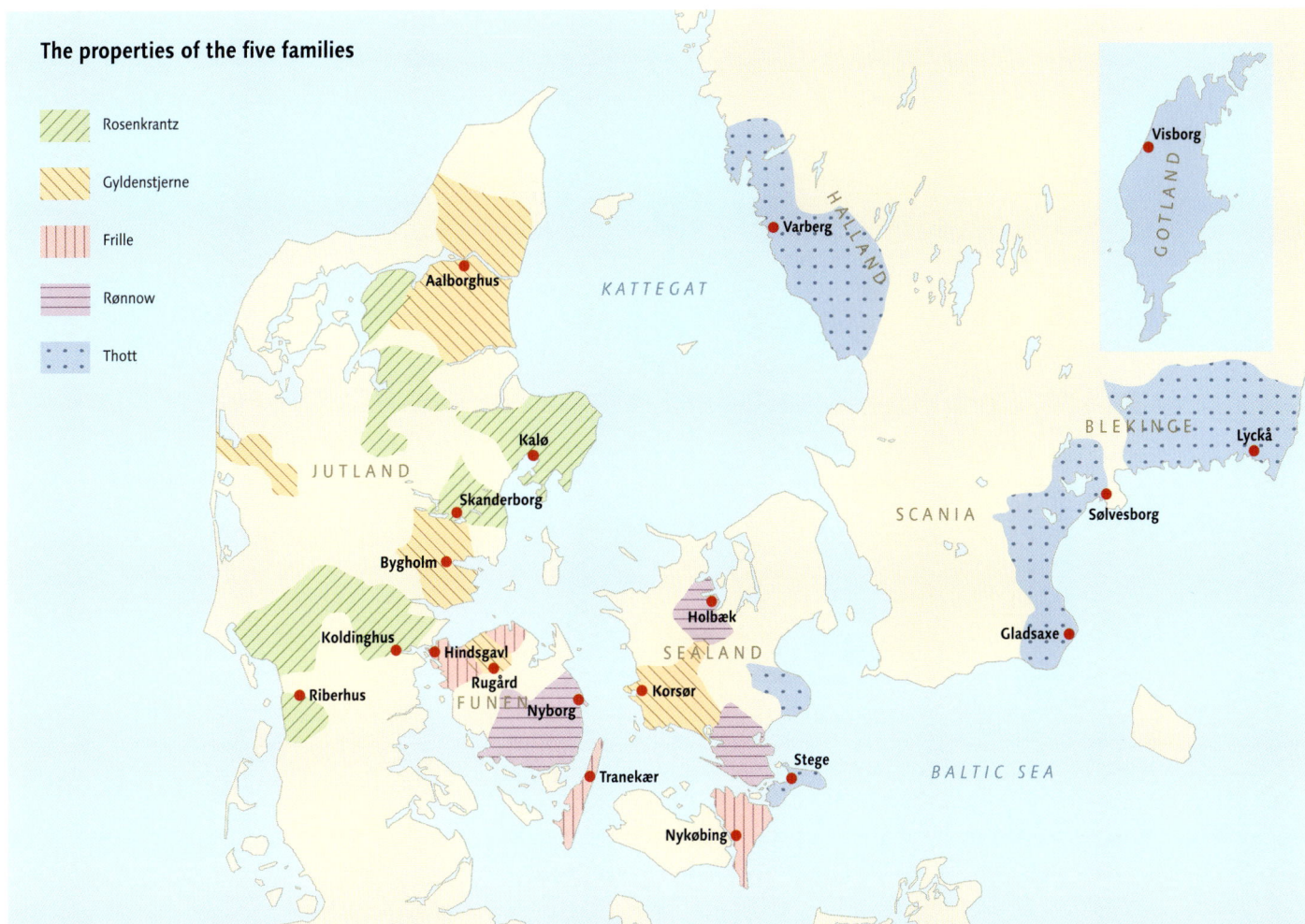

The properties of the five families

- Rosenkrantz
- Gyldenstjerne
- Frille
- Rønnow
- Thott

GOTLAND — Visborg

KATTEGAT

HALLAND — Varberg

Aalborghus

JUTLAND

Kalø

Skanderborg

Bygholm

BLEKINGE — Lyckå

SCANIA

Sølvesborg

Koldinghus

Hindsgavl

Rugård

FUNEN

Riberhus

Nyborg

Holbæk

SEALAND

Korsør

Gladsaxe

Tranekær

Stege

BALTIC SEA

Nykøbing

THE FIVE FAMILIES *Map of the areas controlled by the Rosenkrantz, Gyldenstjerne, Frille, Rønnow and Thott families in the second half of the 15th century. From Harry Christensen:* Len og magt i Danmark i 1439-81. *Aarhus 1983.*

In time there came to be five families, all of them closely linked to each other, who had possession of many of the important castles in the kingdom, and of large segments of royal properties, and who occupied these estates on conditions that included virtual inheritance rights. These were families such as the Rosenkrantz and Gyldenstjerne families, who were figureheads of the country's nobility for so many years that they even featured in Shakespeare's "Hamlet". Anyone with a slight knowledge of Denmark in Shakespeare's day would have known that they were important people and had been so for a considerable time. By collecting mortgaged Crown land around their own properties these families ended up controlling huge areas of land, but the kingdom did not fall apart, as had happened in the previous century, even though in the course of the 15th century royal authority could largely only be exercised with the assent of the aristocracy. They assured payment of the necessary taxes and provided the active military service that was necessary if the king was to rule.

Even though King or Crown might be weak, central authority was solid. The

HALKÆR or HEDEGAARD in Jutland is more a farm site than a castle. Only the situation, low in a stretch of marshy meadow, provided protection for the buildings. The farm was inhabited around 1400 and was very old-fashioned, with a central fireplace in one of the wings.

On Claus Berg's altarpiece from c.1520 in St Knud's Church in Odense KING HANS looks very pious, but it is not certain that the figure was a faithful likeness. Photo Danish National Museum.

major landowners determined the policy of the kingdom and administered Crown property. They were the central authority. As long as the King worked with the Council there was peace in the kingdom, and when the Council was united it was difficult for the King to adopt a different and independent policy. And yet this happened from time to time. The Council was not permanently in session, and in many cases disagreement gave way to common interests pursued by both King and Council. They agreed about the need to preserve the Nordic Union, the Kalmar Union, which Margrete had created in 1397, and the King was indispensable as the military commander of the realm. Nor could he be overlooked as the chief enforcer of the law. Successive kings naturally sought to reduce the influence of the Council and to increase their own power, for instance by appointing as representatives people who were dependent on the estates in their care, but throughout the rest of the Middle Ages the powerful men who were on the Council were so firmly entrenched in authority that in case of conflict it was the King who got the worst of it. For this reason among others, both Erik of Pomerania and Christian II were deposed, in 1439 and 1523 respectively, and Frederik I's rule was also to some extent dependent on the good will of the aristocracy.

It all worked as long as the Crown and the most powerful people in the land had the same objectives, and for a long time that was the case. Erik of Pomerania was succeeded on the throne by his nephew, Christoffer of Bavaria. When he died childless in 1448, Count Christian of Oldenburg became Denmark's king. By this time the male descendants of the old royal house had become few and far between. In Christoffer's time a provisional form of order was established in

On a mural painting from c.1500 in BIRKET CHURCH on Lolland one finds mercenaries wearing armour, walking along with their weapons in their hands. This was how the Danish army were equipped to fight in Sweden during the wars of unification, and this was what mercenaries looked like when they went to war in Denmark during Grevens Fejde, the Count's War.

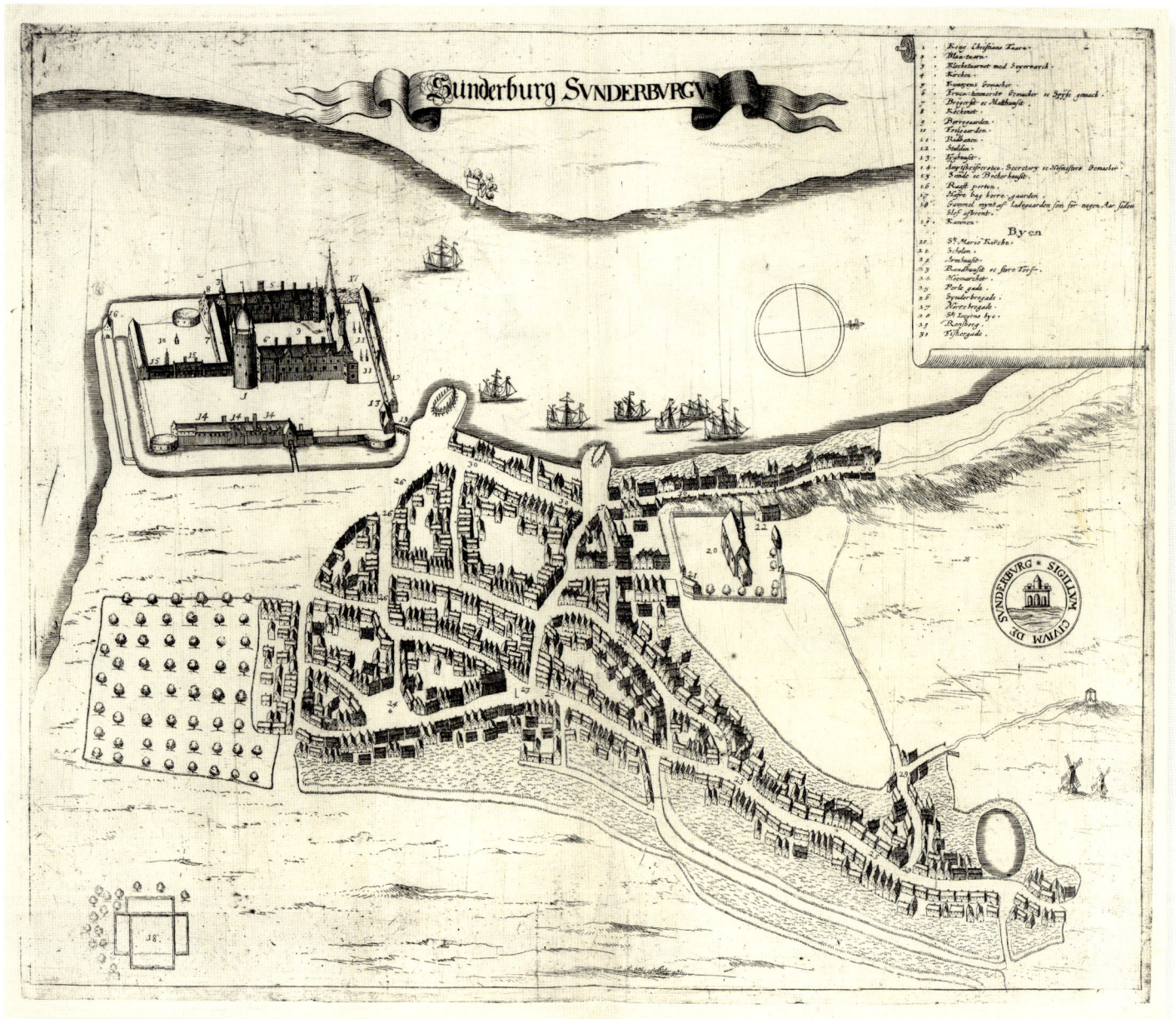

relations with Schleswig/Southern Jutland, but it became more and more difficult to keep the Nordic Union intact. Erik of Pomerania had achieved that for 40
years, and it still functioned under Christoffer, but from the early days of his reign
there was grumbling from Sweden about Denmark being the leading nation, and
about dominant Danish influence in the other countries. Access to the holding
of entailed Swedish estates meant increased influence and significantly enlarged
incomes for the Danish aristocrats. This was not welcomed either by the Swedish
aristocrats or the people of the country, and it led to unrest and stubborn opposi-

On Resen's engraving of **SØNDERBORG** *from c.1670 both the town and the castle can be seen. As in Skanderborg, the town developed to a great extent to service the many people in the castle. Alone among the Crown castles* **SØNDERBORG** *was provided with a rampart with robust round towers for cannons before* Grevens Fejde, *the Count's War.*

tion to the Danes. Many hard battles were fought on open fields in Sweden and there were sieges and skirmishes around castles and towns, but in Denmark there was peace apart from an uprising in northern Jutland in 1441. This caused damage to some of the properties owned by aristocratic landowners, but Christoffer of Bavaria quelled the revolt, and the long period of peace became decisive for the role of the castle in the kingdom.

Some of the royal castles ceased to be fortresses, while others lost their significance because of administrative reorganisations, such as when the estates of Søborg and Gurre were taken over by Krogen, in Elsinore. The old royal castles continued to function, but apart from Sønderborg, where the deposed Christian II lived for a while, after 1530, as a prisoner of the state, the castles were not modernised. That proved to be unfortunate, since social and religious unrest flared up into the war that is called *Grevens Fejde,* and that raged in the kingdom from 1534 to 1536. It was also connected with problems over the succession.

Stormy weather ahead

From the 1520s onwards the internal problems in Denmark grew. The incessant wars with Sweden had burdened the population economically, and the rich Catholic Church was increasingly accused of misusing its power and resources. The ideas behind the Lutheran Reformation, which were spreading abroad and leading to bitter conflicts, reached Denmark as well. They even spread within the Danish Church, which broke away from the papacy and became a national institution; in reality it had almost always been so in practical terms. There was much resentment in the population against the mendicant friars, who had already been driven out as early as in the time of Frederik I, but monarchy and church were also in conflict about authority over the monasteries and their revenues.

In Denmark at that time there was only one man who built new castles on his own land in order to protect himself against his enemies within the country. That was the Bishop of Viborg, Jørgen Friis. He was a strong opponent of Lutheran ideas and thus in dispute with his fellow clergymen, the monarchy and the people in his diocese. Things went so badly that he could not go out in public in his own cathedral city of Viborg. In order to protect himself against his enemies he commissioned fortifications on the model of the old familiar ones, but using new methods. In the 1520s he built the large castles at Hald near Viborg and at Spøttrup in Salling.

At both those sites houses of stone and brick were built within the castle area, and there were gate towers, wall-walks, drawbridges, etc. The location was also part of the defence-measures. Hald was situated in a lake, and is now a ruin, but still has its immense ramparts to hide behind. Spøttrup still stands as a monument to the years when the techniques of warfare changed because of new weapons.

(continued on page 198)

JØRGEN FRIIS' CASTLES

HALD

In the lake to the east of the grounds of the present-day manor-house of Hald, some 10 kilometres from Viborg, lie the ruins of the strong fortress that the Bishop of Viborg, Jørgen Friis, built in the 1520s to protect himself against attack both from the King's forces and from the local population of Viborg. It was a very up-to-date construction with massive ramparts designed for defence against guns, but the Bishop's castle did not manage to withstand attack by the Viborg citizens during the unrest stirred up in the civil war of 1534-36. After the Reformation Hald became Crown property, and later it became privately owned. The castle fell into decay in the 17th century, was demolished in the 18th, and new buildings were then erected on other sites in the area. The present building is the fifth version of Hald and is from c.1787; it was originally the gate-house of the fourth Hald.

In the lake at the outer edge of the Bishop's Hald a number of stout vertical poles have been found, hammered in close to each other. They can be interpreted as reinforcement of the edge of the shore on the peninsula on which the fortress stands, but they have been dendrochronologically dated to 1423, and so are significantly older than Jørgen Friis's fortress. Perhaps they should be seen in connection with a dam at a nearby water-mill, Non Mølle, which raised the water level in the lake at Hald, but that does not explain why the shores of the peninsula would need protection. Viborg's bishops at that time would hardly have built castles – that was banned after 1396 – and Niels Bugge's Hald had been transferred to the diocese on condition that the fortifications were demolished, but then what was it that was on the peninsula?

New finds often raise new questions.

SPØTTRUP

Spøttrup is surrounded by low marshy areas and on the entrance side it is protected by a lake in such a way that access to the castle is only possible from a narrow road between the moat and the lake, and it was difficult to get close to the castle from any direction with heavy artillery. It was the immense ramparts, however, that made both Spøttrup and Hald something special and something new.

They were meant as protection against cannon-fire. Earth ramparts can absorb cannon-balls without suffering immediate major damage, whereas masonry is shaken into pieces. And that happens also in situations where heavy artillery is placed on the top of towers or curtain walls, and with the new weapons the old principles of defence from a height were abandoned; it was no longer so important to aim and fire down on

Jørgen Friis, Bishop of Viborg, was a modern man who was familiar with the art of warfare of his time. His two castles, **HALD** *and* **SPØTTRUP,** *were the most modern in Denmark in the early 16th century. Both locations had the best form of protection against cannonballs – immense earth ramparts.*

The ramparts at **HALD** *still contain the ruins of walls and cellars.*

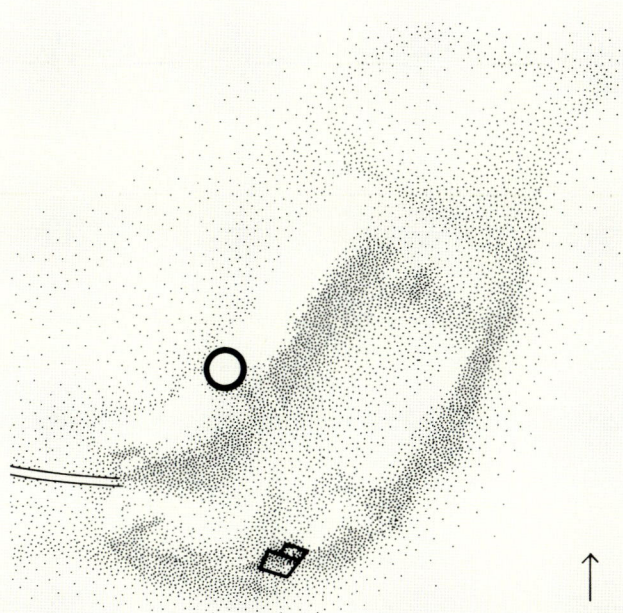

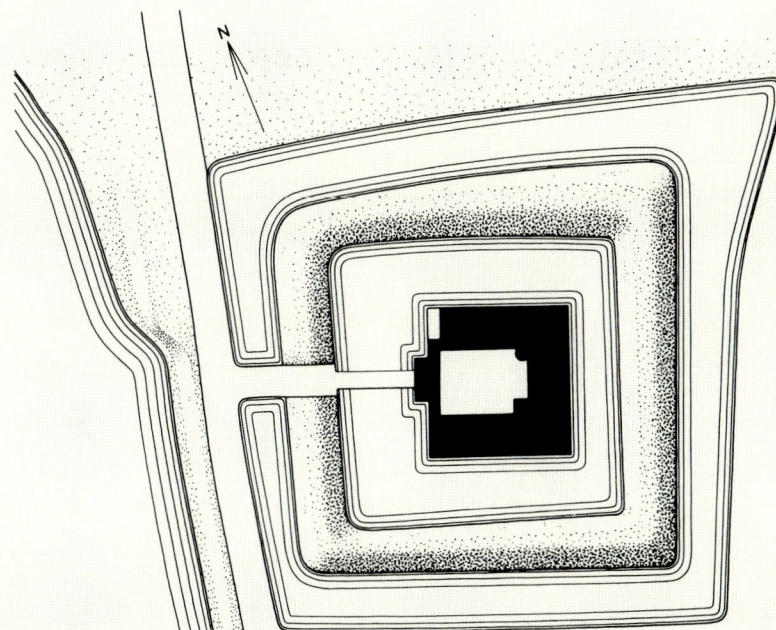

the enemy. With cannons attack and defence were mostly carried out on a horizontal level. Hence the ramparts, and hence the absence of crenellations and embrasures or machicolations on the upper parts of Spøttrup's walls, which hardly rise above the ramparts. But there is plenty of space for a garrison in the attics, and eight of the castle's nine garderobe shafts go up to the upper storey.

The entrance side with its gatehouse and drawbridge is more traditionally designed. There may have been wall-walks on the gables and on the connecting wall, since from there one could overlook the enemy, who would have to approach in a thin column up the narrow road in front of the castle, so that it would be easy for the defenders to pick off the attackers one by one with gunshots or crossbow fire and to reduce the attackers' artillery to smithereens using guns on the ramparts.

With the Reformation Spøttrup came into the Crown's hands and later it came to have a succession of private owners until the state purchased it in 1937. Since 1941 the castle has been open to the public.

SPØTTRUP *was a serious fortification and could house a large contingent of defenders in its loft storey. Eight of the castle's nine lavatory shafts led down from the loft. There may well have been a foul smell from the moat on a warm summer day. The east wing.*

SPØTTRUP *was hidden away behind its ramparts. The castle buildings were entirely medieval and only equipped with fortifications in the gateway and in the connecting wall between the gate and the main buildings. All the strength of the castle lay in its ramparts and the cannons on them. The gate is to the west.*

Firearms had been known in Europe from the 14th century, but the earliest types could not cause much damage. From the 15th century onwards instructions on the use of guns are to be found in books on warfare, weapons and methods of attack. Much is also made in those books of the production of gunpowder, and firearms then began to have significance. Cannons were made in several places; the Duke of Burgundy, for instance, had a major production, and when the Turks attacked Byzantium in 1453 the city fell after a week of bombardment of the city wall from a gigantic cannon.

In Denmark there are reports of the Hanseatics having cannons on their ships in the wars against Valdemar Atterdag. Cannons were also said to have been used in the battle at St Jørgensbjerg in Thy in 1441, when Christoffer of Bavaria defeated the uprising, and this may well be true. At any rate he had in his service a specialist in the science of warfare and guns, Johannes Bengedans, and in the Court household accounts of Copenhagen Castle from 1447 there is an item of expenditure for 32 pick hammers "with which to shape stones for cannons". Bengedans, who had previously also advised Erik of Pomerania, wrote a book on

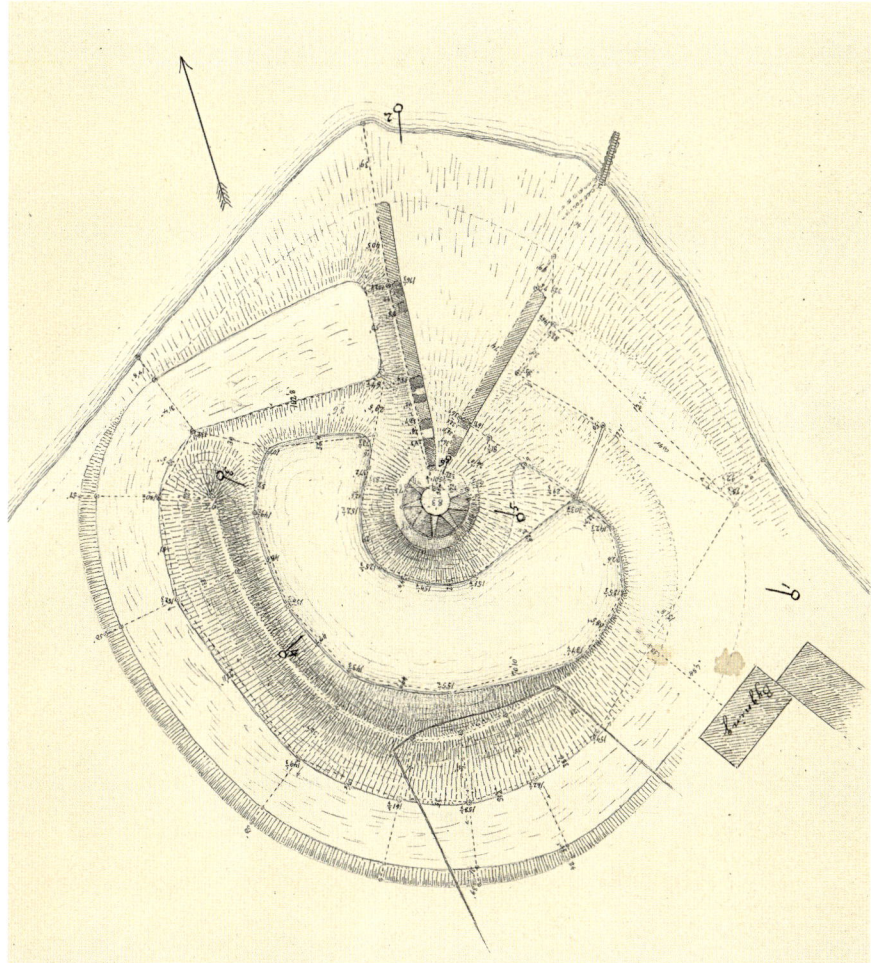

*King Hans's fortified ship wharf, **ENGELBORG** on Slotø in Nakskov Fjord, was constructed around 1510. Its location was ideal for a ship wharf, in that there was deep water just close to it, but not many ships were built there. Until 1523 this was the administrative centre for West Lolland. In 1534 it was conquered by forces from Lübeck, and subsequently burned by the local people, but the ruins are still impressive. Drawing in the Danish National Museum.*

warfare and guns which describes in detail what the new weapons could do; today it is difficult to form a clear concept of how much those weapons meant for war in the Nordic region in those days. In the reigns of later kings their importance became apparent.

In the course of the first decades of the 16th century guns became more dangerous because people learned how to clean the powder, giving it greater explosive power, and then the defences had to adapt accordingly. This development happened further afield in Europe and took off at the same time that the religious wars were raging. Jørgen Friis, who was a well-travelled man, may have seen the new types of defence-works and brought the model home to Denmark. By European standards his castles were rather primitive, but they were ahead of the style of other fortifications in Denmark, included the royal ones. Only at Sønderborg were the defences strengthened by a rampart with circular gun towers at the corners, while in Copenhagen a rampart was constructed behind the town wall.

King Hans's fortified ship wharf at Slotø in Nakskov fjord, from 1509, was constructed purely in line with medieval principles and did not withstand attack

Important castles c.1500

1. Abrahamstrup (Jægerspris)
2. Bygholm
3. Dragsholm
4. Duborg
5. Falsterbo
6. Gjorslev
7. Glimmingehus
8. Gottorp
9. Gurre
10. Haderslevhus
11. Hald
12. Hammershus
13. Helsingborg
14. Hindsgavl
15. Jungshoved
16. Kalundborg
17. Kalø
18. Koldinghus
19. Korsør
20. Krogen
21. Copenhagen
22. Laholm
23. Lyckå
24. Møgeltønderhus
25. Nordborg
26. Nyborg
27. Nykøbing F.
28. Næsbyhoved
29. Ravnsborg
30. Riberhus
31. Skanderborg
32. Skjoldnæs
33. Solvig
34. Spøttrup
35. Stege
36. Søborg
37. Sølvesborg
38. Sønderborg
39. Tranekær
40. Tønderhus
41. Varberg
42. Visborg
43. Vordingborg
44. Ørkil
45. Aalborghus
46. Aalholm

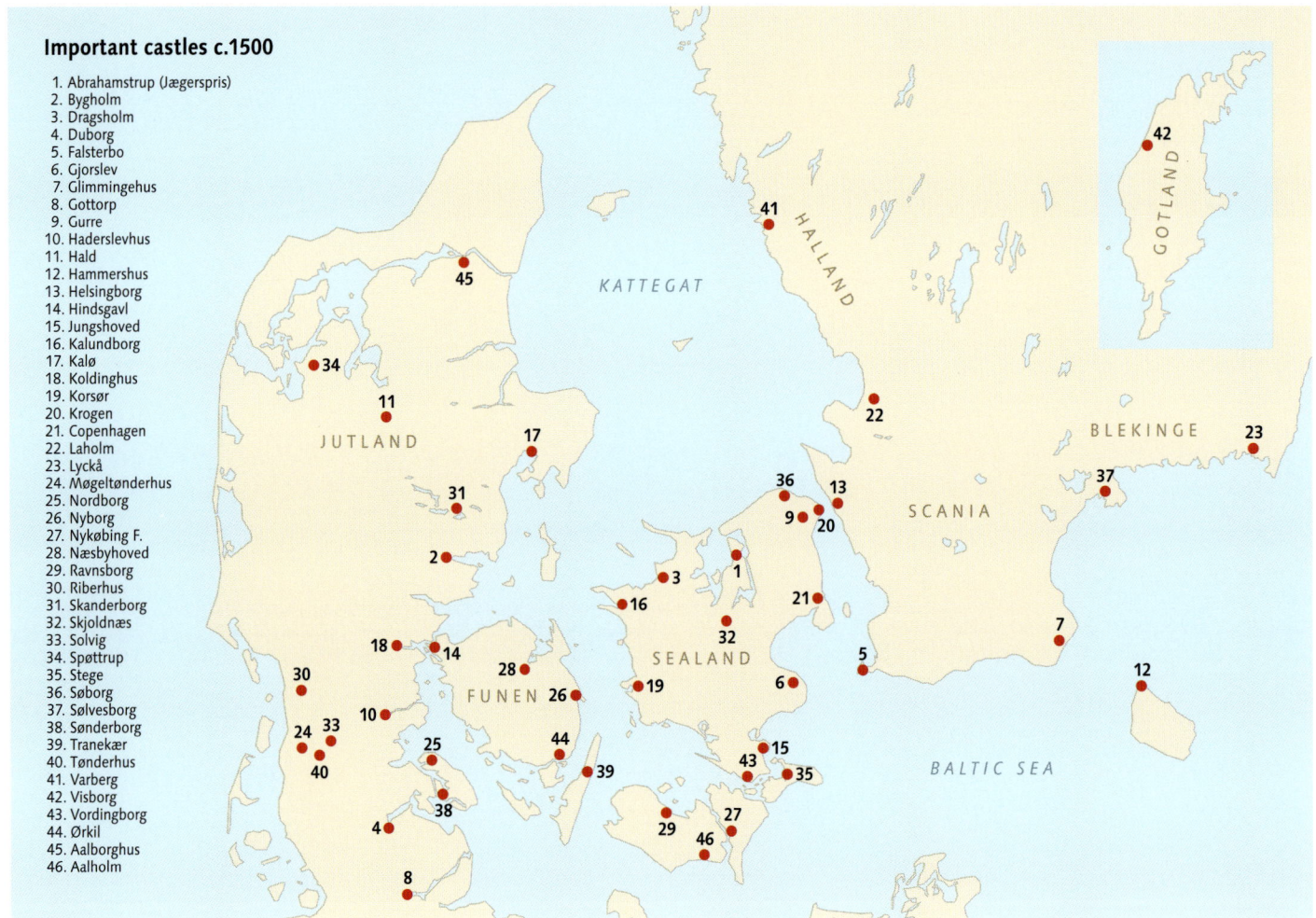

from Lübeck forces in 1534. The other fortifications in the kingdom were as far as is known merely medieval. There had not been a need for anything more for over a hundred years.

Map of the **IMPORTANT CASTLES IN DEN-MARK** *c.1500. Their placing shows the location of the centre of gravity of the kingdom.*

The Civil War (*Grevens Fejde* – "The Count's War")

But in 1534 all hell broke out in Denmark. When Frederik I died, the State Council could not agree on the choice of his eldest son, Christian, as king. He was a publicly committed Lutheran and a person of strong will, so the Catholic State Council preferred his younger brother, Hans, still a child, who could be brought up Catholic to be an obedient instrument of the Council. While the issue dragged on at length unrest broke out among the population, and foreign interests became involved in the case, rapidly leading to armed conflict in many places; none of the belligerents was able to win the whole kingdom, and the State Council was not able to bring the war to an end. There were many horses to back, and the warring

Attack on a town with cannons. The attackers manoeuvre a siege tower forward so that they can be at the same height as the wall, and they scale it with siege ladders. Jean de Wavrin, the conquest of Ribedane in 1475. Chronique d'Angleterre vol. III. British Library IV page Folio no. f. 281 v.

parties had very diverse motives, some of which changed in the course of time. Religious attitudes and hatred against oppressors became mixed into the people's uprisings in towns and rural areas. Lübeck stirred up the muddied waters for its own ends and sent Count Christoffer of Oldenborg with troops and a fleet, hoping to gain the throne back for Christian II.

This gave the war its name, *"Grevens Fejde"*, the Count's War.

Count Christoffer lost no time in winning power in Eastern Denmark, but never did so in Jutland, where rebellious forces were dominant in the population and in fact won the upper hand against the nobility's array of forces in the battle at Svenstrup, south of Aalborg, on 16 October 1534. The balance of power shifted frequently, however, and the various warring forces never formed a united front for a common goal. The Count's troops burned down the bishops' estates and the royal properties on Sealand, Svendborg's townspeople ravaged the estates of the major landowners in that part of Funen, Stege's inhabitants besieged the castle there and pulled it down "the same day", Skipper Clement and his band stole horses and other things in Northern Jutland, and it is said that he attacked Spøttrup. Mistress Anne Meinstorp was killed by a mob at Sealand's *Landsthing* in Ringsted, while her two nieces managed by the skin of their teeth to escape up into the town's church tower. These were hard times indeed, and tradition has it that the enemy's guns and the unruly masses finished off the castles in the country because they were out-of-date.

That is true enough, but only up to a point. The castles of the nobility were few in number, and only very few of them were in fact attacked. The rebellious peasants and townspeople did not attack the property of the nobility systematically, but they ravaged bishops' estates and unpopular noblemen's houses. Others were left undisturbed. For instance Mogens Gøye, who was the wealthiest of all and owned vast estates over the whole country, suffered no damage to his own property or to any of those he held on behalf of the Crown.

If one tries to follow the course of the battles as closely as possible, from the written sources, one can see that cannons actually are only seldom mentioned.

HELSINGBORG *and its castle was among the many towns in the world that the geographers Braunius and Hogenberg depicted. This is a section of a picture from 1589. There is still life in the castle and many of the buildings around it, but decay has set in and trees are growing in some of the towers in the castle courtyard.*

Christian III's castles and buildings

1. Koldinghus
2. Copenhagen
3. Landskrona
4. Malmø
5. Nyborg
6. Randers town
7. Riberhus
8. Sønderborg
9. Aalborg

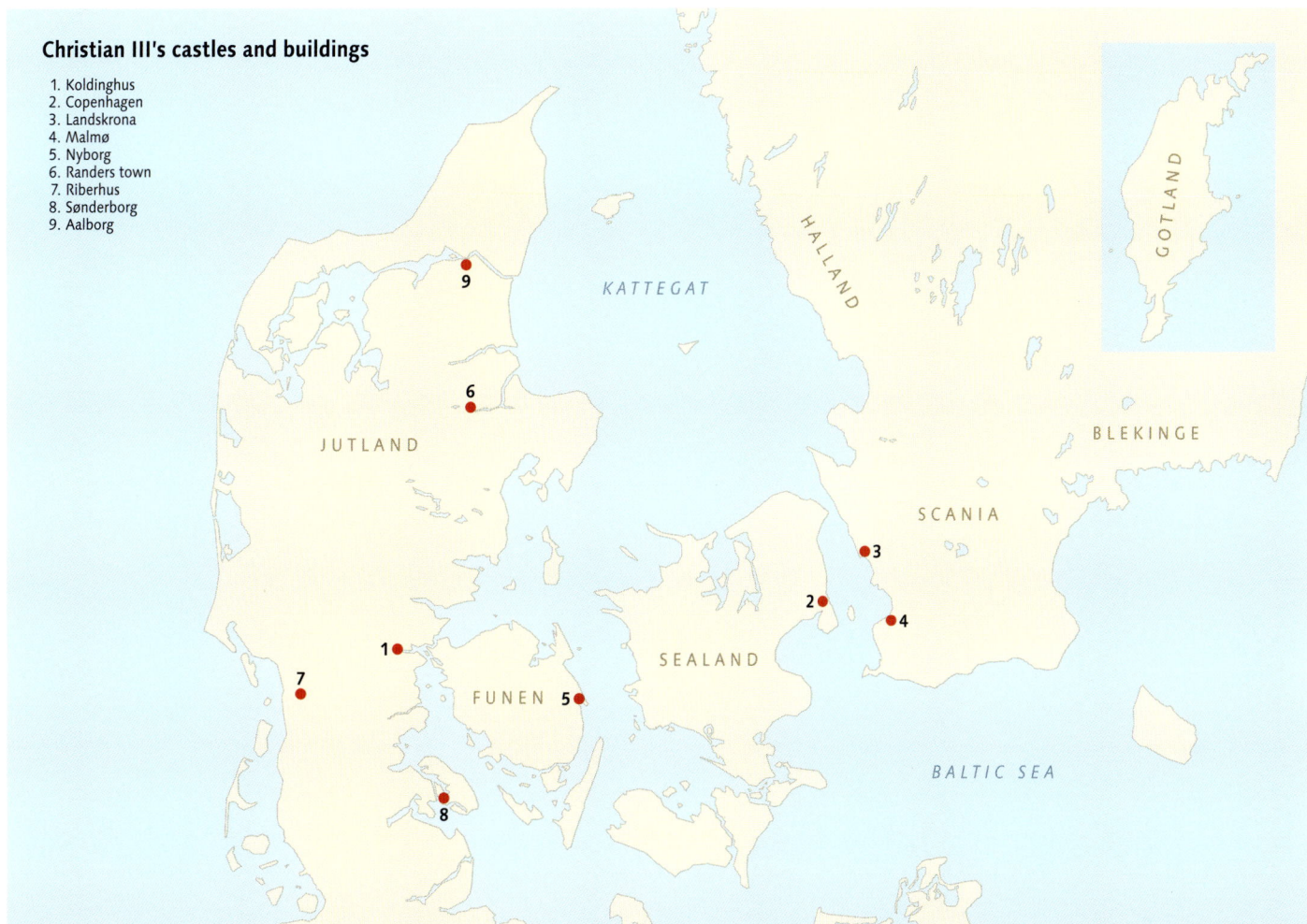

Map with **CHRISTIAN III'S CASTLES.** *A new era had arrived when Christian III needed to fortify his kingdom after* Grevens Fejde, *the Count's War. Not so many structures were needed, and it was also more costly than ever to build. The old Crown castles still functioned for a long time to come as administrative centres, but their fortifications fell into disrepair.*

Nonetheless there is evidence that Søholm in Southern Sealand, which belonged to Sealand's commanding officer, Anders Bille, was fired at by the Count's troops; however, many of the accounts of surrender and conquest of even important royal castles sound somewhat like games of "cops and robbers". Tyge Krabbe, the Lord High Constable, surrendered Tranekær on Langeland just because he heard that the enemy had cannons with them – a rumour that turned out to be false. Korsør Castle was opened up for some citizens who pretended to be horse-traders, and even Varberg, the strongest fortress in Halland, fell without a stroke of a sword to twenty untrained citizens who sneaked in via a garderobe shaft while the King's representative was preparing to go out riding. There are many other tales of this kind. They are perhaps not all equally close to the truth, but they give us an impression of the state of the nation's defences in general and of the strength of will to defend properties on the part of those responsible. On the other hand we do not gain from them much knowledge about how strong the castles were if they were properly manned and prepared for battle. That was the case, evidently, at

MALMØHUS *seen from the southwest. The large round towers on the corners of the castle housed the guns, and from there one could use flanking fire – shooting along the wall or rampart and covering the narrow access route in front of the castle so that the main body of the castle could be unprotected by ramparts. Remains of the old royal castle are still to be found in the large building at the side of the gate-tower, and there are evident marks in the masonry where the building has been extended. It was also modernised and given triangular bay windows, a new feature in 16th century building. The garrison was accommodated at the top of the building, where there were several stoves and small chambers. On the floors below there were two apartments, one for the king and one for the royal representative in the area.*

Plan of **MALMØHUS.** *There were stout ramparts around the castle area and passages between the round towers. Most of the cannons fired in low horizontal trajectories. This was why the ramparts were important.*

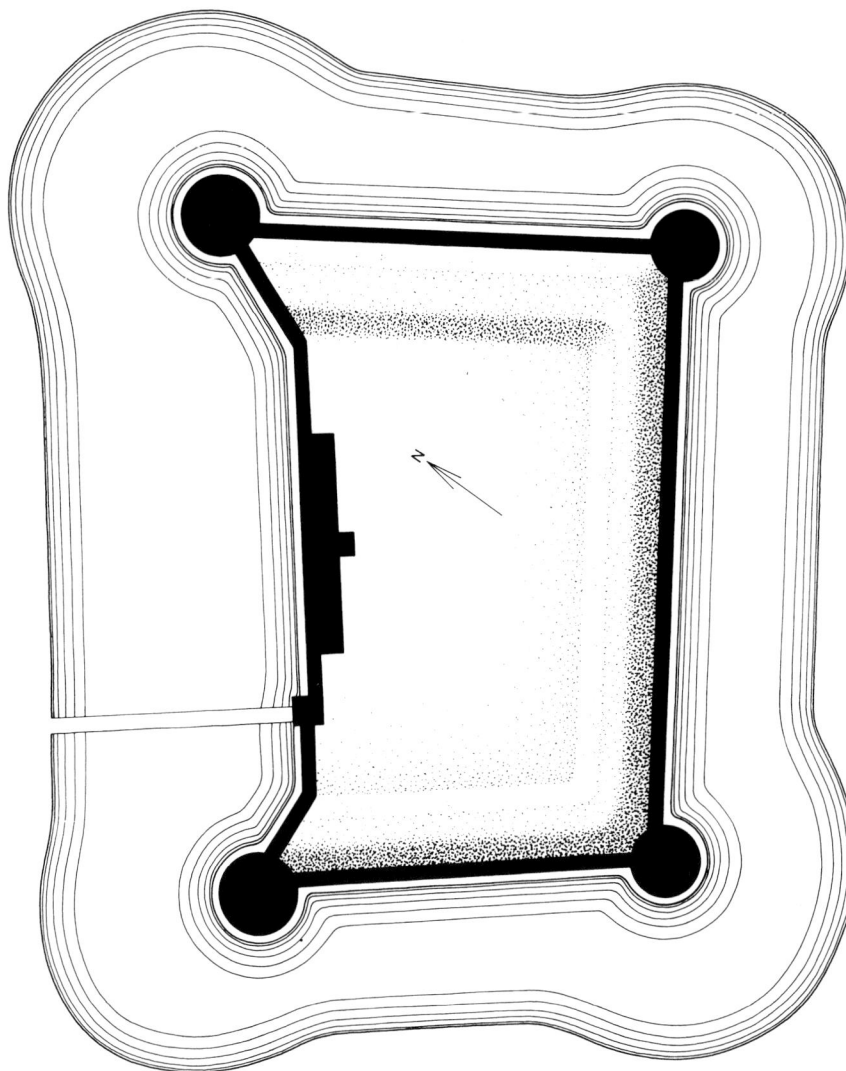

Helsingborg in Scania. The castle there was now the strongest in the country, and it held out throughout the whole war.

It was actually not just the castles of the realm that were out-of-date; the war itself was also an out-moded enterprise, until Christian III in 1534 agreed to become involved in it. When the Council had finally reached agreement on choosing him as king, he turned up with his military commander, Johan Rantzau, and a large body of mercenary troops with many modern cannons. With all of that he won the war, took the castles and ended up in a position to decide for himself on what conditions he would rule. The struggle between King, Church and nobility over power in the country ended with victory for the monarch, and this signalled the end of the Middle Ages in Denmark.

This was also the end of the medieval castle.

Christian III's castles

King Christian immediately set about building new fortresses that were modern and designed for defence against artillery. They were regular constructions – often square with gun towers at the corners of stout earthen ramparts, as can still be seen, for instance, at Malmøhus in Scania. This type of fortress had already served as the model for Spøttrup and Hald, and it was still in use elsewhere in Europe when castles on this pattern began to be built in Denmark after the civil war. They were constructed in accordance with all the contemporary rules of warfare, using foreign specialists as advisers. The costs were enormous. Although Christian III was wealthier than his predecessors, because most of the lands of the Church had been taken over by the Crown after the Reformation, the royal revenues were still insufficient to cover the fortress-building. At frequent intervals extra taxes had to be imposed so that the defence of the realm could be brought up to date, and the peasants' labour-duties were exploited more than ever before.

The niches for the cannons in the round towers were equipped in accordance with all the precepts of the time, with ventilation holes for gun-smoke.

*The living quarters at **MALMØHUS** seen from the courtyard. There are many evident traces of rebuilding.*

The new fortresses were fewer in number than the old royal castles, but they were strategically placed, as the old ones had been, near borders, coasts and roads. Some of them replaced or extended older structures, e.g. Nyborg, where the whole town was made into a huge fortress. Others were built where there had not been a castle before, e.g at Landskrona in Scania. In addition to being turned towards foreign foes, some of Christian III's buildings were also intended to be able to keep the domestic population at bay. Both in Malmø and in Aalborg the inhabitants had been particularly rebellious.

The old royal castles and estates continued to be administrative centres from which Crown property was managed and judicial authority was exercised. The obsolescent defence constructions were allowed to fall into disrepair, as did the living quarters that rapidly became outdated, resulting in the Crown representatives preferring to live in their own comfortable properties. This was what hap-

EGESKOV, *near Ringe in southern Funen, is a double building from the second half of the 16th century; it is covered in loopholes and machicolations with no practical significance. They just show that grand people lived in this splendid Renaissance dwelling – a monument to the nobility's idolisation, at that time, of the "good old days". Building adjoining houses as double or multiple houses was a known contemporary solution. It provided better space on each floor, and the breadth of each building was determined by the length of the available ceiling beams. The Swedish architect Hugo Zettervall restored Egeskov at the end of the 19th century, and now it resembles a French château manoir. Seen from the west.*

BORREBY *near Skælskør was built after 1556 by the chancellor of the realm, Johan Friis, who also built Hesselagergård on Funen. His buildings belong to the group of 16th century manor houses that flaunt sentry walks, loopholes and flanking towers so that they look like medieval castles, but are in fact built for prestige and status. Twenty years after Grevens Fejde, the Count's War, there was no danger of a peasant revolt, and in actual warfare the manor houses would not have served any functional purpose. Seen from the east.*

pened, for instance, at Kalø. There and in many other places the buildings were pulled down in the 17th century and the materials were re-used elsewhere.

This is why we know so little about how the living quarters were arranged in the old castles.

Castle-like manors and royal castles

Even the most powerful of the nobles and landowners could no longer have a military role to play, and none of them had the wherewithal to build modern fortresses. The nobility had also gained, however, from the Reformation. They had won some land back from the Church, and since the 16th century became a time of economic growth, they had increasing opportunities to build fine brick residences for themselves. A number of manor-houses from the 16th century look

NYBORG'S *west wing seen from the rampart. The sentry walk and the blind arch frieze are among the details that were also used in the construction of manor houses.*

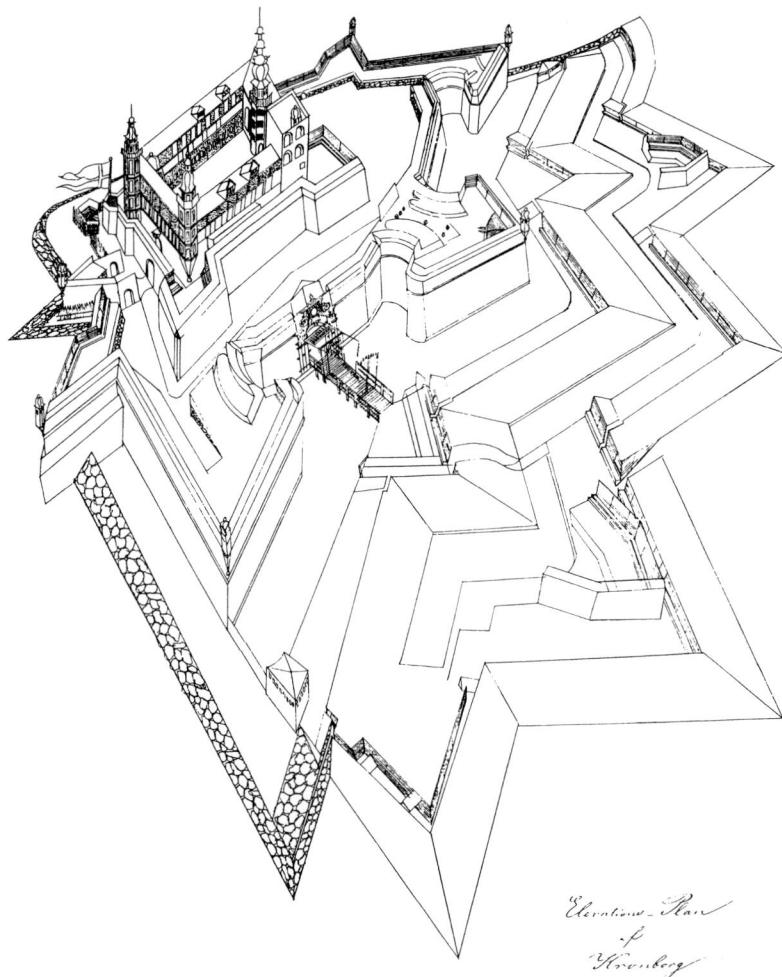

KRONBORG in all its glory, surrounded by its bastions, as they had evolved by around 1700. The original simple round towers at the corners had been overtaken by a complicated system of bastions based on consideration of all dead angles and aiming at total flanking coverage. Elevated plan from the beginning of the 18th century in the historic drawings archive of the Danish Engineer Corps.

The castle courtyard at **KRONBORG** looks demilitarised and peaceful. Gradually the living quarters and the defence functions became split up, and by the time of Christian IV Kronborg was a palace concealed within a fortress.

like castles. This is true not least of Borreby in Southern Sealand and Egeskov on Funen.

They have corbelled storeys, towers that give the impression of being designed to enable flanking fire, with in some cases actual sentry walks and real loopholes, but they were not meant to function in earnest. With their large regularly-positioned windows and living quarters in the "towers" these castle-like manors were not at all designed for defence, not even against rebellious peasants. There was no need to have fears on that account in the middle of the 16th century, when building began, for instance, on Egeskov – the example that most closely resembles a real castle. And there was absolutely no reason to have any such fears at the end of the century, when the house was completed.

The castle-like exteriors of the manor houses was intended to show, like their moats, that this was where the best families in the land lived – those who had the right to wear gold chains. The magnificent houses are monuments to their noble owners' dreams about the glorious past, when landowners had power over the king and had the right to fortify their properties.

The King also needed new residences. In some cases he installed them in the old castles, for instance at Koldinghus and Copenhagen, where the castle fortifications were not rebuilt. At Nyborg, where Christian III often stayed, new

fortifications were built. The old *palatium* from the 13th century was not part of the new fortification, however; it was protected by it. In the same way Krogen's successor, Kronborg, Denmark's most splendid royal castle from the Renaissance, lies in the shelter of its bastions, which became stronger and more extensive during the next century.

From now onwards it was the perimeter defences that formed the fortress. The two parts of the castle had been split off from each other and would never again be reunited.

VII

The castle in use

The castle and its owners

The castle or manor was above all the family's home, where all the family members belonged, even though as a rule provisions were made for the inheritance to go to one person, usually the eldest son. In Denmark this could be difficult to arrange, because all the children had inheritance rights, and because husband and wife each had their own property rights, but where there is a strong enough will there is often a way around laws and provisions. One could emphasize one's connection to a place by taking the name of it, and in the late Middle Ages in Denmark, as elsewhere, one could write "of" with the name of the family's main estate, whether one owned part of it or merely stayed there. That showed who one was, and that one was somebody. Actual family names were given to the nobility only after Frederik I's decree about this in 1526. Then the choice of name often fell on the emblem used in the coat of arms: Basse (a boar), Gyldenstjerne (a star), Rosenkrantz (roses) etc. Immigrant families like the Ahlefeldts, from Holstein, had brought their name with them, but titles were given up, because they were not used in Denmark. The Counts of Eberstein, for instance, became Albert Ludvigsen and Ludvig Albertsen, with Christian names and surnames like all the other landowners in the country. Some naturally used nicknames, Vendelbo, Svarteskåning, etc.

The landowners were proud of their names and of their homes. This is luminously clear, for instance, from the description by the historical chronicler Gerald of Wales of his beloved childhood home, the castle of Manorbier near Pembroke in Wales, from around 1200: [The castle has] "excellently well defended turrets and bulwarks, and is situated on the summit of a hill extending on the western side towards the seaport, having on the northern and southern sides a fine fishpond under its walls, as conspicuous for its grand appearance, as for the depth of its waters, and a beautiful orchard on the same side, enclosed on one part by a vineyard, and on the other by a wood, remarkable for the projection of its rocks, and the height of its hazel trees. On the right hand of the promontory, between the castle and the church, near the site of a very large lake and mill, a rivulet of never-failing water flows through a valley …"

As a child Gerald had had a favourite place, possibly up on the rampart, where he liked to sit and look out to right and left over all these alluring features.

*Window niche at **NYBORG** with geometric decoration – almost three-dimensional in effect – from Christian III's modernisation of the castle.*

Pembroke is a far cry from Denmark, where there are few rocks and in the Middle Ages there were no vineyards, but apart from that one could find everything else in the contemporary Danish constructions. They were also the context for a family's everyday life and the headquarters of a large agricultural enterprise, but towers and ramparts would only have been found on the largest of them. In Denmark it is not until considerably later that one can find written sources as to what the castles and manors looked like, how many people lived in them, and how they lived. The few accounts, deeds and wills that are preserved have to be inter-

Vaulted ceiling of the hall on the first floor of **BOLLERUP.** *It is now used as a cellar, because the level of the mound has been raised.*

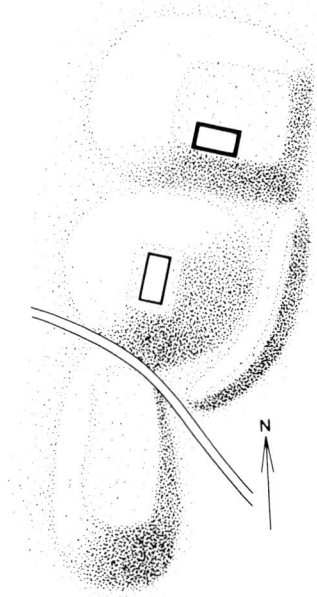

SKARSHOLM *near Jyderup was old Crown property and in the 14th century it belonged to the last male line of the royal house, but in 1369 there was evidently just a minor stone-built house on one of the mounds.*

CLAUSHOLM *near Hadsten is now a splendid baroque mansion, but in the 16th century, when Mogens Gøye's heirs had to divide up the estate, the main house, with an enclosed courtyard, stood on one islet and farm buildings on another. The whole area was split in two, but the two families that came to live there could not agree.*

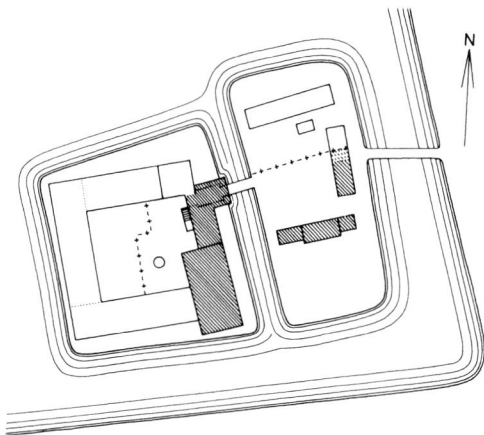

preted with care. They relate only to the uppermost layer of society, and words can have a different meaning from what we first believe; they may also change meaning within the same text. We have to use what we have, however, and keep making comparisons with what archaeology can tell us and with conditions established in other places. The medieval upper classes were often well-travelled and well-educated and thus familiar with conditions elsewhere; much of what they saw out in the world they would have tried to replicate when they were at home.

The documents relating to the inheritance of Skarsholm in 1369 concern a wealthy property, the home of a family in the highest social circles of the realm. The reigning king, Valdemar Atterdag, was an appropriate person to guarantee the validity of the inheritance rights, since the deceased owner of the property was a great-great-grandson of Valdemar the Victorious, like the King himself. The court sat in the castle, and negotiations were carried on in the presence of many good men as to how the estate of Herr Erik Barnumsen should be divided up between his widow and his children.

An exclusion from this division was the main house at Skarsholm with the part of the wood that had traditionally belonged to it. It was to go to the eldest son, Barnum, but on condition that the widowed Mistress Gertrud would keep the upper dwelling-room in the stone-built house, along with two guest houses in the eastern part; likewise, she would keep half of a section of kitchen garden with the adjacent apple orchard, together with a house between the kitchen and the lake, built for the benefit of "her and hers", for her use as long as she wanted. By Danish standards Skarsholm was a large private castle, worthy of its owner, and it included many buildings for various uses, as was the custom in the Middle Ages.

The castle-mound structure at the northern end of Skarresø Lake consists of two four-sided mounds with a moat between them and the remains of moats and ramparts around them. There was possibly a third mound south of the two others. In the course of excavations carried out around the year 1900 the remains came to light of buildings on both mounds; on the southern mound of the two there was a stone-built cellar, 13 x 6 m, which possibly belonged to the stone house that was divided up between the widow and the son in 1369. The question is then whether it was split by storey, with the "upper dwelling room" meaning the upper floor, or whether it was the "fine room" at one end of the house that was to be the widow's. Considering the size of the building one can reasonably surmise that it was the upper floor, and that there was probably an external gallery that gave access to the upper storey – as there was, for instance, at Spøttrup and at Tjele.

It was easy to divide a house in the way that this estate was settled. Each room or couple of rooms in a stone-built house of this type had its own function, just as each building did. There would have been at least one form of access from the outside to each storey in large buildings. Except, of course, in the case of fortified towers. They would only have had one entrance, at a high level, and they might be equipped with a staircase tower to link the floors internally, as for example at Kärnan in Helsingborg.

The sharing of a castle or manor between several households was very common. In Germany there are examples of family-held castles in which up to ten

families lived at a time, and there must have been problems for instance in relation to kitchen facilities. This type of communal living could also provide a wealth of opportunities for falling out and actual emnity, and that was the case at Mogens Gøye's Clausholm, near Randers. After his death in 1544 the castle was divided so carefully between two of his children that it almost seems as if all the bricks and timbers were counted up in order to give them exactly the same. Initially there had been only one access to the castle courtyard, across the moat and through the gateway. That was of course awkward, but it was rearranged with the courtyard

Staircase towers only became common after the Middle Ages; until then it was common that each floor had its own entrance, often from an external gallery. In the case of the west wing at **SPØTTRUP** *the gallery was outside the walled-up door on the second floor.*

The staircases in the walls of the towers and houses were often spiral since that took up least space. Tradition has it that they should turn to the right, as here at **KÄR-NAN.** *This is said to be designed to give the defenders room to fight with their swords in the right hand, if they had to retreat up the staircase. In reality there are at least as many staircases that turn to the left.*

being divided in two by a fence. When Mogens Gøye's daughter and daughter-in-law had to live each in their own half of Clausholm some years later, however, it all went wrong. They quarrelled violently, and a commission headed by the Lord High Constable had to be called in to solve the problems! Among the points of contention was that one of the ladies had constructed a building so close to the other's quarters that the second lady could not open her window. In addition she had installed a "privy" – a toilet – too close to the other's dwelling. This must have been particularly offensive; at that time people were not as a rule squeamish about natural odours, even if they were personally careful about hygiene and frequently took baths. But when one lives surrounded by strong smells one reacts differently to them from the way most people today would, in our deodorised era. The second lady in this case, or perhaps her deceased husband, had not behaved

better, but had had a chimney cut into the wall of the first lady's house. After many more such issues this case eventually found resolution when both ladies died.

The surroundings and out-buildings of the castle

The document relating to the settlement of the Skarsholm estate deals with the inheritance of the home, and does not at all mention the fortifications, so their maintenance was no doubt the responsibility of the younger Barnum. Mistress Gertrud was granted her share of the kitchen garden and orchard, however, which evidently were sited within the castle enclave itself or else perhaps below it as at Manorbier. It was good to have the kitchen garden near to the kitchen, so that one could easily fetch a cabbage or perhaps herbs and other useful plants that were needed for the household. In documents and in ballads there is ample evidence that apples and orchards were highly prized. In the borders between Scotland and England, where there was a long period of uncertainty about which laws applied where, and in consequence conditions of lawlessness prevailed extensively, in the 16th century it was still common to go out with weapons to steal cattle and scrump apples from the neighbours if one didn't have any oneself. In Denmark there could have been good reason to protect the apple harvest in the unruly 14th century.

Among the buildings that made up Skarsholm there was apparently only one kitchen, evidently sited some distance from the living quarters. It was common

*Diverse items of **KITCHENWARE** from the 16th century. The metal gridiron could be used for roasting or to stand hot pans on, the oblong dish with a handle could be placed under a spit to catch hot fat from roasts. The cauldron could be suspended above the fire, and in the mortar one could crush herbs, which were important for cooking. The whisk and carving knife in the foreground, and the grater, are self-explanatory. The two clay pots with handles could be used for many purposes.*

***TABLEWARE** from 1350-1450. These diverse items were not on the table at any one time. The stoneware jugs were imported from Germany and were drinking vessels, as was the pewter jug and the fine little glass. The brass dish at the back was a wash bowl for the hands. The little wooden bowl with spoon and the wooden board with knife were for eating with. One did not use forks, only spoons and pointed knives. Knives were both for cutting and for taking food up to the mouth. The wooden board, or just a piece of bread, would function as a plate for everyday meals, but in more sophisticated surroundings there might be plates of either silver or gold.*

***GLAZED EARTHENWARE JUG** with yellow "flowers" of pipe-clay mounted on it, from the 14th century. Found in Roskilde and no doubt made in Denmark. Fine jugs like this would have graced the tables in many castles.*

All objects from Danish National Museum.
Photos Danish National Museum.

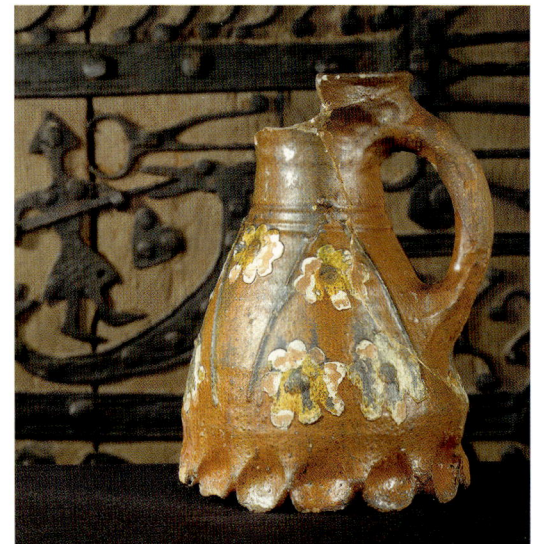

In the kitchen at **SPØTTRUP** *there is a drainage channel in the floor leading out through the wall and down into the moat.*

Good fishing waters were an important asset, counting towards the value of a castle or estate. Here the wealth of herring in Øresund is depicted in Olaus Magnus's History of the Nordic Peoples, *from 1555.*

ØSTRUPGÅRD, *in the parish of Hastrup on Funen, like Lynderupgård, has a little late medieval stone-built house incorporated into the half-timbered buildings of later date. Here too there is a large complex of farm buildings preserved from the 18th century. Seen from the northeast.*

that the food was carried over in covered dishes to wherever it would be eaten, so in fact it would only have been the kitchen staff that could be certain of having really hot food.

The kitchen, like the rest of the housekeeping, was the woman's domain; it was the responsibility of the lady of the house to administer the stores, and the evidence of this was the bunch of keys hanging from her belt, which she wore both for practical reasons and as a sign of her status. She had to supervise the many people who attended to housekeeping and all the indoor work, and in principle she should direct and distribute the tasks involved in the extensive and diverse activities.

Much of the work was carried out by manual effort, especially in the smaller places, and the whole preparation process from raw materials to finished products, whether food or clothing or other textiles, took place within the domestic household and was carried out by its members. In principle even large estates were to a great extent self-sufficient except for salt and iron. But those who could afford it of course bought luxury goods.

Another settlement of an estate in a distinguished family on Sealand reveals more about the features of value that were associated with large estates. At Vallø, south of Køge, on 13 November 1421, it was agreed between Henning Podebusk of Skjern and his wife Christine on the one hand and Oluf Axelsen Thott on the other, that the estate with the bailey, the farm buildings and the orchard should be scrupulously divided into two equal parts, a western one and an eastern one, and Oluf Axelsen was to have the eastern half. "And we will give Oluf Axelsen 25 marks for his half of the house that stands on our part and is roofed with tiles. Furthermore we, Henning and Christine, agree to divide into two parts the forests, fields, fishing waters, wet and dry, water-mills and other property..."

Vallø was called a manor *("gård")* in the document, although the Danish word for a "bailey" *("forborg")* is also mentioned. In 1421 the living quarters were more important than the fortifications, but some of the terminology of castles lingered in use, even without connection to the former functions. Vallø was by no means a castle in 1421, and it is not known whether it had been one earlier. The

document makes no mention of stone or brick buildings. The house with roof tiles was probably a half-timbered structure, maybe only of one storey, but it was in any case a fine house; roof tiles were costly, and most houses, including castles and the houses of the elite, had thatched roofs. Since compensation had to be paid for it, Oluf Axelsen's house was probably situated so far into the Podebusk family's western part of the courtyard that he could not have made any practical use of it. Again the orchard was sited close to the buildings, and the other features that are mentioned imply that here there was all that was needed for a large household.

GOOD HUNTING GROUND *also had amenity value. It was mentioned in wills and deeds of property exchange, and was managed with serious care and with respect for the animals hunted – in this case red deer, from Gaston Phébus:* Le livre de chasse. Ms. Fr. 616. *Photo Bibliothèque nationale de France.*

The forests formed the setting for special occasions when the lord of the manor, or the bailiff and the estate hands, would go out hunting game with the estate's hunting dogs and falcons, and wood was felled there for the stoves and fireplaces. The fields provided grain and hay and the meadows grazing for the cattle. The rivers and lakes held fish to supply food in fasting periods, which were long and had to be observed in Catholic times. In addition every Friday and sometimes other weekdays as well were fasting days, which meant fish days, so that even if there were fishing waters on the property one would also have to buy herring from the fisheries on the Øresund shores. In Visborg on Gotland quantities of salmon and eel were also bought in the 1480s.

The "wet and the dry" may have referred to meadows and other grazing for cattle, sheep and horses, which provided meat, milk, cheese, butter, wool, leather and candles. Tallow candles were made of sheep or beef fat, while wax candles of beeswax were much more expensive. Horses were used for riding and as draught animals, and for generating power by turning horse-mills. Some also went to war as warhorses, or were used in tournaments. Waterpower from watermills was much used, but in the later Middle Ages in some places there were windmills which ground grain not just from the estate's own harvest but also, in return for payment, for other people. Milling was one of the privileges of major landowners, and it was important and profitable to have a mill near the house, but the watermills of course had to be situated where the water flowed best.

With this array of facilities almost everything necessary was to hand, and the estate was a whole microcosm, since one could be self-provisioning from brewing and baking, salting and smoking one's own produce. Wool from one's own sheep was spun and woven, as might also be one's own linen, and fabric was dyed and

THE SPLENDID BEAKER, *almost 20 cm in height, with a man's head to one side and a woman's head to the other, is from the 14th century and was found at Sandgravvold near Aarhus, where several other fine objects have also come to light. The beaker was probably produced in Central Europe, but no close parallels are known. Danish National Museum. Photo Danish National Museum.*

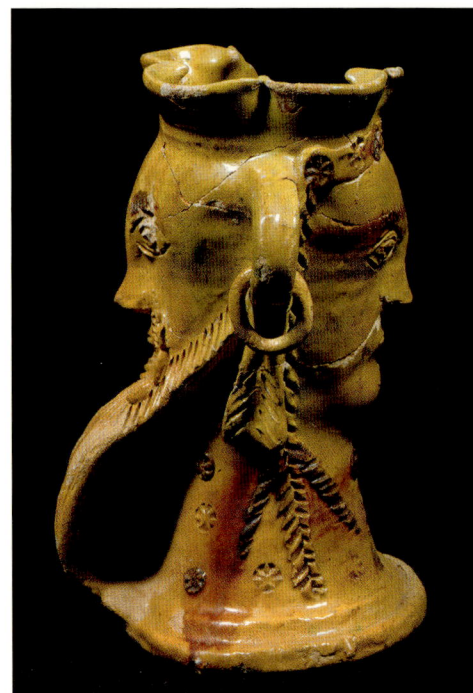

THE DUC DE BERRY *hosting a fine banquet. The war scene in the background depicts events that were being recounted at the table. Here grand people and their large and small dogs are being waited on by other grand people. The guests sat on one long side of the table and possibly also at the ends of the table, so that it was easy to serve a succession of courses. The large ship-shaped object on the table is a container for salt. Salt was costly and had to be presented accordingly. From the* Très riches heures du Duc de Berry.

sewn to make clothes, tablecloths, cushions, etc. Only salt and iron had to be bought, as already mentioned, to keep the household running, but for an especially fine occasion good German beer might be bought in as something appropriate to offer to social equals. One might buy or commission jewellery, procure expensive weapons, costly foreign textiles or furs that were more refined than the local wolf, otter or stoat skins. Spices were also precious and necessary in a good kitchen. Sometimes luxury trading was on such a large scale that the Crown found it necessary to intervene with prohibitions and restrictions.

Mogens Maltesen's letter from 1373 (see Two castles, page 252) about what he intended to replace in the castle of Ørum mentions a considerable quantity of meat, which was consumed on a large scale in the Middle Ages. There were five cows, probably live ones, but there were also eight cattle-carcasses and forty sheep-carcasses. Many of them would have been boiled for soup with cabbage or other vegetables, e.g. peas. Some ended up as sausages, and large roasts were cooked on spits. Bread was eaten along with the juicy meat, and home-brewed

<

THE **"MARGRETE BEAKER"** *has nothing to do with Queen Margrete. It is from around 1500, but it is a fine piece of goldsmithing, and for many years every other goldsmith's shop in Denmark had a copy among its stock. Danish National Museum. Photo Danish National Museum.*

The Danish National Museum has a large collection of medieval **SILVER SPOONS.** *Many of them are decorated with religious motifs in the bowl. Photo Danish National Museum.*

Two fine **CARVING KNIVES** *with gilt mounts on the handles. This kind of implement would have been used for festive meals in sophisticated households. Danish National Museum. Photo Danish National Museum*

beer was the everyday drink. Mogens Maltesen's letter mentions peas, barley and malt as well as two barrels of already brewed beer.

Accounts from the uppermost layers of society provide us with an impression of the quantity of meat that found its way to the table, but there was also a truly large amount of fish that was consumed. When there was something to be celebrated there was certainly no lack of substances to drink. At Bollerup in Scania a wedding took place just after 1500; several litres of beer and wine were reckoned for each participant per day. There were several hundred guests and the party lasted for many days. On such occasions there were many meals, often with imaginatively decorated courses, perhaps built up to look like swans or other birds, and some of them purely for decoration. Elaborately shaped and extremely sweet desserts were reserved for exceptionally festive occasions.

Work, enjoyment and learning

The raw ingredients were prepared in the kitchen, pantry or bakehouse, which might be in separate buildings or be parts of the same building, as at Kalø. If the castle buildings were wooden or half-timbered the bakehouse would often be separate because of the danger of fire. The cook was usually a man, e.g. at Gunderslevholm in 1441. There were many cooks in Visborg in the 1480s, when Iver Axelsen Thott was the royal representative there and maintained a household in princely style; he was in fact married to the daughter of the king of Sweden, Karl Knutsson. There were young boys who worked in the kitchen too, turning the

large spits or fetching water and firewood. Otherwise there were many women who worked in the various out-buildings, and they slept there too, perhaps on a kitchen bench or several of them together in the attic above. The lady of the house no doubt had the role of supervising the work, but was rarely to be found stirring pots. If the household was a large one, she would sit with her ladies or maids in the bower – the ladies' quarters – working on fine needlework or embroidery, or spinning on a silver spindle, as described in ballads. The young girls checked the linen and cloths, cut out clothes and sewed them together with silk stitching. A woman was expected at least to sew the bridal shirt for her husband, but exceptionally fine decoration, e.g. with beading, would be done by trained specialised workers. Sometimes tailors came to cut the material out before it was sewn into clothing.

Many activities took place in the ladies' bower, which was also the everyday living area for the family and its guests. They might have been accompanied in their occupations by people reading aloud, or singing and playing music while others played board games or threw dice, or in the late Middle Ages played cards. At Visborg Iver Axelsen played both in the bower and on the outdoor gallery. And he gambled for money, which his account-keeper supplied to him. Mouritz Nielsen from Aagaard in Vendsyssel was also a keen card-player in the years around 1500. Sometimes he had a major win. Then he gave the winnings back to his account-keeper, who put the money away with the rest in the money-casket.

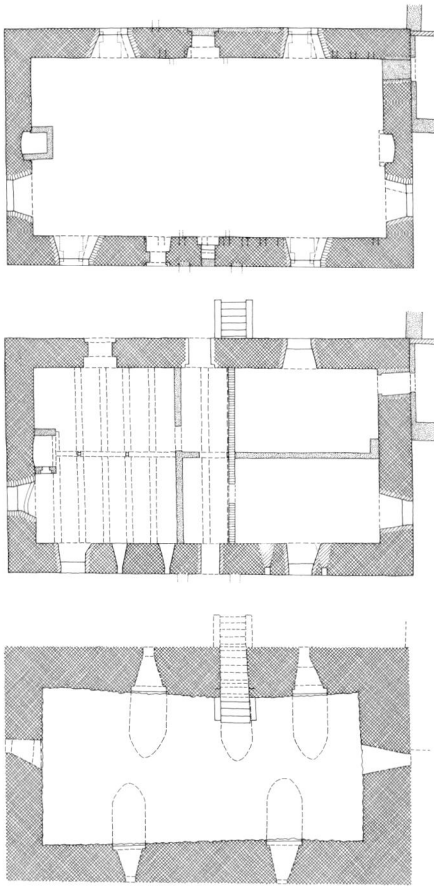

Plans of **TJELE'S** *three storeys. The ceiling of the lower floor was barrel-vaulted.*

In the hall at **TJELE** *there is a fragment of a mural painting similar to the one at Nyborg. The rural nobility also wanted to follow fashion.*

The ladies' bower consisted of one of the two rooms that the family used as their ordinary living space even in the uppermost social layers until well into the 16th century. In addition there was a garderobe, a small room with a built-out latrine shaft, a "privy", which often let waste products out into the moat, as at Spøttrup, but might also discharge into the bailey or outer castle courtyard as at Kalø, or into the middle of the cellar as at Gjorslev. If the waste did not end up in the moat someone had to clear it away, and whatever the system it would have given rise to unpleasant odours.

Among the young women and maids in the house, in addition to the family's own daughters there might be others who had been taken into the household to be trained up in domestic skills. In the same way there could be boys from other families who were there to be educated in masculine pursuits. The upper echelons of society were often extremely well-educated, as was necessary for those who would be expected to control and direct kingdoms and properties and their own enterprises. At any rate in the late Middle Ages the children of such families often attended schools in monasteries from an early age in order to learn to read and write and acquire some knowledge besides, most of it about religion, and before and after that they would be sent to the houses of relatives or friends of the same social level. In that way the circle of family was broadened, one gained wider background experience and at the same time learned manners and customs and how to behave in different places. It was a fine privilege to have royal children in care, as Absalon's family had, but it was also not bad if one's children had the chance to serve at court from a young age. That might involve anything – holding a train, helping in the archives, or looking after the royal dogs, perhaps for years. Tyge Krabbe, who had been the Lord High Constable – the military commander of the realm – during the civil war, had taken care of King Hans's dogs for several years while he was a boy, and had had "many a god-awful day with them in bogs and marshes".

Children's lives were not always fun or easy in the Middle Ages, and when there was constant moving around this could no doubt leave scars on the souls of sensitive children, but good teachers in monasteries were aware of that problem. The prioress in Ring Convent near Skanderborg, for instance, wrote to a mother about her little boy, who was well-behaved and gentle and liked by everyone, but also a little slow to learn and very sensitive, ".... but I beg you, Mistress Sofie, do not send Peder to a hard man, because he could not withstand that yet". That was in 1529.

There were always many people around in the castles and in the manors, both for the work during the day and at night. In the living area the bower was often where the family slept, and the lord and lady and children living at home in many cases also shared a bed. Private life in our sense of the term was not something anyone knew much about or even perhaps thought desirable. It was only in monasteries that people were alone for much of the time, and the fact that Mogens Gøye had his own room at Clausholm, referred to as "blessed father's old chamber above the prison", was possibly because as a widower in the last twenty years of his life he was alone in his status as master and travelled frequently be-

The candlestick from **GURRE** *shed light in the castle during the time of Valdemar Atterdag. It is c. 50 cm in height. Photo Danish National Museum.*

ELMELUNDE CHURCH *on Møn is almost completely covered in mural paintings. They are depictions of biblical scenes, naturally, but they also show us something of daily life in the late Middle Ages, when they were painted. Here Adam, in the form of a little squire, is engaged in ploughing. Photo Danish National Museum.*

<

There are several mural paintings from the 16th century at **BOLLERUP.** *This one from the hall has garlands of flowers around the niche for a blocked-up window.*

tween his nine residences and other possessions, just as did the King. A prison or dungeon was also part of the medieval castle or manor, but it was not normally the case that prisoners sat there chained up for years with only rats as company. The jails mainly served to make peasants who were unwilling to cooperate more malleable, or else at times to house local criminals for short periods.

The menfolk of the castle and the land around it took care of the outdoor work under the direction of the owner or, in the case of larger properties, his bailiffs. The land was cultivated and the animals looked after, crops were harvested and taxes were collected from the peasants who belonged to the estate, the working of the mill was supervised, etc. The minor landowner with perhaps one farm could go out into the fields himself, as described in the ballad about Torben's daughter, in which the daughter's suitor kills Torben the landowner while he was ploughing, but a major landowner might not even visit all his properties in the course of a year. There were vast economic and therefore social differences between the landowners, but they all had the same rights to immunity from tax, in return for duty of service to the king and for military service in war. This was a common bond, and from the later Middle Ages onwards they began to call themselves noblemen. In 1536 it was decided that one should have sixteen noble ancestors – forefathers – in order to belong to that class. That requires three generations, and many of those who considered themselves noble had difficulty in dredging up so many. Those who could do so proudly put all sixteen coats of arms on their gravestones.

All the work on the estates took a long time and required many hands. In

most places the farmhands also defended the property if it was under attack. In the case of royal castles and a few very large private properties there was a permanent war-trained crew, possibly including specialists such as the artillery-master who figured on the wages list for the Bishop of Ribe's property named Brink, near Tønder, as early as 1379. He could use firearms, cannons and hand guns, and this is an early date to find such a person in Denmark. It is more in line with what one might expect that at Visborg in Iver Axelsen's time there were both powder chambers and powder masters, but there as in other similar places there would hardly have been soldiers in any significant number in peacetime. The work of the permanent hands would have included keeping the weapons and equipment in order and possibly exercising the many horses and dogs that would normally belong to such places. They might also work on the maintenance of buildings and

There are several variants of the mural painting of a "perspective" pattern which is to be found on the storey containing living quarters in **NYBORG.** *Here the wall has been made to look as if it consists of ashlars carved with a pointed pattern.*

The view through the gateway of the manor house of **ODDEN.**

fortifications, so that this could be done without resorting to outside labour. The big farms and castles had their own blacksmiths, while smaller ones would use the village blacksmith. There were many who knew all about carpentry from working on building houses and palisades. This can be seen from written sources which from time to time describe how evil people stole other people's houses at dead of night, taking them apart and carrying them away under cover of darkness. At Vallø Henning Podebusk and his wife paid for Oluf Axelsen's house. They could perhaps also have reached agreement with him to have it demolished.

The men lived, as did the women, alongside their work. The stable hands slept near the horses and the dog-keepers lived in the kennel with the dogs. At Spøttrup, which was a strong fortress built in a context of danger, there was room, with a degree of comfort, for a large garrison of men in the archers' loft. In Chri-

*The servants' hall at **GLIMMINGEHUS** has an octagonal table surface encircling the pillar that carries the groined vaulting. The rings in the ceiling were possibly for chandeliers.*

stian III's Malmøhus there were rooms for the garrison, with fireplaces for heating, up under the roof. Otherwise there was the communal living space in the servants' hall and the servants' cellar, where they ate and whiled away time during breaks from work.

In the grander castles belonging to the elite there was often a chapel or church. In bishops' castles there would certainly always be one. In 1361 Valdemar Atterdag received permission from the Pope to install a chapel at Gurre, and indulgences and absolutions could be granted to people who visited there. At Kalø there was a chapel in the east wing, which also contained the great hall – to be found in any real castle or manor – and at Gjorslev there was a chapel originally built onto the outside of the main building on the south side. At Tårnborg the church still stands a little away from the mound with the ruin, and at Vordingborg there was a church in the outer bailey, but there is also mention of a chapel in the castle itself. At Søborg and Pedersborg there were small round churches, and the parish churches in many places around the country were originally estate churches for the landowners. Where there was a church there was also a priest who would take care of the spiritual welfare of the inhabitants and in many cases provide useful service by drafting letters for the lord of the estate, reading the letters he received, and keeping order in the documents in the castle – e.g. concerning testimonies of ownership, issues about adjoining land and rights.

Owners of smaller castles and estates in villages seldom had their own chapels, but the local church was recognised as "theirs". In Denmark's case Christianity took hold first in the higher social layers, and it was the members of local elites that built the Danish churches as their private houses of God, the earliest most often of wood, like other buildings on the estates. In several of the earliest stone churches, and probably also in their wooden predecessors, the landowner had a special place set apart for himself and his family, a "squire's gallery", such as one can see in Fjenneslev Church near Sorø, where Absalon and Esbern Snare were born and grew up together with Valdemar the Great. The estate there no doubt had everything that one could expect to find on the property of the most powerful family in the country after the royal family, but the estate in Fjenneslev did

*This late medieval chest in **KETTRUP CHURCH** was once housed in the nearby manor of Aagaard and probably held the treasures of the house. Chests and cupboards built into walls formed much of the furnishing of large households in the Middle Ages. Photo Danish National Museum.*

not have fortifications. Diverse examples are now known of connections between estates and churches, and in Scania in particular, e.g. at Tosterup near Ystad, the close connection is clear.

The parish priest, like the priest belonging to one of the major castles, was the source of spiritual and literary support for the inhabitants of the small castle or large farm. The administration of a substantial estate had many similarities with the running of the kingdom, and the larger the property the greater the number of people who could write or calculate who were associated with it. At Visborg Iver Axelsen employed all of six. They were not necessarily all clergymen, but they were often men of the church who also had some legal knowledge, since that was necessary in many issues about ownership and other agreements. For a long time the Royal Chancellor was a clergyman – for instance in Queen Margrete's time it was the Bishop of Roskilde, Peder Jensen Lodehat. Throughout the Middle Ages the Chancellor's office grew, and the royal archives became so extensive that they had to be permanently housed in the tower of "Folen" at Kalundborg. In lesser properties the important documents would be kept in a chest, or a couple of chests, in a tower room or a stone building.

Gatherings and celebrations

Large-scale national meetings took place in important royal castles. "Danehoffet", the Danish National Assembly, which was a powerful gathering of the country's leading men, was almost always held at Nyborg, as it was for instance in 1287, when Marsk Stig Andersen and Count Jacob and the others were made outlaws. In the same way the leading families made agreements and held meetings on their own estates. The castles provided the setting for many festivities, and for really grand occasions there would be entertainment in the form of jousting or tilting. This warlike game consisted of showing off one's skill in knocking one's opponent off his horse with a lance and then possibly completing the fight with a sword duel on foot. There were acclaimed heroes of this sport who were followed with a degree of interest certainly no less intense than that to be found in our overwhelming obsession with sport today. The Sealand Chronicle, which otherwise gives serious accounts of a small selection of major events, informs us that in 1352, in the middle of Valdemar Atterdag's struggle with the rebellious Jutlanders and his campaign in Germany, jousting contests were held both in Køge and in Stege, and in 1355 it was the turn of Roskilde, where a certain Arnold of Lübeck became the hero of the day. Erik Menved's fantastic celebrations at Rostock in 1311 resounded for a long time in people's memories, and Erik of Pomerania's wedding with Philippa of England in 1406 also reverberated in the Nordic countries.

Weddings meant more than merely the joining together of two individuals. They were an expression of estate politics and in princely circles national politics, and they brought many people together. Then the great hall of the castle was taken into use. On normal days it would be empty and unheated, with bare chalk-washed walls, maybe decorated with mural paintings, as at Nyborg and Tjele, for instance. But when there was to be a celebration the fire would be lit, splendid

merito adiuse et si remerchie
de voftre deliurance monseigner
de bourbon et monseigneur de
couchy car ilz ont moult fort en
tendu pour vous. Et auffi la
conteffe de faint pol car la bon

ne dame sen est moult grunde
ment acquitte de vous aidier.
Le seigneur de clary ref
pondi en telle maniere et dist
grans mercis a messeigneurs
mais ie cuidoie auoir bien fait

tapestries would be hung on the walls, and long tables would be set out for the guests. There would be eating and drinking on a grand scale, there would be music during the meal, and dancing afterwards. The dancing would take the form of chain dancing rather than dancing in couples – that belonged to later eras. At Visborg there were several musicians attached to the houschold: two sackbut players, a flute player and a trumpeter, who at one point was sent to be taught to play the organ by a monk in Visby's Franciscan monastery.

Major festivities would last for several days. People often came from far away, and many had to stay for the duration. Even if there were guest houses, as there were at Skarsholm, no estate would be able to house e.g. 50 travelling guests with servants and horses, so some of them would be found accommodation on properties in the neighbourhood, while others would live in tents during their stay. There were around 300 guests at the wedding at Bollerup just after 1500, and at Aagaard there were 113 for Christmas in 1496.

This was also the scene when major national meetings were held in royal castles far from a town, so that participants could not stay with other townspeo-

PANCAKES WITH FILLING

These pancakes are not like those with which we are familiar nowadays. Instead they are more like bread. They are called pancakes because they are made on a pan.

Pancake ingredients:

400 g flour
30 g yeast
2½ ml milk
½ teaspoon salt
1 dessert spoon sugar

Filling ingredients:

200 g hazelnuts and/or walnuts
3-4 tart apples
100 g sugar
1-2 teaspoons cinnamon
1 teaspoon ginger

Begin by making the dough. Dissolve the yeast in the milk, which should be at room temperature. Mix in the other ingredients and knead. Let the dough rest for 1 hour. Divide the dough into 8 pieces and roll them out flat. Make sure that they can fit into the pan you are going to use. Chop the nuts roughly, grate the apples, and mix with the sugar and spices. Place the filling on one half of the round bread and fold the other half over on top. Press the edges together with a fork. Cook the pancake in butter on a pan. Be careful that they do not get too hot. They should cook for c. 4 minutes on each side.

(From the book "Middelaldermad"
[Medieval food]
by Bi Skaarup and Henrik Jacobsen)

ple or in their own town houses. Many landowners had such a house. When large delegations came to a royal castle there was a colourful tent-town with flapping pennants around it, as there certainly was at Gurre in October 1375, when Valdemar Atterdag became ill during negotiations with the Hanseatic representatives and died without them discovering what had happened. It no doubt looked like a military camp – during war and sieges the enemy also lived in tents outside castles, but in those circumstances living conditions for both sides would have been quite different.

War and siege

The royal castles protected the country, or part of its territory, while the smaller structures protected smaller areas and their owners. The fortresses contained armed men who were capable of knocking out an enemy, so a conquest was not complete if the castles of the area around, or the country as a whole, had not been taken. Without control of them an area or a country could not be controlled effectively.

No matter what their size, the medieval castles were arranged in accordance with the same principles of defence techniques. First of all it was a matter of keep-

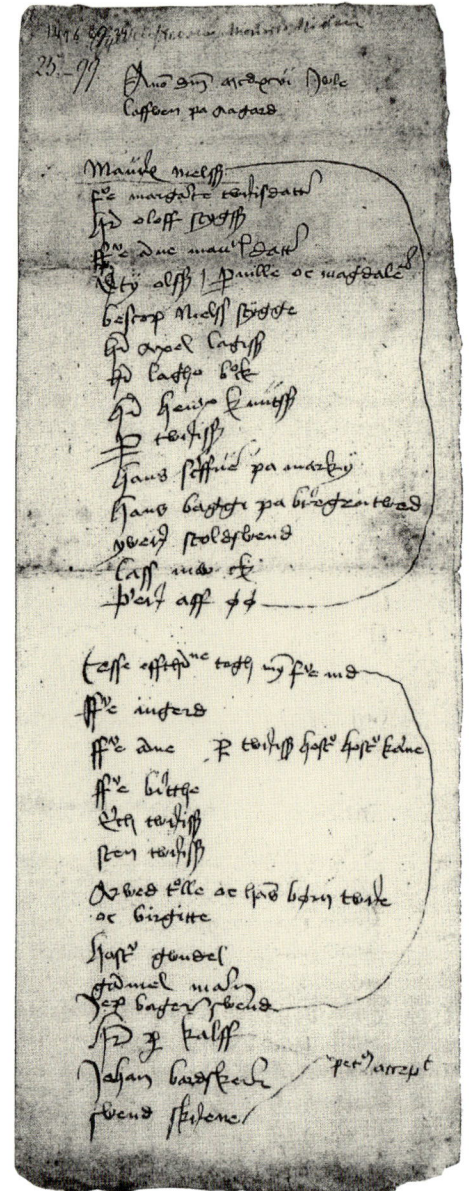

*In 1496 there were many guests at **AAGÅRD** at Christmas time. Here on the front page of a long list are the names of the owner of the estate, Mourids Nielsen Gyldenstjerne, his wife Margarete, son-in-law Oluf Stigssøn, daughter Anne and their three children, Stig, Pernille and Magdalene. The Bishop of Børglum, Niels Stygge, is also included, as are a large number of the family's relatives and friends from various social layers. In all there were over 100 people on the list, and even if they did not all turn up there must have been many to feed and house.*

AAGAARD'S *castle mound lies in the garden of the present manor house and consists of two tree-covered mounds. There must have been a fair amount of outdoor space for the many guests at Christmas in 1496.*

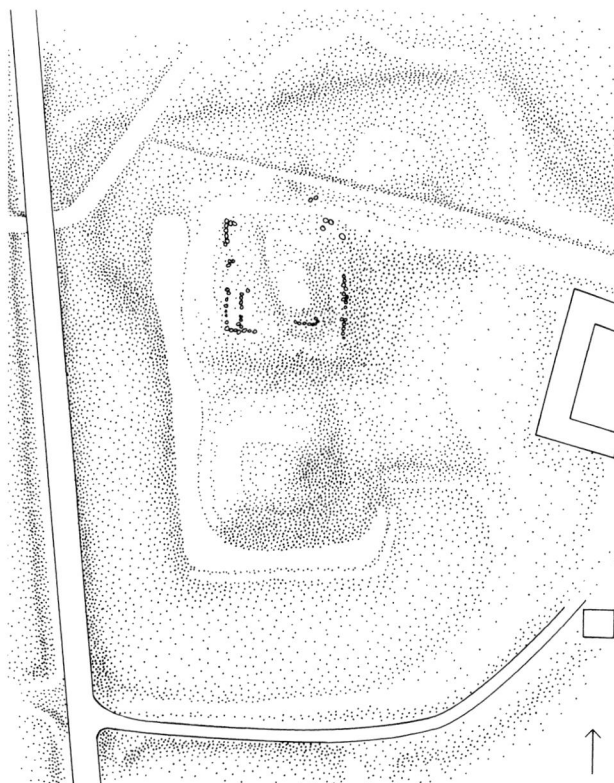

ing the enemy at bay. For that reason people built castles in marshes and bogs, on hilltops or on islands, with wide moats and high ramparts around them, and they surrounded the central part with palisades or stout walls. It was important that the attackers as they advanced should constantly be in a difficult situation, so that they could not fight effectively: they had to climb steep slopes so that they could not use their weapons, they were standing in water and mud to their knees at the bottom of the moat so they could not move, or they could only reach the gateway via a narrow passage overlooked by the defenders. In some cases the castle was situated at a low point in relation to its surroundings. When enemy troops approached they were divided up and spread out so that they were easy to spot and shoot at from the castle.

The defence features and defending troops were concentrated at the highest levels, so the castle's men had good vantage-points from the battlements and the tops of the towers over the enemy's movements and could shoot at the troops while they themselves stood under cover of the crenellations and shutters or on the walk-ways protected by the battlements. In addition the defence was divided up into many sections, all of which had to be defeated before the castle was won. With each tower or section of wall that the enemy took he would be confronted with a new obstacle. The best example in Denmark is the fortification of the island of Hjelm, which functioned as one single large castle. Access to the castle plateau was difficult, and the defenders could make a stand in several places. The attackers had to stay on the island until all of it was conquered, as happened in 1305, when everything was demolished. Otherwise they would have to blockade access with ships and starve the defenders out.

It was important that there was room for food stores, and particularly that there was a safe supply of water inside the castle, so that a long siege could be withstood. Large important buildings that belonged to those who shaped the policies of the country were particularly at risk of being besieged for prolonged periods. It was no coincidence that attempts were made – over a period of sixteen months – to take Hammershus at the time around 1324 when Christoffer II had promised to get the Archbishop's castle back for him, or that the many people in Vordingborg in 1326 at the end of the long siege had only gruel made of chaff softened in water to eat when the same Christoffer finally left the castle. There were also good reasons why Copenhagen was frequently fought over, long and hard, and why Helsingborg was shot at "day and night" by the Hanseatics in 1362 with no fewer than 16 trebuchets. In the case of less powerful people with smaller properties to defend, preparedness was the vital factor. It was important to be able to man the palisade when the enemy came. If it was the neighbour or a band of thieves there was no risk of a siege.

Back in the 13th century, when Erik, Abel and Christoffer and their sons and descendants were fighting each other, smaller-scale fortified sites were not necessarily subjected to attack. But that changed when the war once more came from outside, with the Norwegian king and the outlaws, and when the dissolution of the kingdom eventually became total in the 14th century. In that period the small wooden castles were adequate protection in many places, possibly even on Crown property. It was only after the 1340s, when King Valdemar had initiated a coherent planned and purposeful campaign of conquest, that the smaller properties could no longer hold their own, and Gunderslevholm and Padeborg and the

Cannon aperture, beside the gateway at the **BISHOP'S HALD.**

In the Middle Ages a whole strip cartoon could be depicted in one picture. This is from a **SWISS PICTORIAL CHRONICLE** *from the 15th century, showing how a castle is attacked, the wall bombarded by mortar to fragments, the defenders fight bravely, but the castle surrenders all the same, and the defenders are led out. And that was the end of that battle. The cannonball in the wall shows that it would also soon be the end of the medieval castle. Diebold Schilling:* Amtliche Berner Chronik. *Stadtsbibliothek, Bern.*

Holstein fortresses on Lolland, along with many other castles, fell. Small and vulnerable structures are also known from after that time – for instance Boringholm near Horsens was built on low-lying wet ground in the later years of Valdemar Atterdag's reign. At that time he was yet again in conflict with the landowners from Jutland, but it is difficult to see what gave rise to the fortified structures of Sandgravvold and Silkeborg in around 1385.

Even in the times of greatest unrest not everyone could build fortifications, and therefore the old communal refuges continued to be used, as already mentioned, for some considerable time into the Middle Ages. In the diocese of Aarhus there were a number of churchyards which were each surrounded by a huge wall, so that they could be a place of communal defence, and that must have been authorised by the bishop, in spite of the fact that the Church normally tried to prevent people using churches and church towers as fortresses. In 1343 the monks in Sorø were afraid that this would happen in Pedersborg, and they were given permission to demolish the church and level the mound with its surroundings. Fortunately that did not happen, but the fear of violence on Church property was

VESBORG *was situated on the southwest point of Samsø. Its solid structure was built in the reign of Valdemar Atterdag, while he was in conflict with many of the important families. The castle did not remain intact for long. The lighthouse now on the mound is also disused. Here the remaining fragment of one of the castle's buildings is seen from the shore.*

widespread. In 1342 the Bishop of Aarhus, and probably several others as well, issued a stern order that excommunication and interdict would be the consequence for all who "with armed men or archers fortify, occupy and take control of church towers or churches in order to turn them into fortresses and defences without the authorisation and consent of their prelates and chapters...". Such consent was never granted to people at large, but one could always seek sanctuary in churches and churchyards, and at a church meeting in Helsingborg in 1345 hefty ecclesiastical punishments were imposed on those "who with violence capture people who are in churches or within places of sanctuary... or by depriving them of food and drink force them to leave those places of sanctuary". It was still equally punishable, however, to barricade oneself in churches or church towers and turn them into fortresses without the authorisation of the bishop and his chapter. It was certainly impossible to prevent people from taking initiatives for self-protection, and particularly in the diocese of Aarhus, where in the 14th century the bishop had become overlord of the majority of the estates and castles that were situated there.

The bishops themselves had strongly fortified castles, and the church meeting in Helsingborg determined that those castles should not be relinquished with-

With the exception of the Bornholm round churches the Danish churches were not normally fortified. A number of churches in the Aarhus diocese, however, were surrounded by such solid walls that the local population could have sought shelter behind them. Here we can see the wall with the remains of a robust tower at **MALLING CHURCH,** *south of Aarhus. The church was as a rule strongly opposed to people using consecrated buildings as defensive fortifications, but during the conflicts in the 1340s the archbishop and the bishops together granted a general authorisation. The hefty church walls in the Aarhus bishop's diocese should be seen in that context. Seen from the east.*

*To the west of **MALLING CHURCH** a small moat can be seen, and old excavations brought to light moats on the other sides of the church. They should not be interpreted as military defences, but rather as protection against the free-roaming pigs and other village animals which might have damaged the churchyard. Ditches of this type are known from several other places. Seen from the south.*

out secure guarantees that they would be delivered back to the bishops themselves or their successors or to the diocese if the post of bishop was vacant. The Church took great care to prevent situations arising in which it would be without power, but perhaps it was not a bad move to allow the population to defend itself. It would be both expensive and dangerous for the Church to take that role upon itself. There are still remains of walls around churchyards in Odder, Maarslet and Randlev, all in the Odder region. In the wall round the churchyard in Malling there are also the ruins of a tower which it has been possible to date to the first half of the 14th century, i.e. precisely the time when the kingdom was disintegrating. In the second half of that century the tower was used for burials. At Malling Church, west of the churchyard, a piece of a small ditch can be seen. This is hardly a moat, but more likely the remains of a church ditch that has once run right round the churchyard. Ditches of this type were for a long time the normal form of boundary for churchyards and served, like shallow ditches round manor houses, to keep the free-ranging village animals at a distance.

In the same area there is Kærsgård, south of the manor of Aakær and directly west of the road between Odder and Horsens. The castle there was attacked and destroyed, probably at the beginning of the 1330s, perhaps because there was a

Holsteiner in residence. There is a steep little tower-mound there, surrounded by the remains of ramparts, but the farm-mound has been destroyed by the modern road. Excavation of the top of the mound brought to light traces of a wooden tower that had burned down. A number of crossbow arrows testify to a battle in connection with the fire and no doubt the fall of the castle, since the tower was not rebuilt. The fortifications of Kærsgård are exactly like the oldest we have evidence about in France, and which are depicted on the Bayeux tapestry. The construction was also similar to the structures that the Normans took to England. Kærsgård's tower stood on posts that went down right to the bottom of the mound that was built up around them, just like at the castle of Abinger in Surrey, England, from c.1150. And here it came to function two hundred years later in Denmark. Several larger structures also made do with fortifications of timber and earth, as can be seen for instance from two letters from 1373 about the rebuilding of Ørum and Aggersborg.

The large royal castles and the main residences of the bishops and major landowners could be very refined constructions with towers flanking the walls to protect them and other devices that secured particularly vulnerable points such as the gateway. The flanking towers projected forwards from the curtain wall, and it was possible to fire along the length of the wall through loopholes in their sides. The sentry-walk along the top of the curtain wall and towers was often corbelled, and through the machicolations at its base there was a good view of any enemy that was close to the bottom of the wall, so that they could be treated in the way the Swedish clergyman Peder Månsson recommends in his book about warfare from the beginning of the 16th century: "If the enemy approaches the wall, then boiling water, molten lead and all manner of foul-smelling ordure is thrown down on his head".

Small towers sitting on top of the wall can be seen at Visby on Gotland, on the town wall. They can both defend the flanks and provide vertical defence, and the same is true of the little tower-like projections at the corners. There was also a "pepper-pot" of that type at Dragsholm, and there were no doubt many places where there was a "lead nose" or scalding-hole above the gateway. This was a small built-out bay with outward-angled loopholes and machicolations at its base similar to those in sentry-walks; there are traces of a construction of this type above the sea-gateway to Hammershus, and there have no doubt been many others throughout the country.

The gateway was the weak point of the castle, and there were many special measures taken to secure it. It was often placed in a separate tower, and the approach road to it, or the bridge giving access, was cut off just before the entrance by a drawbridge or bascule bridge that could be pulled up so that it protected the gateway. The hole in front of the door prevented the attacker from battering it with a ram – a stout wooden pole with the front end covered in metal, hung by chains from a scaffold which was pushed up to a wall or gateway. Then the hammering began, and went on until the wall collapsed or the gate gave way. The ram apparatus had a roof over it, so the attackers were protected while they worked. At Søborg one can still see the channel where the counterweight slid down when the drawbridge was tipped up.

TWO SWORDS, *one from c.1150 found on the estate of Ingvorstrup near the Grund Fjord; the other is slightly later and from Esrum. The sword was the weapon of the upper classes and was indispensable in close combat. Danish National Museum. Photo Danish National Museum.*

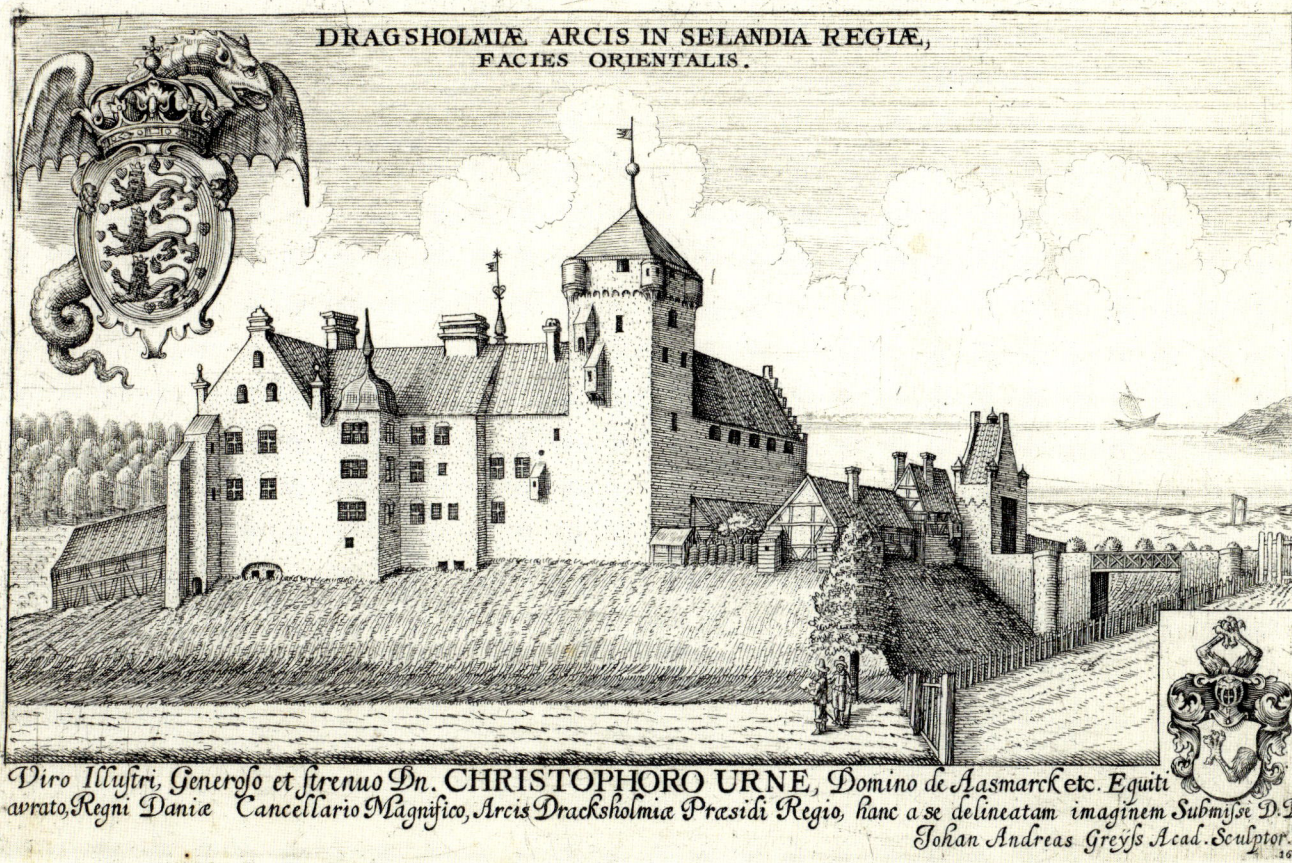

DRAGSHOLMIÆ ARCIS IN SELANDIA REGIÆ,
FACIES ORIENTALIS.

Viro Illuſtri, Generoſo et ſtrenuo Dn. CHRISTOPHORO URNE, Domino de Aasmarck etc. Equiti avrato, Regni Daniæ Cancellario Magnifico, Arcis Dracksholmiæ Præsidi Regio, hanc a se delineatam imaginem Submiſſe D.D. Johan Andreas Greyſs Acad. Sculptor. 1656

DRAGSHOLM *near Fåreveile developed over time into a strong castle, and it even withstood the ravages of the civil war known as* Grevens Fejde. *After a siege of four months the castle was still in the hands of the Bishop of Roskilde. On Resen's engraving from the late 17th century one can see sturdy ramparts and "pepper-pot" turrets at the corners of the great tower. The little projecting bays are privies, however.*

At Hammershus the gateway to the inner castle is placed in the strongest tower of the fortress, the Mantel Tower. Mantel means "cape" in German, and the curtain wall is also known in Germany as the "Mantelmaur", because it lies around the castle like a cape. The great tower at Hammershus acquired its name in the period of many years when the Lübeckers occupied Bornholm and held its castle. The tower grew to its great height in several stages, starting as more of a tower-house than a tower, and containing the living quarters – a rare example in Denmark. Kärnan in Helsingborg, in Scania, is also a tower with living quarters, a *donjon*, as was the Bastrup tower perhaps as well, but when there are only foundations or traces in the earth left of a building it is often difficult to determine how high it was and whether it was a tower or a house.

The main gate was normally blocked inside with a stout bar, but if the enemy troops managed to break that they would be stopped by a portcullis – or two – inside the gateway passage, and they would be caught like rats in a trap, exposed to firing through the holes in the ceiling or the sides of the passageway. Although every entrance was a weak point, it was necessary to have at least two, so that

(continued on page 255)

TWO CASTLES

When one stands confronted by a grass-covered castle mound with few or no traces of buildings, sometimes one is struck by doubt. Could such sites really be defended, and how were they arranged internally; what were the buildings that stood there and what were they used for? It is rare to find evidence in the written sources, but two valid legal documents from 1373 tell us more than we can normally expect.

In both cases a landowner pledges that he will reconstruct a royal building that he has destroyed in the conflict between the intractable Jutlanders and Valdemar Atterdag. The locations in question are Ørum in Thy and Aggersborg on Aggersund, both in Northern Jutland, and there is a very detailed account of what has to be rebuilt on the two sites in the form of "planking", i.e. palisades, fences, ramparts, moats and buildings. Aggersborg had "an outer area", where there were bridges and a farmyard placed in front of the castle; those were also to be reconstructed. Both Ørum and Aggersborg had a stone tower.

The texts of these letters are formulated in legal terminology, intended to ensure that everything is included and nothing is forgotten. They do not provide us with precise descriptions of the two castles in question, but they all the same present a good picture of what many smaller castles across the kingdom consisted of, and what fortification features were standard – they can be seen from the Danish words in the Latin texts of the documents.

Mogens Maltesen Juul commits himself to rebuilding Ørum: "in all respects equally good and strong, in particular with buildings, moats, houses and fences, defences known as the keep or tower, posts known as palisades, as the same property Ørum was built and constructed before it was demolished by me and mine". The Aggersborg document is more detailed. In it Niels Eriksen Gyldenstjerne promises: "...Within a year from this day to construct and build the castle of Aggersborg as well as its outer area, in all respects, viz. with buildings, houses, the defence work known as the keep, with posts called palisades, with bridges, moats, ramparts and in brief in all respects as the same castle and outer area were previously, before the said castle burned down. Similarly we promise in accordance with this letter by the previously mentioned date to recon-

ØRUM does not look particularly castle-like on Resen's engraving. Perhaps it was never rebuilt in accordance with the stipulations made in 1373.

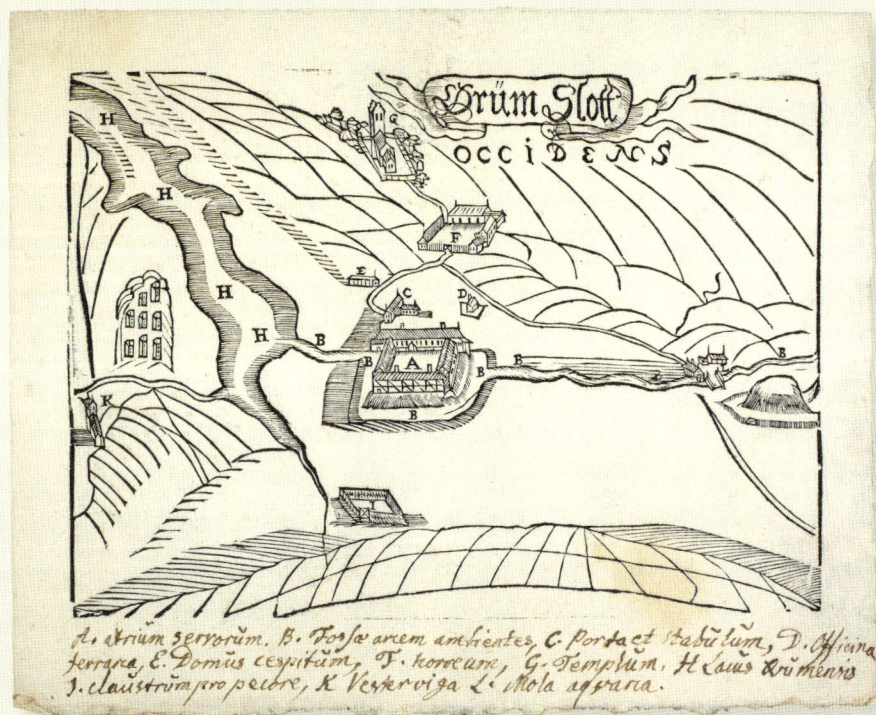

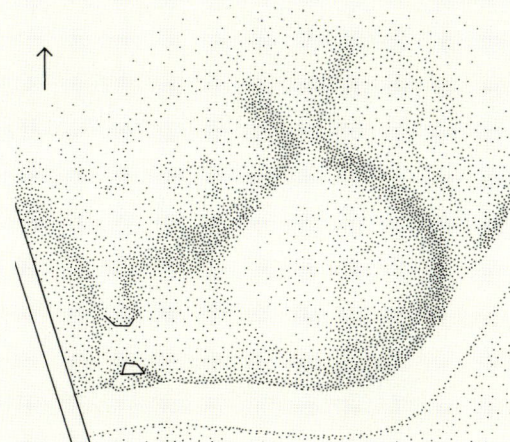

struct the farmyard in front of the castle of Aggersborg to correspond to the way it was before the fire at the same castle..." The farmyard in front of the castle consisted of the agricultural buildings, and it could sound as if Aggersborg was more strongly fortified than Ørum. That is difficult to see on the castle mound as it has come to light in recent years in connection with excavations around the major Viking fortress on the site, but earth and wood were typical components of defence features here as at so many other places in the 14th century.

Mogens Maltesen Juul, who had caused the destruction at Ørum, was also required to replace for the King all the grain he had illegally claimed while he occupied the place. In addition he should supply five head of cattle, eight beef carcasses, 40 sheep carcasses, ½ a load of barley, two pounds of flour, a barrel of peas, three pounds of malt, a

frying pan, a kettle, two pots, a quilt, three crossbows, a crossbow windlass, two dozen spears, two jars, two barrels of beer, three empty barrels, 20 plates. As well as all else that the King can prove he had acquired.

The pantry had definitely been left empty after Mogens Maltesen Juul and his men had been there, but there is no list of actual furnishings – chests, cupboards, etc. Even though we can learn much from these two letters there is even more that we are not told about in them.

*The plan of **ØRUM** shows two mounds. This accords well with the letter from 1373.*

*In the western vault-section of the chancel in **SØNDER ASMINDERØD CHURCH** the martyrdom of St Sebastian was painted at the end of the 15th century. The poor man was shot at with bows and arrows and with crossbows, and the crossbowman is in the act of stretching his bow. He is placing his foot in a hoop in front of the weapon and tightening the string with a hook on his belt like the one from Boeslum. Photo www.kalkmalerier.dk*

there was a back door to escape through, as King Christoffer did from Vording-borg with the contents of the Treasury, in 1326. A rear door, postern or "sally port" could also be used, however, to allow the defenders to exit and to encircle the enemy from behind.

The fact that the castle was divided up was seen as a form of strength, both when it was divided up on several islands or mounds, as at Skarsholm, Kærsgård, Bjørnkær, Ørum, Aggersborg and several others, or when it had an outer and an inner castle courtyard as at Kalø. In addition there could be various outer build-ings, a bailey and possibly a succession of moats and ramparts. A castle consisted in reality of a whole series of defence structures. Each tower in the wall was a fortress in itself, and so that it could not be exploited by the enemy the towers in the curtain wall were often open into the castle courtyard. In that way they could not give cover to any attackers who had managed to get onto the wall. The larg-est and strongest tower was the last refuge of the defenders and was sometimes a complete little castle in itself, with a raised entrance and crenellations around the top. Towers containing living quarters were rare in Denmark, as already said, but in the ruin on Bjørnkær castle mound near Hov, south of Aarhus, there is a well in the cellar. Bjørnkær is one of the places where it is difficult to see if the ruin is the remains of a tower or of a house, possibly with a stone-built cellar and half-timbered upper storeys, but the building on the tower mound was the safest place in a castle, and the well was very important, not least in a situation of war. Without food one can endure for some time, but without water the enemy cannot be held at bay for very long.

The attackers had to overcome all the obstacles and conquer the many parts of the castle, and do so as fast as possible. A long siege was costly and only pos-sible if one had control over the surrounding territory. Otherwise one had prob-lems with provisioning and could maybe end up suffering as badly from hunger as the people inside the castle. To besiege, storm and conquer a medieval castle required both a major effort of engineering and good soldiers. Moats had to be drained and filled in so one could reach the castle walls under cover of mantlets – portable shelters. In darkness or perhaps during decoy attacks the enemy could sometimes dig under the walls of the castle to undermine them, or possibly light a fire in the tunnel under them. The enemies of King John of England did just that, successfully, at the castle of Rochester near Canterbury at the beginning of the 13th century. Saxo gives an account of one of the successful campaigns against the Wends in the era of the Valdemars, describing the attack on "Otimar's town", a place in Pomerania, exactly as if following a manual about warfare involving fortresses. He says the town invites siege "because of the absence of walls", but it is situated far out in a lake, just like Refshaleborg in Maribo lake. Otimar had broken up the bridge, but the bridge pillars were still in place, and the Danes used them to build up a new bridge with e.g. some wattle fencing from a village nearby. In order to stop them the defenders in the stronghold built a large timber tower so that they could rise high up above the Danes and pelt them from a height with stones from their slings. The Danes used wattle fencing as mantlets over their heads, however, and went on building the bridge until they were able to reach the

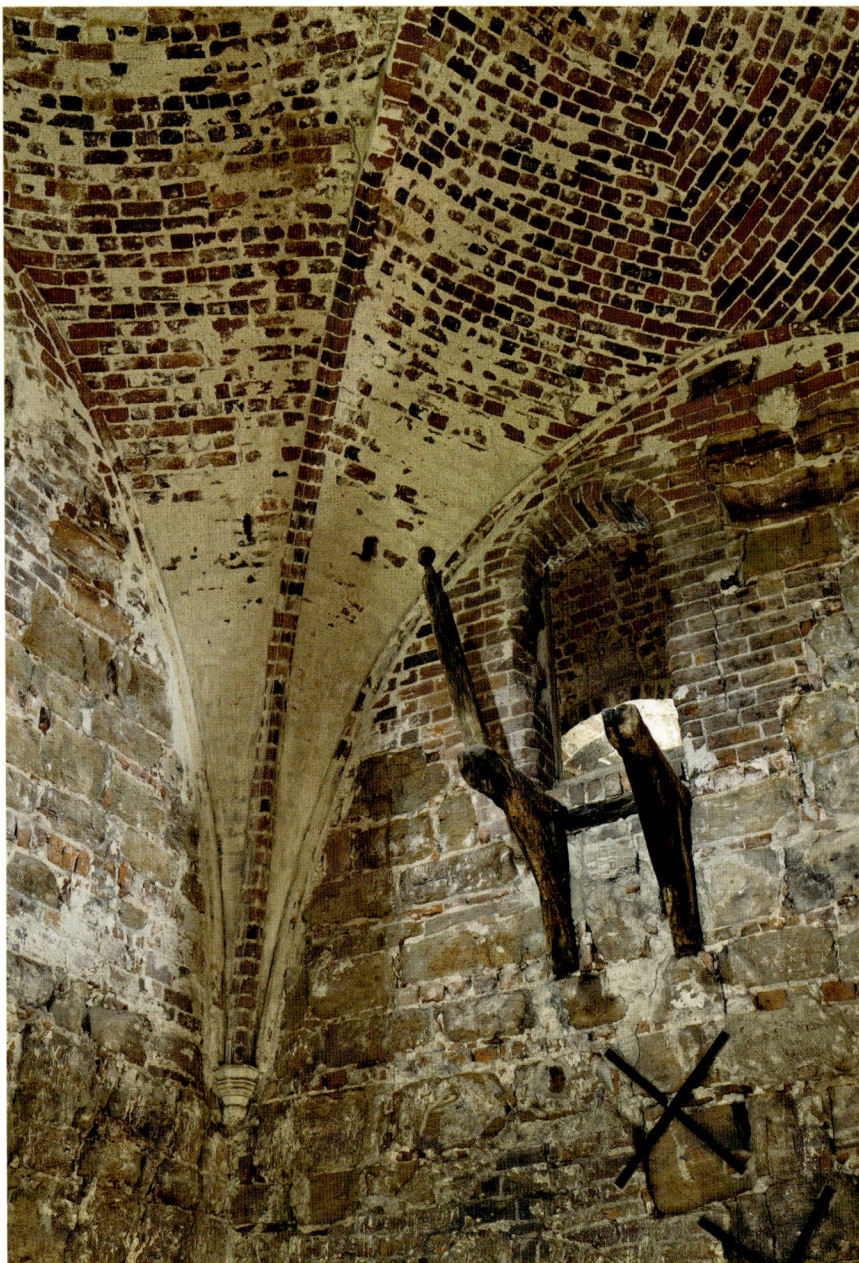

*In the King's Room in **KÄRNAN,** high up on the wall, there are the remains of the staircase up to the next floor. Before the days of staircase towers the connections between storeys were inside the rooms, if there was not a staircase in the wall.*

*At **SØBORG** there was, naturally, a drawbridge over the moat to the gate-tower. The pits for the counterweights can still be seen in the ruins.*

stronghold. They then conquered it after taking over the top of the tower, which they reached with the help of scaling ladders. This was not the last time the Danes would experience that their enemies built towers; Rostock's citizens did the same when they had had enough of Erik Menved and the other princes in around 1311.

Mantlets were part of the context of weapons of attack that included battering rams, designed to batter gates and walls to pieces, so long as it was possible to get close to the castle. They were used to provide cover over all kinds of "wheeled

machines" – siege engines – and thus to protect troops in line of fire. But in the final onslaught, the storming, the attackers had to rely on their own numbers, their speed and their skill in close combat. In order to avoid the dangerous exploit of climbing the scaling ladders that were leant up against or thrown over the walls, the attackers sometimes built one or more storm towers that were rolled right up to the walls. In that way they reached the same height as the defenders on top of the walls and on the sentry-walks, and battle conditions were rendered more equal.

Enemies and defenders used the same weapons, and the castles were equipped with giant catapults – ballistas and trebuchets – as well as crossbows, just like the attackers. Until the end of the 14th century shields and chainmail were used as protection, and after that plate armour came into use. Close combat involved swords, daggers, different kinds of blunt instruments and spears, and from the 13th century onwards the crossbow was the most commonly used manual firearm, except in England, where the longbow was favoured for a long time, and used to good effect e.g. in the Hundred Years' War against France. The English victories at Crécy in 1346 and Agincourt in 1415 were thanks to the longbow. Stones were used as ammunition both for hand-held slings and larger machines, such as ballistas, but the first cannons also fired stones, and in large castles there could be several stone-cutters working on cutting stones into ball shapes for fir-

*The old-fashioned siege weapons – **TREBUCHETS,** etc. – remained in use long after cannons became common. They were at least as precise and had just as long a range. Johannes Bengedans depicts several different types in his work on the art of war from c.1450. This is a trebuchet.*

ing. Otherwise it was difficult to hit a target with them. Saxo relates that Absalon, on his way home from fighting the Wends, broke his journey at Stevns Klint, on the coast some 45 kilometres south of Copenhagen, and gathered stones for slings there for the defence of the castle in Copenhagen. He was not the only one to do such a thing. Richard the Lionheart collected stones for ammunition in Sicily on his way to the Crusade in the Holy Land in 1190. Fire was also an effective form of warfare. Buildings were often of light construction and there could be many thatched roofs within the castle that would readily go up in flames if burning material was fired over the wall. Sometimes also carcasses were thrown in to those under siege in the hope that they would spread disease and sickness and hasten the surrender of the victims.

Many sieges ended with negotiations and relatively peaceful agreements, but a fight over a castle could also be a long-drawn-out affair and a very unfortunate development for the defenders. Either they were starved out or they were cut down at the end, as was the fate of the garrison at Gunderslevholm in 1345. The defence of the castle was not always only in the hands of its menfolk. Even though the duties and responsibilities of running the home were divided between men and women, wife and husband were equal in the sense that in the absence of the castle's master it was the lady of the household who was responsible for the home and its defence. This was how it was in 1358 when Duchess Richardis had to surrender Sønderborg to Valdemar Atterdag. In perhaps the hardest siege in the Nordic region in the Middle Ages the defence was led by a woman; that was when King Hans's Queen Christine held Stockholm from the autumn of 1501 until the following spring, while King Hans was in Copenhagen trying to preserve the union by other means. Women and children stayed in the castles even in war situations. The castle was their home and much work had to be done just like in peacetime. Food still had to be prepared, there might be wounded to care for, and the living animals that had been brought into the castle as provisions had to be tended. War involving the castles was not just a military matter, but consisted of a battle for many people's home.

The age of the fortified home was over by the end of the civil war 1536, and that was *inter alia* because of Christian III's modern cannons. Firearms had been in use from the 14th century onwards, and the loopholes of the late Middle Ages were designed for harquebuses and not crossbows, so the new weapons must have had some significance, even though as a rule the smoke and noise they emitted was more conspicuous than the damage they caused. The powder was not pure and the explosive power was limited. While the earliest cannons were breech-loaders with changeable chambers and considerable firing-speed compared with the later muzzle-loaders, they were not sufficiently well-sealed to have a long range of fire. The degree of accuracy of fire also left much to be desired. In fact the trebuchet and the other older catapult engines were much more precise. Cannons did not become really dangerous until the 16th century, when the technique of purifying powder became known and muzzle-loading weapons, which could be cast in one piece and were therefore better-sealed, came into use.

During the civil war some of the strongest castles in the country still managed to hold their own. The Bishop of Roskilde's Dragsholm, for instance, was besieged in 1536 for four months and for a time was shot at by Count Johan von der Hoya's troops and many citizens from Copenhagen. They "...had ten cannons with them and fired heavily at the castle. But they could not weaken it by firing so that they could storm it, because those in the castle defended it so manfully that the Count's people could do them no harm but had to leave the place. And they built a block house in front of it, which they filled with people, and then the rest of them went away". It was Arild Hvidtfeldt who described the event in his Chronicle of Denmark from around 1600. In his time there were no doubt still many good stories that were told about the terrible war that was just as remote in time from Hvidtfeldt as Erik Emune's attack on Haraldsborg had been for Saxo. For that reason there is no way of telling what kind of cannons were used against Dragsholm, how many people it took to service them, or what the "block house" was intended to do once most of the attackers had gone home. Dragsholm did not surrender, but the walls on the approach side are in fact extremely thick.

After Christian III's victory with the new weapons and large numbers of mercenary troops the old fortresses were no longer effective, and the castle could no longer be used in war. Private castles had already fallen out of use from around 1400. The royal castles were in many cases pulled down in the 17th and 18th centuries, as the fortifications decayed and the living quarters fell out of favour because they were outdated.

Very few of the kingdom's castles fell in war; instead they were allowed to fall into disrepair in peace.

KARLSTRUP *in the Køge area consists today of a rather small tower mound. The castle mound with living quarters and other buildings was situated in part where there is now a churchyard. The castle existed in the 13th and 14th centuries. There had been a farm at the site long before that. Seen from the southeast with the church-tower in the background.*

(Next page) **VARBERG** *was established in the 1280s by Count Jacob of North Halland in the context of the wars that followed the murder of King Erik Klipping. The buildings of the inner castle resemble the plans of medieval castles, but there have been many changes and rebuildings in the course of time. Christian IV had the old castle surrounded by bastions in around 1600. Until c.1800 the fortress had military significance. Now it contains Halland's Museum of Cultural History.*

Sequence of kings during the age of the castle
Genealogical table

Svend Estridsen	1047-1074/76	Five of his sons in turn succeeded him on the throne:
Harald Hen	1074/76-1080	
Knud the Holy	1080-1086	
Oluf Hunger	1086-1095	
Erik Ejegod	1095-1103	
Niels	1104-1134	The first known castles are from the reign of King Niels
Erik Emune	1134-1137	
Erik Lam	1137-1146	
Svend, Knud, and Valdemar	1146-1157	
Valdemar the Great	1157-1182	
Knud VI (IV)	1182-1202	
Valdemar the Victorious	1202-1241	
Erik Plovpenning	1241-1250	
Abel	1250-1250	
Christoffer I	1252-1259	
Erik Klipping	1259-1286	
Erik Menved	1286-1319	
Christoffer II	1320-1326	
Valdemar III	1326-1330	
Christoffer II	1330-1332	
Interregnum	1332-1340	Period without any king
Valdemar Atterdag	1340-1375	
Oluf	1376-1387	
Margrete –		Established the Kalmar Union in 1397
"Sovereign Mistress" of the kingdom	1387-1396	Ruled with Erik (her great-nephew) until her death in 1412
Erik of Pomerania	1396-1439	Held power in all Kalmar Union Countries until deposed in Denmark and Norway in 1439, in Sweden in 1441. Lived on Gotland from 1437/38 until 1449, and in Rügenwalde (Pomerania) until his death in 1459
Christoffer of Bavaria	1440-1448	
Christian I	1448-1481	Reign in Sweden disrupted by rebellion except between 1457 and 1464
Hans	1483-1513	Reign in Sweden disrupted by rebellion except between 1497 and 1502
Christian II	1513-1523	Reign extended to Sweden only between 1520 to 1521. The "Stockholm bloodbath" brought the Union to a definitive end. Christian was deposed; in 1532 he tried to win his kingdoms back, but was imprisoned, first in Sønderborg and then in Kalundborg, until his death in 1559.
Frederik I	1523-1533	
Christian III	1534-1559	

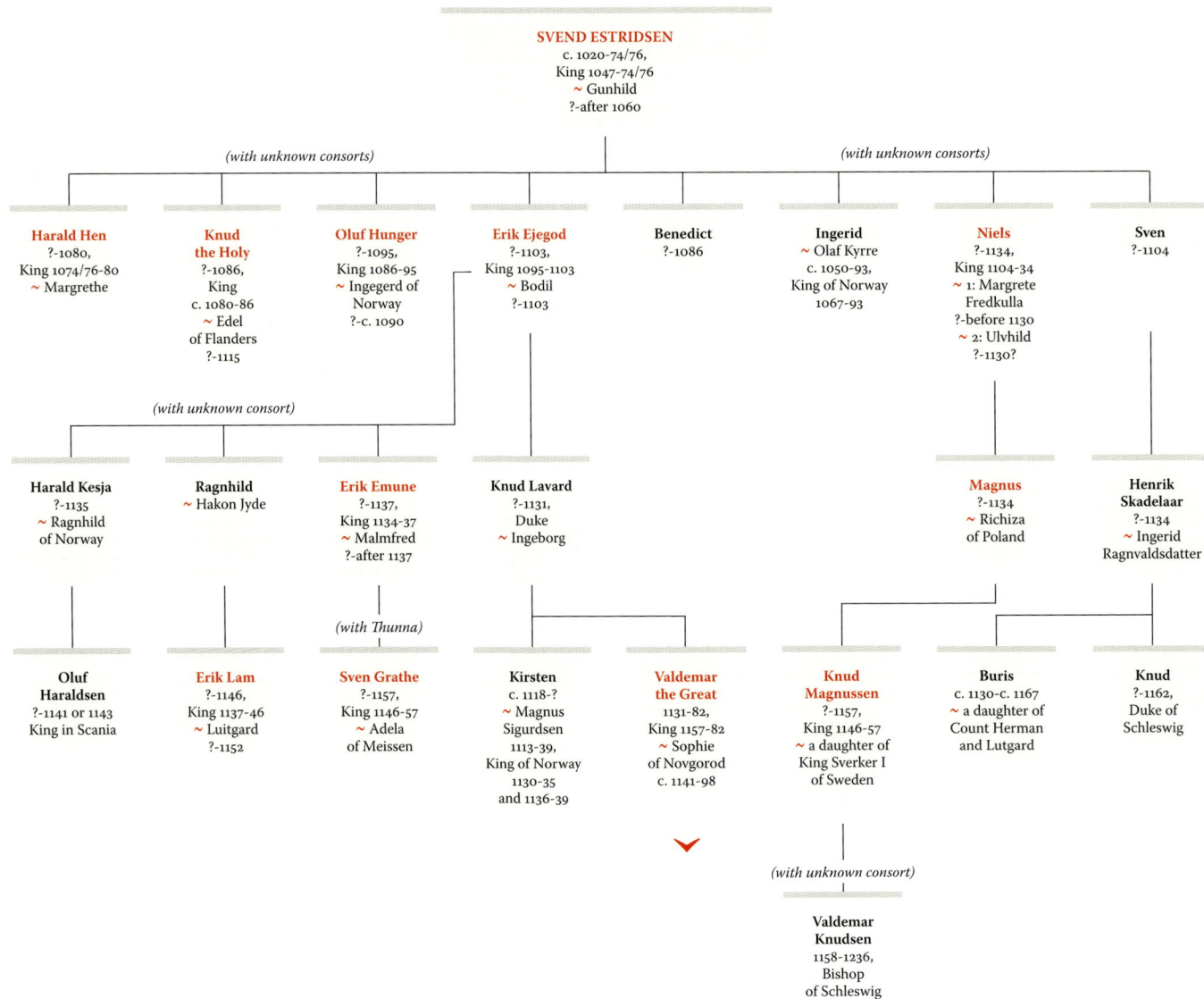

SVEND ESTRIDSEN
c. 1020-74/76,
King 1047-74/76
~ Gunhild
?-after 1060

(with unknown consorts)   *(with unknown consorts)*

Harald Hen
?-1080,
King 1074/76-80
~ Margrethe

**Knud
the Holy**
?-1086,
King
c. 1080-86
~ Edel
of Flanders
?-1115

Oluf Hunger
?-1095,
King 1086-95
~ Ingegerd of
Norway
?-c. 1090

Erik Ejegod
?-1103,
King 1095-1103
~ Bodil
?-1103

Benedict
?-1086

Ingerid
~ Olaf Kyrre
c. 1050-93,
King of Norway
1067-93

Niels
?-1134,
King 1104-34
~ 1: Margrete
Fredkulla
?-before 1130
~ 2: Ulvhild
?-1130?

Sven
?-1104

(with unknown consort)

Harald Kesja
?-1135
~ Ragnhild
of Norway

Ragnhild
~ Hakon Jyde

Erik Emune
?-1137,
King 1134-37
~ Malmfred
?-after 1137

Knud Lavard
?-1131,
Duke
~ Ingeborg

Magnus
?-1134
~ Richiza
of Poland

**Henrik
Skadelaar**
?-1134
~ Ingerid
Ragnvaldsdatter

**Oluf
Haraldsen**
?-1141 or 1143
King in Scania

Erik Lam
?-1146,
King 1137-46
~ Luitgard
?-1152

(with Thunna)

Sven Grathe
?-1157,
King 1146-57
~ Adela
of Meissen

Kirsten
c. 1118-?
~ Magnus
Sigurdsen
1113-39,
King of Norway
1130-35
and 1136-39

**Valdemar
the Great**
1131-82,
King 1157-82
~ Sophie
of Novgorod
c. 1141-98

**Knud
Magnussen**
?-1157,
King 1146-57
~ a daughter of
King Sverker I
of Sweden

Buris
c. 1130-c. 1167
~ a daughter of
Count Herman
and Lutgard

Knud
?-1162,
Duke of
Schleswig

(with unknown consort)

**Valdemar
Knudsen**
1158-1236,
Bishop
of Schleswig

VALDEMAR THE GREAT
1132-82,
King 1157-82
~ Sophie of Novgorod c. 1141-98

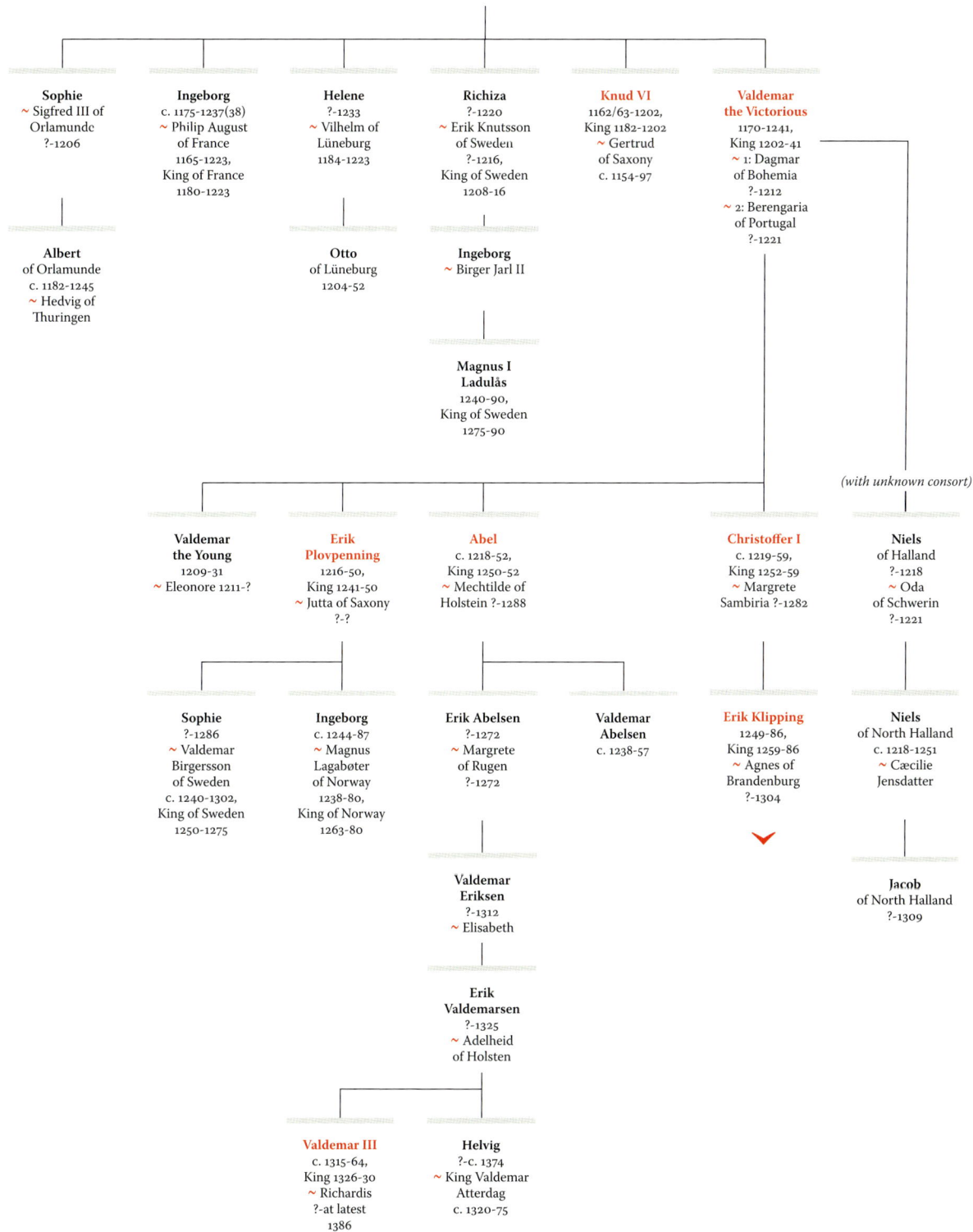

Sophie
~ Sigfred III of
Orlamunde
?-1206

Ingeborg
c. 1175-1237(38)
~ Philip August
of France
1165-1223,
King of France
1180-1223

Helene
?-1233
~ Vilhelm of
Lüneburg
1184-1223

Richiza
?-1220
~ Erik Knutsson
of Sweden
?-1216,
King of Sweden
1208-16

Knud VI
1162/63-1202,
King 1182-1202
~ Gertrud
of Saxony
c. 1154-97

**Valdemar
the Victorious**
1170-1241,
King 1202-41
~ 1: Dagmar
of Bohemia
?-1212
~ 2: Berengaria
of Portugal
?-1221

Albert
of Orlamunde
c. 1182-1245
~ Hedvig of
Thuringen

Otto
of Lüneburg
1204-52

Ingeborg
~ Birger Jarl II

**Magnus I
Ladulås**
1240-90,
King of Sweden
1275-90

(with unknown consort)

**Valdemar
the Young**
1209-31
~ Eleonore 1211-?

**Erik
Plovpenning**
1216-50,
King 1241-50
~ Jutta of Saxony
?-?

Abel
c. 1218-52,
King 1250-52
~ Mechtilde of
Holstein ?-1288

Christoffer I
c. 1219-59,
King 1252-59
~ Margrete
Sambiria ?-1282

Niels
of Halland
?-1218
~ Oda
of Schwerin
?-1221

Sophie
?-1286
~ Valdemar
Birgersson
of Sweden
c. 1240-1302,
King of Sweden
1250-1275

Ingeborg
c. 1244-87
~ Magnus
Lagabøter
of Norway
1238-80,
King of Norway
1263-80

Erik Abelsen
?-1272
~ Margrete
of Rugen
?-1272

**Valdemar
Abelsen**
c. 1238-57

Erik Klipping
1249-86,
King 1259-86
~ Agnes of
Brandenburg
?-1304

⌄

Niels
of North Halland
c. 1218-1251
~ Cæcilie
Jensdatter

**Valdemar
Eriksen**
?-1312
~ Elisabeth

Jacob
of North Halland
?-1309

**Erik
Valdemarsen**
?-1325
~ Adelheid
of Holsten

Valdemar III
c. 1315-64,
King 1326-30
~ Richardis
?-at latest
1386

Helvig
?-c. 1374
~ King Valdemar
Atterdag
c. 1320-75

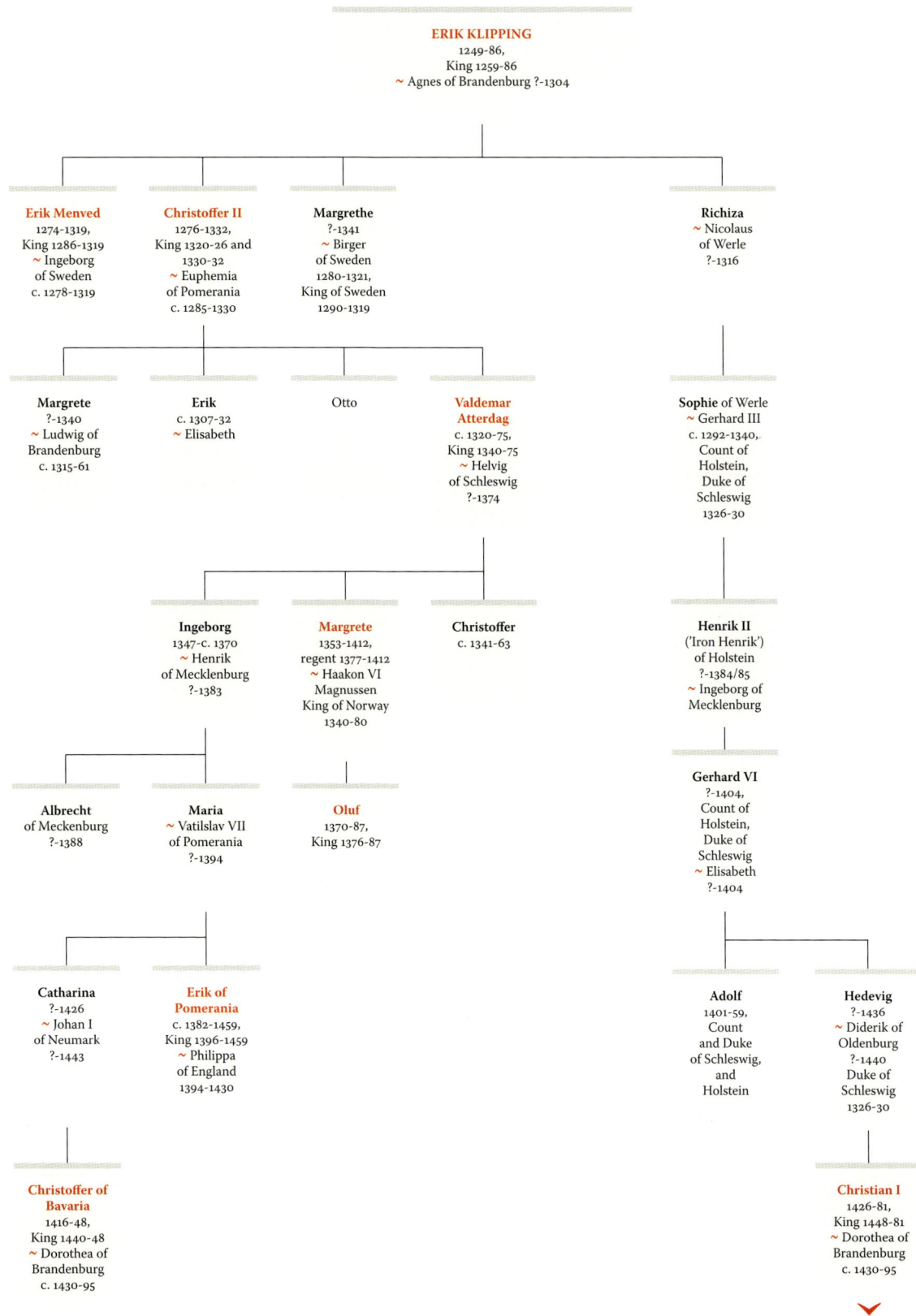

ERIK KLIPPING
1249-86,
King 1259-86
~ Agnes of Brandenburg ?-1304

Erik Menved
1274-1319,
King 1286-1319
~ Ingeborg
of Sweden
c. 1278-1319

Christoffer II
1276-1332,
King 1320-26 and
1330-32
~ Euphemia
of Pomerania
c. 1285-1330

Margrethe
?-1341
~ Birger
of Sweden
1280-1321,
King of Sweden
1290-1319

Richiza
~ Nicolaus
of Werle
?-1316

Margrete
?-1340
~ Ludwig of
Brandenburg
c. 1315-61

Erik
c. 1307-32
~ Elisabeth

Otto

**Valdemar
Atterdag**
c. 1320-75,
King 1340-75
~ Helvig
of Schleswig
?-1374

Sophie of Werle
~ Gerhard III
c. 1292-1340,
Count of
Holstein,
Duke of
Schleswig
1326-30

Ingeborg
1347-c. 1370
~ Henrik
of Mecklenburg
?-1383

Margrete
1353-1412,
regent 1377-1412
~ Haakon VI
Magnussen
King of Norway
1340-80

Christoffer
c. 1341-63

Henrik II
('Iron Henrik')
of Holstein
?-1384/85
~ Ingeborg of
Mecklenburg

Albrecht
of Meckenburg
?-1388

Maria
~ Vatilslav VII
of Pomerania
?-1394

Oluf
1370-87,
King 1376-87

Gerhard VI
?-1404,
Count of
Holstein,
Duke of
Schleswig
~ Elisabeth
?-1404

Catharina
?-1426
~ Johan I
of Neumark
?-1443

**Erik of
Pomerania**
c. 1382-1459,
King 1396-1459
~ Philippa
of England
1394-1430

Adolf
1401-59,
Count
and Duke
of Schleswig,
and
Holstein

Hedevig
?-1436
~ Diderik of
Oldenburg
?-1440
Duke of
Schleswig
1326-30

**Christoffer of
Bavaria**
1416-48,
King 1440-48
~ Dorothea of
Brandenburg
c. 1430-95

Christian I
1426-81,
King 1448-81
~ Dorothea of
Brandenburg
c. 1430-95

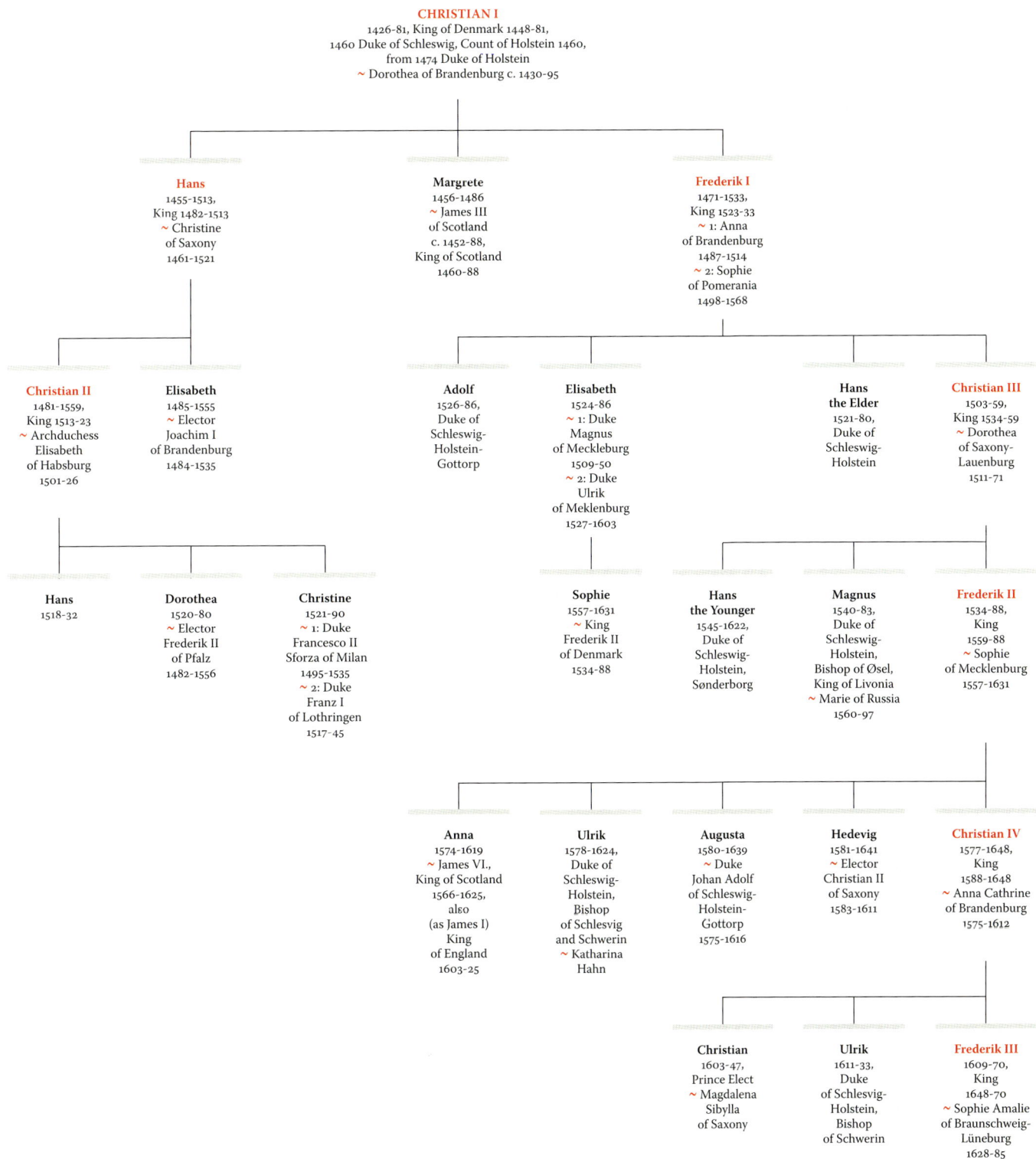

CHRISTIAN I
1426-81, King of Denmark 1448-81,
1460 Duke of Schleswig, Count of Holstein 1460,
from 1474 Duke of Holstein
~ Dorothea of Brandenburg c. 1430-95

Hans
1455-1513,
King 1482-1513
~ Christine
of Saxony
1461-1521

Margrete
1456-1486
~ James III
of Scotland
c. 1452-88,
King of Scotland
1460-88

Frederik I
1471-1533,
King 1523-33
~ 1: Anna
of Brandenburg
1487-1514
~ 2: Sophie
of Pomerania
1498-1568

Christian II
1481-1559,
King 1513-23
~ Archduchess
Elisabeth
of Habsburg
1501-26

Elisabeth
1485-1555
~ Elector
Joachim I
of Brandenburg
1484-1535

Adolf
1526-86,
Duke of
Schleswig-
Holstein-
Gottorp

Elisabeth
1524-86
~ 1: Duke
Magnus
of Meckleburg
1509-50
~ 2: Duke
Ulrik
of Meklenburg
1527-1603

**Hans
the Elder**
1521-80,
Duke of
Schleswig-
Holstein

Christian III
1503-59,
King 1534-59
~ Dorothea
of Saxony-
Lauenburg
1511-71

Hans
1518-32

Dorothea
1520-80
~ Elector
Frederik II
of Pfalz
1482-1556

Christine
1521-90
~ 1: Duke
Francesco II
Sforza of Milan
1495-1535
~ 2: Duke
Franz I
of Lothringen
1517-45

Sophie
1557-1631
~ King
Frederik II
of Denmark
1534-88

**Hans
the Younger**
1545-1622,
Duke of
Schleswig-
Holstein,
Sønderborg

Magnus
1540-83,
Duke of
Schleswig-
Holstein,
Bishop of Øsel,
King of Livonia
~ Marie of Russia
1560-97

Frederik II
1534-88,
King
1559-88
~ Sophie
of Mecklenburg
1557-1631

Anna
1574-1619
~ James VI.,
King of Scotland
1566-1625,
also
(as James I)
King
of England
1603-25

Ulrik
1578-1624,
Duke of
Schleswig-
Holstein,
Bishop
of Schlesvig
and Schwerin
~ Katharina
Hahn

Augusta
1580-1639
~ Duke
Johan Adolf
of Schleswig-
Holstein-
Gottorp
1575-1616

Hedevig
1581-1641
~ Elector
Christian II
of Saxony
1583-1611

Christian IV
1577-1648,
King
1588-1648
~ Anna Cathrine
of Brandenburg
1575-1612

Christian
1603-47,
Prince Elect
~ Magdalena
Sibylla
of Saxony

Ulrik
1611-33,
Duke
of Schleswig-
Holstein,
Bishop
of Schwerin

Frederik III
1609-70,
King
1648-70
~ Sophie Amalie
of Braunschweig-
Lüneburg
1628-85

Glossary

Castle mound is a term used to refer to a site where there have been fortifications, i.e. a castle or a similar structure with e.g. ramparts/earthworks. Now there may be only ramparts and/or mounds to be seen in the landscape, possibly with ruins of buildings. Or there may be no visible remains at all. **Castle mound** can also be used of the site on which a castle or manor house is built.

Fortifications (or **fortress, stronghold, defence work**) refers to any form of military structure, ranging from a castle to an earthwork, rampart or moat, gun tower, bastion or redoubt.

A **medieval castle** is a fortified dwelling. It may have been a farming enterprise or an administrative centre for the surrounding area, which it would protect and control. If a castle had purely military functions, to protect a border or a sentry force, or to house a garrison, and did not contain living quarters for the owner, it is termed a **citadel** or **fortress**. A **castle** consists of a building or a building complex which is fortified with and surrounded by **curtain walls, moats, ramparts, palisades**, etc.

A **castle** may be built on one or several mounds, man-made or natural. A **castle** may have a forward outpost or a projecting feature, often functioning as a look-out post. **Castles** are **strategically** positioned and are used **tactically**.

Communal strongholds or **places of refuge** gave protection to the people in the surrounding area and belonged to prehistoric times, but in some cases continued to be used in the Middle Ages.

Ramparts were often turf or earth banks built up around a wooden construction or a stone core. There could be a **palisade** on top of it. Mounds can have similar structures. Single castle mounds with farm buildings and fortifications are usually surrounded by **ramparts** and **moats.**

Sites with two mounds are sometimes known as *castrum curia* or **"motte and bailey" structures** (the latter term is mostly avoided in Denmark). Such sites usually have one mound with a farm area and another with fortifications – often a **tower mound** – and are usually surrounded by ramparts and moats.

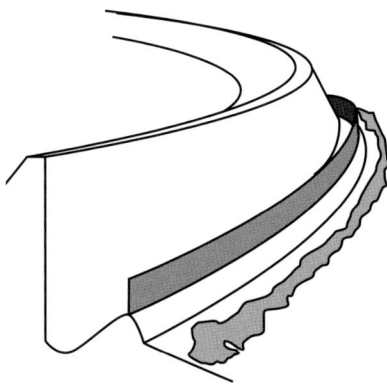

Rampart, Moat

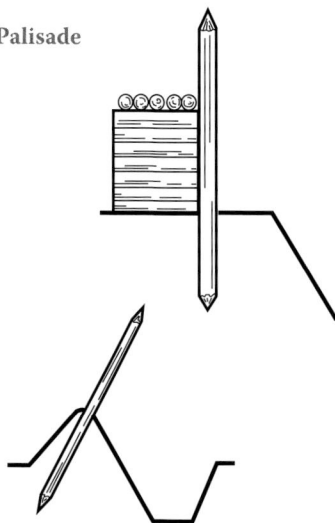

Palisade

Curtain wall with flanking towers

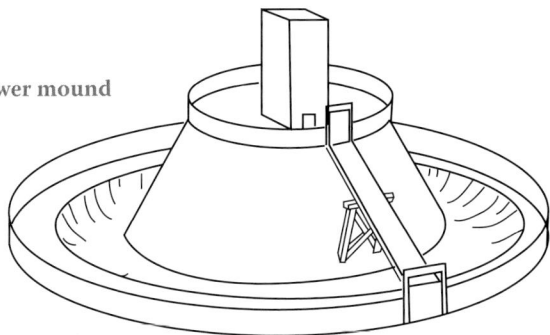

Tower mound

Renaissance castle mounds may be the remains of a **manor house** – an aristocrat's dwelling from the late Middle Ages or the Renaissance. The residential features were far more pronounced than the defensive functions, which were often merely decorative. **Manor house sites** contain the remains of a prestigious house – a manor – with extensive farmland. The site may have been equipped with minor defence elements.

A **palace** is a splendid mansion, in Denmark usually from the Renaissance and later. The word comes from the Latin *palatium*, which in Danish is used of the main stone-built dwelling in a large building complex from the 12th -13th centuries. There might be an external gallery giving access. There would be latrine shafts in stone channels, normally on the outer sides of the walls. They led down to the courtyard, moat or cellar.

The **tower** might stand alone on a mound or within the castle area, i.e. in the **castle courtyard**, and it might be surrounded by its own curtain wall. A *Bergfried* is the German term for a tower that does not contain living quarters, while a tower with living quarters is a **keep** in English and a *donjon* in French. A **keep** or a *donjon* could be a castle with a tower containing living quarters, stores, a chapel, etc. In the Nordic region and in other parts of Europe these functions would usually be divided up in several buildings around a castle courtyard. A **tower** can also be a gatehouse, or **barbican,** defending the access to the castle, or it can form part of the **curtain wall.**

The **curtain wall** surrounds the castle, whether it lies on one mound or several or is divided up into several courtyard areas. The **inner courtyard** is the central one with living quarters, chapel, etc. In the outer courtyard(s) there could be guest quarters, stables, stores, etc. Possibly also a stronghold or place of refuge. The **curtain wall** normally has a rear exit, a **postern** or **sally port. Curtain walls** and **towers** may have a high sloping base known as a **talus.**

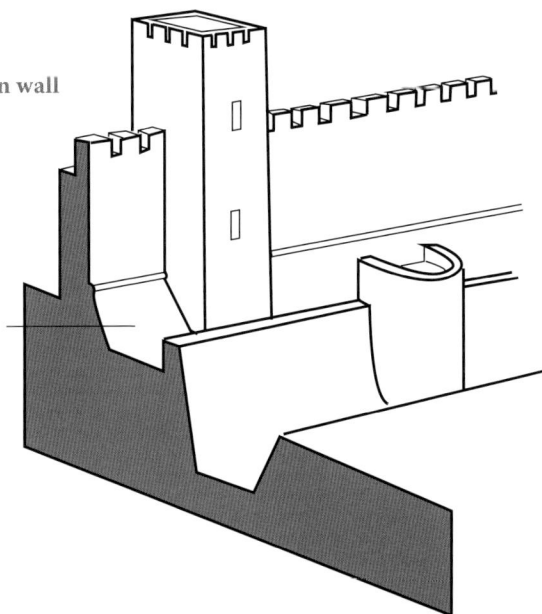

Curtain wall

Talus

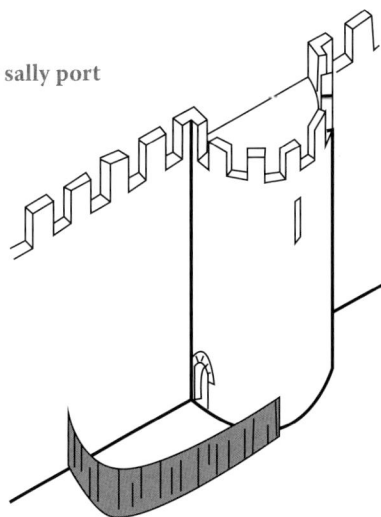

Postern or sally port

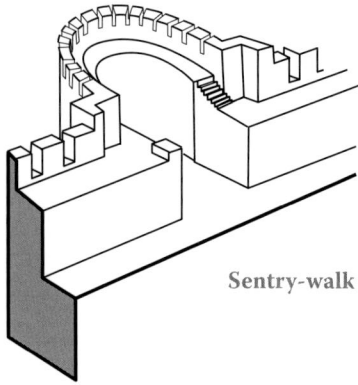

Sentry-walk

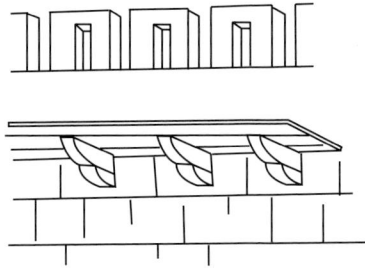

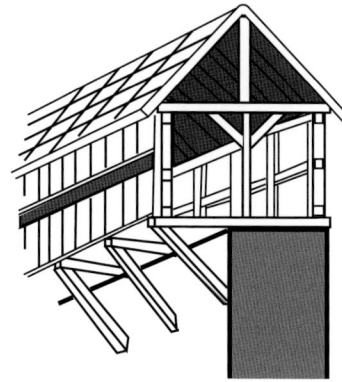

Sentry-walk wooden construction

The castle may have a **sentry-walk** or **wall-walk**, made of wood or of stone, with **loopholes** or **embrasures**. There may be **machicolations** above gateways and **"pepper pot" turrets** (*echauguettes*) at the corners. They are supported by **corbels**.

Loopholes

"Pepper pot" turrets

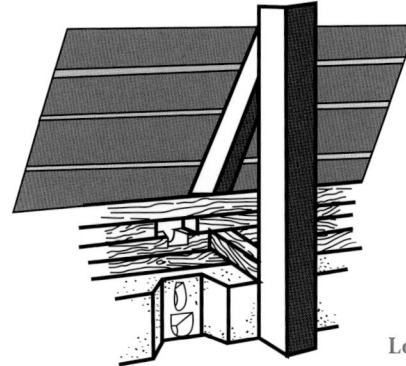

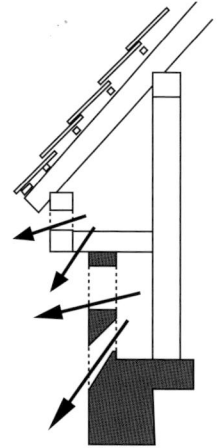

Loopholes and machicolations

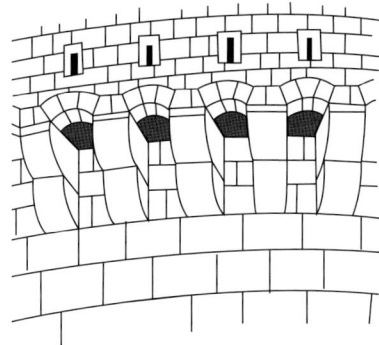

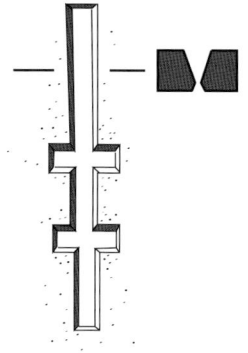

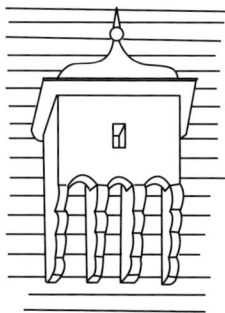

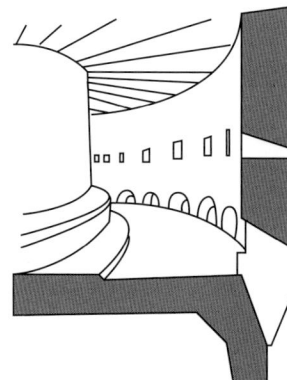

Machicolations

Sentry-walk

Loophole

The walls may be topped by **parapets** with **crenellations – merlons** and **crenels –** which can be covered by **shutters** or **flaps.** There can be **loopholes** for bows, crossbows or guns, and gun-niches for larger firearms, positioned in the curtain wall or tower wall. (In Denmark the bow was not used as a military weapon during most of the Middle Ages. There were therefore no niches for archers.)

Shutter

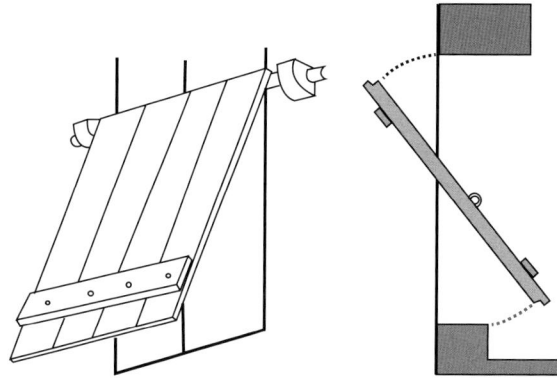

Shutters/flaps

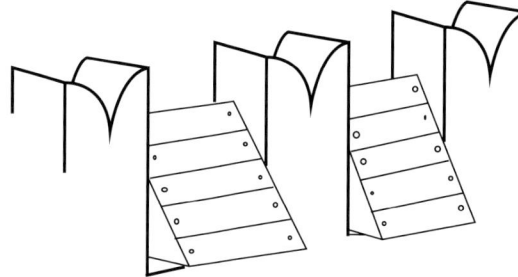

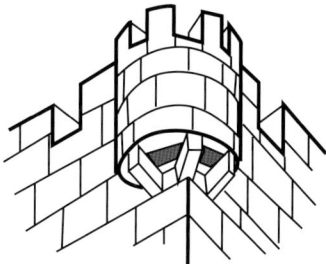

Gun-niche

Parapet/crenellations

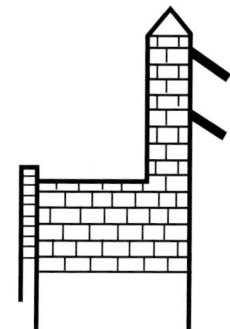

The **access to the castle** was protected by a **drawbridge** or **bascule bridge** across the moat, which could be drawn up or tipped up so that it protected the gateway. The **gate** could be blocked with a **bar** and a **portcullis**, in some cases at both ends of the access passage, so that the enemy could be attacked from the side and from the holes, known as **murder holes** or **scalding-holes**, in the ceiling of the passage.

Gateway

Portcullis

Gateway with murder-holes

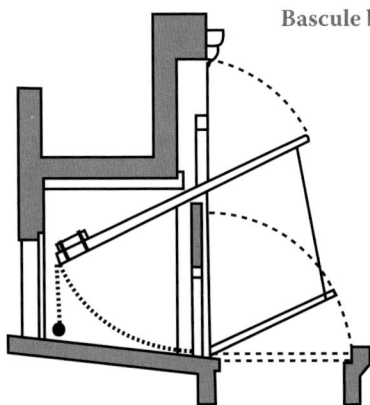

Bascule bridge

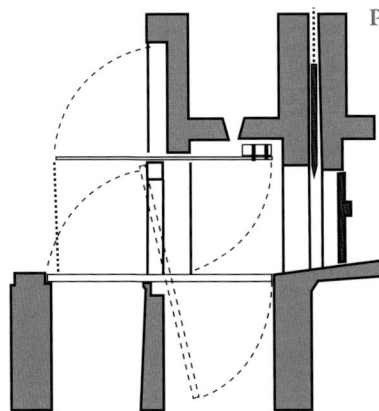

Portcullis

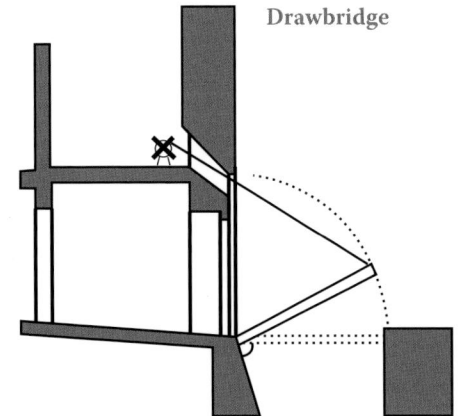

Drawbridge

Ballista

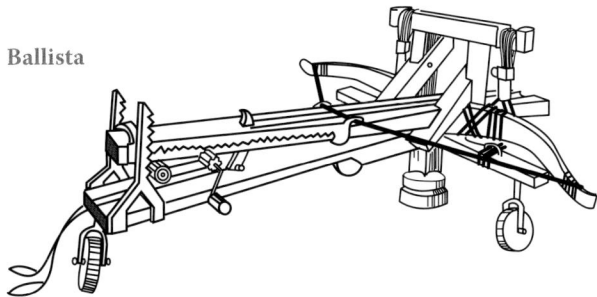

Mangonel

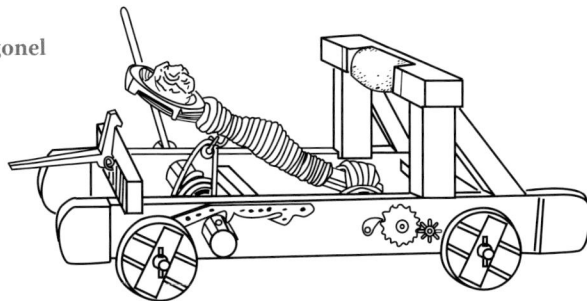

Trebuchet

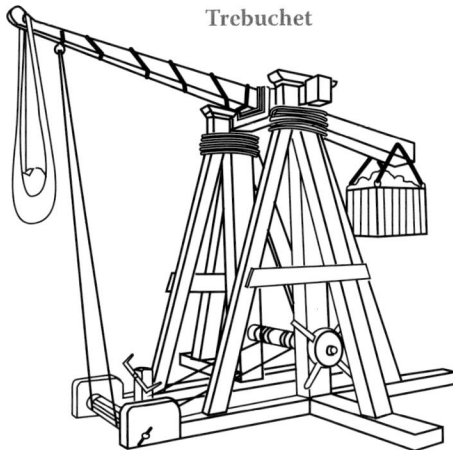

Catapult

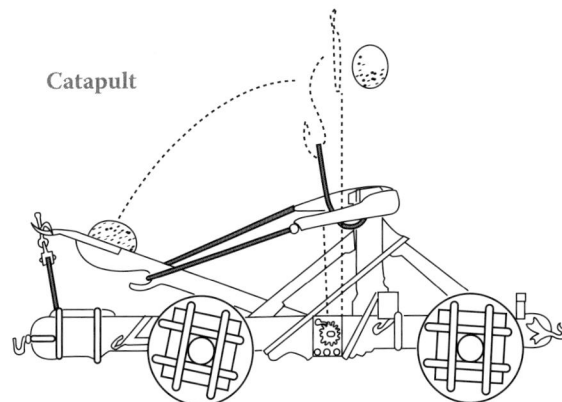

The castle was attacked and defended with siege engines and firearms of the following types:

ballista
trebuchet
catapult
mangonel
**bow (not much evidence
of this in the Nordic region)**
crossbow
gun
sling
cannon

The castle's walls were attacked with
battering rams
siege ladders
siege towers

The attackers and defenders protected themselves with:
chain mail
plate armour
shields

Close combat was decisive and was fought out with
spears
swords
daggers
clubs
axes

Battering-ram

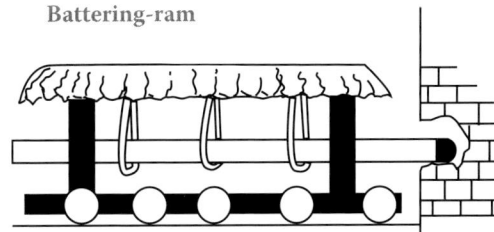

Siege Tower

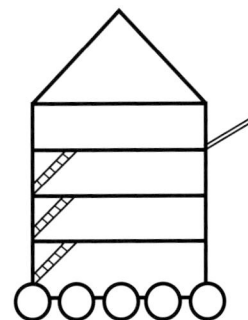

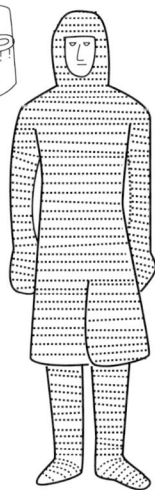

Chain mail

Plate armour

Catalogue of Castles

This catalogue covers the castles, castle mounds and royal estates from medieval Denmark that are mentioned in this book, along with various other interesting and important structures.

Numbers in *italics* refer to pages with illustrations.
Arabic numerals in ordinary script refer to the main text.

Abrahamstrup/Jægerspris, Dråby parish, North Sealand. Late medieval brick building with later buildings added. Royal estate, date of origin unknown. 187-*188*

Aggersborg, Aggersborg parish, Vendsyssel, North Jutland. In 2009 the remains were found of a medieval castle mound south of Aggersborggård. It was very probably the royal building that was mentioned e.g. in 1373. Royal until 1579, since then privately owned. 250, *252-253*, 255

Arnsholm I og II (Ørnsholm) Søndervolde and Nørrevolde, Arrild parish, South Jutland I: Two mounds, a round one and a square one, surrounded by moats. Probably constructed c.1340 by Valdemar Sappi, step-brother of Duke Valdemar of North Schleswig, and Helvig, Valdemar Atterdag's wife. Soon abandoned and succeeded by new construction, II, c.1350, on three mounds surrounded by moats and outer ramparts. Abandoned after 1368. Privately-owned.

Arreskov, Ø. Hæsinge parish, Funen. Now a Renaissance structure from 1558. Two substantial medieval earthworks. Destroyed by Erik Plovpenning in 1248 and by Erik Klipping in 1264. Precise age unknown. Royal possession in the age of the Valdemars, inherited by Abel and thus the ducal family. Privately-owned from the late Middle Ages. 87-88, 91, 94

Asdal, Asdal parish, Vendsyssel, North Jutland. Large rectangular mound surrounded by moats and ramparts, first mentioned in the 14th century. The buildings on the mound were demolished around 1800. Privately-owned.

Asserbo, Tibirke parish, North Sealand. Ruin on an almost square mound surrounded by moats. Late medieval structure, belonged to Sorø monastery from the end of the 12th century until the late Middle Ages. Abandoned in the 18th century because of sand drifts. Privately-owned for a time, royal possession from 1560. *164*

Aagård, Kettrup parish, Thy, North Jutland. Double castle mound surrounded by moats on three sides, with the road running over part of the ramparts. Traces of foundations on the castle mound. 14th century structure, destroyed during the uprising of 1441, but rebuilt. Demolished after 1633. Privately owned. 229, 240, *242-243*

Åhus, Scania. A mound and the ruin of a stone house are the remains of Archbishop Eskil's building from the 12th century. It was destroyed in 1567 during the Nordic Seven Years' War. 32, *33*

Aakær, Falling parish, Central Jutland. Three-winged half-timbered building from c.1700 on boulder foundations from a late medieval structure. The medieval complex, of which nothing else is known, was transferred to the Bishop of Aarhus in c.1400 and after the Reformation to the Crown. The medieval house fell into disrepair from 1661. Privately owned. 249

Aalborghus, Aalborg. Jutland. Remains of Christian III's new fortifications. The east wing is quite well preserved. The medieval Aalborghus was situated in the southern part of the town and was destroyed in the 1530s during Grevens Fejde. Royal property. 142

Aalholm, Nysted Landsogn, Lolland. Radically changed and restored curtain-wall castle from the first half of the 14th century on a rectangular mound. Latest changes in 1895. Probably built by Count Johan of Plön, who held Lolland on mortgage. Became Crown property in 1725, later privately owned. *100-101*

Bastrup, Uggeløse parish, North Sealand. Ruin of a fortress tower of calcareous tufa (travertine) built originally in the early 12th century, diameter 21 m. Abandoned at an unknown date in the Middle Ages. Probably originally privately owned. 27, *34-35*, 44, *58*, *72-73*, 251

Bisgård, Onsbjerg parish, Samsø. Double castle mound consisting of two low mounds. Sturdy foundations of stone buildings on the tower mound. Probably from around 1300. Samsø was royal property throughout the Middle Ages, but became part of the Duchy of Samsø-Halland for a number of years in the 14th century. Royal property or from the period of the Duchy. 52

Bistrup, Roskilde. Almost square mound below the main building of what used to be Bistrup Herregård (Manor). First mentioned in 1277; burned down in the 1530s during Grevens Fejde. Remains of fine buildings have been found on the site. Belonged to the Bishops of Roskilde throughout the Middle Ages. 54

Bjørnholm, Tirstrup parish. Central Jutland. On the mound at this site, which belonged to Marsk Stig Andersen in 1331, the manor of Høgholm now stands. 167

Bjørnkær, Gosmer parish. East Jutland. Double castle mound with ruin of a brick building on the tower mound. In use in the 14th century, disused before 1427, when the Bishop of Aarhus acquired the deeds. Privately owned. 12, *128-129*, 173, 255

Boeslum, Dråby parish, Djursland, East Jutland. Mound with traces of diverse buildings and wells. Built on Crown land in the 1320s. Was lived in until after the Middle Ages. In private ownership from the 1330s. *127*

Bollerup, Bollerup parish, Scania. Stone house built in the second half of the 15th century, on a rectangular mound surrounded by a moat. The remains of an old brick house are incorporated in the wall. Formerly had an enclosed courtyard. Privately owned. *175-176*, 184, *216*, 229, *234-235*, 241

Borgeby, Borgeby parish, Scania. 16th century house on the mound that belonged to an earlier castle with a tower and curtain wall, destroyed in 1452. Beneath that are circular fortifications from the Viking Age. Belonged to the Archbishops until 1536, became royal property until 1589. Now owned by a foundation responsible for the museum there.

Borgvold, Viborg, Jutland. Large castle mound where the Nørresø (North Lake) and Søndersø (South Lake) meet. The castle was built as a "subjugation castle" by Erik Menved in 1313-14. Period of function unknown. Royal property. *110*, 112

Boringholm, Hvirring parish, Central Jutland. Low-lying castle mound, on a natural islet, and two artificial ones sited in marshy ground – the remains of a weakly fortified structure without solid masonry buildings. End of the 14th century, privately owned, subsequently partly shared by the Crown. Period of function unknown. No information after 1400. 153, *185*

Borreby, Magleby parish, Sealand. Manor house, a distinguished dwelling from the mid 1590s without real defence features. Privately owned. 27, 44, 73, 98

Borren, Højby parish, West Sealand. Castle area of about 2.5 acres on a headland in a lake, cut off from surrounding land by a stone wall. At one time the area was divided in two by a moat, and on one part there are boulder foundations of a round tower 8.5 m in diameter.

Established in the 12th century. Length of function and ownership conditions unknown. 27, 44, 46, 73, 98

Brattingsborg/Hald, Dollerup parish, Central Jutland. One of several castle mounds with this name, which became common in legends and poems, but was first used in 1573 by Erasmus Lætus. Double castle mound originally surrounded by a 20m-wide moat. Probably from the beginning of the 14th century. Period of function unknown. Privately owned. *135-138*

Brink, Ballum parish, South Jutland. Mound surrounded by broad moats but with no traces of any large structure or masonry houses. Neither the extent nor the arrangement of the buildings is known. 14th century. Belonged to the Bishops of Ribe until the Reformation. Then came under Riberhus, and the estate later became part of the Schackenborg estate. 236

Brobjerg, Rynkeby parish, Funen. Levelled-out site that once had rather slight brick buildings on it. Appears more like a manor than a castle. Possibly originally royal. 151-152

Brundlund, Aabenraa. Post-medieval structure on a late medieval castle site. Built by Queen Margrete after 1411, when the old castle elsewhere in the town was demolished. Radically rebuilt, by C.F. Hansen among others, in 1805-07. Royal property. 186

Brådeborg, Ullerup parish, South Jutland. Large rectangular structure, royal in the 14th century, later privately owned and possibly destroyed in connection with the fighting between Erik of Pomerania and the Holsteiners at the beginning of the 15th century. 167

Bygholm, Horsens. High mound in the NE corner of Bygholm Park. Traces of foundations at the top. Built as a "subjugation castle" by Erik Menved in 1313-14. Altered and raised in the 16th century, demolished after 1617, royal property until 1661. 167

Christiansborg see København.

Clausholm, Voldum parish, Central Jutland. The present buildings from c.1700 stand on the re-

mains of structures from the Middle Ages and Renaissance which were sited on two islets. Privately owned. 153, 176-177, *217-218*, 220, 235

Copenhagen Castle see København.

Dragsholm, Fårevejle parish, West Sealand. Three-winged structure with remains of earlier houses in the walls of the building, including a Romanesque *palatium.* Belonged to the Diocese of Roskilde in the Middle Ages, to the Crown from the Reformation, and in private ownership from 1664. 54-55, 250-251, 260

Dronningholm, Kregme parish, North Sealand. Ruin of a curtain-wall structure with Romanesque brick buildings on the islet in what was then the bay on the south side of Arresø Lake. Royal property. *84-85*

Drostholm, Tamdrup parish, Central Jutland. Double castle mound, one round and the other quadrilateral, surrounded and divided by ramparts. Probably 14th century. Conditions of ownership uncertain, but transferred from private ownership to the Crown in 1366.

Duborg, Flensborg. Only the street-names now testify to the castle that was built shortly after 1410. The remains disappeared at the end of the 18th century. Two other early castles in the town have also vanished. Royal property. 186

Dynæs, Linå parish, Central Jutland. Substantial castle mound on a tongue of land stretching out into Julsø Lake, originally surrounded by moats and thereby cut off from land. Royal ownership before 1360, privately owned until 1444, Aarhus diocese until the Reformation. Subsequently transferred with other estates to private ownership. Possibly in disrepair before the Reformation.

Egeskov, Kværndrup parish, Funen. Manor house, a distinguished residence from the 16th century. Double house on a mound with driven-in poles in the lake. Privately owned. *208*, 212

Egholm, Skørping parish, North Jutland. Two castle mounds. 1: Egholm Castle, double mound with the foundations of a substantial round tower on the tower-mound and other evidence of buildings on the lower mound. 14th century, building work mentioned in the 1350s. 2: Small low-lying man-made tower-mound that has had a wooden tower on it. Built in 1334, possibly the predecessor of 1. Private ownership until 1374, then Crown until 1391, when Queen Margrete gave estates and land to the Bishop of Aalborg with the stipulation that the fortifications should be demolished. *162, 167*

Egholm, Sæby parish, Sealand. Later buildings on an impressive castle mound with evidence of several medieval structures, including the ruins of a brick building from the 13th century. The first known owner was Count Jacob of North Halland, so perhaps it was originally royal property. Privately owned since the Middle Ages. The buildings were demolished in 1765. Present building from 1846. *96-98*

Engelborg/ Slotø, Sandby parish, Lolland. At the north tip of the island of Slotø stands the ruin of a fortified ship wharf built by King Hans in 1510. Burned down in the 1530s during Grevens Fejde. Fell into complete disrepair after the Middle Ages. *199*

Eriksvolde, Østofte parish, Lolland. Huge double mound, built early in 1340, no doubt by the Holsteiners during the fighting in the kingdom. Never completed and soon demolished. *147, 150*

Falkenberg, Årsta parish, Halland. 13th century, mentioned in 1298, often attacked, destroyed in the 15th century. Now restored ruin of the central tower, probably from the early 14th century. *109*

Falsterbo, Scania. Remains of an almost square curtain-wall structure with masonry buildings and a central tower on a square castle mound surrounded by moats. 14th century buildings on older structures. Demolished at the end of the 16th century. Royal property. *124, 156, 185*

Flynderborg, Helsingør (Elsinore). Double castle mound in the southern outskirts of the town, destroyed by house- road- and railway- con-

struction in recent times. The predecessor of Krogen (Kronborg). Royal property. *186*

Fåborg, No trace of the castle that functioned in the time of the Valdemars and on into the 14th century. It was possibly destroyed when the town was fortified in the 1530s during Grevens Fejde. Royal property. *167, 169*

Gamborg, Gamborg parish, Funen. Two quadrilateral mounds from structures dating from the end of the 13th century. Sold and demolished in 1664. Royal property. *151*

Gamle Trudsholm, Kastbjerg parish, Central Jutland. Castle site with three mounds and several outer fortifications. Royal property in 1377, but privately owned a few years later. Date of destruction of the buildings unknown. The present-day manor of Trudsholm, in the same parish, was built in the 17th century on the foundations of an earlier building in the possession of the Krumpen family. *167*

Gammel Brattingsborg, Tranebjerg parish, Samsø. Largely eradicated castle mound on a field SW of Tranebjerg Church, but finds have been made there of moats and ramparts, remains of solid buildings and of a little church. Period of function probably from late in the 12th century to some point in the 13th. Possibly destroyed in 1289. Royal property. *44, 50-52*

Gammel Estrup, Fausing parish, Central Jutland. The structure contains buildings from c.1500 and later. The oldest is the gateway wing. "Essendrup" (possibly = Estrup) is mentioned in 1340, and was destroyed in 1359. Traces of buildings from the 14th century have been found on the site. Privately owned until 1930, then used as Jutland's Manor House Museum. *154-155, 175*

Gammelhald/Niels Bugges Hald, Dollerup parish, Central Jutland. Large islet with faint traces of ramparts, stone foundations, a baking oven and hypocaust. Possibly originally two mounds. Owned by Niels Bugge from 1346. Queen Margrete gave the castle to the Viborg Diocese in 1393 on condition that the building

was demolished. Privately owned. *135-137*

Gamleborg, Vester Marie parish, Bornholm. Refuge-fortress from before 1100. Still in use in the Middle Ages. Earthworks and remains of walls. *47-49*

Gjorslev, Holtug parish, South Sealand. Cross-shaped limestone building on almost square mound, built for the Bishop of Roskilde in c.1400. Ground plan unique in Europe. North and south wings added later. Transferred to the Crown in 1540 at the time of the Reformation, privately owned until 1679, then owned by Queen Charlotte Amalie. Privately owned again from 1743. *178-179, 233, 239*

Glimmingehus, Vallby parish, Scania. Stone house built on a mound of driven-in posts on an islet in a lake, by Jens Holgersen Ulfstand in c.1500. Adam van Düren was employed on the building operation. Privately owned until 1924. Now a museum. *168-169, 180-183, 230, 238-239*

Gottorp, Schleswig-Friedrichsberg, Schleswig. Buildings from the period 1500- 1700 with significant evidence of the medieval castle in the walls. Founded in the mid-13th century by the Duke of North Schleswig. In periods alternately ducal and royal. From 1713 again property of the royal family. Functioned as barracks in 1847-64, then base for the German garrison. From 1947 onwards has housed a museum and archives. *30, 75, 93, 104, 141*

Grenå, royal estate in the 14th century. No knowledge about location or period of function. *127, 187*

Grimstrup, Maribo landsogn, Lolland. Three castle-mound sites in Lysmose forest, two of them with multiple mounds and the third with a single mound. Dates of origin and relations within the group not known. "Grimstrup" was privately owned in 1359, but Crown property in 1388. In 1408 Queen Margrete donated the Grimstrup estate for the purpose of establishing a Bridgettine convent in Maribo. It was set up in 1416. *167*

Græsegård, Græse parish, Sealand. No traces

now of the house that was demolished in 1580. Privately owned.

Grønholt, Grønholt parish, North Sealand. Square mound surrounded by a moat. History unknown, but probably royal property around 1200. *120*

Gunderslevholm, Gunderslev parish, Sealand. Irregular mound beside the River Suså NE of the present main building. Castle built on it between 1333 and -39. Destroyed after battle in 1345, demolished in 1391. Rebuilt in the second half of the 15th century. Present main building from the 18th century. Privately owned. 147-148, 165, 175, 231, 245, 259

Gurre, Tikøb parish, North Sealand. Ruin of 14th century curtain wall with brick corner towers, surrounding a possibly older tower/tower-house on stone foundations. Part of a larger structure with several buildings. Disused from the 16th century. Royal property. 119, 158, *160-162*, 173, 193, *235*, 239, 242, *260*

Haderslevhus, Haderslev. All traces of the 14th century castle, probably in the east area of the town, have disappeared. At times royal property, at other times ducal. Demolished after 1540. 141

Hagenskov/Frederiksgave, Sønderby parish, Funen. Two medieval castle mounds in the grounds of the present main building from the 18th century. The old main building burned down in 1741. Belonged to the Crown until 1667, and the State from 1824 to -54. Since then privately owned. 88, *90*, 94, 167

Hagerup, Jørlunde parish, North Sealand. No visible evidence of ramparts or moats around the manor. Period of function unknown. Privately owned.

Hagestedgård, Hagested parish, West Sealand. 18th century manor on the foundations of a 16th century house which was built when the unfortified royal estate was transferred to private ownership in 1540. 187

Hald/Jørgen Friis's Hald, Dollerup parish, Central Jutland. On a headland in the lake to the east of the present Hald there is a large rectangular castle mound with ramparts and ruins. Round tower of later date. Built in the late 1520s for the Bishop of Viborg, Jørgen Friis. State-of-the-art protection against cannon-fire at that time. Became Crown property after the Reformation, until 1664. Privately owned until 1948, then state owned. Private foundation from 1975. Fell into disrepair in the 17th century. New main building in the 18th century on a different site in the area. 9, 135-136, 162, 167, 193-*195*, 206, *245*

Halkær/Hedegård, Bislev parish, North Jutland. On the western edge of the parish of Bislev, between Sønderup and the River Halkær, there was a four-winged complex on a man-made mound, with timber strucutres for dwelling quarters and farm buildings, built in c.1363. Crown property in 1406, sold to the Bishop of Viborg at the beginning of the 16th century. 126, *190*, *250*

Hammershus, Allinge-Sandvig parish, Bornholm. Extensive ruins of a curtain-wall castle with brick buildings and towers. Founded at the beginning of the 13th century by the king and archbishop in collaboration. Conflict between the two parties over ownership throughout the Middle Ages. Recognised as royal in the time of Valdemar Atterdag, but continued to be controlled by the archbishops. Conquered by forces from Lübeck in 1522, gained back by the Crown in 1576, and used among other purposes as a state prison. Fell into disuse and was used as a stone quarry from 1743; became a protected building in 1822. 47-49, 53, *61*, 73, *76-79*, 90, *93*-94, 122-*123*, 136, 138, 158, 244, 250-251, 254-*255*

Haraldsborg, Roskilde. Buildings of recent date have obliterated all traces of the original structure, which dated from c.1130. The founder, Harald Kesja, belonged to the royal family, and the place was a royal administrative centre until it burned down in the 1530s during Grevens Fejde. 27, *38*-39, 44, 54, 73, 178, 260

Hastrup, Thyregod parish, East Jutland. There is no building evidence nor any certain knowledge about the location of "Hastrup Castle", which was demolished in 1419 and is mentioned as a "castle mound". Privately owned. 12

Helsingborg/Kärnan, Scania. Huge central tower with living quarters, *donjon*, from the first half of the 14th century, on a high-lying castle site which was previously surrounded by a curtain wall with towers. There were several buildings within the castle area, including a round church. Royal structure with roots in the 12th century, fell into disrepair in the 16th. The strongest fortress in the kingdom in the late Middle Ages. Bastions added in the mid 17th century, disused from c.1700. *67*, 72-73, *80-81*, 88, 92, 110, *118*, 124, *144-145*, 156, 158, 185, 202, 205, 217, *219*, 245, 248, 251, *256*

Hestehave (Nørre Vosborg), Ulfborg parish, West Jutland. Low, large and irregular castle mound. Nothing is known about its history or owners; tradition has it that this is the mound of an earlier Nørre Vosborg manor.

Hindsgavl, Middelfart parish, Funen. A large mound in a marshy meadow near the shore of Little Belt. On the mound there are traces of a curtain-wall castle with stone buildings. Known from the end of the 13th century. Destroyed and rebuilt several times over. Fell into disrepair in the 17th century. New main building on a different site in the 18th century. Royal property until 1664. 104, *106-107*, 153, 167

Hjelm, island in the waters outside Ebeltoft. Three castle mounds from the end of the 13th century turned the whole island into a fortress. The Norwegian king owned the island, and the outlawed Stig Andersen, former Lord High Constable, was the first "chieftain" on the island. Erik Menved conquered the island in 1305 and destroyed all the fortifications. 52, 103-*104*, 107, 143

Hjortholm, Onsbjerg parish, Samsø. Double castle mound constructed on a natural mound, without visible traces of building, on an uninhabited island in Stavns Fjord. No historical information, apart from a mention of the island in King Valdemar's *Jordebog* (land register). The building was never completed or used. *50*

Holbæk. In the west side of the town there is a large mound surrounded by moats, buildings and walls pulled down after 1659, when the castle was destroyed in the Swedish War. Royal property.

Holmegård, Holme Olstrup parish, South Sealand. Three-winged half-timbered structure from 1635. Privately owned.

Hunehals, North Halland. Built by Count Jacob of North Halland after 1287. Last written reference in 1328, possibly identical with Kungsbacka Castle, which is mentioned a couple of times later in that century. No clear building traces. *103*

Højstrup, Lyderslev parish, South Sealand. No visible remains of the farm with a little stone building which Queen Margrete I took over in 1406. Privately owned. *173*

Hønborg, Taulov parish, East Jutland. Large, steep four-sided mound surrounded by a moat and outer ramparts. Functioned from the end of the 13th century, destroyed in the 1530s during Grevens Fejde and again in the Thirty Years' War. Christian II sailed from here back and forth to Middelfart after he had received the denunciation letter from the Jutland noblemen in 1523. Royal property. *166-167*

Jels, Jels parish, South Jutland. Large castle site on the lake, screened off towards land by a semi-circular rampart and moat. On the lake side there is a group of posts. Looks most like a castle-refuge. No building traces, only some finds of artefacts from the 14th century. A single document from 1403 mentions the castle in Jels.

Jomfruhøj, Revninge parish, Funen. Double castle mound from the 14th century surrounded by moats. No known facts about origin or period of function, but may have been a predecessor of the manor house of Lundsgård. *88*

Jungshoved, Jungshoved parish, South Sealand.

In the southwest of Jungshoved parish, beside a little bay, there is an irregular high mound with steep sides. Original perimeter rampart. Mentioned in c.1230 in King Valdemar's *Jordebog*, possibly older. The church looks as if it belongs to the castle area, and traces have been found of a trading place at the foot of the mound. Destroyed during the Swedish Wars, the ruins removed c.1714. Royal property. *152, 153*

Jurisborg. On the island of Möweninsel near Schleswig harbour. Mound with remains of walls on the surface. Possibly from the beginning of the 12th century; protected the harbour. Mention of "the old castle" in 1291. Royal–ducal property. Further history unknown. *30-31*

Kalundborg. West Sealand. Ruins of two castles, one in the east and the other in the west end of the town. Also remains of walls from the extensive town fortifications. Founded by Esbern Snare in 1170. Attached to the Crown in 1262. The eastern castle was reinforced at the end of the 13th century. Disrepair in the second half of the 17th. Blown up by Swedish troops in 1658. Royal property. *65, 69, 70-73,* 118, 145, 150, 153, 157, 173, 240

Kalø, Bregnet parish, East Jutland. Ruin of a large curtain-wall castle with a substantial tower on a shaped natural mound surrounded by ramparts and moats on a small island. Built by Erik Menved in 1313/14 as a "subjugation castle". Important in Jutland in the 14th century. Demolished after the 1670s. Royal property. *112, 114-117,* 124, 126, *132-133,* 138, 142, 147, 167, 185-186, 209, 229, 233, *239,* 255

Karlstrup, Karlstrup parish, Sealand. The only visible evidence of the 14th century fortification of the 12th century property is a small tower mound close to the church. Privately owned. *260-261*

Katholm, Ålsø parish, Central Jutland. The present main building from the second half of the 16th century stands on an irregularly rounded islet in a small lake. Possibly the castle mound

of the medieval castle. Privately owned. *153*

Kegborg, Kegnæs parish, Als. Small round mound surrounded by moats. Uncertainty as to whether this is the place that is mentioned in letters from 1377. But presumably royal property. *167*

Kelstrup, Vig parish, West Sealand. Double mound with the ruin of a small stone building on the tower mound, which looks as if it is cut out of the corner of the large castle mound. 14th century, privately owned, but transferred to the Crown at the end of that century and then on to Vor Frue Convent in Roskilde on condition that it was demolished. *173*

Ketting, Ketting parish, Als. During excavations at Lykkegård a tower mound came to light with traces of a wooden tower surrounded by a rampart and associated with a settlement from the Middle Ages and earlier. Perhaps the end of the 12th century. Privately owned.

Klejtrup, Klejtrup parish, Central Jutland. Two sites, 1: with two large mounds on a headland in a lake, and 2: a mound that has been considerably levelled out. Age and history unknown. *156*

Kokkedal, Torslev parish, Vendsyssel, North Jutland. Late medieval manor house with three brick-built wings on a high mound surrounded by a moat. May have been the site of an earlier construction. Privately owned. *177*

Koldinghus, Kolding, Jutland. Ruin with restored and rebuilt buildings from the frequently rebuilt curtain-wall castle from c.1268 which was an important royal possession and defended the border with Schleswig. From Christian III's time onwards without defence significance. Burned down in 1808. Now a museum. *84,* 212

Kongshelle, Ragnhildsholmen, Bohus Län. Sweden. Norwegian royal castle from the 13th century, superseded by Bohus after 1308. 101

Korsør, Sealand. Fortress tower in brick, constructed in two phases, in the 13th century (?) and in the 15th. The castle was demolished in the 18th century and replaced by coastal fortifications with bastions. Royal property. 31, 52, *56*, 61-62, *65*, 67, 147, *149-150*, 157, 203

Krapperup, Brundby parish, Scania. Manor house with buildings from the 17th and 18th centuries on a medieval castle mound. Privately owned.

Krenkerup, Radsted parish, Lolland. A small stone-built house from the last part of the 15th century is now incorporated into the eastern part of the north wing of the larger complex of buildings from the 16th century, with alterations in the 17th. Privately owned. 169, *171*

Krogen/Kronborg, Helsingør (Elsinore), Sealand. Erik of Pomerania's square curtain-wall structure from c.1420 now forms part of the walls of the Renaissance castle behind the bastions. Fires and battles caused restorations and rebuilding. Now a museum, since 1935. Royal property. *186-187*, 193, *212-213*

Kærsgård, Hundslund parish, East Jutland. Small quadrilateral mound which has been the site of a wooden tower. The main castle mound now lies beneath a main road. Destroyed, probably in the 1330s. Privately owned. 128, 130, 249-250, 255

Kærstrup, Bregninge parish, Funen. Four mounds surrounded by moats and ramparts. Remains of stone buildings. End of the 13th century, originally privately owned, transferred to the Crown in the 1370s and to the diocese of Odense in 1387, until the Reformation. Privately owned in 1573, demolished in 1630. 167

København (Copenhagen Castle). Ruins of Absalon's castle from 1167 and later additions and rebuilding can be seen in the cellar below Christiansborg Palace. The Crown and the diocese fought over the right to the castle from the mid-13th century. From Erik of Pomerania's time, and perhaps even from Valdemar Atterdag's, the castle clearly belonged to the Crown. Royal property. *68-69*, 198

Laholm, Halland. Royal structure from the 13th century, demolished in the 17th. 109

Landskrona, Scania. Artillery fortress built by Christian III as a closed quadrilateral structure on a low mound behind broad moats. Not equipped with royal living quarters. Now surrounded by bastions of later date. 208

Lilleborg, Vester Marie parish, Bornholm. Ruin of a curtain-wall structure with towers and stone buildings on a rocky outcrop in a lake, probably from the 12th century. Ruined in 1259, but still lived in for some years. Royal property. *48-49*, *53*, 90

Lindholm, Svedala parish, Scania. Rectangular castle mound surrounded by moats. Was a curtain-wall castle with a slender tower in the centre of the castle area. First mentioned in 1332, but is older. Transferred to the castle of Malmøhus in 1540 and became disused in the 17th century. Royal property. 118, *185*

Lundenæs, Skjern parish, West Jutland. Double castle mound near the River Skjern. Broken bricks have been found on the tower mound. 14th century, mortgaged to the diocese of Ribe until 1407. Royal property until 1661.

Lynderupgaard, Lynderup parish, Central Jutland. Three-winged half-timbered structure with a stone house built into the east wing. Stands on a low square mound surrounded by moats. Built in the middle of the 16th century. Privately owned. *170*, 224

Magelund/Lykkesholm, Ellested parish, Funen. Large irregular castle mound, originally with a lake on one side and moats on the others. 14th century, demolished c.1400. Privately owned, but for a brief time belonged to Queen Margrete.

Malmøhus, Malmø, Scania. On the old royal estate and citadel-area in Malmø Christian III constructed a modern fortress, partially preserved today, with ramparts and round corner towers, re-using some of the pre-existing buildings. From 1660 a Swedish fortress, now a museum since 1937. Royal property. *204-207*, 239

Mogenstrup/Månstorp, Vellinge parish, Scania. Ruin and encircling rampart preserved from Eske Bille's attempt to build a functional fortress in the mid-16th century. Privately owned.

Møgeltønderhus/Schackenborg, Møgeltønder parish, South Jutland. The Bishop of Ribe's castle on the mound under the present castle is known to have been in use from the second half of the 13th century. Transferred to the Crown at the time of the Reformation, curtain wall in disrepair in the 16th century, extensive alterations made in 1661 after ownership transferred to Hans Schack. Owned by the Danish royal family since 1978. 91-92, 94

Nebbe, Herslev parish, Sealand. Three mounds surrounded by moats and outer ramparts to the north, west, and south. To the east protected by Kattinge Lake. On the southernmost and smallest mound the remains have been found of a brick-built tower. First mentioned in 1315, originally privately owned. Transferred to the Crown in Valdemar Atterdag's time, but presented to the diocese of Roskilde in 1375 by Queen Margrete. Then fell into disrepair.

Nebbegård, Gårslev parish, Central Jutland. Castle mound with traces of foundations. Transferred to the Crown in 1401 and then demolished. Privately owned. There is another castle mound, without any known history, in the parish.

Nordborg, Nordborg parish, Als. The present castle, from the end of the 17th century, stands on the mound of a medieval castle, which was perhaps built by the Crown in the 12th century. Through the Middle Ages the estate belonged alternately to the Crown and to the Schleswig Dukes. From 1564 to 1766 it belonged to Hans the Younger's descendants or members of the royal family. In 1766 it was privately owned; in 1921 the building underwent alterations and in 1922 it became a college. 152, 167

Nyborg. Funen. Large brick building with the remains of a Romanesque *palatium* and the lower part of a solid tower preserved from the curtain-wall castle with projecting semicircular towers. From c.1200 and until Christian III renewed the fortifications this was one of the most important Danish castles and a meeting place for the national assembly, the Danehof. Demolished in 1772. Until that time there were four wings. Royal property. 31, *75*, *92, 101-102*, 151, 167, *208-211*, 213, *214-215*, 220, *233, 236*, 240

Nykøbing Falster. At the end of the headland projecting into Guldborg Sound there was a construction from the 13th century which developed into a large curtain-wall castle. It was demolished from 1767 onwards and has now disappeared. Royal property. 52, 88, 149

Nyköping, Södermanland, Sweden. Curtain-wall structure with a tower, from the second half of the 13th century. Rebuilt as a Renaissance castle in 1568. Destroyed in the second half of the 17th century. Various public uses; became a museum in 1918. Royal property. 109

Næsbyhoved, Odense. Large square castle mound dug out of a natural mound, so that it is surrounded by moats and outer ramparts. Age unknown, but possibly 13th century. No building remains. Destroyed in 1534 during Grevens Fejde. The last ruins were removed in 1764. Royal property.

Næsholm, Højby parish, West Sealand. Artificially-shaped natural mound in a former lake. One corner seems to have been dug out to make a tower mound. There are remains of a brick tower, and diverse foundations on the castle mound. Period of function c.1250-1345. Unknown whether privately owned or royal. 97-98, 134, 136, 149, 152

Nørreris, Foldby parish, Central Jutland. Originally square mound surrounded by dry moats with traces of boulder foundations. Probably 14th century. According to tradition belonged to Niels Ebbesen, but nothing is known about the history of the place or who the owners were. 136

Odden, Mygdal parish, Vendsyssel, North Jutland. Three wings of a manor on a mound surrounded by moats. In the east a stone-built house from the mid-15th century; the west end of the south wing is from early in the 16th century, and the west wing is from the 18th

century. Privately owned. *175, 237*

Øland, Hassing parish, Thy, North Jutland. Small artificially-shaped mound in the garden of the later manor house on the mound. Privately owned, but transferred to the Crown under Valdemar Atterdag in 1365, then in 1525 to the Bishop of Børglum, and later privately owned. *142, 143*

Ørkelljunga, Ørkelljunga parish, Scania. Important castle around 1300, but nothing preserved. Unknown whether private or Crown property. 109

Ørkild near Svendborg on Funen. The largest castle mound on Funen. Its age is uncertain, but it certainly goes back at least to the 13th century. On the main mound there are traces of a curtain wall and buildings, but nothing is now visible. Destroyed by people from Svendborg in the 1530s during Grevens Fejde. Originally royal, then ducal, and then belonged to the Bishops of Odense, until transferred again to the Crown, and to the Bishop once again; he had possession when it was demolished.

Ørum, Ørum parish, Thy, North Jutland. Two low mounds remaining from a 14th century structure that was replaced by half-timbered buildings. Royal until 1661, then sold and torn down in 1748. *252-253*

Østrupgård, Håstrup parish, Funen. Half-timbered buildings around a little stone house from c.1500. Privately owned. 169, 224-225

Padeborg/Sparresholm, Toksværd parish, South Sealand. Beneath the main building from the 17th century the remains have been found of a 13th century curtain-wall castle with a *palatium*. Privately owned. 145, 173, 246

Pedersborg, Pedersborg parish, Sealand. On a natural mound in the area behind prehistoric earthworks there are the foundations of a building or curtain wall from the 12th century, along with a little round church which has now partially collapsed down the side of the mound. On the mound there is now a church from the 13th century. At the foot of the mound there was a large Romanesque

palatium protected by a wall. Demolished in 1206. Privately owned. 27, *36-37*, 44, 72, 175, 239, 246

Randers, Jutland. No trace of Valdemar Atterdag's castle. It may however be incorporated in the town fortifications of which some stretches are known. 142, 153

Ravnsborg, Birket parish, Lolland. On a large natural mound on the shore there are extensive traces of building remains, walls and palisades, all of them constructed on top of earlier structures. Curtain-wall castle from the 14th century, demolished from the 16th century onwards. Royal property. 125-126, 128, 167

Refshaleborg, Engestofte parish, Lolland. At the west end of the island of Borgø in Maribo Lake there is a large almost circular castle site with traces of a brick wall around its edge. On the land side to the east there are 5 ramparts and moats. Between the island and the mainland to the north there are many posts left from bridge structures. Built in the 12th century, destroyed in 1256. Royal property. 44, *49*, 73, 255

Riberhus, Ribe, Jutland. Castle mound and ruins of Christian III's rebuilt medieval castle, constructed in 1268, perhaps as a replacement for a royal seat. The castle was uninhabitable from the 1660s onwards and then was pulled down. *84*

Riber Ulvs Borg, Ribe. Faint remnants of a castle mound, almost totally destroyed in the 1870s. Timber from the site has now been dated by dendrochronology to the middle of the 12th century, when a landowner called Riber Ulv was active in Danish politics.

Rugtved, Albæk parish, Vendsyssel, North Jutland. Large, irregular, longish mound surrounded by moats and ramparts. Ruined condition, probably from the early 14th century. In 1393 it was given by Queen Margrete to the Bishop of Børglum for demolition. Possibly royal property. 128, *130*, 167

Sandgravvold, Storring parish, Central Jutland.

The original structure had several mounds that have now been totally ploughed down. End of the 14th century. Demolished in the Middle Ages. Privately owned.

Silkeborg, Jutland. Faint remains of the castle courtyard in the large castle structure that grew up here and developed from a modest private structure, originally from 1385, into a large castle. Belonged to the Bishops of Aarhus from the early 15th century until the Reformation. Royal property for most of the period up to 1767, when the last remains of the castle were demolished. 246

Sjørring, Sjørring parish, Thy, North Jutland. Large mound surrounded by ramparts and moats. Age and history unknown.

Skanderborg, Jutland. The church is the last remnant of the 16th century castle. All traces of the medieval castle have gone, and only the castle mound now remains of the strong castle that grew up from the end of the 12th century, surrounding a large tower and developing into a curtain-wall castle. Demolished after 1767. Royal property. 44, *74, 86*, 88, 121, 124, *130*, 167

Skanør, Scania. Close to the water on the Falsterbo peninsula, oval castle mound surrounded by a rampart and moat. Traces of several buildings. Built in c.1230 and abandoned after 1425. Royal property. 88, *108*, 110, 124, 156, 185

Skarsholm, Bjergsted parish, West Sealand. Double mound on the north bank of Skarre Lake, possibly from the beginning of the 14th century. Traces of stone buildings. Privately owned, but by a family of royal descent. Sold to Queen Margrete in 1408 and demolished. 167, *217*, 221, 224, 240, 255

Skjern, Skjern parish, Central Jutland. Almost square mound, surrounded by moats and ramparts and with outer mounds to the north. On the main mound there were several wings and a staircase tower until the building was demolished in the mid-19th century. Built in the 14th century. Privately owned. 142

Skjoldnæs, Valsølille parish, Sealand. Double mound on the shore of a lake. Two nearly oval and almost equal-sized mounds. Many finds of brick on the site suggest brick buildings. Probably from c.1300 and probably royal. From 1429 clearly royal. Placed under the Roskilde estate in 1567 and demolished. 149

Skodborg, Vejen parish, South Jutland. Castle site with remains that are difficult to decipher, on the river Kongeå at the border between the kingdom and the duchy, close to an important road. At one stage after the Middle Ages there was a small customs-house on one of the mounds, built out of stone from the castle's buildings. Partly destroyed by road construction in the 19th century. Royal property in the Middle Ages, later privately owned. 167

Skælskør. Sealand. No remaining evidence of Henrik Æmeltorp's castle and no knowledge about it.

Solvig, Hostrup parish, South Jutland. There is nothing left to be seen on the four low man-made mounds in the meadow on the south bank of the River Arn that were the site of the medieval structure, from c.1300; excavations on the southernmost mound have shown that there was once a house built of wood and peat. It was replaced by a tower, which in turn was replaced by a wooden building with a tiled roof. One mound was in use until some point in the 16th century, but the other three were given up and farm buildings etc. were moved to firmer ground. There, after 1583, a large manor house was built, where the estate named Solvig still stands, with buildings from 1851. Originally privately owned, but built by a member of the ducal family. Transferred to the Crown in 1583, but soon afterwards in private ownership again. *138-139*

Sprogø, Storebælt, Korsør. Castle mound, now with a lighthouse standing on it, with remains of a curtain wall from a square structure with a fortified tower erected by Valdemar the Great. Later history unknown. 31, 50, *56, 61*, *65*, 72, 158

Spøttrup, Rødding parish, Salling, Central Jutland. Three-winged brick structure linked by a barrier wall with a sentry walk and a gate-tower. Surrounded by moats and sturdy ramparts, meant as protection against cannon-fire. Built by the Bishop of Viborg, Jørgen Friis. Transferred to the Crown after the Reformation. Privately owned from 1579 until 1937, when the state bought the castle. Museum from 1941. 2, 193-*194*, *196-197*, 202, 206, 217-*218*, 223, 226, 233, 239

Stautrup, Kolt parish, Central Jutland. Manor house site with perimeter ramparts. Modern buildings on the site. Originator and period of function unknown.

Stege, Møn. Nothing visible preserved of the curtain-wall castle with towers which was demolished by the town-dwellers in the 1530s during Grevens Fejde after it had developed through the Middle Ages from before the mid-13th century. Royal property. 52, 149, 167, 202, 240

Svaneholm, Skurups parish, Scania. Manor house built in 1530. Later rebuilding and extensions. Privately owned.

Svendborg, Funen. Nothing visible preserved or known of the castle that gave the town its name.
87-88, 94, 151

Søborg, Søborg parish, North Sealand. In the dried-up lake at Søborg lies the ruin of the curtain-wall castle with towers and a *palatium*, built in the 12th century on the outermost of three islets. Initially it was probably a tower behind ramparts or a palisade. In front of the next islet there were large ramparts of unknown age, probably older than the castle. The first known owner was Archbishop Eskil. Valdemar the Great conquered the castle in 1161, and it remained in royal possession thereafter. In the 16th century it was placed under Kronborg and the castle was demolished after 1577. *24*, 27, 32, 36, *40-44*, 63, 71-73, 78, 92, 104, 147-148, 160, 193, 239, 251, *257*

Søbygård, Søby parish, Ærø. On a narrow ridge there is a trapezoid mound with perimeter ramparts protected by moats and ramparts and a bailey. Period of function from a point in the 12th century until around 1300. At the same time there was a trading place in Vitsjø bay, below the castle. Probably a royal building. *54*

Søgaard, Kliplev parish, South Jutland. Large castle site, probably 14th century, razed in 1643-44 during the "Torstensson War" between Sweden and Denmark. The mounds were partly destroyed by road construction in the 19th century. In the 16th century the castle was the residence of several members of the Ahlefeldt family. Privately owned. 167

Søholm, Magleby parish, South Sealand. Double castle mound with a main mound and a bailey, originally on a spit of land in a lake but now completely surrounded by water. Destroyed in the 1530s during Grevens Fejde. Age unknown, privately owned. 203

Sölvesborg, Blekinge. Ruins of a castle from the 13th century, possession disputed between Danes and Swedes, Valdemar Atterdag's from 1359. Damaged by fire in 1564, then destroyed. Swedish after 1658.

Sønderborg, Als. The medieval castle's curtain wall is the outer wall of the present castle, and several of its buildings are also incorporated. The castle grew up around a tower from around the end of the 12th century and became a strong curtain-wall castle. It was given outer defences with projecting round towers in the 1530s, and in 1550-71 it was rebuilt as a Renaissance castle. Belonged to Hans the Younger after that, to the Crown from 1667, and to the Duke of Augustenborg from 1764. Became a museum after the Reunification in 1920. 142, 152, 167, *192-193*, 199, 259

Søvdeborg/Sigosta, Søvde parish, Scania. Nothing is preserved of this structure, which stood on a headland in Søvde Lake, around where the churchyard is situated now. On a narrow neck of land traces have been found of a brick wall. Absalon's? Belonged to the archbishopric of Lund, and to the Crown after the Reformation. 54-55

Tibrantsholm. Jämtland, Sweden, which Queen Margrete transferred to Archbishop Henrik of Uppsala in 1402, when he held the mortgaged Jämtland. The castle was to be torn down and some of the income from it was to be used to reduce the Queen's debt. 167

Tjele, Tjele parish, Central Jutland. Little brick house from the beginning of the 16th century with alterations in the course of the centuries. Now stands amidst other later buildings on an unfortified manor-house site. Privately owned. 169-170, *172-173*, 175, 217, *232-233*, 240

Torbenfeld, Frydendal parish, West Sealand. Three-winged manor house in which the south wing is a rebuilt medieval house. It is situated on one of three islets which formed the site of the medieval structure. Royal for a brief period in the 17th century. Privately owned.

Tordrup, Ørum parish, Central Jutland. Slightly raised area in the meadow beside the manor house of Frisenvold. Here posts have been found along with faint traces of the ruins of the castle, probably from the 14th century, which Queen Margrete acquired in 1406, and which was demolished after that. Probably royal property. 162, 187

Torupvolde, Søvind parish, Central Jutland. Tower mound with trees growing on it, and castle mound partly destroyed by garden activity associated with the present-day buildings at the edge of the mound. No doubt a 14th century structure, but original owner and period of function unknown. *128*

Tosterup, Tosterup parish, Scania. Medieval buildings with a tower are incorporated into the present manor-house buildings, which follow the ground plan of the medieval structure. Built on an islet in a lake, and probably from c.1300. Privately owned. 240

Tovskov, Sommersted parish, South Jutland. An oval tower mound surrounded by moats is all that is known of the castle that in 1374 was promised to Valdemar Atterdag as "a castle of the kingdom and ready to be demolished at his order". This did not happen until later. Age and origin unknown, but no doubt a 14th century structure.

Tranekær, Tranekær parish, Langeland. Two wings built at right angles, on a high natural mound surrounded by moats, are what is left of a medieval curtain-wall castle. The north wing was the *palatium* in the 13th century. Function as a fortress abandoned after Grevens Fejde in the 1530s. In 1725 the curtain wall and the south and east buildings were torn down. Originally royal property, belonged to the Duke of Schleswig for some period in the Middle Ages. Privately owned from 1645. *50*, 88, 94, *108-109*, 119, *151*-152, 167, 203

Trøjborg, Visby parish, South Jutland. Ruin of a castle dating from 1580, built on the ruin of a medieval castle with tower and curtain wall from c. 1300. Owned privately or by the Duke, then by Queen Margrete I in 1407 and after that by the Bishops of Ribe. Crown property after the Reformation, private ownership in 1579. Demolished in 1854. *141*, 167

Tønderhus, Tønder, Jutland. Nothing is preserved of the medieval castle from 1268-70, which was built on three mounds. On the main mound a Renaissance building was erected in the 1520s, and the gatehouse of that structure is preserved. The owner was the Duke of Schleswig and the castle remained in principle ducal. The later Frederik I initiated the rebuilding. For the next many years Tønderhus was ducal. From 1721 until 1748 it was royal property and then was demolished. The fortifications were demolished at the end of the 17th century. 92

Tørning, Hammelev parish. South Jutland. Huge structure with a main mound, moats and several other mounds. Probably 14th century, originally royal, with frequent changes of ownership until 1494, when the castle again became Crown property. After 1523 it was administered under Haderslevhus, the buildings decayed and it all burned down in 1579. 128

Tårnborg, Tårnborg parish, West Sealand. Almost square castle mound with traces of a curtain wall and brick central tower on boulder foundations. Part of a larger structure which also included the nearby church. Similar to Sprogø, and possibly built in the 12th century. Abandoned at the latest in the mid-15th century. Royal property. *64, 65,* 67, 149

Vallø, Valløby parish, South Sealand. 16th century manor, restored in the 19th century, situated on a medieval mound. Age unknown, no knowledge of possible fortifications. Privately owned. 224-225, 238

Varberg, Halland. The inner castle courtyard of this impressive fortress is the medieval curtain-wall castle that was probably built by Count Jacob of North Halland between 1287 and 1300. Royal ownership later in the Middle Ages. Modernised fortress with bastions 1588-1618. Fortifications abandoned early in the 19th century. Used as a museum from the early 20th century. 103, 203, 260, *262-263*

Vardehus, Varde parish, West Jutland. Two mounds, one south and the other west of the town, are probably 14th century and functioned until the beginning of the 15th century. Only the former has been investigated. Royal property.

Vesborg, Kolby parish, Samsø. Lighthouse and remains of a building on top of one of a pair of mounds. Part of it has been eroded by the sea. Built in the mid-14th century and disused after a few years. Royal property. *7,* 51-52, *247*

Visborg, Visby, Gotland. Ruin of a large curtain-wall castle built by Erik of Pomerania. Expanded to become almost a town in itself, with the town. Destroyed in 1676-79 by Danish troops. Royal property. 182, *184,* 186, 226, 231, 233, 236, 239-240

Vittsjø, Vittsjø parish, Scania. Double castle mound with traces of iron production on the mounds. There are coin finds dated to the 14th century, but the age and circumstances of ownership are not known. 139

Voergaard, Voer parish, Vendsyssel, North Jutland. A brick house from c.1525 is the eastern part of the north wing in an angled structure on an unfortified low square mound surrounded by moats. The east wing is a splendid Renaissance house from the end of the 16th century. Belonged to the Bishop of Børglum from 1510, and the Crown after the Reformation. Privately owned from 1578. *174,* 176

Volstrup/Ulstrup, Hjerm parish, West Jutland. A 19th century manor house with three wings, standing on the medieval castle mound where Erik Menved built a "subjugation castle" in 1313-14 on "the Bishop of Ribe's land". Nothing is known about the character of the structure. Belonged to the Crown at the Reformation, but then immediately became privately owned. 112

Vordingborg, Sealand. Formidable ruin of one of the largest and oldest of the important royal castles. The structure certainly dates back to the 12th century. The ruins of the curtain wall, the central castle and the Goose Tower lead back to Valdemar Atterdag in particular. Demolished in the 18th century. Royal property. 48, *53*-54, 62-63, 65, *67,* 73, 78, 81, 92, 123, 145-147, 150, *157-159, 239, 244, 255, 259*

Index of names and places

Historical Sources

Raven van Barnekows Råkenskaper för Nyköpings fögderi 1365-1367 (Accounts of Nyköping bailiwick 1365-67). Utgivna genom Birgitta Fritz och Eva Odelman Kung. Samfundet för utgivande av handskrifter rörande Skandinaviens historia. Handlingar del 17. Stockholm 1994

IVAR AXELSSON THOTTS RÄKENSKAPSBOK FÖR GOTLAND 1485-1487 (Account book for Gotland 1485-87). Utgiven med inledning och register av Evert Melefors under medverkan av Dick Wase. ACTA ERUDITORUM GOTLANDICA, Actum VII MCMLXXXXI

Roskildekrøniken – the Roskilde Chronicle, translated into Danish and annotated by Michael Gelting, Wormianum 1979

Jyske Krønike – the Jutland Chronicle, translated into Danish and annotated by Rikke Agnete Olsen 1995

Ryd Klosters Årbog i kulturhistorisk belysning – the chronicle of Ryd monastery, translated into Danish by Rikke Agnete Olsen 1989

Sjællandske Krønike – the Sealand Chronicle, translated into Danish and annotated by Rikke Agnete Olsen 1981

Valdemar Sejrs Sønner og den store Ærkebispestrid Udvalg af Kilder til Danmarks Historie 1241-1274 (selected sources of Danish History 1241-1274), translated into Danish by Jørgen Olrik 1906-08

Erik Klipping og hans Sønner, Rigets Opløsning, selected sources translated into Danish by Ellen Jørgensen 1927

Valdemar Atterdag, Udvalg af Kilder – selected sources translated into Danish by Ellen Jørgensen, 1911

Annales Danici medii aevi, Ellen Jørgensen (ed.) 1920

Danmarks middelalderlige annaler. (Denmark's medieval annals) Erik Kromann (ed.) København 1980

Danske middelalderlige regnskaber Vols. I-II (Danish medieval accounts) Georg Galster (ed.) København 1953

Den danske Rigslovgivning indtil 1400 (Danish national laws before 1400) Erik Kromann (ed.) København 1971

Den danske rigslovgivning 1397-1513 (Danish national laws 1397-1513) Aage Andersen (ed.) København 1989

Diplomatarium Danicum indtil 1400 Frantz Blatt et al. (eds.) København 1938-2000, Danish version in Danmarks Riges Breve Frantz Blatt et al. (eds.) København 1938-2000

Diplomatarium Danici/ Danmarks Riges breve 1400-1412 digital edition

Repertorium diplomaticum regni Danici medievalis Kristian Erslev (ed.) I-IV København 1894-1912

Testamenter fra Danmarks middelalder indtil 1450 (Danish medieval testaments before 1450) Kristian Erslev (ed.) København 1901

Bibliography

Andersen, Charlotte B.H.: Material Culture in Danish Castles, *Castella Maris Baltici* 6 2004 pp. 9-17

Andersen, Jens: Nye undersøgelser af bispens borg Sejlstrup, *Vendsyssel Nu og Da* 1997 pp. 62-67

Andersen, Valdemar: *Hald Hovedgård 1435-1975. Niels Bugges borg, slot og len*, Herning 1977

Asingh, Pauline and Engberg Nils (eds.): *Marsk Stig og de fredløse på Hjelm*, Ebeltoft/Aarhus 2002

Bekmose Jens and Svend Nielsen: Borgen i Stege, *Antikvariske Studier* 2 1978 pp. 97-130

Bencard, Mogens and Rikke Agnete Olsen: Højstrup. En hovedgårds bygningshistorie, *Historisk Samfund for Præstø Amt, Årbog* 2005 pp. 5-30.

Bengedans, Johannes: *Krigskunst og Kanoner/ Kriegskunst und Kanonen* I-II, Hans Blosen and Rikke Agnete Olsen (eds.) with Aage Andersen, Bendt Falkesgaard Pedersen and Frede Storborg, Aarhus 2006

Bengtsson, Bengt: *Hallands fästningar Hallands Historia*, Halmstad 1954

Bertelsen, Thomas: Det middelalderlige Gammel Estrup, *Bygningsarkæologiske Studier* 2001-02 pp. 19-32

Blomqvist, Regnar: Falsterbohus, *Kulturen* 1950 pp. 142-181

Bonde, Niels; Eriksvolde – en dendrokronologisk datering, *Nationalmuseets Arbejdsmark* 1979 pp. 150-155

Bonde, Niels, Aoife Daly and Kaare Lund Rasmussen: Nyborg Slot i nyt lys. Naturvidenskab og bygningsarkæologi, *Aarbøger for nordisk Olskyndighed og Historie* 2000 pp. 137-154

Bonde, Niels: Dendrokronologisk datering af Nyborg Slot, *Bygningsarkæologiske Studier* 2006-2008, 2010 pp. 212-126

Boringholm, en østjysk træborg fra 1300-årene, Jan Kock and Else Roesdahl (eds.), Jysk arkæologisk selskab 2005.

Carelli, Peter: Krapperup och det feodala landskapet, *Historia kring Krapperup* 2003

Christensen, C.A.: Arnsholm and Valdemar Sappi. Et nordslesvigsk drama fra Valdemar Atterdags tid. *Festskrift til Johan Hvidtfeldt på halvfjerdsårsdagen 12. december 1978*, Peter Kr. Iversen, Knud Prange and Sigurd Rambusch (eds.) 1978 pp. 39-52

Christensen, Harry: *Len og magt i Danmark 1439-1481*, Aarhus 1983

Christensen, Keld: Årringsdateringer af træ fra kongeborgen Vordingborg, *Kulturhistoriske studier* 1998 pp. 59-68

la Cour, Vilhelm: Voldsted ved Højskovgaard, *Fynske Årbøger* 1952

la Cour, Vilhelm: Om studiet af vore danske voldsteder, *Historisk Tidsskrift* 12th series.Vol. I. 2nd part. pp. 155-188.

la Cour, Vilhelm and Hans Stiesdal: *Danske Voldsteder fra Oldtid og Middelalder, Thisted amt*, 1957 and *Hjørring amt* 1963.

la Cour, Vilhelm: *Næsholm. Det middelalderlige borganlæg Næsholm ved Nykøbing S.*, Nationalmuseet 1961

la Cour, Vilhelm: *Danske borganlæg til midten af det 13. århundrede* I-II, København 1972

Dahlerup, Troels, Jeppe Büchert Netterstrøm and Bjørn Poulsen: Mourids Nielsen Gyldenstjernes regnskaber. Rejseregnskaber 1493-94, inventarium 1494, julelagsliste 1496 og mandtal 1499, *Danske Magazin* Vol. 50 part 2, København 2008 pp. 303-342

Didriksen, J.: *Bjørnkær. Østjysk Hjemstavn* 1941 pp. 55-67

Dobat, Andreas S., Per Th. Mandrup and Simon K. Nielsen: Et kongeligt borganlæg fra middelalderen ved Aggersborg. Årbog 2009 *Vesthimmerlands Museum* pp. 37-45

Dähn, Arthur: *Ringwälle und Turmhügel, Mittelalterliche Burgen in Schleswig-Holstein*, Husum 2001

Egevang, Robert and Søren Frandsen: Det ottekantede tårn, *Nationalmuseets Arbejdsmark* 1985 pp. 73-90

Eliasen, Kirsten and Marianne Goral Krogh: Nyborg Slot-status vedrørende de arkæologiske undersøgelser, *Bygningsarkæologiske Studier* 2006-2008, 2010 pp. 57-74

Engberg, Nils: Danske privatborge før 1250? Et bidrag til det omdiskuterede spørgsmål. Festskrift til Hans Stiesdal, *hikuin* 19 1992 pp. 15-30

Engberg, Nils: Næsholms datering-dendrokronologisk eller numismatisk? brugerens dilemma. Festskrift til Hans Stiesdal, *hikuin* 19 1992 pp. 75-82

Engberg, Nils: The Danish Castle before 1250 – Status Symbol or Necessary Defence, *Castella Maris Baltici* 1 1993 pp. 51-61

Engberg, Nils: Borren and Næsholm. Two examples of Danish Castle-building, *Château Gaillard* XVI 1994 pp. 155-166

Engberg, Nils: The nobleman's estate in Denmark in the period 300-1500 AD, *Castella Maris Baltici* 5 2001 pp. 31-42.

Engberg, Nils: Hagerup Castle. *Wider das „finstere Mittelalter". Festschrift für Werner Meyer zum 65. Geburtstag*. Basel 2002 pp. 31-40

Engberg, Nils: Three Castles on Hjelm Island – their Military, Social and Political Significance, *Castella Maris Baltici* 6 2004 pp. 63-83

Engberg, Nils and Frandsen Jørgen: Engelborg – et befæstet orlogsværft på Slotø i Nakskov Fjord, *Nationalmuseets Arbejdsma*rk 2006 pp. 115-133

Engberg Nils, Vivian Etting and Marianne Iversen

Greve: Kongens borg på Kalø – Nye undersøgelser, *KUML* 2008 pp. 187-210

Engberg, Nils, Vivian Etting, Lis Nymark and Hans Skov: Kongeborg, kirke og borgerkrig på Gl. Brattingsborg – en forrygende start på et nyt forskningsprojekt på Samsø, *Nationalmuseets Arbejdsmark* 2009 pp. 91-108

Engberg, Nils: The King's Castle on Kalø Island, Denmark, *Château Gaillard* 24, 2010 pp. 77-87

Engberg, Nils and Jørgen Frandsen: *Valdemar den Stores borg på Sprogø*, Wormianum 2011

Engqvist, Hans Henrik: *Tjele. En midtjysk herregårds bygningshistorie*, København 1974

Engqvist, Hans Henrik: Fire fynske herreborge, *Architectura* 2 1980 pp. 55-125

Engqvist, Hans Henrik: Østergaard, *Bygningsarkæologiske Studier* 1993 pp. 7-28

Engqvist, Hans Henrik: Herregårdene Odden og Kokkedal – samt lidt om de små senmiddelalderlige stenhuse, *Bygningsarkæologiske studier* 1994 pp. 7-43

Ericsson, Ingolf: Burgen und Herrenhöfe auf den süddänischen Inseln. *Medeltiden och Arkeologin. Festskrift til Erik Cinthio*, A. Andrén et al. (eds.) (Lund Studies in Medieval Archaeology 1) 1986

Ericsson, Ingolf: Engelborg på Slotø-skibsværft, fæstning og lendmandssæde på kong Hans' tid, *hikuin* 14 1988 pp. 261-275

Ericsson, Ingolf: Nogle bemærkninger om privatborge i Skåne og styltetårne i Danmark. Festskrift til Hans Stiesdal, *hikuin* 19 1992 pp. 31-42

Ericsson, Ingolf: Mittelalterliche Wehrbauten in Schleswig-Holstein, *Castella Maris Baltici* 1 1993 pp. 67-78

Ericsson, Ingolf: Wehrbauten des Mittelalters in Skandinavien und dem Gebiet südlich der Ostsee. *The Study of Medieval Archaeology*, Hans Andersson and Jes Wienberg (eds.) (Lund Studies in Medieval Archaeology 13) 1993 pp. 219-291

Eriksson, Anna-Lena: Town and Castle as Framework for Social Structure, *Castella Maris Baltici* 3-4 2000 pp. 49-56

Eriksson, Torkel and Thomas Bartholin: Takbjälkar och golvbjälklag. Dendrokronologisk datering af Kärnan. Festskrift til Hans Stiesdal, *hikuin* 19 1992 pp. 43-54

Erikssson, Torkel: "Castrum nostrum Helsingburgh" – Erik Menved und Schloss Helsingburgh, *Castella Maris Baltici* 1, Stockholm 1993 pp. 79-88

Eriksson, Torkel: *En ruin försvinner: Kärnan i Helsingborg 1880-1894*, Helsingborg 1994

Eriksson, Torkel, Knut Drake, Peter Carelli: *Kärnan och borgen, Helsingborgs slotts medeltida byggnadshistoria* (Skånsk senmedeltid och renässans 22) 2007

Etting, Vivian: The Royal Castles of Denmark as Centers of Regional Administration, Tax collection and mobilization in the late Middle Ages, *Castella Maris Baltici* 5 2001 pp. 43-50

Etting, Vivian, Lone Hvass and Charlotte B. Andersen: *Gurre Slot – kongeborg og sagnskat*, København 2003

Etting, Vivian and Nils Engberg: Fra storgård til herregård. I: *Herregården. Menneske – Samfund –Landskab – Bygninger*, Bd. I, John Erichsen and Mikkel Venborg Pedersen (eds.), København 2004 pp. 119-162

Etting, Vivian, Jørgen Frandsen, Hans Mikkelsen and Kjeld Borch West: Kelstrup – en middelalderborg i Ods Herred, *Nationalmuseets Arbejdsmark* 2005, pp. 11-29

Etting, Vivian, Lone Hvass and Charlotte Boje H. Andersen: Jagten på Gurre. Nye arkæologiske undersøgelser af Valdemar Atterdags borg, *Nationalmuseets Arbej*dsmark 2002 pp. 149-170

Etting, Vivian, Nils Engberg, Jørgen Frandsen and Lis Nymark: Vesborg-kongeborgen med den korte historie, *Nationalmuseets Arbejdsmark* 2010 pp. 37-52

Etting, Vivian: Riberhus. I: *Ribe bys historie* 710-1520, Søren Bitsch Christensen (ed.) (Skrifter om dansk byhistorie 7), Aarhus 2010 pp. 82-90

Etting, Vivian: *The royal castles of Denmark during the 14th century. An analysis of the major royal castles with special regard to their functions and strategic importance.* (Publications of the National Museum) (Studies in Archaeology and History Vol. 19) 2010

Fangel, Henrik: Det middelalderlige Ejsbøl og den holstenske indvandring i hertugdømmet Slesvig, *Sønderjyske Årbøger* 1969 pp. 104-130

Fangel, Henrik: Slægten Emmiksen og dens gods, *Sønderjyske Årbøger* 1972 pp. 5-59.

Fangel, Henrik: Herremænd på Haderslev Næs i middelalderen, *Sønderjyske Årbøger* 1978 pp. 5-47

Fangel, Henrik: Herremænd på Als og Sundeved i middelalderen og 1500-tallet. *Fra Als og Sundeved* 57, 1979 pp. 9-49

Fangel, Henrik and Lennart S. Madsen: Voldsteder og herremænd i Nordslesvig. *Kongemagt og samfund i middelalderen festskrift til Erik Ulsig på 60-årsdagen 13. februar 1988* (Historiske Skrifter) 1988 pp. 363-390

Finderup, Thomas and Henriette Rensbro: Træværket fra Stege Borg, Håndværk, teknologi og ressourcer i 1314, *KUML* 2005 pp. 225-268

Fisker, Erik Bjerre: Nyborg Slot-bygningsarkæologiske undersøgelser, *Bygningsarkæologiske Studier* 2006-2008 2010 pp. 9 -56

Gadgaard, Hans, Jesper Hjermind and Jens Vellev: Undervandsarkæologiske registreringer ved bispens Hald. Festskrift til Hans Stiesdal, *hikuin* 19 1992 pp. 125-268.

Galster, Georg: Fra Christopher af Bajerns hof, *Nationalmuseets Arbejdsmark* 1966 pp. 512-60

Gamrath, Helge: *Københavns Slot, Christiansborg Slot* I 1975 pp. 48-166

Grinder-Hansen, Kjeld: Hvor der handles, der spildes – hvad 3300 mønter fortæller om Tårnborg ved Korsør, *Nationalmuseets Arbejdsmark* 1994 pp. 186-196

Haas, Charlotte: Korsør middelalderlige fæstningstårn, *Bygningsarkæologiske Studier* 1990 pp. 33-44

Hansen, Karl: *Danske Ridderborge*, 1832

Hansson, Martin: *Medeltida Borgar, Maktens hus i Norden* 2011

Hammershus, Kjeld Borch Vesth and Ebbe G. Rasmussen (eds.), Bornholms Historiske Samfund 1997

Hauberg, P. : Hammershus. *Bornholmske Samlinger* 7 1912 pp. 139-158

Hertz, Johannes: Tre borge på Egholm, *Nationalmuseets Arbejdsmark* 1962 pp. 94-119

Hertz, Johannes: Solvig, *Skalk* 1, 1967 pp 8-13

Hertz, Johannes: The excavations of Solvig, a Danish crannog in southern Jutland/Further excavations at Solvig, *Chateau Gaillard* VI 1973 pp. 84-105

Hertz, Johannes: Some examples of medieval hypocausts in Denmark, *Château Gaillard* VII 1975 pp. 127-140

Hertz, Johannes: Om danske middelalderlige vindebroer på baggrund af nye fund ved Hald og Søborg, *Antikvariske Studier* 4, 1980 pp. 161-178

Hertz, Johannes: Danish Medieval Drawbridges, *Château Gaillard* X, Caen 1982 pp. 419-432

Hertz, Johannes: Brundlund, et næsten ukendt slot, *Nationalmuseets Arbejdsmark* 1986 pp. 84-103

Hertz, Johannes: Kalundborg, Danmarks Carcassonne, *Nationalmuseets Arbejdsmark* 1990 pp. 79-93

Hertz, Johannes: Bisp Peder Jensen Lodehats kapel på Gjorslev, *Bygningsarkæologiske Studier* 1991 pp. 13-20

Hertz, Johannes: Kalundborg a Danish Fortified Medieval Town and Castle, *Château Gaillard* XIV pp. 195-202

Hertz, Johannes: Gjorslev, en borg i korsets tegn, *Nationalmuseets Arbejdsmark* 1992 pp. 190-207

Hertz, Johannes: Træk af Trøjborgs bygningshistorie 1347-1854. Festskrift til Hans Stiesdal, *hikuin* 19 1992 pp. 153-178

Hertz, Johannes: Gammelt nyt om Kogsbøl voldsted. Festskrift til Hans Stiesdal, *hikuin* 19 1992 pp. 103-108

Hertz, Johannes: Træk af Trøjborgs bygningshistorie 1347-1854. Festskrift til Hans Stiesdal, *hikuin* 19 1992 pp. 153-178

Hertz, Johannes: Gjorslev, eine dänische Bischofsburg mit architektonischen Bezügen zum Deutschen Ritterorden? *Castella Maris Baltici* 3-4 2000 pp. 57-62

Hinsch, Connie: Fundene fra Hammershus, *Hammershus* 1997 pp. 211-220

Hyldgaard, Inger Marie: Hedegård – et træbygget borganlæg fra 1300-tallet, *hikuin* 14 1988 pp. 263-271

Hørby, Kai and Rikke Agnete Olsen: Hammershus i middelalderen. *Bornholmske Samlinger* series III. Vol. 6, Rønne 1992 pp. 43-55

Jacobsen, J.C.: Aagaard og dens ejere, *Historisk Aarbog for Thisted Amt* 1930-34 pp. 66-96, 115-148, 227-241

Jantzen, Connie and Jan Kock: Mosens fæstningsværker, *Skalk* 1 1988, pp. 3-8

Jantzen, Connie: Det første Egholm. Forgængeren til Egholm Slot. Festskrift til Hans Stiesdal, *hikuin* 19 1992, pp. 130-152

Jantzen, Connie: Timbered Fortresses from the 14th Century in Northern Jutland, *Château Gaillard* XV 1993 pp. 205-216

Jantzen, Connie and Rikke Agnete Olsen: Mourids Nielsen Gyldenstjerne, The Owner of Aagaard, and his House, *Château Gaillard* XX 2002, pp. 123-129

Jantzen, Connie and Rikke Agnete Olsen: Vand og Voldsteder. *De ferske vandes kulturhistorie*, Silkeborg 2004 pp. 209-216

Jantzen, Connie and Rikke Agnete Olsen: Boeslum by Ebeltoft – unexpected Information from an "ordinary" Site, *Château Gaillard* 25, 2012, pp. 203-210

Jaubert, Anne Nissen: "han byggede nye borge –" *Skalk* 3 1987 pp. 18-27

Jaubert, Anne Nissen: The Royal Castles during the Reign of Erik Menved (1286-1319), *Journal of Danish Archaeology* 7 1988 pp. 216-224

Jaubert, Anne Nissen: Princes' Residences in Denmark – from ca.1000 to ca.1350, *Castella Maris Baltici* 1 1993 pp. 89-100

Jensen, Christian Axel: *Gjorslev*, København 1924

Jensen, Christian Axel: Riberhus Slotsbanke. *Fra Ribe Amt* 1943 pp. 1-16

Jensen, Jørgen Steen; Næsholms datering – dendrokronologisk eller numismatisk? Festskrift til Hans Stiesdal, *hikuin* 19 1992 pp. 83-88

Jensen, Vivi: Koldings middelalderlige fæstningsværker og jordværkerne omkring Koldinghus, *hikuin* 7 1981 pp. 9-109

Jensen, Vivi: Koldinghus, a Danish Border castle of the late Middle Ages, *Château Gaillard* XIII 1987 pp. 81-98

Jensen, Vivi and Poul Dedenroth-Schou: *Koldinghus. Grænseborg – Kongeslot – Ruin – Museum*, Viborg 2004

Johannsen, Marianne: Vallø før stiftet. I: *Vallø. Historien om et slot og dets ejere dets skæbne og funktion fra middelalder til nutid og fremtid. Et kvindehus gennem 250 år*, Sys Hartmann (ed.) 1988 pp. 9-36

Klitgaard, C.: Bidrag til Aagaards bygningshistorie, *Historisk Aarbog for Thisted Amt* 1930-1934 pp. 242-514

Kock, Jan & Mette Svart Kristiansen: Skjern Slot. En undersøgelse af en borg og dens omgivelser gennem middelalder og renæssance, *KUML* 2010 pp. 129-177

Kock, Jan: Skjern Castle: An Archaeological-Historical Investigation, *Château Gaillard* 24 2010 pp. 135-147

Kollberg, Ludvig: Vadstad borg och Abraham Brodersen Tjurhuvud eller Oxhuvud, Halland 1967 pp. 25-44.

Kristensen, Hans Krongaard: Sandgravvold. Festskrift til Hans Stiesdal, *hikuin* 19 1992 pp. 55-74

Kristensen, Hans Krongaard: Østtårnet på Nyborg Slot, *Bygningsarkæologiske Studier* 2006-2008, 2010 pp. 87-100

Kromann, Anne: Et senmiddelalderligt bryllupsregnskab, *Nationalmuseets Arbejdsmark* 1980 pp. 33-42

Larsen, Lars Agersnap and Jesper Hjermind: De fem Halder. Kan man kigge gennem jorden? Pilotprojekt til implementering af ikke-destruktive arkæologiske undersøgelsesmetoder (IDA) i Dansk Middelalderarkæologi, *Viborg Middelalderseminar* 3 2010

Larsen, Lars Krants, Jette Linaa, Johannes Hertz and Inger Lauridsen: *Tønderhus – en købstadsborg i hertugdømmet Slesvig*, Museum Sønderjylland 2010

Liebgott, Niels-Knud: Keramikfundene fra voldstedet Pedersborg ved Sorø. *Aarbøger for Nordisk Oldkyndighed og Historie* 1977 pp. 118-170

Liebgott, Niels-Knud: Pedersborg, *Château Gaillard* X 1982 pp. 471-482,

Liebgott, Niels-Knud: An Outline of Danish Castle-Studies, *Château Gaillard* XI 1983 pp. 193-206

Liebgott, Niels-Knud: *Dansk middelalderarkæologi*, København 1989

Liebgott, Niels-Knud: Brick-making and Castle-building, *Château Gaillard* XVIII 1996 pp. 109-117

Liebgott, Niels-Knud and Rikke Agnete Olsen: Castellology in Scandinavia at the Beginning of the 2nd Millennium, *Château Gaillard* 23 2008 pp. 341-348

Lundberg, Erik B: Lindholmens Slott och Grävningarna år 1935, *Skånes Hembygdsförbunds Årsbok* 1959 pp. 71-82

Lundberg, Erik B.: Visborgs Slott. *Kung. Vitterhets Historie och Antikvitets Akademiens Handlinger*, Stockholm 1950 pp. 224-287

Lundberg, Erik B.: Vem anlada Visborgs Slott- Tyska orden eller Erik af Pommern? Nogra synpunkter, *Gotländsk Arkiv* 1984 pp. 151-160.

Madsen, Lennart S.: Dagligliv på Nørrevold-hvad udgravninger og genstande kan berette, *Sønderjyske Årbøger* 1990 pp. 5-20

Madsen, Lennart S.: Grimsborg, Jels, Refsø og Dresvold. Hans Neumanns voldstedsudgravninger i 1940'erne. Festskrift til Hans Stiesdal, *hikuin* 19, 1992 pp. 89-102

Madsen, Lennart S. and Rasmussen Carsten Porskrog: Herremænd og borge. I: *Middelalderens Danmark. Kultur og Samfund fra trosskifte til reformation*, Per Ingesman, Ulla Kjær, Per Kristian Madsen and Jens Vellev (eds.) 1999 pp. 82-99

Mathiesen, Poul: Bygholm Østjysk Hjemstavn,

1957 pp. 11-26; 1958 pp. 33-55; and 1959 pp. 81-89

Mathiesen, Aage: Oplysninger om middelalderlige Fæstningstårne. *Aarbøger for Nordisk Oldkyndighed og Historie* 1902 pp. 45-68

Melander, Jan (ed.): *Den medeltida borgen. Aspekter på aktuel borgforskning*, Gävle 1989

Mogren, Mats and Jes Wienberg (eds.): *Lindholmen Medeltida riksborg i Skåne*, 1995

Mogren, Mats: The Bailiff's Craftsmen, A Study of Two Administrative Castles from the Fifteenth Century, *Meddelanden från Lunds Universitets Historiska Museum* 1993-1994 New series 10 pp. 119-133

Mortansson, T.: *Helsingborgs Slott under Medeltiden* 1934

Mortensen, Michael H.: *Dansk artilleri indtil 1600*, København 1999

Møller, Elna: Hindsgavl Slotsbanke, *Nationalmuseets Arbejdsmark* 1944 pp. 39-48

Neumann, Hans: Adel og voldsteder. Fra Gelsbro til Lilllebælt. *Hjemstavnsbog for Haderslev by og amt* 1958 pp. 49-60

Nielsen, Carl Lindberg: Hvor lå Vardehus? *Fra Ribe Amt* 1936 pp. 18-45

Nielsen, Finn Ole Sonne: Hammershus set ud fra et arkæologisk perspektiv, *Hammershus*, 1997 pp. 137-148

Nielsen, Henning: A private fortification in Gammel Forlev near Korsør, Denmark, *Castella Maris Baltici* 5 2001 pp. 115-122.

Nielsen, Henning: Arkæologi i Haderslev & en stormandsgård i Ketting. Under fælles hat, Årbog for Museum Sønderjylland, Sønderjyske Museer 2008, pp. 57-80

Nielsen Heidi Maria Møller: Fra borg til herregård i Danmark: privatborge ca. 1350-1600. Moesgaard 1998

Heidi Maria Møller Nielsen: Krogen/Kronborg in the 16th Century: The transformation of a Medieval Danish Royal Castle into an Early Modern Fortress. *Castella Maris Baltici* 2007, pp. 119-130

Heidi Maria Møller Nielsen: A Network of Power: The Royal Castles of Denmark in the 15th Cen-

tury. *Die Burg im 15. Jahrhundert. Veröffentlichungen der Deutschen Burgenvereinigung e.V. Europäisches Burgeninstitut. Reihe B, Band 12*, Braubach 2011 pp. 91-97(and translated into German: Ein Netzwerk der Macht: Dänische Königsburgen im 15. Jahrhudert, same publication pp. 97-101.)

Nielsen, Heidi Maria Møller: Krogen: The medieval Predecessor of Kronborg, *Château Gaillard* 23 2008 pp. 315-328.

Nielsen Heidi Maria Møller: Om studiet af middelalderens borge og voldsteder. Eksempler fra Bromme sogn. *Virke og Vækst II, (Heide Maria Møller Nielsen ed.)*, Sydvestsjællands Museum 2012 pp. 141-154

Nielsen Heidi Maria Møller: Holbæk og Kalundborg – Om kronens borge i middelalderens nordvestsjællandske købstæder, *Middelalderens nordvestsjællandske købstæder* 2012 pp. 107-134

Nielsen Heidi Maria Møller: Holbæk – new light on a sparsely known medieval royal castle. *Castella Maris Baltici* 11 – in print

Nielsen Heidi Maria Møller: "Lost and forgotten": The Castles of Eric of Pomerania (King of Denmark 1396-1439) in the Duchy of Schleswig. *Château Gaillard* 26 – in print

Nilsson, Sten Åke (ed.): Glimmingehus 500 år, *Skånsk Senmedeltid och Renässans* 17 1999

Norn, Otto: Østerholm Slotsruin på Als, *Nationalmuseets Arbejdsmark* 1956 pp. 103-114

Norn Otto: *Christian III's Borge* I-II, København 1949

Nymark, Lis: Samsøs voldsteder, *hikuin* 14 1988 pp. 241-252

Nystrøm, Arne: *Spøttrup*, København 1924

Olsen, Olaf and Rikke Agnete Olsen: Saon-Sahyun-Qalaat Saladin in: *From Handaxe to Kahn*. Essays presented to Peder Mortensen on the occasion of his 70th birthday. Kjeld von Folschack, Henrik Thrane and Ingolf Thunesen (eds.) 2004 pp. 241-254

Olsen, Rikke Agnete: Borgens fald, *Skalk* 6, 1973 pp. 18-28

Olsen, Rikke Agnete: Borgen bygges, *Skalk* 2, 1980 pp. 18-27

Olsen, Rikke Agnete: Danish Manor Houses of the late Middle Age. *Feestbundel voor prof. dr. J.G.N. Renaud*, Zutphen 1981 pp. 154-164.

Olsen, Rikke Agnete: Kalø, *Skalk* 3 1982 pp. 11-22 (Skalk-Vejleder)

Olsen, Rikke Agnete: Danish Medieval Castles at War, *Château Gaillard* IX, Caen 1982 pp. 223-236

Olsen, Rikke Agnete: The Buildings on Danish Moated Sites, *Château Gaillard* X, Caen 1982 pp. 509-526

Olsen, Rikke Agnete: The Danish Royal Castles in the late Middle Ages: Fortresses or Administrative Centres, *Château Gaillard* XII 1985 pp. 65-76

Olsen, Rikke Agnete: Voldsteder i Roskilde Amt, *Historisk Årbog fra Roskilde amt*, 1986 pp. 3-18

Olsen, Rikke Agnete: Big Manors and Large-scale farming in the Late Middle Ages, *Château Gaillard* XIII 1987 pp. 157-167

Olsen, Rikke Agnete: Rehabilitering, *Skalk* 4 1988 pp. 28-29

Olsen, Rikke Agnete: Castle, Manor and Society in the Danish Middle Ages, *Château Gaillard* XIV, 1990 pp. 341-350

Olsen, Rikke Agnete: Kings, Nobles and Buildings of the Later Middle Ages: Denmark. I: *Scotland and Scandinavia 800-1200*, G. Simpson Grant (ed.), Edinburgh 1990 pp. 48-59

Olsen, Rikke Agnete: Livet på borgen – og omkring den. Festskrift til Hans Stiesdal, *hikuin* 19, 1992 pp. 269-280

Olsen, Rikke Agnete: Voldsteder. I: *Da klinger i Muld. 25 års arkæologi i Danmark*, Steen Hvass and Birger Storgaard (eds.), Aarhus 1993 pp. 260-63

Olsen, Rikke Agnete: The feudal Castle – A Fiction? *Castella Maris Baltici* 1 1993 pp. 155-158.

Olsen, Rikke Agnete: *Borge i Danmark*, 1996 (2nd edition)

Olsen, Rikke Agnete: *Danske Middelalderborge*, 2011

Olsen, Rikke Agnete: Hammershus on Bornholm – or who owned the Archbishop's Castle, *Château Gaillard* XVII 1996 pp. 145-149.

Olsen, Rikke Agnete: "Schnaps auf der Burg" – a Danish Example. I: *Wider das „finstere Mittelalter", Festschrift für Werner Meyer zum 65. Geburtstag*, Basel 2002 pp. 151-158

Olsen, Rikke Agnete: The best of Friends – or? Queen Margrete at Work. *Interdisciplinäre Beiträge zur Siedlungsarchaeologie, Gedenkschrift für Walter Janssen*, Rahden/Westf. 2002 pp. 279-287

Olsen, Rikke Agnete: *Den historiske Marsk Stig og Hjelm*. I: *Marsk Stig og de fredløse på Hjelm*, Pauline Asingh and Nils Engberg (eds.), Ebeltoft/Aarhus 2002 pp. 49-74.

Olsen, Rikke Agnete: Kalø. To reconstruct or not to reconstruct. *Mélanges d'archaeologie médievale. Liber amicorum en hommage à André Matthys*, Les Cahiers de l'Urbanisme, horsserie. Septembre 2006 pp. 156-161.

Olsen Rikke Agnete: Asdal i middelalderen, *FRA EGNENS FORTID*, Lokalhistorisk selskab for Hirtshals og omegn 2013 pp. 33-43

Pavón Martin: Søborg – ærkebiskop Eskils borg i Nordsjælland. *Aarbøger for Nordisk Oldkyndighed og Historie* 2013 pp 263-292

Porsmose, Erland: Slaget ved Brobjerg, *Skalk* 6 1984 pp. 3-8

Poulsen, Bjørn and Fritz S. Pedersen: Regnskabet for Ribebispens gård Brink 1388-1389, *Danske Magazin* Series 8, vol. VI part 3. 1993 pp. 316-336

Poulsen, Karen Lykkegaard: Eriksvolde – et uafsluttet fæstningsværk. Festskrift til Hans Stiesdal, *hikuin* 19 1992 pp. 109-124

Randsborg, Klavs: Bastrup – Europe. A massive Danish Donjon from 1100, *Acta Archaeologica* vol. 74,1 2003 pp. 65-122

Rasmussen, Ebbe Gert: Landet og borgen. Bornholm og Hammershus indtil 1684, *Bornholmske Samlinger* 1997, Series 3 Vol. 11 pp. 9-78

Rasmussen, Kaare Lund: Termoluminicensdatering af mursten fra Nyborg Slot, *Bygningsarkæologiske Studier* 2006-2008, 2010 pp. 127-132

Rasmussen, Ulla Fraes: Karlstrup voldsted. En stormandsgård ved Karlstrup Kirke sammenlignet med andre middelalderhuse, *Årbog for Køge Museum* 1991

Reisnert, Anders: The City of Malmø and the Castle Malmøhus, *Castella Maris Baltici* 3-4 pp. 159-166

Rensbro, Henriette: Udgravning af Stege borg, *Kulturhistoriske Studier* 2001 pp. 65-81

Rensbro, Henriette: Stege Borg 1314 – En Tvangsborg på Møn, *Historisk Samfund for Præstø amt, årbog* 2002 pp. 9-20

Rensbro, Henriette: Stege Borg-a Danish Wooden Castle, *Castella Maris Baltici* 6 2004 pp. 165-172.

Riismøller, Peter: Høgerede i Himmerland, *Skalk* 1966, 1 pp. 12-20

Roesdahl, Else (ed.) *Bolig og familie i Danmarks middelalder*, Aarhus 2003

Rosborn, Sven and Anders Reisnert: *Borgeby: Medeltidsborgen ved Lödde å*, Malmø 1986

Rosén, Jerker: Drottning Margaretas svenska räfst, *Skandia* XX/2 1950 pp. 169-246

Roussell, Aage: En middelalderlig jysk træborg, *Nationalmuseets Arbejdsmark* 1939 pp. 55-59

Roussell, Aage: *Danmarks Middelalderborge*, København 1942

Roussell, Aage: Middelalderborgen ved Halkær, *Nationalmuseets Arbejdsmark* 1947 pp. 73-79

Rydbeck, Otto: *Den medeltida borgen i Skanör. Historik, undersökninger och fynd*, Lund 1935

Schultz, C.G.: Malling, en befæstet Kirkegaard, *Nationalmuseets Arbejdsmark* 1945 pp. 85-100

Simonsen, Vedel: *Borgruinerne*, København 1913

Skansjö, Sten: Örkelljunga 1307 – borg, bygd och brödrastrider. *Ale, Historisk tidskrift för Skåne, Halland och Blekinge*, 3 2007 pp. 1-16

Søvsø Morten: Riber Ulfsborg Middelalderarkæologisk Nyhedsbrev no. 82, February 2014 pp. 17-19

Skaarup, Bi: *Middelaldermad: kulturhistorie, kilder og 99 opskrifter*, København 2000

Skaarup, H.E.: Borgen og dens våben, *Hammershus*, Ebbe Gert Rasmussen and Kjeld Borch Vesth (eds.) 1997 pp. 115-136

Skaarup, Jørgen, with contributions by Sara Vebæk Gelskov and Anders Reisnert: *Øhavets middelalderlige borge og voldsteder,* Langelands Museum 2005

Slettebo, Jørgen: Adel, slotte og voldsteder. I: *Bogen om Als,* Robert Huhle (ed.), Aabenraa 1956 pp. 145-170

Smidt, C.M.: Nationalmuseets udgravning af Blåtårn, *Fra Arkiv og Museum* III 1905-08 pp. 42-70

Smidt, C.M.: Borgholm og Klosterø. Spredte træk af Skanderborgs forbindelser med Øm Kloster. Undersøgelser, Fund m.m., *Historiske Årbøger for Aarhus Stift* XIX 1926 pp. 178-210

Smidt, C.M.: Ravnsborg, *Nationalmuseets Arbejdsmark* 1929 pp. 15-30

Smidt, C.M.: Søborg, *Nationalmuseets Arbejdsmark* 1930 pp. 5-18

Smidt, C.M.: Kalø: grundlagt 1313, *Nationalmuseets Arbejdsmark* 1932 pp. 67-77

Smidt, C.M.: Gurre, *Nationalmuseets Arbejdsmark* 1933 pp. 67-74

Smidt, C.M.: Forsvaret i danske borge, *Nationalmuseets Arbejdsmark* 1934 pp. 29-43

Smidt, C.M.: Kalundborg, *Nationalmuseets Arbejdsmark* 1936 pp. 21-36

Smidt, C. M.: By- og borgbro, *Nationalmuseets Arbejdsmark* 1937 pp. 57-72

Smidt, C.M.: Port og faldgitter, *Nationalmuseets Arbejdsmark* 1939 pp. 29-42

Smidt, C.M.: Dronningholm, *Nationalmuseets Arbejdsmark* 1940 pp. 63-77

Smidt, C.M.: Vordingborg, *Aarbøger for nordisk Oldkyndighed og Historie* 1941

Smidt, C.M.: Kalø, *Nationalmuseets Arbejdsmark* 1944 pp. 88-98

Stiesdal, Hans: Kærsgaard Voldsted. *Aarbøger udgivne af Historisk Samfund for Aarhus Stift* XLV 1952 pp. 5-22

Stiesdal, Hans: *Kalø slotsruin,* Nationalmuseets blå bøger 1954

Stiesdal, Hans: Grøngaard, Hans den Ældres jagtslot, *Nationalmuseets Arbejdsmark* 1956 pp. 115-127

Stiesdal, Hans: En gruppe voldsteder i Sønderborg amt, *Fra Als og Sundeved* 37 1958 pp. 111-129

Stiesdal, Hans: Padeborg, *Årbøger for Nordisk Oldkyndighed og Historie* 1960 pp. 72-96

Stiesdal, Hans: *Absalons Borg, Christiansborg Slot* vol. 1 1975 pp. 1-47

Stiesdal, Hans: The medieval Palatium in Denmark. Some recent discovcries at Tranekaer Castle, *Château Gaillard* VII, Caen 1975 pp. 201-208

Stiesdal, Hans: Die ältesten dänischen Donjons, *Château Gaillard* VIII, Caen 1977 pp. 279-286

Stiesdal, Hans: Nørrevolde, *Nordslesvigske Museer* 6 1979 pp. 67-78

Stiesdal, Hans: Voldsteder ved Varde. Beretning om en egnsundersøgelse, *Mark og Montre* 1981 pp. 5-17

Stiesdal, Hans: Types of public and private fortifications in Denmark. I: *Danish Medieval History, New Currents*, Niels Skyum-Nielsen and Niels Lund (eds.) 1981 pp. 207-220

Stiesdal, Hans: Eriksvolde, *Château Gaillard* IX 1982 pp. 255-264

Stiesdal, Hans: Voldsteder ved Varde II, *Mark og Montre* 1983 pp. 23-31

Sørensen, H.E.: *Slotte, herregårde og voldsteder i Sønderjylland* I-II 1994

Thorsen, Svend: Den tredje folkeborg, *Skalk* 5, 2001

Tuulse, Armin: *Borgar i Västerlandet. Ursprung och typutveckling under medeltiden,* Stockholm 1952

Ulsig, Erik: *Danske adelsgodser i middelalderen,* København 1968

Vedsø, Mogens: Det middelalderlige Voergaard, *Bygningsarkæologiske Studier* 1984 pp. 29-40

Vedsø, Mogens: Spøttrup, *Bygningsarkæologiske Studier* 1986 pp. 33-72

Vedsø, Mogens: Nyborg Slot – en bygningsarkæologisk analyse af det romanske palatiums østfacade, *Bygningsarkæologiske Studier* 2006-2008, 2010 pp. 75-86

Vedsø, Mogens: Det store tårn på Nyborg Slot, *Bygningsarkæologiske Studier* 2006-2008, 2010 pp. 133-140

Vegger, Per Bugge: "Gravene" ved Alsted. Festskrift til Hans Stiesdal, *hikuin* 19 1992 pp. 125-130.

Vellev, Jens: Borgvold – Viborgs borg. *Museer i Viborg Amt* 13 1985 pp. 66-93

Vellev, Jens: Viborgbispens og lensmændenes Hald – og noget om Brattingsborg og Niels Bugges Hald. Festskrift til Hans Stiesdal, *hikuin* 19 1992 pp. 219-264

Vellev, Jens: Silkeborgen, *Skalk* 4, 2008 pp. 3 -7

Vemming Hansen, Peter: *Middelalderens mekaniske apparater til krigsbrug,* Middelaldercentret Nykøbing F. 1998

Venge, Michael: Erik Menved og Stegeborg. *Historisk Samfund for Præstø Amt* 2005 pp. 31-46

Vesth, Kjeld Borch: Danske Voldsteder, *Antikvariske Studier* 7 1985 pp. 197-255

Vesth, Kjeld Borch: Hammershus – fra borg til ruin, *Hammershus* 1997 pp. 79-114

Vesth, Kjeld Borch: Hammershus Castle, *Castella Maris Baltici* 3-4 Gdansk 2000 pp. 193-198

Wille-Jørgensen, Dorthe: Kongeborgen i Vordingborg – de arkæologiske undersøgelser, *Kulturhistoriske Studier* 1995, 1996, 1997, 1998

Wille-Jørgensen, Dorthe: Slotsruinen i Vordingborg – de arkæologiske udgravninger i 1998, *Kulturhistoriske Studier* 1999 pp. 36-59

Wille-Jørgensen, Dorthe: Kloakering – en sag for arkæologer. Udenværker omkring Vordingborg Kongeborg, *Kulturhistoriske Studier* 2001 pp. 85 -99

Wille-Jørgensen, Dorthe: Wiederverwendete Kalksteinsquader in der Burg zu Vordingborg, *Castella Maris Baltici* 3-4, Gdansk 2000 pp. 241-246

Wille-Jørgensen, Dorthe: Vordingborg Slot-fortsat! *Historisk Samfund for Præstø Amt Årbog* 2002 pp. 21-34

Ødman, Anders: Järnskat och borglän I-II, *Ale, Historisk Tidsskrift for Skåneland* 1/1993 p. 1-32.

Ødman, Anders: Glimmingehus and its Predecessor, *Castella Maris Baltici* 2 1996 pp. 135-140

Ødman, Anders: Borgar i Skåne, *Historiska Media* 2002

REFERENCE WORKS

Byggnadskultur, Nordisk Kultur XVII, Sigurd
    Erixon (ed.) 1953

Bygningsarkæologiske Studier 2006-2008, Tvær-
    videnskabeligt Seminar på Nyborg Slot 30.
    marts 2006, Kirsten Eliasen et al. (eds.)

Danske Slotte og Herregårde, Aage Roussell (ed.),
    2nd edition, København 1963-68

Kulturhistorisk leksikon for nordisk middelalder
    I-XXII 1956-1978

TRAP, Danmark, 5th edition, København 1958-72

VOLDSTEDER I DANMARK, En vejviser: Fyn
    og Omliggende øer, Rikke Agnete Olsen (ed.)
    1992; Sjælland og Lolland-Falster, Connie
    Jantzen and Rikke Agnete Olsen (eds.) 1998;
    Jylland I, Connie Jantzen and Rikke Agnete
    Olsen (eds.) 1991; Jylland II, Connie Jantzen,
    Lennart S. Madsen and Rikke Agnete Olsen
    eds. 1999

Dänische Mittelalterburgen
German summary

I

In Dänemark finden sich heute nur noch wenige Spuren der zahlreichen Burgen, die im Mittelalter die Landschaft prägten und den Rahmen um das Leben vieler Menschen bildeten. Damals hatte das Reich eine größere Ausdehnung als heute. Ganz Schleswig gehörte dazu, obwohl die Herzöge dort immer den Status selbständiger Fürsten anstrebten. Schonen, Halland und Blekinge – zusammengefasst „Schonenländer" genannt – waren auch seit alter Zeit Teile von Dänemark und zwar die reichsten Provinzen des Landes, vor allem Schonen mit dem Sitz des Erzbischofs in Lund.

Seit 1660 gehören die Provinzen östlich des Öresunds zu Schweden. Schleswig wurde zusammen mit Holstein 1864 von Preußen erobert, aber der Großteil des Herzogtums Schleswig fiel 1920 nach einer Volksabstimmung wieder an Dänemark. Dort und in den Schonenländern entspricht die Situation der mittelalterlichen Burgen dem übrigen Dänemark; die allermeisten sind verschwunden. Einige sind vielleicht noch als mehr oder weniger deutliche Burgen-Standplätze in der Landschaft zu erkennen, andere als Ruinen; und einzelne wurden bis zur Unkenntlichkeit umgebaut und in Schlösser aus späterer Zeit einbezogen.

Der Grund ist darin zu sehen, dass mittelalterliche Burgen und ihre Nutzung in Dänemark wie in allen anderen Ländern den Verlauf der historischen Entwicklung widerspiegeln und davon geprägt sind. Aber in Dänemark und im übrigen Skandinavien sind die Verhältnisse anders gelagert als auf dem europäischen Festland und auf den britischen Inseln. Das Rechtssystem und die Gesetzesgrundlage waren anders, und ebenso unterschieden sich die Sozialgefüge. Bedeutsam ist auch, dass das Christentum später in den Norden übernommen wurde, das dann Bedeutung für das Rechtswesen gewann und insgesamt europäischen Einfluss mit sich brachte.

Erst mehrere Jahrhunderte nachdem die Burg als privater befestigter Wohnsitz und zur Verteidigung der Staatsmacht und fürstlicher Besitzungen in Europa üblich geworden war, erscheint sie in Dänemark, und hier wird sie – wie das Christentum – durch die Zentralmacht eingeführt. Erst nach langer Zeit scheint sie sich als Wohnsitz der grundbesitzenden Oberschicht zu verbreiten. Das hängt mit der Rolle des Königs zusamen, der allein die Macht zur Wahrnehmung der Verteidigung des Reichs besaß und der allein die Verantwortung dafür trug. Die Errichtung von Burgen zeigt auf diese Weise, wie es um die königliche Macht im Reich bestellt war, d.h. ob die Zentralmacht funktionstüchtig war oder nicht.

II

Trotz intensiver Suche nach älteren Anlagen sind eigentliche Burgen in Dänemark erst aus der ersten Hälfte des 12. Jahrhunderts bekannt. Zwar existierten damals längst Wallanlagen zum Schutz der Grenze, und es gab auch noch vielfach allgemeine Fluchtburgen im Reich; sie stammen jedoch aus vorhistorischer Zeit. Mehrere von ihnen wurden aber noch im 13. Jahrhundert von der Lokalbevölkerung genutzt. Das ist in jener Zeit durch Unruhen im Reich und in Unsicherheit im Verhältnis zum Ausland begründet. Zugleich deutet es an, dass es keine privaten Verteidigungseinrichtungen für alle gab, vermutlich gab es solche Einrichtungen nur für einige wenige.

Die wenigen Burgen, die aus dem Anfang des 12. Jahrhunderts bekannt sind, sind Zeugen des jahrzehntelangen Streites um die Krone zwischen Mitgliedern der Königsdynastie und ihren verschiedenen Anhängern. Diese Burgen verdanken ihre Entstehung teils Mitgliedern des Königsgeschlechts – Haraldsborg bei Roskilde (Plan S. 38) – und teils Mitgliedern des mächtigsten Geschlechts auf Seeland, dem sogenannten Hvide-Geschlecht – Bastrup in Nordseeland (Plan S. 35) – und eventuell Borren in Ods Herred. Das ebenfalls in Nordseeland gelegene Søborg (Plan S. 40) scheint dem Erzbischof gehört zu haben; und das etwas jüngere Pedersborg bei Sorø (Plan S. 36) wurde von einem Mitglied des mächtigen Hvide-Geschlechts erbaut. Dagegen lassen sich Anlagen aus jener Zeit, die sich in königlichem Besitz befanden, nicht mit Sicherheit ausmachen. Man kann allerdings Vermutungen anstellen, z.B. über Lilleborg in der Mitte von Bornholm (Plan S. 53) oder Refshaleborg im See von Maribo (Plan S. 49), also Orte, die wie Fluchtburgen in weitem Abstand von gefährdeten Küsten lagen. Vielleicht gab es auch eine königliche Anlage bei Vordingborg (Plan S. 52), wo man unter den Ruinen der späteren bedeutenden und mächtigen Reichsburg Spuren eines älteren Befestigungswerks entdeckte. Hier handelt es sich jedenfalls um eine königliche Burg, die im weiteren Mittelalter große Bedeutung für die Krone besaß.

Mit seinen 6 Meter dicken Mauern war der Turm von Bastrup ein einzigartiges Bauwerk – auch in europäischer Perspektive. Søborg war eine völlig zeittypische Ringmauerburg, zudem mit einer kleinen Rundkirche innerhalb der Anlage. Das galt auch für die älteste Anlage von Pedersborg oben auf einer steilen Erhebung in einem großen Gebiet, das durch starke Wälle aus vorgeschichtlicher Zeit abgeschirmt war. Haraldsborg wurde durch den Bau moderner Wohnviertel gänzlich ausgelöscht. Die Nutzung von Bastrup wurde bald aufgegeben, und die Anlage geriet in Vergessenheit. Pedersborg verlor seine Funktion als Befestigungsanlage und ging um 1200 in den Besitz des Klosters Sorø über. Aber Søborg und Haraldsborg wurden Zentren der königlichen Verwaltung, nachdem Waldemar I., der Große, 1157 Alleinherrscher geworden war. Vielleicht lassen sich dadurch auch alte Ansprüche der Krone auf diese beiden Anlagen ableiten.

III

In der Waldemar-Periode, d.h. unter Waldemar dem Großen und seinen Söhnen Knut VI. und Waldemar dem Sieger 1157-1241, gewann das Königtum und das Reich erheblich an Macht im Verhältnis zum Ausland. Die Könige bauten wichtige Burgen an den Grenzen und an den Überfahrtsstellen. Nun wurden nicht nur die Plünderungszüge der heidnisch-slawischen Wenden an den Ostseeküsten zum Stillstand gebracht, unter denen Dänemark während des Thronstreits zu leiden hatte, vielmehr konnte man nun Vergeltungszüge großen Stils einleiten und bedeutende Gebiete entlang der Ostseeküste erobern und eine Zeitlang unter dänischer Herrschaft halten. Estland blieb dänisch bis 1346. Einige Forscher betrachten die Kriege dieser Könige als reine Kreuzzüge; aber so einfach lagen die Dinge kaum, wenn die Züge auch mit päpstlichem Segen durchgeführt

wurden. In der Auffassung der Zeitgenossen waren diese Züge und Eroberungen mit Sicherheit von politischer Notwendigkeit bestimmt.

In diesen Jahren der Machtentfaltung entstanden die Burg auf der Insel Sprogø (Foto S. 56-57, Karte S. 72) und Tårnborg im Haff von Korsør (Plan S. 65); Kopenhagen (Plan S. 68) und Kalundborg (Plan S. 69) wurden angelegt, zwar nicht auf Veranlassung des Königs selbst, wohl aber von ihren wichtigsten Unterstützern; es entstanden Helsingborg (Plan S. 145) und Nyborg (Plan S. 75). Ebenso wuchs die Bedeutung von Vordingborg; von hier gingen alle Kriegszüge aus. Als eine seiner ersten Maßnahmen hatte Waldemar der Große den alten Grenzwall Danewerk (s. Karte S. 30) durch eine Ziegelmauer verstärkt, und während seiner Zeit und während der Regierung seiner Söhne wurden weiter zahlreiche Burgen im ganzen Reichsgebiet gebaut, z.B. Sonderburg auf Alsen (Karte S. 72) und Skanderborg in Mitteljütland (Karte S. 72), wo vielleicht schon vorher eine königliche Festung lag.

Der Bau von Hammershus auf Bornholm (Plan S.53) war wohl ursprünglich ein Gemeinschaftsunternehmen des Erzbischofs und Waldemars des Siegers aus den Anfangsjahren des 13. Jahrhunderts und war vielleicht als Ausgangspunkt für Kreuzzüge geplant. Aber im übrigen gab es kaum Anzeichen für die Anlage von Burgen außerhalb der königlichen Familie. Auch in den letzten, von erheblicher Schwäche geprägten Regierungsjahren Waldemars des Siegers herrschte Ruhe im Reich. Jedenfalls gab es keine Anzeichen für zunehmende Burgenbauaktivität unter den Großen im Reich, wenn sie auch vielleicht solche Absichten hegten (s. Karte mit den Burgen der Waldemar-Periode S. 72).

IV

Aber am Horizont drohte Unruhe. In Waldemars letzten Jahren befestigten seine Söhne offenbar ihre Besitzungen. Mehrere von ihnen waren kampfbereit, als der älteste Sohn, der Mitregent seines Vaters gewesen war, nach dessen Tod die Krone übernahm und der zweitälteste Herzog in Südjütland war. Während des vieljährigen Bruderstreits wurden z.B. im Jahrzehnt nach 1260 Burgen in Ribe und Kolding gebaut (Karte S. 28), was dazu beitrug, die Grenze zwischen dem Königreich und dem Herzogtum für mehrere Jahrhunderte deutlich zu markieren. Damals entstand Gottorp (Hinweis auf Karte S. 28) als „Schutz des ganzen Reichs" – aber vom Herzog erbaut. Der Streit im

Königshaus teilte auch das Reich; und ein Teil der Kirche, an der Spitze der Erzbischof, trat auf die Seite der herzoglichen Linie. Die Folge waren fortwährende interne Kämpfe in Dänemark und Bestrebungen der großen Grundbesitzer, das Recht zur Befestigung zu erlangen und die Arbeitskraft der Bauern dafür zu verwenden.

An der Gesetzgebung lässt sich ablesen, wie die Macht der Krone über die Verteidigung des Reichs und die Festungen in dem Maße abnahm, wie der Streit im Reich zunahm und sich durch die Gesellschaft ausbreitete. Die Kosten waren erheblich, und die Finanzkraft der Krone war im voraus dadurch geschwächt, dass man ein enormes Lösegeld hatte aufbringen müssen, um Waldemar den Sieger und seinen ältesten Sohn um 1226 aus der Gefangenschaft in Schwerin loszukaufen. Es verschlimmerte die Lage, dass die Kriegskosten ständig stiegen, während die Einnahmen der Krone nicht erhöht werden konnten. Die einzige Möglichkeit des Königs, mehr Mittel für die Kriegsführung aufzubringen, war, Besitz zu verpfänden. Aber das war nur ein befristeter Ausweg; denn, da Christen keine Zinsen nehmen durften, die Geldgeber aber trotzdem einen Gewinn für die Bereitstellung von Geldmitteln erzielen wollten, erhielten die Pfandgläubiger die verpfändeten Besitzungen mit Einnahmen – Steuern – und mit Jurisdiktion, aus der sich ebenfalls Einnahmen ableiteten. Auf diese Einnahmen musste die Krone verzichten, und neue Verpfändungen blieben als einziger Ausweg.

Die Lage gestaltete sich katastrophal, als Erich Klipping 1286 ermordet wurde und ein mehrjähriger Krieg zwischen Dänemark und u.a. dem norwegischen König ausbrach, der die Großen unterstützte, die als Urheber des Mordes friedlos erklärt worden waren. Daraus folgte unter anderem, dass der norwegische König die Insel Hjelm tief in dänischem Gewässer befestigte (Plan S. 104). In Dänemark waren im Lauf der Jahre zweifellos weitere königliche Burgen entstanden, z.B. Hindsgaul auf Fünen (Plan S. 107).

Verpfändungen sind allerdings eine ewige Zwickmühle, die auch in diesem Fall für die Krone im Bankrott endete. Der trat ein, als alle Besitzungen teils an zwei holsteinische Grafen und deren nachgeordnete Pfandgläubiger, teils an mehrere dänische Große verpfändet waren. Das dänische Reich stand vor dem Zerfall. Nachdem der eine Pfandgläubiger Schonen an den schwedischen König verkauft hatte, blieb dem dänischen König nichts mehr, worüber er als König herrschen konnte. Als er 1332 starb, war das Reich bis 1340 ohne König.

V

Während all dieser Jahre, fast ein ganzes Jahrhundert lang, als die Krone ihre Macht einbüßt, zerfallen die zentrale Regierung und Recht und Ordnung selbstverständlich; und in dieser Periode erbauen die großen Grundbesitzer soweit möglich Burgen, um sich selbst und ihren Besitz zu verteidigen. Das gilt für Dänen und Holsteiner, Besitzer und Pfandgläubiger. Nun entstehen überall private Burgen, teils größere, teils kleinere; und zwar handelt es sich im Wesentlichen um solche, deren Reste sich heute unter grünen Hügeln verbergen oder die völlig aus der Landschaft verschwunden sind. Viele von ihnen waren Anlagen mit Holzbauten und Erdwällen, allenfalls für die Verteidigung gegen umstreifende Räuberbanden und feindliche Nachbarn berechnet. Viele dieser Anlagen ähneln denen, die früh in Frankreich und Deutschland entstanden waren und die man z.B. aus Wiedergaben auf dem Wandteppich von Bayeux kennt. Sie bestehen aus zwei oder mehr – teilweise künstlichen – Hügeln mit dem eigentlichen Verteidigungswerk auf dem einen und Hofgebäuden auf dem oder den anderen. Diese Art privater Festungen kamen mit den Normannen nach England und wurden dort und in Frankreich Motte/Bailey-Anlagen genannt. In Dänemark sprechen wir von Castrum/curia-Anlagen, d.h. Burg/Hof-Anlagen oder Turmhügel und Hofhügel. Diese Burgen stellten die befestigten Höfe für die Großen im Reich dar. Bjørnkær in Ostjütland (Plan S. 128) ist ein Beispiel einer solchen Anlage. Dagegen ist Aalholm auf Lolland eine starke, aus Steinen errichtete Burg, allerdings wurde sie auch von dem einen der beiden wichtigsten Pfandgläubiger gebaut, dem Grafen Johann von Plön (Illustration S. 129).

Diese Entwicklung dauert merkwürdigerweise fast hundert Jahre an, nicht zuletzt, weil Erich Menved, der von 1286 bis 1319 regierte, enorme Summen für Krieg im Ausland und Burgenbau in Dänemark verwendete. Er erweiterte und verstärkte die alten Reichsburgen und erbaute neue in Jütland, um sich dort gegen Aufruhr zu sichern. Es handelt sich um Burgen wie Kalø in der Bucht von Aarhus, Bygholm bei Horsens und Borgvold bei Viborg (Pläne S. 110).

In Dänemark gibt es nicht so viele schriftliche Quellen wie im übrigen Europa, und es ist oft schwer oder unmöglich zu entscheiden, wer die Burgen besaß, die nun als Reste früherer Anlagen in der Landschaft liegen. Die großen Grundbesitzer besaßen viele Sitze, die über das ganze Land verstreut waren. Sie konnten nicht alle befestigen; und es lässt sich heute kaum noch ausmachen, warum sie eine Anlage vor anderen bevorzugten. Aber die Burgen-Standplätze liegen dort als Zeichen unruhiger Zeitläufe mit mangelnder Zentralmacht.

VI

Die Schwäche der Zentralmacht war jedoch nicht feudal bedingt, und sie dauerte auch nicht im restlichen Mittelalter an. Teile der Bevölkerung begehrten auf und wünschten Frieden herbei, denn die Pfandgläubiger, die wussten, dass ihre Anwesenheit im Land begrenzt war, stellten erdrückend hohe Forderungen. Für sie war es wichtig, für ihre Darlehen einen so hohen Erlös wie möglich zu erzielen. Die Handeltreibenden, die Hansestädte, erstrebten aus wirtschaftlichen Gründen Frieden; der Kaiser wollte Frieden, damit sein Sohn, der mit der Tochter des letzten dänischen Königs, Christophs II., verheiratet war, seine Mitgift erhielt. All dies bewirkte, dass nach dem Interregnum der jüngste Sohn Christophs II. 1340 zum dänischen König gewählt wurde. Dänemark war keine Erbmonarchie, sondern die großen Grundbesitzer wählten den König, und der neue, Waldemar Atterdag, musste sich bei der Wahl harten Bedingungen unterwerfen, nämlich der Zahlung einer enormen Summe, die das Land den Pfandgläubigern schuldete. Aber der König verfügte über Unterstützung von außen und von Seiten der Kirche und erhielt 1346 finanzielle Mittel durch den Verkauf von Estland an den Deutschen Orden.

In Chroniken und Urkunden kann man seine Bemühungen verfolgen, die in hohem Grad darauf abzielten, Burg um Burg im Kampf zu gewinnen. Auf diese Weise erhalten einige der Burgen historisches Profil und lassen sich sozial einordnen, während die Macht der Krone langsam wiederhergestellt wurde und der König seine Autorität unter anderem durch den Ausbau existierender Burgen festigte. Nach Waldemar Atterdags Tod 1375 in Gurre in Nordseeland (Plan S. 160), wo er sich gern aufhielt, übernahm seine Tochter Margrete die Regierung für ihren unmündigen Sohn. Sie vollendete das Werk ihres Vaters, indem sie jede Burg, die sie mit Rechtsanspruch in ihre Hand bringen konnte, entweder abreißen ließ oder zur Rückzahlung der Schulden der Kirche übergab, die sie und ihren Vater mit reichen Mitteln unterstützt hatte. Der Kirche fiel dann das Recht und die Pflicht zu, die Burgen abzureißen. Baumaterial war wertvoll, und die Kirche erhielt auf diese Weise Einnahmen zur Begleichung der königlichen Schulden. Das betraf z.B. Hald bei Viborg (Plan S. 137).

Als Margrete 1396 eine Verordnung erlassen konnte, die den privaten Burgenbau verbot, war die Autorität der Krone, also die Zentralmacht, endlich in vollem Umfang wiederhergestellt. Die Begründung für diesen Erlass war, dass niemand mehr Burgen bauen dürfe, „weil von den Burgen, die bestehen, so unendlich wenig Recht ausgegangen ist". Darin hatte die Königin recht; man kann zwar durchaus ein Land erobern, ohne die Burgen zu erobern, aber man kann bekanntlich ein Land nicht regieren, ohne Macht über die Burgen zu haben. Auch Bischof Peder Jensen Lodehat, dem Margrete alle Jahre hindurch stärkste Unterstützung verdankte, fügte sich in die Verordnung und errichtete Gjorslev auf der Halbinsel Stevns (Plan S. 179) um 1400 nicht als Burg, sondern als prächtigen Palast.

Margrete selbst baute nur wenige Burgen, aber sie schuf die Union der drei nordischen Länder, die Kalmarer Union, als ihr Adoptivsohn Erich von Pommern mündig geworden war. Die Union bestand – wenn auch unter Schwierigkeiten – bis 1520; und im Lauf dieser langen Periode wurde eine Vielzahl jener privaten Burgen, die trotz der Verordnung nicht abgerissen worden waren, von ihren Besitzern aufgegeben, weil sie aus Sumpf und Moor und anderen unzugänglichen Stätten wegzogen und zivilisiertere Orte suchten, wo es sich leben ließ, die landwirtschaftliche Nutzung in der Nähe erreichbar war und wo man nun wieder sicher wohnen und Landwirtschaft als Lebensgrundlage betreiben konnte. König Erich erbaute Krogen bei Helsingør, woraus später durch Erweiterung und Umbau Kronborg entstand (Plan S. 186).

VII

Margretes Verbot wurde zwar durch die Handfeste aufgehoben, die König Hans 1483 unterzeichnen musste, jedoch mit der Einschränkung, dass privater Burgenbau auch dem Nutzen des Reichs dienen sollte. Es handelt sich also um eine bedingte Zurücknahme, aber trotz der damit eröffneten Möglichkeit entstanden keine neue Burgen. Für die Großen war das Recht des Burgenbaus eine Frage des Prestiges, aber, obwohl einige auf früheren Standplätzen bauten, wurden keine Burgen, sondern Herrensitze errichtet, z.B. Aagaard, Kokkedal und Odden (Plan S. 243, an illustrationen S. 177 und 237) nördlich des Limfjords. Es bestand auch kein Bedarf an Burgen in Dänemark, wo Friede herrschte, während die Unionskriege in Schweden geführt wurden. Glimmingehus in Schonen von ca. 1500 (Plan S. 183) sieht wirklich einer Burg ähnlich, ist aber viel zu klein, um eigentliche militärische Bedeutung zu haben. Es war der Traum des Bau-

herrn von einer Mittelalterburg und ist fast als „Folly" zu be-
zeichnen. Die königlichen Burgen in Dänemark wurden auch
keiner eigentlichen Modernisierung unterworfen.

Jedenfalls waren sie offenbar nicht modernisiert, als es
beim sozialen und religiösen Aufruhr zum Kampf um sie und
um die Macht im Reich kam, der in den Jahren nach 1530 in
der sogenannten Grafenfehde gipfelte. Sie endete mit der Reformation und in Wirklichkeit mit dem Sieg der Monarchie
in der Rivalität zwischen Krone, Kirche und großen Grund-
besitzern, die das Mittelalter geprägt hatte. Der neue König,
Christian III., modernisierte einige königliche Burgen, z.B.
Nyborg, Aalborg und Malmø und baute neu in Landskrona (Karte S. 203). Die Großen verloren erheblich an Macht,
und der König erstarkte und wurde reich, da die Krone den
Hauptteil der unermesslichen Kirchengüter übernahm. Auch
die Großen, jetzt zum Adel gewandelt, erhielten ihren Teil,
und die Landwirtschaft erlebte eine steigende Konjunktur.
Dadurch konnte der Adel sich vornehme Wohnsitze aus Stein
mit Türmen und Zinnen leisten, die der Burg eines mächtigen
Herren ähnelten. Sie verkörpern den Traum vom Mittelalter
– wie Glimmingehus; und mehrere dieser Herrensitze, die
mehr Pracht als Kampfeignung ausstrahlen, sind noch heute
als Schmuckstücke in der dänischen Landschaft zu sehen, z.B.
Egeskov auf Fünen und Borreby auf Seeland (Illustrationen S.
208 und 209).

Hier und auf den neuen oder neu eingerichteten Schlös-
sern der Krone lebte man wie früher von den Erträgen der
Landwirtschaft, aber in größerem Maßstab als früher und mit
mehr Einkäufen aus den Städten oder sogar aus dem Ausland
und weniger hauseigenen Waren für den täglichen Bedarf. Die
Krone behandelte das Land wie eine Domäne, und die großen Güter sammelten nach und nach durch Tausch und Kauf
Besitz in der Nähe des bevorzugten Herrensitzes. Auf diese
Weise änderte sich die wirtschaftliche Struktur im Verhältnis
zu früherer Zeit, als der König und die großen Grundbesitzer
von Ort zu Ort reisten, um den Ertrag der Besitzungen zu
sammeln und davon zu leben.

Da war die Zeit der Burgen längst Vergangenheit, und die
Verteidigung des Landes war allein Angelegenheit der Krone
oder des Staats geworden.

DANISH MEDIEVAL CASTLES

© Rikke Agnete Olsen

© Photos Janne Klerk unless otherwise indicated

English translation by Joan F. Davidson

Summary in German translated by Hans Blosen

Plan-drawings by Helge Bregnehøj-Olesen and Orla Svendsen

Drawings for glossary by Sara Heil Jensen

Drawings pages 115 and 186 by Flemming Bau

Layout, typesetting and cover design by Jørgen Sparre

The book is set in Warnock Pro

Printed at Narayana Press on Arctic Volume Ivory

Photo, front cover: Hammershus by Janne Klerk

Photo, back cover: Kalø by Janne Klerk

Printed in Denmark 2014

ISBN 978 87 7124 179 2

AARHUS UNIVERSITY PRESS

Langelandsgade 177

DK-8200 Aarhus N

www.unipress.dk

INTERNATIONAL DISTRIBUTION

UK & Eire:

Gazelle Book Services Ltd.

White Cross Mills

Hightown, Lancaster, LA1 4XS

United Kingdom

www.gazellebookservices.co.uk

North America:

ISD

70 Enterprise Drive, Suite 2

Bristol, CT 06010

USA

www.isdistribution.com

Published with the financial support of

A.P. Møller og Hustru Chastine Mc-Kinney Møllers Fond til almene Formaal

The groundplan drawings reproduced in this book are on the scale 1:2000 unles otherwise indicated.